DORDT INFORMATION SERVICES

3 6520 0023493 .

D1033067

DORDT COLLEGE
Sioux Center, Iowa

ISAAC BUTT
AND HOME RULE

ISAAC BUTT: drawing by John Butler Yeats the Elder
(Courtesy of the National Gallery of Ireland)

ISAAC BUTT

AND HOME RULE

DAVID THORNLEY

MCMLXIV

MACGIBBON & KEE

LONDON

FIRST PUBLISHED 1964 BY MACGIBBON & KEE LTD
COPYRIGHT © DAVID THORNLEY 1964
PRINTED IN GREAT BRITAIN BY
W. & G. BAIRD LTD
LONDON AND BELFAST

COLLEGIO SANCTAE ET INDIVIDVAE TRINITATIS
IVXTA DVBLIN HVNC LIBRVM GRATO PIOQVE ANIMO
DEDICO IN EISDEM AVLIS IN QVIBUS ILLE CVIVS
RES GESTAE IN HIC NARRANTVR DISCEBAT
DOCEBATQVE ET IPSE DISCERE ET
DOCERE SOLITVS

CONTENTS

PREFACE   *Page* 9

     Introduction   13

   I   The Disestablishment Election   25

  II   Irish Public Opinion and the Liberal Administration: November 1868—February 1870   62

 III   The Home Government Association   83

 IV   The Founding of the Home Rule League   138

  V   The General Election of 1874   176

 VI   Home Rule, Class, and the Ballot   205

 VII   The New Party and its Leader   212

VIII   Two Sessions of Argument   227

 IX   Two Sessions of Argument (contd.)   251

  X   Conciliation's Last Rally   272

 XI   The Call for Action   286

 XII   The Obstruction Crisis   300

XIII   The Struggle for Power   330

XIV   Stalemate   346

     Conclusion   379

BIBLIOGRAPHY   389

INDEX   399

PREFACE

OF ALL the men who claimed the tribuneship of Irish nationality perhaps none has suffered such neglect as Isaac Butt. His greatest successor in the leadership of the Home Rule movement, Charles Stewart Parnell, has been the subject not merely of generations of romantic adulation, a multitude of biographies, and at least one motion picture, but also of two first-rate modern studies—Dr Cruise O'Brien's *Parnell and his party* and Dr F. S. L. Lyons's *The fall of Parnell.* The post-Parnellite party has received equally scholarly treatment in Dr Lyons's *The Irish parliamentary party, 1890-1910.* By comparison the career of Isaac Butt has been virtually ignored. Mr Terence de Vere White's attractive biography, *The road of excess,* alone pays tribute to his personality; in the modern historiography of Home Rule the years of Butt's authority, the years in which the movement was born, are unexplored. Gifted with many of the attributes of historical popularity—fluent, convivial, and more than slightly dissipated—Butt has nevertheless left little trace upon the histories of Anglo-Irish politics. Brief pre-Parnellite asides convey a shadowy impression of an amiable but elderly conservative, set incongruously at the head of a Home Rule party whose origins are as obscure as its future is predestined. The anonymity of the first Home Rule leader is an enigma. It is not explained by the briefness of his reign; Parnell's lasted no more than a decade. It is not justified by his failure; every Irish leader failed, Parnell perhaps most totally.

It is, then, perhaps, hardly necessary to apologise for attempting a modern treatment of the first Home Rule movement. The terms of reference of this book may require some explanation. The general election of 1868 has been adopted as its point of departure because that contest was in many ways one of the most important of Irish nineteenth-century elections, directly influencing much of what followed in the era of Home Rule. The extent to

9

which the Irish people were immutably committed to separatism in that century can be grossly exaggerated; a study of the election of 1868 reveals, perhaps, how close Ireland came in at least one period to the acceptance of Liberal unionism. It also sets the scene, and marks off most of the antagonists, in the struggles which are to follow not merely under Butt but under Parnell. The book ends with Butt's death, and does not enter into a discussion of the Land League and the 'New Departure', which belong to the study of the Parnellite party rather than that of Butt. These eruptions of political energy, extraneous, in that period, to the Home Rule movement as such, rather herald the rise of the new leader than the fall of the old, a fall by that time already effectively consummated.

In writing this book I have been fortunate enough to gain access to a number of manuscript collections, some of them in private hands. I wish to express my thanks to Viscount Hampden, Earl St. Aldwyn, and Lord Strachie for their kindness in allowing me to consult, and where necessary quote from and refer to, their family papers—to Lord Hampden, in respect of the papers of H. B. W. Brand, Viscount Hampden, Speaker of the House of Commons, 1872-84; to Lord St. Aldwyn, in respect of the papers of Sir Michael Hicks Beach, Earl St. Aldwyn, Chief Secretary for Ireland, 1874-78; to Lord Strachie, in respect of the papers of C. S. Fortescue, Baron Clermont, Baron Carlingford, Chief Secretary for Ireland, 1865-66 and 1868-71. I am grateful to the Director and Trustees of the National Library, Dublin, the Trustees of the British Museum, and the National Trust, for permission to make use of manuscript collections in their keeping, and to the Director and Governors of the National Gallery of Ireland for permission to reproduce the portrait of Butt by John Butler Yeats the Elder. I wish also to express my thanks to the Directors, Librarians, and staffs of the National Library, Dublin, the library of Trinity College, Dublin, the Manuscript Division of the British Museum, the National Registry of Archives, London, and the National Trust, Hughenden, and to Sir Edward Fellows, sometime Clerk of the House of Commons, and his assistant, Miss Patricia Brandt. I am particularly indebted to Mr Alf Mac Lochlainn and Mr T. P. O'Neill of the National Library and to Miss W. D. Coates and Colonel R. P. F. White of the National Registry of Archives.

I am grateful to the Trinity College, Dublin, Trust and to the Research Committee of Trinity College for their assistance to my research, and to Professor F. B. Chubb, Dr F. S. L. Lyons, Dr R. B. McDowell, Professor R. Dudley Edwards, Dr Aidan Clarke, Mr W. G. Fuge, and Mr J. H. Whyte for their advice and help. Above all I must express my great indebtedness at all times to Professor T. W. Moody, without whose scholarly guidance and friendship as teacher, as research supervisor, and as colleague this book would not have been written.

Finally I must thank my wife both for her practical assistance in the production of this book, and for her patience and understanding in the years since its preparation was first undertaken.

DAVID THORNLEY

Trinity College
Dublin
July 1963

INTRODUCTION

THE ATTITUDE of mind which we regard today as Irish nationalism is largely the product of forces which first reached
their full expression in the nineteenth century. Attractive
though it may be to the emotionally patriotic, there is no
more dangerous oversimplification of our history than to regard the desire of the Irish people for independence as an im-
mutable force, an historic nationhood, working through different leaders and different generations, but always recognis-
able as the incorruptible will of the folk to satisfy its group
consciousness by the purging from its soil of the invader. The
resentment of the common people against their rulers was
produced by no question-begging folk myth: it drew its vigour from three great stimuli, at once emotional and practical.
Of these a sense of nationality was only one; the others were
land and religion. The rivalry of these three great forces at
some times paralysed the popular will; their sporadic coincidence produced great cataclysms in the history of Ireland.
In their interaction lies the explanation of many of the apparent paradoxes of that story.

Nowhere is this interaction more clearly at work than in
the period which is the subject of this book. The Roman Catholic Church, mute and suffering in the eighteenth century,
had become, largely through the genius of O'Connell, fully
articulate as the religious spokesman of the great majority of
the Irish people; there remained two challenges—to disposs-
ess the minority church of its legalised religious ascendancy
and to gain control of the education of the children of its own
faith. The land movement had won no comparable power.
Purged by the famine, the peasantry had yet to rediscover the
stimulus of desperation which was to produce the Land League. The one serious attempt to organise its grievances politically, that of the Tenant League in the early 1850's, had
failed for a multiplicity of reasons, not the least of which was
its conflict with the rival priorities of religious feeling. But
the experience of the famine, if politically prostrating, had

13

burned into the popular memory a resentment to which ownership of the land had become significantly both the means to
economic survival and a nationalist symbol.

The representatives of Ireland at Westminster in the period from Gavan Duffy to Butt were not difficult to ignore.
Men of indifferent calibre for the most part, without a commanding spokesman, they came together intermittently upon
the three issues of catholic education, disestablishment of the
church, and tenant right, the 'charter' of Cardinal Cullen.[1]
The cardinal, as leader of the catholic church in Ireland, was
eager to eschew nationalism and to enter into an alliance with
the English Liberal party. Such an alliance might be incongruous in terms of nineteenth-century ideologies, but it was
not difficult to justify upon the basis of the peculiar local divisions of Irish politics, where toryism, landlordism, and protestantism seemed so often to present, to the eyes of the majority, a composite image.

Great forces, however, lay beneath the apparently stagnant
surface of this period. They could find no outlet through constitutional spokesmen content to express their O'Connellite
heritage in terms of catholic liberalism. But two rival solutions were preparing. In Ireland the fenians were arming for
final separation; in England a great statesman pondered a new
approach to the responsibilities of unionism.

In the late 1860's the period of quiescence came to a violent
end as the eruption of the fenian conspiracy shattered the
complacent illusions of both islands. The rising itself failed
ignominiously. But the striking demonstration which it gave
of the impermanence of the Irish settlement and of her unplacated grievances produced two major and opposing results.
It permitted the constitutional nationalists to revive their demand for a native legislature, and it drew from Gladstone the
offer of a new and more generous settlement.

In a third and less calculably important way the fenian
rising also helped to determine the nature of the conflict that
was to follow. In September 1865 the government arrested

[1] O'Leary, *Recollections of Fenians and Fenianism*, 1896, Vol. 2, p.
165.

the authors of the fenian *Irish People,* the first in a long series
of such arrests. The brief for the defence was first offered to
Whiteside, the leading Irish lawyer of the day, who declined
it. It was then offered to his next most outstanding colleague,
Isaac Butt. For nearly fifteen years Butt had appeared only
irregularly at the Irish bar. It was the election of 1865 which,
in depriving him of his parliamentary seat, had forced him
irrevocably back to Ireland to rebuild, at over fifty years of
age, a once great legal career. But this same setback gave him
a still greater opportunity. When Butt took the fenian brief
which Whiteside had rejected, he took the first step back upon
the path which years before had brought him to the forefront
of an earlier generation of Irish tribunes, and which was now
to take him to the leadership of home rule.

The youthful Butt had first risen to prominence in the
early 1840's when as a brilliant young lawyer and a distinguished graduate of Trinity College Dublin he appeared the
most promising of the younger conservatives. Even at this
early stage some of his work as editor of the *Dublin University
Magazine,* notably his pamphlet in 1837 upon the Irish poor
law, had demonstrated that his conservatism rested upon two
pillars, an emotional sympathy with the grievances of the
peasantry, and the conviction that this and other weaknesses
in the Irish economy were essentially imperial problems.[2]
But in public controversy he found as yet no inconsistency in
conducting himself as a violent Orange bigot. Sir William
Gregory, who enjoyed his support in the Dublin City by-election of 1842, recalled him in this period as 'the very type of
ultra-domineering, narrow-minded, Protestant ascendancy'.[3]
When the municipal reform measures of the whig administration in 1840 proposed to destroy this citadel of ascendancy,
Butt's combination of bigotry and legal brilliance caused him
to be chosen to argue the case of the old Dublin Corporation
before the House of Lords. His career as a conservative
spokesman reached its zenith when in 1843 he was chosen to

2 Butt, *The poor law bill for Ireland examined,* London, 1837. pp. 8,
29, 35.
3 Gregory, *Autobiography,* London, 1894, p. 60.

put forward the conservative reply to O'Connell in the great corporation debate on repeal.

By this time, however, a natural breadth of mind and generosity of spirit, a love of country and a susceptible emotional nature, had stripped much of the bigotry from his politics. The conservatism which he put forward in this debate he justified on national grounds as an Irishman. Its basis was a belief in the imperial partnership of Great Britain and Ireland in a joint civilising destiny, a partnership of reciprocal rights and duties inherent in the union settlement. Repeal would give Ireland only the status of a province; union gave her equal partnership in a great empire. The idealism of Irish nationalists, especially Tone, he warmly conceded, but their agitation he denounced:

> It is our duty now to abandon agitation that can lead to no practical or real good, and cordially unite in a generous rivalry and co-operation to improve the condition of our people.[4]

Butt's arguments upon this occasion were not highly praised by his own party, but they were quite warmly received by the repealers, who remarked upon 'the broad and candid admissions with which his speech was thickly studded'. It was these admissions which inspired the famous prophecy of O'Connell:

> Depend upon it that Alderman Butt is in his inmost soul an Irishman, and that we will have him struggling with us for Ireland yet.[5]

The debate over, with repeal, inevitably, triumphant, O'Connel had a word for his youthful opponent. 'Isaac', he is recorded as saying, 'you are young and I am old. I will fail in winning back the parliament, but you will do it when I shall have passed away'.[6]

In the 1840's Butt became the chief exponent of a new kind of Irish conservatism which conceded not a whit to its nationalist opponents in love of country. It was a philosophy which could not master the basic conservative dread of O'Con-

4 Butt, *Repeal of the union,* Dublin, 1843, pp. 17, 35-36.
5 *Nation,* 4, 11 Mar. 1843.
6 J. G. Swift MacNeill, *What I have seen and heard,* (1925), p. 123.

nell, but it could appeal more closely to the spirit of young Ireland, with which, especially in its literary attitudes, it had much in common. Two lectures of Butt's on protection to Irish industry, published in 1846, were actually purchased for distribution to repeal reading-rooms on the motion of John Mitchel, who characterised them as 'a very admirable repeal essay, potent to convince any Irishman (except perhaps the author of it) that Ireland's only hope lay in the restoration of a national legislature'. 'A soul has come into Ireland', said T. F. Meagher of the new conservatism.[7] But it was left to another of the younger nationalists, T. McNevin, to sum up this emotional sympathy most aptly, and to express a shrewd understanding of Butt's attitudes which was to remain more or less true for the rest of his life. Writing to Smith O'Brien he semi-jocularly grouped the younger conservatives of the Butt—Samuel Ferguson school under the heading of 'Orange Young Ireland'.[8]

This new conservatism might have had much to contribute to Ireland in more peaceful times. But the famine, the imperial neglect of Ireland, and the rebellion which followed created a new political situation in which it had no place. For Isaac Butt these events were the final disillusionment which destroyed the basis of his conservatism and left him for twenty years without a practicable political philosophy. In April 1847, in the midst of the famine disaster, he wrote:

Irishmen were told, indeed, that in consenting to a Union which would make them partners with a great and opulent nation, like England, they would have all the advantages that might be expected to flow from such a union. How are these expectations to be realised, how are these pledges to be fulfilled, if the partnership is only to be one of loss, and never of profit to us? If, bearing our share of all imperial burdens—when calamity falls upon us we are to be told that we then recover our separate existence as a nation, just so far as to disentitle us to the state assistance which any portion of a nation, visited with such a calamity, had

7 *Nation*, 4, 11 Apr. 1846.
8 O'Brien papers, National Library, no 2291; Duffy, *Young Ireland*, 1880, pp. 503-504.

a right to expect from the governing power . . . this calamity
ought to be regarded as an imperial one, and borne by the empire at large. If this be not conceded—if the state be not, as we
have said, our government—if we are not to receive the assistance which government can render upon such an occasion—
what alternative is there for any Irishman but to feel that the
united parliament has abdicated the functions of government
for Ireland, and to demand for his country that separate legislative existence, the necessity of which will then be fully proved.[9]

Butt participated in the early works of the Irish Council, a
non-party association formed to consider famine remedies, but
the futility of this body soon became apparent. In April 1848
a new 'Protestant Repeal Association' was founded; Butt's
old friend Samuel Ferguson gave in his support, and Butt's
own impending adhesion was rumoured.[10] But events were
moving too fast for the gentler nationalists. In May, Smith
O'Brien and Meagher were put on trial for sedition and Butt
was briefed for their defence, on the understanding that nothing they had said would be retracted or disavowed.[11] In this
trial Butt unmistakeably placed himself in the eyes of the
Irish people at the head of the new conservative repealers.
O'Brien, he argued, was guilty not of contempt of the crown
but of contempt of the union, and the kernel of his defence
was a justification of repeal. In each case the jury disagreed,
and both prisoners were discharged.

Butt was now thirty-five years old and at the peak of his
career. Throughout Ireland his name was applauded as that
of a national hero. The *Nation* sounded a timely note of
warning:

Mr Butt performed his task nobly . . . he has done Ireland
good service, but she cannot afford to permit him to stop here.
No man since Grattan has a greater career open to him if he
be true to the principles he himself has taught; but Ireland is

9 Butt, *A voice for Ireland, the famine in the land,* Dublin, 1847, pp.
22, 53.
10 *Nation,* 8, 22, 29 Apr. 1848.
11 Ibid., 13 May.

no longer content with half a heart; she is rich enough in power and genius to reject it.[12]

That was on 20 May 1848. On 27 May John Mitchel was sentenced and immediately transported. Soon afterwards the Confederate leaders at last decided upon the import of arms. In July violence broke out and the political reactions of men like Butt became largely irrelevant. For twenty years he was to pay the moral price of his hesitation.

Elected for Youghal in 1852 as a 'Liberal-Conservative' he transferred his residence to England, but as an old-fashioned protectionist and a Palmerstonian imperialist, a brilliant Irishman of uncertain consistency, he could find no satisfactory outlet in either party. For a time he enjoyed some contact with Disraeli as a fellow-protectionist, but he sought in vain from that chameleon figure the recompense of minor office as Law Adviser to Dublin Castle.[13]

Unable to advance politically, he could find compensation in the opportunities which London offered for cheerful living. Always a man of vigorous appetites—he married at twenty-four and begot eight legal offspring—he fathered at least two illegitimate children in this period and acquired a burden of debt and a reputation for profligacy which were to damage him both financially and politically for the rest of his life. Moral degeneration, however, not uncharacteristically brought mellowing, and as the bright hopes of preferment dwindled old sympathies revived, and at Westminster he became increasingly the champion of the Irish tenantry and of Catholic education. When at last in 1865 he surrendered his tiny borough to the allurement of a wealthier patron, no less a patriot than John O'Leary could mourn his passing.[14]

But the compulsion to return to legal practice in Ireland which followed upon this defeat was, in fact, a blessing in disguise. Butt gained the fenian brief, and with it something

12 Ibid., 20 May.
13 Butt to Disraeli, several undated letters from this period, Disraeli MSS.
14 O'Leary, *Recollections of fenians and fenianism*, 1896, vol. 2. p. 165.

which Ireland has given to few of her leaders—a second chance.
He was principal in nearly all the state trials of the next two
years, to the virtual abandonment of his private practice.
Speaking often for four hours at a time, bullying informers,
haranguing juries, he made himself a household name to an
avid national audience which followed the full-length reports
of the trials in the press. The beginning of 1868 found him a
prisoner for debt in the Marshalsea, but once again, as in
1848, the legal tribune of nationalist Ireland.

The generation of Irishmen at whose head he was now to
be placed was, however, a new one, largely unfamiliar with
the conflicts of his youth and the attitudes which they had
bred in him. In those earlier, formative years lie many of the
roots of Butt's subsequent failure as a national leader. Most
obviously, though not most important, the debts which he had
acquired were to compel him always to divide his energies
between politics and legal practice. This strain upon his resources, together with his tarnished moral reputation and his
recurring indebtedness to many of his political lieutenants,
was to contribute much to the weakness of his leadership. But
more fundamentally important, he had evolved during those
years the curious imperial nationalism which was so often to
prove inexplicable to the younger men around him in the
home rule movement. He returned to Ireland already a be-
liever in his country's right to legislative independence,[15] but
no simple separatist. The conception of an imperial partnership in a great destiny which he had developed in the 1840's
was still the basis of his nationalism, overlaid now by an eag-
erness, learned from Young Ireland, to awaken in every denomination of his countrymen a realisation of their own cul-
tural unity which would bring them into that 'united nationalist party' the creation of which had become his life's aim.[16]
Federal home rule was for him no mere tactical second-best; it
was at once the thought-out expression of his own emotional
view of the relationship between the two islands, and an offer
of partnership to Irish protestantism. Davis could have grasp-

15 *Irish Times,* 6 Sep. 1871.
16 *Nation,* 13 Nov. 1869.

ed the generosity of his thought. His new allies were for the
most part only to detect in it those suspect conservative origins from which long ago it had sprung. For the moment it
might be enough for Ireland that Butt was the protector of
the fenian convicts, whom free she had repudiated, but who
now in captivity earned their martyrdom. So too, for the moment, were hidden fundamental differences of attitude which
the stresses of a working political relationship were to bring
once more to light.

But if the shock of the fenian rising threw up a new nationalist leader, it created an alternative to nationalism in the person of William Ewart Gladstone. For the first time since the
1830's it became possible for a great body of national Irishmen
to argue the merits of support for the English Liberal party
and the mischievousness of separatist agitation. The cause
which produced this new situation and which precipitated the
general election in which the new struggle opened was Gladstone's historic offer of ' justice for Ireland '.

In May 1868, Gladstone, as leader of the opposition, secured
the passage in the House of Commons of three resolutions calling for the abolition of the Church of Ireland as an establishment, and requesting the Queen to create no further personal
interests pending such a measure. This Liberal victory made
a dissolution of parliament inevitable. The election which
followed was fought by the Liberals almost entirely upon the
issue of Irish administration. Speaking at St. Helen's at the
outset of the campaign, Gladstone described the state of Ireland as ' the question which is of paramount importance at
this juncture '. In the face of the continued suspension, two
years after the rising, of the habeas corpus act, no statesman,
he declared, could congratulate himself on the condition of
Ireland. ' Do not conceal from yourselves this fact . . . you
have arrived at a point only one step from civil war '. On behalf of the Liberal party he said : —

We have asked ourselves whether in this state of things we
stand clear in the face of Ireland and of the civilised world;
whether the laws and institutions in Ireland are such as ought
to prevail; whether they are such as in the face of national

danger we should be bold enough to maintain . . . I have asked myself this question, and I do not find that the laws and institutions in Ireland are such that I am willing to be responsible for maintaining them.

Gladstone was then in the first stage of that massive reconsideration of Irish problems which was to lead him to the Land Act of 1881 and ultimately to the incorporation among the basic tenets of the English Liberal party of the principle of Irish home rule. In 1868 hc had come to realise, as no English leader of comparable authority had ever before realised, the immensity of the grievances under which the bulk of the Irish people laboured. At this period, however, he still believed that these grievances could be removed by a belated act of reparation on the part of the English to the Irish nation, without disturbing the ties which bound the two partners together. The programme which he now outlined soon became known as that of 'justice for Ireland'.

The Irish question has many branches; I will not mention all of them. The two principal questions that arise for the consideration of the coming parliament are, the one concerned with the tenure of land, the other that which is connected with the religious institutions of the country. As respects the tenure of land, that question is to the rere, whilst the other occupies the front.

On the land question, he affirmed the desire of his party to 'give to the Irish cultivator the security for his efforts and results of his industry which he does not adequately enjoy'. With regard to the church issue, he denied the practicability of partial reforms such as the redistribution of funds between the different denominations, which as late as a year before he had been privately considering;[17] the real struggle between the two parties was between:

the removal of the Irish Church on the one hand and maintaining it on the other, between perpetual attempts to bolster

---

[17] Sir John Gray to Gladstone, 2 Sept. 1877; Gladstone to Gray, 6 Sept., B.M. Add. MSS, 44413 ff 121, 134.

it up by throwing sops to other parties in the shape of state
grants and state endowments, and abolishing that church as
an establishment.

He concluded by asking his hearers to assist in the mitigation
of 'these inveterate causes of alienation' between the two
races. ' I trust you will exhibit an earnest determination to do
justice, and open a future of happiness, prosperity, and con-
tentment, which shall stand in joyful contrast with the past
of that unhappy land '.[18]

The bid which Gladstone thus made for the loyalty of the
Irish people was to dictate the course of the conflict which
followed in the next six years. It had been possible in the past
for Irish leaders to justify a temporary alliance with one or
other of the English parties upon the basis of local reforms,
but never before had an English leader so totally identified
his party with the redress of Irish grievances. Those Irish liberals, and there were many, in whom the ideological attach-
ment to repeal had become drugged by time and security,
could now welcome, perhaps, an ultimate fruition of the union
settlement. Others were still emotionally attached to the idea
of legislative independence, but no less sharply aware of the
immediacy of their practical grievances. The catholic church
seemed to have found a champion who would lift the last gal-
ling yoke of protestant ascendancy from its neck. It was not
difficult for Irish clerics to overlook the ideological chasm
which separated them from nonconformist English Liberalism, to forget for the moment its implacable opposition to the
endowment of denominational education. For the tenant farmer there was the offer of security for himself and his family
in his holding. Only the irreconcilable nationalist could withhold his support from the Liberal party.

Two forces, then, were to struggle for supremacy in the
next six years, two alternative solutions to the Irish problem:
the operation of the united parliament to grant redress of
grievances on the one hand; on the other, the achievement
first of legislative independence as a prelude to reform. It was

[18] *Freeman's Journal,* 7 Aug. 1868.

not that this was a new conflict. But in the 1850's and 60's the
paralysis of the national movement, and the equal hostility to
Irish demands shown by both the English parties, had robbed
it of much of its vitality. Now fenianism had revivified political controversy. It had re-awakened in Irishmen an emotional
awareness of their nationality. But at the same time it had
swept away the Liberalism of the Durham Letter. In its place
stood a statesman who offered what might at last be a true
reconciliation between the two islands.

CHAPTER I

The Disestablishment Election

A: THE STATE OF THE FRANCHISE

IF DISRAELI'S reforms of 1867 are among the landmarks of English parliamentary history, the concessions extended to the unfranchised Irish in the parallel Representation of the People (Ireland) Act were scarcely comparable. In borough constituencies the poor rate qualification for the franchise was reduced from £8 to 'over £4' for rated occupiers, and the franchise was also extended for the first time to lodgers, the minimum qualification being twelve months continuous residence in sole tenancy of an apartment having an unfurnished letting value of at least £10 per annum. The qualification for the county franchise remained unchanged at a £12 rating. By comparison with the English act, this was a mockery, wrote one liberal.[1] Registration drives were launched by both parties in most of the Irish boroughs, but the list of new claimants was never great. In Limerick there were only 36 claimants under the lodger franchise, and 247 under the new rating provisions, in proportion to an existing electorate of 1,944. In Ennis 59 ambitious citizens sought to join the 178 who had previously despatched the town's representative to Westminster.

But it was in Dublin, where party registration was most highly organised, that the effectiveness of the act was most fully tested. Its complexities were aggravated from the outset by the scrupulosity of the four barristers who adjudicated on claims. Where in London the presence of the claimant was not required unless his claim had been questioned in writing, in Dublin all applications were treated as challenged and personal attendance required. The difficulties thus placed in the

---

[1] *Freeman's Journal,* 1 Nov. 1868.

way of working-class claimants were enhanced by the refusal
of one of the four barristers to sit at night. He was subsequently a conservative candidate in the election. Prospects of
a large increase under the lodger franchise were made all the
more dubious by the definition of that class adopted; against
the protests of the liberals, the four barristers ruled that:

> A lodger is a person who occupies part of a dwelling house
> as his residence, either where the landlord resides on the pre-
> mises, or where although the house is wholly let out in tene-
> ments the landlord retains a control over the outside door en-
> titling him to enter the premises without thereby becoming a
> trespasser.[2]

It was a ruling which, once published, brought a rapid accre-
tion of business to the locksmiths of Dublin.

> Henry Watts, liberal, 19 Lower Liffey Street, stated that he
> never saw the landlady use a latchkey, but he knew that she
> had one.
> 'When did she get the latchkey'?
> 'I think she got it today' (laughter)[3]

A comparison of the electoral statistics for the Irish boroughs before and after the introduction of the act clearly
illustrates its ineffectiveness. Between 1866 and 1868 the borough vote increased by 19 per cent. Greater increases were
on the whole recorded in Ulster and Leinster than in Munster and Connaught. The electorates of Limerick and Cork
rose by only $4\frac{1}{2}$ and 9 per cent respectively; Dublin increased
by approximately the average percentage; Belfast by rather
more.[4] A slow growth was maintained in subsequent registra-
tions, a further increase of just over 8 per cent being recorded
between 1868 and 1874. But the Irish borough electorate re-

2 ibid., 11, 15 Sept.
3 ibid., 18 Sept. 1868.
4 The extension of the parliamentary borough of Belfast to the municipal boundaries under the 1868 act makes valid comparison difficult.
The real increase was probably, however, something over three thous-
and, or rather more than in Dublin. (*Return as to rating, population,
number of electors, etc.*, p. 2, H.C. 1867-8, (236), lvi, 509).

mained extremely restricted, representing less than 4 per cent of the borough population, and no effort was yet made towards the most obviously needed reform—a redistribution of seats. Of the thirty-three Irish boroughs, two had electorates of less than two hundred, another nine had between two and three hundred voters, and five between three and four hundred. Almost half the Irish boroughs had less than four hundred voters, and just over four thousand people chose sixteen representatives. In several boroughs, notably Dublin and Carrickfergus, the corrupt and anachronistic freeman franchise remained almost decisive.

In short, despite the act of 1868, little real expansion occurred in the size of the Irish electorate in this period. It required, firstly, the introduction of the ballot, and still more, a redistribution of seats, radically to alter the character of the Irish representation. In the meanwhile, it was a strictly limited Irish electorate which was summoned, in November 1868, to accept or reject the Gladstonian message of reconciliation.

B: THE ISSUES IN THE ELECTION

If the issue of Irish grievance, and of Gladstone's new Irish policy, dominated the election in both islands, that policy was practically speaking identified, above all else, with the cause of disestablishment. The agitation for disestablishment, which now reached a climax under the stimulus of Liberal support, had proceeded intermittently for many years. Motions in its favour had been put in the Commons by the English liberal, Dilwyn, in 1865, and in 1866, and 1867 by Sir John Gray, who had been put in charge of the subject by the Irish members, and was unremittent both in debate and in private lobbying. Gray, member for Kilkenny City and proprietor of the *Freeman's Journal,* was undoubtedly, with Cardinal Manning, the principal influence in persuading Gladstone to take up the cause,[5] and those in Ireland to whom disestablishment was the great issue of the election looked naturally to him as the

5 cf. Gladstone to Gray, Gray to Gladstone, 20 Mar. 1868, BM Add. MSS 44414 ff. 176-7, and several letters between Gladstone and Manning from 1867 and 1868 in BM Add. MSS 44249.

most authoritative spokesman of their ideas. 'O'Connell will never be dead while Sir John lives', declared one catholic parish priest,[6] employing a favourite form of eulogy which in this case illustrated in truth what was a very real continuity of Irish catholic nationalism, for although Gray himself was a protestant, the party for which he spoke was essentially that of the clerical-liberals. As its spokesman, and as the leading Irish lay agitator for disestablishment, Gray pledged his not inconsiderable forces to Gladstone:

> Anxious to be free from all party trammels, and to be as independent as you are, I nevertheless desire to give a cordial, generous, and trusting support to Mr Gladstone, as the recognised leader of the movement for religious equality,—a statesman who is, I believe, thoroughly sincere in his professed desire to legislate for Ireland in a spirit of justice and equity.[7]

But there was nothing passive in this endorsement. It was the contention of many conservatives that there was no genuine popular demand for disestablishment; but whether or not the Irish peasant had the same kind of enthusiasm for it that he may have had for land reform or fenianism, there can be no doubt that under the influence of the liberal press, the clergy, and the parliamentary candidates, the contest from the beginning resolved itself into a bitter struggle on the church issue. Cardinal Cullen summed up the 'official' Irish liberal attitude in a letter endorsing the two liberal candidates in Dublin City: referring first to land and education, he went on:

> However, these and other matters, though of the greatest moment to the welfare of the country, cannot all be settled at once. They must give preference to the all-absorbing question of the protestant establishment. As soon as that shall have been finally settled, and the principal cause of dissension removed, we may expect the land and education question will be discussed with a proper regard to the material and religious in-

6 Archdeacon Redmond of Glendalough, *Freeman's Journal*, 20 Oct. 1868.
7 ibid., 19 Oct. 1868.

terests of the country, and that measures will be adopted in reference to them calculated to meet the approbation of all classes.[8]

'We have arrived at a momentous crisis, the magnitude of which cannot be overstated', declared Bishop Leahy of Dromore.[9] 'If the established church is not the only grievance we have to complain of, it is the one which lies at the root of all others', said Dr Kieran, archbishop of Armagh and primate of all Ireland.[10]

It was natural, although unwelcome to the protestant conservatives, that the catholic bishops should have adopted this attitude towards disestablishment. 'The priests are exerting all their power at the present moment to keep attention fixed on the one question of the church', wrote the conservative *Mayo Constitution*.[11] Equally, it was natural that Chichester Fortescue, M.P. for Louth, and popularly regarded as Gladstone's Irish spokesman, should have described disestablishment as 'a condition indispensable to the success of all other legislation'.[12] What is more interesting is the extent to which this principle was sustained by the popular liberal representatives throughout the country. The *Freeman's Journal* persistently maintained the primacy of disestablishment over all other issues:

When the church question is settled, we shall agitate the land question, if indeed it be advisable to postpone it so long. One at a time, however, is a salutary maxim. We should not distract popular feeling and diminish its power. The land question will come round in its appointed time.[13]

This attitude was endorsed by the vast majority of the liberal provincial newspapers and of the liberal candidates. Seventy-five per cent of those election addresses which were aimed at the liberal or popular vote—and which were prepared to make

8 ibid., 3 Nov.
9 ibid., 7 Nov. 1868.
10 ibid., 12 Nov.
11 *Mayo Constitution*, 20 Oct.
12 *Freeman's Journal*, 4 Nov.
13 ibid., 30 Sept.

some revelation of the candidate's political beliefs—listed disestablishment first in importance; virtually none omitted to
refer to it. Most followed a standard pattern, citing three
main issues—disestablishment first, with land reform and the
provision of Catholic denominational education second and
third, in order of preference or local expediency.

Clarity, however, was not often a feature of these electoral
pronunciamentos. Even on the main issue of disestablishment,
few candidates went as far as legislative precision. A demand
for 'disestablishment and disendowment', a simple expression of support for Gladstone's church policy, or a combination of both—these were the standard forms. In practice, then,
and perhaps for the first time, a great Irish issue was directly,
and on the whole unquestioningly, linked to the return of the
leader of the English Liberal party.

On the second issue of this election, that of land reform, the
bulk of the popular candidates were no more explicit, and the
notorious complexity of this issue lent itself to far greater
divergencies amongst those who were superficially in agreement upon the necessity for reform. Conservative candidates
could without injury to conscience or party declare themselves
in favour of a measure of land reform, and in this election
many such candidates were glad to be able to give evidence of
their good intentions upon some less vexed topic than that of
the church. Lord Crichton, standing in Enniskillen, declared
that he would give the tenant-farmer 'compensation for all
unexhausted improvements, and in cases where money had
been spent, he would grant leases sufficiently long to recoup
the tenant for his outlay'.[14] Another conservative candidate,
Sir Leopold McClintock, in Drogheda, adjudged 'the indust-
rious occupiers of the soil entitled to have secured to them by
legislative enactment a right to the fruits of their labour and
outlay'.[15]

Many liberals committed themselves no more precisely.
Jonathan Pim in Dublin City promised to 'omit no proper
opportunity of advancing the settlement of the land ques-

14 ibid., 19 Nov. 1868.
15 ibid., 12 Nov. 1868.

DORDT COLLEGE
Sioux Center, Iowa

tion '[16]; Peter Paul McSwiney in Dublin County advocated 'a measure securing all that is equitable to the landlord, securing all that is just to the tenant '[17]; Viscount Burke in Galway County expressed the hope that ' measures will soon be matured to secure an impartial adjustment of the legitimate rights of both landlords and tenants '.[18]

There were, of course, some who fully appreciated that the desire of the occupier for security in his holding could only be realised by a virtual revolution in the landlord-tenant relationship. Butt himself, who at this time was probably the most radical of the leading tenant spokesmen and the most widely-read pamphleteer upon the subject, had produced a detailed plan for security of tenure with 60 year leases based upon the independent revaluation of rents at periodic intervals.[19] In 1867 he had urged the commencement of a serious agitation on the basis of this demand.[20] But the land issue was not ripe for such an agitation in 1868, and the paramountcy of the church question further militated against it. Tenant organisations did exist in wide areas of the country in the shape of the ' Farmers' Clubs '. These clubs, although respectable rather than revolutionary, were quite active in the period of the election; the most prominent was probably that of Limerick, which, under the presidency of William Bolster, organised a great tenant-right demonstration in September, at which Butt was the principal speaker. But schemes such as Butt's, which came to be grouped under the broad heading of ' fixity of tenure ', were still regarded by the bulk of the landlords as dangerously subversive of the rights of property, and by no means possessed, as yet, the support of the generality of Irish liberal candidates, who clung to the vaguer ' security of tenure '. In the face of the general preoccupation with the church issue the tenant party could exert little influence. Its most notable victory was in Cork County, where McCarthy

16 ibid., 14 July 1868.
17 ibid., 18 Nov.
18 Galway Vindicator, 30 Sept.
19 Land tenure in Ireland: a plea for the Celtic race, Dublin, 1866.
20 Butt: The Irish people and the Irish land: a letter to Lord Lifford, Dublin, 1867, p. 289.

15830

Downing, a veteran of the independent opposition movement of 1852, and a future home ruler, defeated the Honourable Robert Boyle, a cousin of Lord Cork, who had the support of the local liberal landowning interest. This was conceded to be a direct victory for tenant farmer organisation and power.

But on the whole, despite the fact that land reform was in theory one of the great issues of this election, argued in principle by every liberal spokesman, lay or clerical, one is left with the impression that in practice, in land reform as in disestablishment, the initiative lay with the English Liberal leader; the criterion was once again a general support, at least for the moment, of that statesman.

The third and last of the major issues of this election was that of education. The demands for denominational education and a catholic university were still before the public, unsatisfied. Negotiations on the subject of a catholic university charter between the catholic prelates and Lord Mayo, the conservative chief secretary, had just broken down at the outset of the campaign, thus dashing catholic hopes that the endowment of such a university formed an integral part of the Conservative theory of concurrent endowment or 'levelling-up', which had been mooted as an alternative to Liberal disestablishment or 'levelling-down'.[21] This disappointment may have helped to reinforce catholic enthusiasm for Gladstone. Yet in the context of this election any form of denominational endowment was out if its place and time. A party which, with exaggerated scrupulosity, proposed to couple with disestablishment the withdrawal of the regium donum and the Maynooth grant, was scarcely likely to endow a sectarian university. Conservative journals did not hesitate to remind independent catholic candidates that the strong nonconformist element in the English Liberal party was fundamentally devoted to the principle of non-sectarian education. Would a party with such an element in it endorse the establishment of the denominational system in Ireland? If English nonconformist opinion is temporarily equated with Ulster liberal opin-

[21] Manning to Disraeli, 4, 21 May 1867; 16 March, 2 Dec. 1868; 7 May 1870; Disraeli MSS.

ion, the result is instructive. The *Northern Whig* opposed denominational education as a feature of Tory 'levelling-up';[22] the *Derry Standard* was firmly for disestablishment, and for its liberal upholder in the city, Richard Dowse, but the whole denominational idea was to it a 'medieval retrogression'. With the catholic rejection of Lord Mayo's proposals 'the intolerable nature of ultramontane despotism' had been self-exposed before the country.[23] Whereas in the south of Ireland the demand for denominational education formed a part of virtually every liberal election address, the six liberal candidates in Ulster studiously avoided it. It was scarcely surprising that the *Galway Vindicator* should have countered the prevailing enthusiasm for Gladstone with the contention that immediately after the passage of disestablishment the Irish catholic members would very probably find themselves in opposition to the Liberal party on the subject of education; ideologically it was the weakest link in the Anglo-Irish liberal alliance.[24]

If disestablishment occupied the liberal mind to the exclusion of much else, still more so were the conservatives preoccupied with it; one would scarcely, in fact, be guilty of oversimplification if one were to characterise the entire election as 'religious equality' versus 'the church in danger'. The liberal presbyterian *Banner of Ulster* printed a terse but accurate summary of the conservatives' attitude to his church's peril:

> Its disestablishment would be contrary to the Act of Union; it would make Roman Catholic members of parliament forswear themselves, inasmuch as, on their entering into parliament, they disavowed, disclaimed, and solemnly abjured any intention to subvert the present church establishment as settled by law within this realm. It would make the queen break her coronation oath. The religious supremacy of Rome in Ireland would be assured, for the Roman Catholic priests are the political as well as the religious leaders of the people; the protes-

---

22 *Northern Whig*, 16 July, 25 Aug. 1868
23 *Derry Standard*, 11 July.
24 *Galway Vindicator*, 12 Aug. 1868.

tant population would rapidly diminish, absenteeism would increase, and the landlords, who are mostly protestant, would, wherever it is possible, become non-resident. Our scheme of government would degenerate into a mere system of police; that sacred union between church and state, which has hitherto been the chief means of our civilisation, and is the only security for our religious liberty, would be dissolved: the Church of England would follow next: the protestant religion would be endangered: the rights of property would be subverted and the landlords spoliated. The church is, after all, self-supporting, for the tithe is paid by the landlord: it has stood for many generations. A sacred feeling towards it has grown up in the hearts of men; and if time-honoured institutions are thus swept away, where will the spoiler stop?—the throne itself will be in danger, and the glory will have departed from England.[25]

Not least of disestablishment's attendant terrors was the fear that agrarian revolution and repeal would follow hard upon its heels. To Anthony Traill, candidate for Dublin University and a future Provost, Gladstone's resolutions were 'certain to lead eventually to the repeal of the legislative union of Ireland with Great Britain'.[26] To the Irish conservative, then, the election presented a stark challenge. 'The Papists . . . will run their entire strength for G. (Gladstone)', wrote Thomas Conolly, M.P. for Donegal, to Disraeli, 'but we have measured them before and they will not prevail'.[27]

The last ditch dug, however, the art of war demanded that it be suitably decorated. Few of the conservative candidates were willing to conceal their determination to uphold 'the protestant constitution in church and state',[28] and 'to oppose all plans which may be brought forward for the endowment of error'.[29] They could, however, avow their readiness 'to assist in removing any anomalies or abuses which, after

25 *Banner of Ulster*, 8 Aug.
26 *Belfast News-Letter*, 2 Nov. 1868.
27 Conolly to Disraeli, 26 Oct. 1868, Disraeli MSS.
28 Stronge (Armagh Co.), *Belfast News-Letter*, 12 Oct. 1868.
29 Lanyon (Belfast), *Banner of Ulster*, 12 Sept. 1868.

careful consideration, may appear to exist ',[30] with, of course, the reservation that any such reform must not 'abolish the parochial system . . . or weaken the power of episcopal government by a diminution in the number of bishops '.[31] But above all, disestablishment was a 'false issue' in Ireland, begotten by an unholy alliance of Gladstone's craving for office with Rome's thirst for ascendancy. Tenant right was the truly vital question of the day—though here, too, there was to be no truckling with 'the wild schemes of all those who follow Mr Butt and Mr Bright on this issue '.[32]

If the catholic liberal or the episcopalian conservative had his duty clearly pointed out to him, Ulster presbyterianism found itself substantially divided. The Ulster conservative candidates made a point of wooing the presbyterian voter by promising to oppose the withdrawal of the regium donum. 'Ninety-nine out of a hundred of the presbyterian laity concur with the episcopalian laity on this church question ', wrote the *Belfast News-Letter*, and urged the protestant people to stick together and resist those who would 'jesuitically' divide them.[33] But against this the *Banner of Ulster* could repeatedly point to the opposition of the Ulster conservatives in the last session of parliament to the Burials Bill of William Monsell,[34] and to their failure to nominate a single presbyterian as a candidate for parliament.[35] The *Banner* described the presbyterian episcopalian alliance as 'a match by which the presbyterians have nothing to gain and everything to lose ';[36] with regard to the loss of the regium donum, 'the sacrifice required is not great. To secure religious equality it (the presbyterian church) must surrender £40,000 a year . . . It is a small price to pay for a great principle '.[37]

[30] Hill Trevor (Down), *Belfast News-Letter*, 2 Nov. 1868.
[31] Traill (Dublin University), ibid.
[32] ibid., 31 Aug. 1868.
[33] ibid., 10 Aug.
[34] It is proposed that under certain conditions a presbyterian clergyman should be allowed to officiate at the burial of a member of his own church in an episcopalian graveyard.
[35] *Banner of Ulster*, 13 Oct.
[36] ibid., 3 Sept.
[37] ibid., 3 Oct.

It is impossible to gauge accurately presbyterian opinion upon the church issue; there appear to have been very strong and active parties upon both sides. The general assembly passed a resolution which all were able to support, and interpret differently,[38] and while the moderator, Dr Morell, threw his weight behind the conservative Keown in Dungannon, being credited by the liberal press with the responsibility for their candidate's defeat, Dowse in Londonderry City seems to have had a considerable amount of active presbyterian support, being proposed by Professor Smyth of Magee, and sustained by fifty-two presbyterian clergymen who published an advertisement denying that the resolution of the general assembly had been a declaration of support for the establishment. On the whole, the liberals probably had considerable grounds for gratitude to the presbyterians at the end of the election; in addition to this aid in Londonderry, two much-prized liberal successes were won by presbyterian candidates in Belfast and Newry. These three seats were the only liberal victories in Ulster.

There remain to be considered briefly those minor topics which were raised by some of the candidates in this election. Two of these topics were of particular local significance to Ulster, the Burials Bill, mentioned above, and the Party Processions Act, a measure much inhibiting of traditional Orange ceremonial, and one which had created a notable martyr in the popular Orange leader, William Johnston of Ballykilbeg. In the rest of the country there were also a number of secondary issues raised. Some, like the question of state railway purchase, crossed the boundaries of party; others, like amnesty, repeal of the union, the secret ballot, and the reform of union rating and of the grand jury system, were generally the

---

[38] '. . . that they declare their unwavering adherence to the principles of an ecclesiastical establishment as set forth in the standards of the presbyterian church—viz. that it is the duty of the state to recognise and endow the truth and to withhold all encouragement from anti-Christian error, while, at the same time, the church is left free from state control in the exercise of all her proper functions, and continues subject to Christ alone, her king and head.' (*Derry Standard*, 4 Nov. 1868).

preserve of the more advanced liberals. Amnesty and repeal deserve separate consideration; the other topics played little part in the electoral struggle. The hardy annuals of Irish politics, they paled in 1868 before the dawning hope of disestablishment.

C: THE CATHOLIC CLERGY IN THE ELECTION

The identity of view which prevailed between Gladstone and the catholic clergy as to the first importance of disestablishment has already been mentioned; the significance of this alliance in the election would be difficult to exaggerate, for it gave to the liberals the invaluable asset of a central authority whose influence could reach into the majority of the constituencies of southern Ireland. William Monsell, the leading Irish catholic in the English Liberal party, took upon himself the duty of writing to members of the hierarchy appealing to them to use this influence on behalf of the party candidates, and urging upon them

> the folly of accepting a candidate who would vote against the church (or any other measure of national importance to Ireland) and at the same time support the party who, as long as they are in office, will make it impossible to overthrow the church.[39]

'My views and feeling are quite in unison with your own', replied the Reverend Dr Delany, bishop of Cork.[40] Dr Butler, bishop of Limerick, wrote to his 'dear friend' Monsell to the same effect; he had visited Cork to see Dr Keane, bishop of Cloyne, and Dr O'Hea, bishop of Ross, and reported:

> I was glad to find them both quite determined to admit no candidate for county or borough except on a distinct pledge of opposing D'Israeli and supporting Gladstone at least until the Established Church is disestablished and disendowed . . . Drs Keane and O'Hea were to have a meeting with Dr Delany and Dr Moriarty so as to have prefect unanimity for Cork.[41]

[39] Keane to Monsell, 13 May, Monsell MSS, 8318.
[40] Delany to Monsell, 27 Mar., Monsell MSS, 8318.
[41] Butler to Monsell, 16 Aug. 1868, Monsell MSS, 8317.

The outcome of this meeting was a public statement, issued
from the palace at Killarney:

> We are of opinion that no candidate aspiring to represent an
> Irish constituency in Parliament ought to be accepted unless on
> a distinct pledge to support the policy enunciated by Mr Glad-
> stone with reference to the Established Church and to oppose
> any ministry which is not prepared to carry it into immediate
> effect.
>
> We are also of opinion that candidates should make a dis-
> tinct declaration of principles in conformity with those enun-
> ciated by the Church and people of Ireland on the all-impor-
> tant questions affecting land tenancy and public education.
>
> While the latter questions must be kept prominently before
> the people without any relaxation of our efforts to carry them
> the disestablishment and disendowment of the Protestant
> Church must be insisted upon as of absolute and pressing
> necessity.
>
> Should a number of candidates solicit the suffrages of the
> constituencies of Cork we recommend to our clergy to ascertain
> the views of the gentry and people, and to arrange, if neces-
> sary, for the holding of a county meeting to whose arbitrament
> the choice of candidates may be referred.
>
> Our representatives should be men whose antecedents and
> position may be a guarantee for their fidelity to this pledge.[42]

This kind of arrangement was by no means unusual. So far
as the selection or endorsement of liberal candidates was concerned, in most contested constituencies outside Ulster these
same clergy were the instruments of order and regulation. In
Dublin alone was there a liberal organisation in a more or less
modern sense: the Central Franchise Association was a formal body, meeting frequently in committee, with a secretary,
John McSheehy, who had permanent offices in Dame Street
and who actively supervised the formation and operation of
the local ward committees which were set up for this election.[43] But this body was mainly concerned with registration;

42 Monsell MSS, 8319, undated.
43 *Freeman's Journal*, 1, 11, 13, 14, 18, 21 July, etc.

it appears to have had no say in the choice of candidates except insofar as its personnel were individually influential. Even in their registration work, the ward committees availed themselves of the parish organisation, often meeting in the presbytery with the local parish priest as chairman.[44] Registration committees as such were quite normal in Irish boroughs, both in the conservative and in the liberal interest. Nowhere throughout the country was there much trace of a permanent secular liberal organisation. Chichester Fortescue, the most prominent Irishman in the upper ranks of the English Liberal party, was anxious that a liberal candidate should be started in Dublin County in order to occupy the attentions of Colonel Taylor, one of the two conservative members for the county, who was the Irish Conservative Whip. In order to bring this about he and his fellow liberal candidate for Louth, Matthew O'Reilly Dease, found it necessary personally to put up the sum of fifteen hundred pounds and to instruct their solicitor in Dublin to set about persuading a suitable candidate to come forward. This munificence was, however, no great hardship to O'Reilly Dease, who found most of the money; he had already smoothed his own path to victory in Louth by offering his principal rival, the sitting liberal member Tristram Kennedy, a thousand pounds to betake himself elsewhere.[45]

In Cavan the bishop, Dr Conaty, presided over a liberal meeting which agreed to set up a county club, with the local clergy to form the basis of parish sub-committees,[46] but despite the 'active organising' of the club's secretary, the Reverend P. Galligan,[47] the county returned two anti-disestablishment members unopposed in November. Another constituency in which such an organisation existed was Queen's Coun-

---

[44] ibid., 11, 16, 22, 27, 28, 29 July, etc.

[45] There is no evidence whether or not Kennedy took the bribe; he certainly withdrew. (R. W. Meade letter-book, MS 3924, Meade to ' My Dear John ', 20 July 1868; Meade to Satchell, 22 July; Meade to Fortescue, 17 Nov.; R Colles to Dease, 17 Nov. Also R. Armstrong to Fortescue, 3 July 1874, Strachie MSS, Carlingford Political.)

[46] Freeman's Journal, 20 July 1868.

[47] Dublin Evening Post, 4 Aug.

ty, where an 'Independent Liberal Club', under the presidency of Richard Lalor of Tinnakill, brother of Fintan Lalor,
had been formed, against the wishes of the local bishop, in
1866.[48] Having met on 30 June, this body published an advertisement promising that 'a good liberal candidate' would
be brought forward, and after several efforts to discover a
suitable person,[49] a subsequent meeting, which included six
priests in its attendance, selected T. Mason Jones, a member
of the English Reform Union and a frequent lecturer upon
the evils of the establishment.[50] The club showed its independence by declaring that Jones was the only candidate whom
it would support, despite the fact that thirty-seven priests of
the county had just announced their continued confidence in
the sitting liberal member, the landowner Wilson Fitzpatrick.[51] Unhappily for his supporters it was discovered that a
few years earlier in Liverpool Jones has drawn large audiences
to his lectures as the friend and apologist of Garibaldi; before
a barrage of clerical disapproval he withdrew from the contest.[52] The club's second choice, Kenelm Digby, was more
fortunate, being accepted by the clergy. A very real conflict
between the more advanced liberals and the whigs seems to
have lain behind all this activity. Fitzpatrick was an old whig
with few popular sympathies, one whose vote for disestablishment represented the ultimate concession to radicalism. This
was, indeed, quite good enough for several of the clergy, who
feared the outcome of a contested election; Father Magee,
parish priest of Stradbally, wrote to Fitzpatrick:

> It seems to us as a just and natural compromise, that the con-
> servative party, who possess so much of the property of the
> county, should have a representative of their views; and in the
> selection of a liberal candidate most of the clergy, if not all,
> would (forgetful of some things in the past) place their con-

48 Michael Dunne to Lalor, 12 January 1866, Lalor MSS, 8566. Lalor
(b.1823, d.1893) was a Home Rule M.P. from 1880-92.

49 Lalor to Sullivan, 9 April 1867 (?), Lalor MSS, 8566.

50 *Freeman's Journal*, 7 July, 12, 13 Aug.

51 ibid., 15, 17 Aug. The other member, General Dunne, was a conservative.

52 ibid., 28 Aug., 5 Sept. 1868; *Nation*, 22 Aug., 5 Sept.

fidence in you, provided your views on the land question and tenant right are as enlightened as those you entertain in regard to the church . . .[53]

Fitzpatrick himself feared for his seat, and appears to have made no secret of his lack of enthusiasm for his liberal fellow-candidate, so much so that Lord Russell wrote urging him to swallow his feelings for the sake of gaining a seat for the party. As Fitzpatrick had dedicated his remaining years to recapturing the earldom from which his illegitimacy debarred him, intervention from such a source no doubt carried weight.[54] In the event Fitzpatrick underestimated the chances of returning two liberals for the county. Queen's County was the scene of one of the most vigorous campaigns in the whole country, with clerical addresses from the pulpits, and a succession of public meetings in the main towns of the county. At these meetings Fitzpatrick did not appear, the clergy spoke on behalf of both candidates, and Messrs Lalor and Michael Dunne of the Independent Club adverted only to Digby. Even among the clergy, some of the most advanced were not too enthusiastic in Fitzpatrick's cause.[55] But the coalition held long enough to compel the conservative to retire, and the two liberals were returned unopposed.

The exact measure of clerical influence in this election cannot be assessed, but it would be difficult to overestimate it. Of the twenty-eight constituencies outside Ulster in which contests were started, the clergy were active in at least twenty-four. But the extent and precise form of this clerical participation naturally varied according to the local circumstances which elicited it. In Louth for example, Chichester Fortescue and O'Reilly Dease seemed to have established claims which no one would oppose when at the beginning of November the conservatives started the Honourable Jenico Preston, a catholic and the younger son of Lord Gormanston. 'Who now dare

[53] Magee to Fitzpatrick, 15 June 1868, Fitzpatrick MSS, National Library. This letter was understandably marked ' most confidential '.
[54] In 1869 Fitzpatrick was created Baron Castletown of Upper Ossory.
[55] *Freeman's Journal*, 13, 21, 27 Oct.; 10 Nov., also T. Franks (election agent) to Fitzpatrick, 11 Oct. 1868, Fitzpatrick MSS.

B*

say that the catholics of Ireland are, to a man, against our church'? asked 'a voter and an Orangeman', in a public advertisement in the *Freeman's Journal*. Thus provoked, Dr Kieran, archbishop of Armagh, published an advertisement denouncing Preston's candidature and calling upon the clergy of County Louth to dissuade from supporting him any of their flocks whom they might find so inclined. Preston withdrew.[56]

The clerical contributions to the contests in Galway Borough and Dungarvan are discussed elsewhere. In the diocese of Tuam, Dr MacHale issued a pastoral letter to be read in all the churches after the twelve o'clock mass on 15 November; this letter attacked the landlords and the establishment in general terms; in addition he called a meeting of the clergy and electors of Mayo which, in Castlebar on 6 August, rejected the claims of Valentine O'Conor Blake, who had already gained the support of some of the local clergy, and selected as the people's candidate George Henry Moore, Gavan Duffy's onetime lieutenant, returning to active politics after a long retirement. Mayo has much in common with Queen's County in this campaign; in each, one seat only was regarded as vacant; in each, the clergy threw themselves into an organised series of mass meetings; in each, the clerically sponsored candidates were successful.

In Cork County, on the other hand, many of the clergy seem to have favoured the Honourable Robert Boyle rather than his successful opponent McCarthy Downing, the 'friend of the tenant farmers'.[57] But when the clerically-convened county meeting was held it declared for Downing, together with Smith Barry, the sitting liberal member, whose seat was not regarded as in question. The *Nation* wrote:

> It is of course true that all the parishes of the county were not represented at that meeting, but it is equally true that many of these, not so represented, were not so because of any unwillingness to accede to the plan proposed by the bishops, but because the clergymen of the parishes, holding opinions opposed

56 *Freeman's Journal*, 11, 12 Nov. 1868.
57 *Tipperary Advocate*, 14 Nov. 1868.

to what they knew to be the opinions of their parishioners, declined to summon the meetings, or, having summoned them, allowed them, as our friend Canon Fitzpatrick stated the other day as his own case, to lapse.[58]

Downing's address had been one of the more independent published in this election:

If elected I will enter parliament as a supporter of Mr Gladstone, on the terms stated by Mr Bright at Limerick, namely, that 'reparation should be made to Ireland for the wrongs inflicted upon her by England, and that Ireland should give in return her forgiveness'. But if Mr Gladstone, once he attains power, wavers in or falters in honestly carrying into effect the policy which he has enunciated, then will I be found in determined hostility to his government.[59]

It would be wrong to imply that clerical participation was necessarily unwanted or unsolicited. In Sligo Borough the sitting member, Sergeant Armstrong, feeling unable through ill-health to contest the seat again, informed the local bishop, Dr Gillooly, who thereupon convened the meeting which chose a liberal candidate to succeed him.[60] In Tipperary the entry of a conservative candidate into the lists galvanised into activity the hitherto quiescent supporters of the two sitting members, Charles Moore and Captain White. Meeting in Thurles they resolved:

That we respectfully but earnestly ask the most Reverend the Archbishop, the Right Reverend the Bishops, and the Very Reverend and Reverend Clergy of the county of Tipperary, to co-operate with the people in maintaining the independence of this great county, for which the clergy and people have made such sacrifices, and with this view to exert their influence on behalf of the candidates of our choice.[61]

It has been remarked above that the liberals in Dublin City were glad to be able to avail themselves of the parish organisation. It was employed also in the rural constituencies of

58 *Nation*, 21 Nov. 1868.
59 *Freeman's Journal*, 4 Nov.
60 ibid., 13 Aug.
61 *Freeman's Journal*, 27 Oct. 1868.

44 ISAAC BUTT AND HOME RULE

Queen's County, Sligo County, Wexford County, and Mayo.
Wexford County shows this technique very well developed.
First the clergy met in St Peter's College, Wexford under the
chairmanship of the bishop, and pledged their support to M.
P. D'Arcy and J. T. Power. Aggregate meetings were then
organised all over the county, generally with the local clergy
on the platform; forty were on the platform in Enniscorthy,
including the bishop of Ferns. In Mayo G. H. Moore pro-
gressed from town to town, greeted by the local clergy, speaking with them from open-air platforms, canvassing each town
in their company, and usually concluding the day by dining
with the parish priest. In King's County the two candidates,
O'Brien and Sherlock, would arrive on a Sunday morning,
attend mass, and afterwards proceed with the parish priest to
the place of meeting. In only three constituencies was a candidate returned in direct opposition to the stated wishes of
the clergy, Dungarvan, Sligo Borough, and Youghal; the peculiar circumstances of the Dungarvan contest are discussed elsewhere;[62] in the diminutive boroughs of Sligo and Youghal
the successful candidate was in each case unseated on petition,
the former borough being disfranchised, after a verdict of
bribery and 'the grossest intimidation'.

Clerical influence was, of course, in no way unusual in
nineteenth-century elections in Ireland, and it is impossible
to gauge its relative degree in different elections, since no
accurate standard of comparison exists. But certainly the
clergy themselves frequently felt it incumbent upon them to
justify the scale of their activity in this election as something
produced by the nature of the main issue involved. 'Under
ordinary circumstances I should be unwilling to address you
on an approaching election for a member of parliament', said
Bishop Leahy of Dromore, recommending William Kirk to
the electors of Newry, 'but these are exceptional times, when
some additional advice may be expected from one holding my
position, for we have arrived at a momentous crisis, the magnitude of which cannot be overstated'.[63] 'In the long course
of a missionary career he had never addressed a political meet-

62 See below, pp. 58-61.
63 *Freeman's Journal*, 7 Nov. 1868.

ing ', said Father Doran, P.P. Rathnure, county Wexford, but 'this election is an exceptional one. It is one purely religious, that is, to secure the equality, on religious grounds, of the catholic million with a handful of anglicans '.[64]

D: ROCKING THE BOAT

That this was the dominant conviction in the 1868 election there can be little doubt. It would be impossible to return even the Pope himself for a liberal Irish constituency as a 'D'Israelite', wrote the bishop of Kerry, Dr Moriarty.[65] But dissenters there were, to whom other issues, less politically respectable, were at least as important as that of the church. The election took place less than two years after the fenian outbreak, less than two years before the launching of home rule. The men who had sympathised with the first movement, the men who were to participate in the second—what room was there for them in the apparent unanimity of the liberal popular front?

The imprecision of the popular liberal programme, its dependence upon emotive first principle rather than clarity of exposition, has already been remarked. It might perhaps have been expected that such a programme would consequently provide an umbrella for all non-conservative opinion. In fact the very vagueness of the liberal programme more often produced the reverse effect. For a bewildered electorate faced, often, with an embarrassment of candidates all equally devoted to 'denominational education', 'security of tenure', and above all 'religious equality', some criterion had to be devised by which the opportunist goats could be divided from the liberal sheep. The flattest declaration for disestablishment and disendowment had little practical value if the candidate were to assist to power, at the opening of the new session, a Conservative administration which would never sponsor such a proposal. The introduction of the measure depended upon the return of a Gladstonian administration pledged to it; to

64 ibid., 2 Nov.
65 Moriarty to Bowyer, 4 Dec. 1868. Included in Bowyer to Disraeli 7 Dec. 1868, Disraeli MSS.

many, then, the real election issue was, logically, the securing
of sufficient seats to give Gladstone an opportunity of fulfill-
ing his pledge of justice for Ireland. Cardinal Cullen commented:

> It is fortunate that in the present election it is not necessary
> to discuss personal claims and the relative position of indi-
> vidual candidates . . . a great fundamental principle on which
> rest our future hopes for the peace and happiness of Ireland is
> now at stake.[66]

In practice this meant that a greater degree than usual of uniformity with English Liberalism was exacted, where possible,
by the disestablishment party from parliamentary candidates:
the emphasis was on loyalty to, rather than independence of,
the English Liberal party. As early as 21 July the *Limerick
Reporter* summed up this attitude in an editorial which spoke
for the feelings of the clerical-liberal party and which was full
of ill-omen for independents. We know now who our friends
are, it said, and the enemy is before us:

> There is now, therefore, no excuse for the playing of the old
> game of Independent Opposition over again; or for repeating
> the fatal tactic of secession which upset the Liberal party some
> twenty years ago, and to a great extent undid the work of
> O'Connell.[67]

The implications of this attitude were most clearly worked
out in the case of the Galway Borough election. The representatives of the borough at the dissolution were two young
catholics, Sir Rowland Blennerhassett, a Kerry landowner,
and George Morris, who had been elected in an uncontested
by-election the previous year.[68] In his brief parliamentary

[66] *Freeman's Journal,* 16 Nov. 1868.
[67] *Limerick Reporter,* 21 July 1868.
[68] He had been returned as a 'Liberal-Conservative' (*Dod's Parliamentary Companion,* 1868, p. 263) following the retirement of his
brother, who had been elected as a 'moderate liberal' (ibid., 1867, p.
260) but took office as Solicitor-General and later Attorney-General in
the Derby-Disraeli administration of 1866 (an appointment which
greatly annoyed the Irish conservatives), was made a judge by the Conservatives and 'was a Conservative for the rest of his life' (*G.E.C.,* Vol.
VII, p. 246).

career Morris had so far concerned himself largely with local matters, defending the borough against a threatened redistribution scheme. The *Galway Vindicator* praised his services in this regard and recommended his re-election as early as 1 July. On the Church issue he had voted for Gladstone's resolutions.

On 5 August the *Dublin Evening Post* devoted an editorial to those members of parliament who

> will vote for every principle of Mr Gladstone's Irish policy, but they will take care, meantime that Mr Gladstone, so far as depends on their votes, shall never have an opportunity of reducing the principle to practice as a minister. There are but three civic constituencies at the outside—Dundalk, that is to say, and Youghal and Galway—in which the trick will be attempted, and but one, we should imagine—the last named—in which it has a chance of success.[69]

This attack provoked two editorials in reply in the *Galway Vindicator* repudiating the idea that the satisfaction of Irish needs was to be identified with the English Liberal party. It agreed that all other issues should give precedence to that of the church, but it prophesied that after the passage of disestablishment the Irish representatives would find themselves in immediate disagreement with the Liberal party upon the subject of education. The Irish electorate, it held, should return:

> Independent representatives, who will ally themselves to no party; but who will labour first for the achievement of religious equality, and who will afterwards vote for any good measure

[69] *Dublin Evening Post*, 5 Aug 1868. The candidates referred to in Dundalk and Youghal were Sir George Bowyer and Sir Joseph McKenna. Bowyer had totally alienated the primate, Dr. Kieran, by his failure to support Gladstone's resolutions on the church (A. McKenna to Fortescue, 10 May 1867; J. W. Kavanagh to Fortescue, May 1867, Strachie MSS, Carlingford Political; Bowyer to Disraeli, 15 June, 25 Nov., 1, 7 Dec., 1868, Disraeli MSS). McKenna lost the local conservative vote through his support for disestablishment, but shewed just enough predilection for toryism to alienate the whigs (McKenna to Disraeli, 6 Sept. 1868).

for the advancement of Irish interests, no matter by what party or statesman proposed.[70]

Upon those who placed the disestablishment question above all else and equated its settlement with the return of Gladstone, this kind of argument made no impression; the *Freeman's Journal* announced tersely that enquiries were being made in Galway City 'with a view to starting a liberal candidate ',[71] and soon afterwards reported the formation, under the patronage of the bishop and clergy, of a ' Galway Independent Club ', determined ' to accept no candidate who will not pledge himself to adopt Mr Gladstone as his leader, and promise to hurl from power the present no-popery administration '.[72]

On 9 September Morris published his address. Pointing to his work on behalf of the city, he promised to continue ' entirely independent of every political party '; he made no specific reference to any of the major issues of the day. This kind of address, although not unusual from a sitting member, was scarcely tactful in the circumstances. Morris quickly realised his error, and augmented his address three days later with a letter repudiating ' misconstructions ' of it; he had voted for Gladstone's resolutions, he declared, and would continue to support the same policy on the church; he was also in favour of tenant right and denominational education. All cavil and criticism were now silenced, said the *Vindicator;*[73] the electorate would not be deceived, said the *Freeman,* by a second address produced as it was by ' the indignation of every elector in Galway '.[74]

The decisive pronouncement was made by Dr McEvilly and the Galway clergy. In a published advertisement on 19 September it was announced that the bishop and clergy had met and passed what became known as the 'College House resolutions', demanding pledges from the candidates on the topics of the church, the land, and education, and, most important of

[70] *Galway Vindicator,* 8, 12 Aug. 1868.
[71] *Freeman's Journal,* 8 Aug. 1868.
[72] ibid., 27 Aug.
[73] *Galway Vindicator,* 12 Sept.
[74] *Freeman's Journal,* 14 Sept. 1868.

all, in the second resolution refusing to support any candidate

> who will not pledge himself both to support Mr Gladstone's resolutions against the Irish establishment, as set forth by him in the last session of parliament, and to assist in hurling from office any, and every ministry, which will refuse to make the said resolutions cabinet measures.[75]

The *Vindicator* approved the other resolutions but deplored this one. Vainly it reminded the bishop of Gladstone's speeches on Italy, of Liberal unsoundness on education.[76] The *Freeman* was delighted and called upon Morris to declare himself or withdraw from the representation; its attack was placarded around Galway by unseen hands.[77] Then on 26 September there arrived, with what seemed to hostile observers suggestively appropriate timing, a new candidate, John Bridge Aspinall, recorder of Liverpool, a staunch English Liberal, a catholic, and the proud possessor of a letter of approval from Gladstone himself. Describing disestablishment as 'the first and greatest question', he declared that on this issue he was completely loyal to Gladstone, 'one of the greatest statesmen whom the world knows:

> We are like an army; we must have a LEADER, and we must *trust and follow him with generous confidence* until at least he has given us some reason to doubt him . . . I need not add that I accede in every particular to the policy set forth in the resolutions recently put forward by your revered bishop and clergy.[78]

Although sent a copy of the College House resolutions by the bishop's secretary, Father Cullen, Morris made no public comment upon them; he later declared that he had not known that an answer was expected.[79] A 'conversion' would now be too late, wrote the *Freeman* on 29 September, and on 30 Sep-

---

75 *Galway Vindicator*, 19 Sept.
76 ibid.
77 *Freeman's Journal*, 22 Sept.
  Galway Vindicator, 23 Sept.
78 ibid., 26 Sept.
79 ibid., 10 Oct.

tember it was announced that a second clerical meeting in the
College House had resolved that the silence of Morris was
equivalent to a refusal on his part to accept the resolutions,
and that he was accordingly adjudged 'an unfit person to
represent this catholic borough at the present juncture in
parliament'. At the same meeting a letter from Blennerhassett approving the resolutions was read. The meeting resolved
to adjourn to 2 October, when it hoped 'to be able to select
another candidate who will faithfully carry out the policy of
our resolutions'.[80] On 5 October Morris withdrew. The
bishop celebrated the event with a triumphant letter to Sir
John Gray; the *Freeman* acclaimed the victory which had
been won despite Morris's 'impertinent appeal to the catholic
people against their bishop'.[81] Morris fired a parting salvo in
the *Vindicator*: Dr McEvilly, he said, had assured him as late
as 5 September that Galway could not be better represented;
he had then left the city, returning on the night before the
passing of the College House resolutions. What influence,
asked Morris, had worked upon him in the interval, causing
him to change his mind?[82]

The conservatives concluded that Dr McEvilly had been
induced to abandon Morris by Cardinal Cullen himself.[83] It
was an understandable inference; it was also probably accurate. In the Monsell papers there is a letter from Cardinal
Cullen to Monsell, undated, but which from internal evidence can definitely be placed at some date early in the election campaign.[84] In the course of it the Cardinal says:

I will write to Dr McEvilly about Mr Morris—but I believe he
has great influence in the town—I do not know how Sir R.
Blennerhassett voted—I dare say he has no great support in the
town.

It is an inescapable conclusion that once again the efforts of

[80] *Freeman's Journal,* 30 Sept. 1868.
[81] ibid., 7 Oct.
[82] *Galway Vindicator,* 10 Oct.
[83] *Mayo Constitution,* 8 Dec.
[84] MS 8317, in a folder with other letters from Cardinal Cullen to
Monsell.

William Monsell had secured for Gladstone the decisive intervention of the catholic hierarchy.

But the events of the Galway election are less important than the kind of argument which was generated, and the divisions which were revealed. It would probably be untrue to suggest that these were the issues that were plainly uppermost in the mind of the average parliamentary candidate, or that in the average constituency they were articulated in this manner. Nevertheless, in the Galway contest, it is possible to perceive, thrown into sharp relief, some of the most fundamental conflicts in the Irish politics of that period.

There is, firstly, the open issue itself. Two clearly opposed points of view are visible. One holds that proceeding primarily from the urgency and importance of disestablishment, and also from the hope of gaining the other Irish liberal demands from Gladstone, it is essential that the greatest possible majority of members pledged to support the English Liberal party should be returned in Ireland. Again one appreciates the shrewdness of Monsell's appeal to the bishops not to be guilty of 'the folly of accepting a candidate who would vote against the Church (or any other measure of national importance to Ireland) and at the same time support the party who, as long as they are in office, will make it impossible to overthrow the Church'. Opposed to this is the advice of the *Nation* on 'How to vote'; it admits that 'ascendancy or religious equality is the question of the hour', but where there is a contest between two or more candidates who support disestablishment it advises that:

> The candidate to be preferred everywhere before all others is the Irish nationalist, independent of all British parties; who holds that 'the best thing England can do for Ireland is to let Ireland do for herself', and who will not only thoroughly represent the national demands on the church, the land, education and the ballot, but will not shrink from opposing even a 'Liberal' government if it palters with these demands.

As for English candidates for Irish seats, these should be viewed with 'suspicion and disfavour'.[85]

85 *Nation*, 3 Oct. 1868.

Next to the issue itself, the grouping of interests which it reveals is informative. Dedicated to the Gladstonian alliance one finds firstly, in most cases, the vast influence of the catholic church, secondly, the considerable influence of the *Freeman's Journal* and of the rest of the orthodox liberal press. When Butt launched the home rule movement less than two years later, it was these two forces which remained most notably aloof in the early stages. Equally revealing is the type of person singled out for attack by the pro-Gladstone party for unsoundness on the church issue: Morris in Galway, three one-time members of the independent opposition party of the 1850's in Sir George Bowyer (Dundalk), Edward McEvoy (Meath), and J. A. Blake (Waterford City), and Sir Joseph McKenna in Youghal. Of these Morris, Bowyer, and McKenna, the three members who were attacked by the *Dublin Evening Post,* all lost their seats to Gladstonian liberals in this election, and all regained them as home rulers in 1874, while Blake was one of Butt's chief agents in the financial negotiations which preceded the launching of the parliamentary home rule campaign. The chief critic of the liberal alliance throughout this election was the *Nation,* which still clung to the memory of Young Ireland and of the independent opposition movement, and which provided a forum for independent nationalist dissidents such as John Martin and W. J. O'Neill Daunt. In Cork City opposition to the uncritical policy of the local liberal organisation was voiced by Joseph Ronayne; in Dungarvan the clerically sponsored liberal candidate was opposed by the influence of advanced nationalist feeling, in Limerick by an alliance of this element with a section of the conservatives. Instances of this kind of opposition could be multiplied at considerable length.

If, then, this election is most noteworthy for the solidarity of the alliance between Irish and English liberalism, there is also a clearly discernible dissenting body of opinion, standing apart from and critical of this alliance, denying the principles upon which it is based, preserving intact the tradition of independent action, and ready to assume the main burden of sustaining the revival of that independent action if the liberal alliance were found incapable of satisfying the needs of the

Irish people. Foremost among this element were those to whom separation in some form remained the irreducible minimum of Irish demands. The issues upon which they rallied were two—the old warcry of repeal and the call for amnesty to the fenian prisoners.

Of these two issues, it was logical that the fate of the imprisoned martyrs should bulk the larger and the more immediate. Popular sympathy, if little moved by the insurrection itself, had been stirred by the successive state trials, in which the character and motives of the fenian leaders had emerged from behind the initial barrage of condemnation. An appeal for the prisoners' dependants was soon launched, and as early as July 1868 it was suggested that nationalist electors should make amnesty the test issue upon which they should give or withhold their votes.[86]

Soon afterwards followed what may be regarded as the first move in the campaign for amnesty when on 3 August, in the Cork Corporation, Daniel O'Sullivan introduced a resolution calling for the release of the prisoners, a course imitated, throughout the following months, by many corporations and town councils. The popular agitation which was to reach such a pitch of activity in the following year was not, however, inaugurated until late in the campaign, too late, perhaps, for effective intervention in the election. A requisition was got up in Dublin City calling upon the Lord Mayor to convene a public assembly to discuss the question of amnesty; a meeting held in the European Hotel, decided that a deputation should wait upon the mayor with the requisition, and that Sir John Gray and Isaac Butt, with some other gentlemen, should be invited to accompany it: it was also agreed to sound the Dublin candidates upon the subject of amnesty.[87] From the successive adjournments of this meeting there grew, more or less informally, the Amnesty Committee, which, after the election, was in its turn to give way to the better known Amnesty Association. The Lord Mayor declined to comply with the committee's request, giving as his reason for refusal the fact

---

86 *Irishman,* 25 July 1868.
87 *Freeman's Journal,* 7, 14, 30 Sept., 5 Nov. 1868.

that he had promised, when first elected, to remain aloof from party politics. Another who consistently opposed the amnesty movement was Cardinal Cullen.[88] The committee then decided to ask Butt to convene a general meeting on behalf of the prisoners in the Mechanics Institute; it resolved also:

> That this test be presented to every candidate in Ireland at the approaching elections—' If a petition be brought forward in the new parliament that an address be presented to Her Majesty praying that she may be graciously pleased to use her Royal clemency in granting an amnesty to all persons convicted of political offences in Great Britain and Ireland, will you vote for and support it '?[89]

It proved, in fact, impossible to carry out this policy to its fullest extent; less than a fortnight remained before polling was to take place in the majority of the constituencies. Several candidates were, however, brought to express their approval of amnesty, and the issue was raised at a number of election meetings. The response varied. At the Dublin City nomination all four candidates hedged when questioned by the representatives of the committee; Pim, of the liberals, pointed to his past behaviour as evidence of his ' kindly feelings towards persons who were in prison ', while Sir Dominick Corrigan, ' would ever stretch out his hand to lift up any fallen creature in suffering or in pain ', but questioned the wisdom of a parliamentary agitation upon the subject. With only tory alternatives, these lukewarm concessions were enough to win a grudging support[90] In Clare, where the two candidates, the liberal Sir Colman O'Loghlen, and the pro-disestablishment conservative Crofton Moore Vandaleur, were enthusiastically heckled by a noted repeal priest, Father Quaid of O'Callaghan's Mills, similar pledges of support in principle, if not promises of active co-operation, were secured from both candidates.[91] In Tipperary one of the two liberal candidates, Cap-

88 Cullen to Fortescue, 14 March 1869. Strachie MSS, Carlingford Political.

89 *Freeman's Journal,* 11 Nov. 1868.

90 ibid., 17, 18 Nov. 1868.

91 ibid., 25 Nov.; *Clare Journal,* 19 Nov.; *Limerick Reporter,* 24 Nov.

tain White, promised to support a petition on the subject.[92] In Kilkenny County, in response to queries from the crowd at the nomination, G. L. Bryan also promised to vote for amnesty, on the one condition that 'foreigners' should have to go back to America and nevermore trouble 'the peace-loving people of this country'.[93] In Mayo Father Lavelle of Partry, another redoubtable repealer, called for cheers for the political prisoners, invoking the memory of Allen, Larkin, and O'Brien before an enthusiastic crowd at the nomination of G. H. Moore, who was wholeheartedly for amnesty.[94] Benjamin Whitworth in Drogheda and William Stacpoole in Ennis also promised their support.[95] In Galway City Sir Rowland Blennerhassett gave the required pledge without much persuasion, and Viscount St Lawrence, after invoking the anglican liturgy in an attempt to evade the issue, was compelled to do the same.[96] In Limerick City, where Richard Pigott of the *Irishman* was put into nomination on rudimentary abstentionist principles by William Bolster, the Town Clerk John Ellard, Councillor 'Dirty Larry' Kelly and the advanced party, in an incongruous coalition with the conservative mayor Peter Tait, amnesty was naturally very much to the fore in the campaign against the liberal nominees Gavin and Russell. The latter was accused in an abusive placard of having refused to sign a petition for the release of William O'Sullivan, junior, of Kilmallock.[97] Gavin and Russell were elected, but amnesty pledges were obtained from both at the nomination. Bolster and Ellard were later staunch home rulers, while O'Sullivan's father was home rule M.P. for Limerick County from 1874 to 1885. In Cork City Daniel O'Sullivan raised the question at an aggregate liberal meeting called to approve the candidature of the sitting members, J. F. Maguire and N. D. Murphy. It was not, he said, the duty of Irish members 'to stand with their hands behind their backs and vote for Gladstone, and

92 *Freeman's Journal*, 25 Nov.
93 ibid., 19 Nov.
94 *Ballinrobe Chronicle*, 28 Nov.
95 *Freeman's Journal*, 13, 19 Nov. 1868.
96 *Galway Vindicator*, 21 Nov.
97 *Irishman*, 14 Nov.

allow Mr Gladstone to concur in opinion with Disraeli, that those three Manchester men should be hanged '.[98]

Amnesty does not seem to have been to the fore in any other constituencies besides these, but it is unlikely that this relative neglect arose from popular indifference. That the issue was not more vigorously agitated was probably the result of the lack of time between the launching of the campaign and the actual election, and also of a general expectation that some measure of amnesty would form part of Gladstone's 'justice for Ireland'. In the words of Sir John Gray, 'the same success which will strike the chains off the whole nation will liberate from their fetters the political prisoners', or as John O'Leary put it a trifle less rhetorically: 'The whigs will hardly dare to keep the Irish political prisoners in jail after their accession to office.'[99]

If the amnesty question had not yet come to the forefront of Irish politics as it was to do in 1869, the issue of repeal was even more quiescent. There were, of course, elder statesmen who clung indomitably to the old cause. John Martin, perhaps the most widely respected of the older nationalists, unfailingly propagandised repeal in the flood of letters which, in the best tradition of neglected Irish prophets, he despatched to the national press from rustic semi-retirement. G. H. Moore was another. There was also Dr O'Brien, the celebrated 'repeal dean' of Limerick, organiser, early in 1868, of the Limerick Declaration, in which sixteen hundred priests joined in asserting that repeal alone could offer final satisfaction to Irish grievance. The *Nation* newspaper retained many of the sympathies of its Young Ireland founders. And in the traditional hustings nominations, making their last appearance before the introduction of the secret ballot, supporting speakers and eager—if usually voteless—hecklers would regularly unfurl the old flag with enthusiasm if not with conscious purpose.

It is clear, however, that repeal was not and indeed could not have been seriously demanded in this election. In the first place, after decades of neglect it now lacked any leadership

98 *Nation*, 21 Nov.
99 *Freeman's Journal*, 9 Nov. 1868.
   Irishman, 31 Oct.

behind which a popular movement could coalesce. The division between on the one hand, those who were prepared for the moment to trust Gladstone and feared to embarrass his position and, on the other, those who had openly foresworn any kind of parliamentary agitation, was clearcut and bitter. It was not yet suspectible of even the partial bridging which was to be achieved by the many-sided personality of Butt. At a dinner given to Richard Pigott in the Rotunda in October, John Martin himself was hissed and shouted down when he demanded that the queen should come over to Dublin and call a free Irish parliament, being greeted with shouts of 'we are all republicans here . . . too late for that . . . a President and Congress . . . no monarchy'.[100] It required a disillusionment with violence to grow on the one hand, a disillusionment with Gladstone on the other, and the emergence of a relatively untainted leader, to achieve even a superficial bridging of this most fundamental cleavage.

The primacy of the disestablishment issue in this election produced a corresponding neglect of repeal as it did of every other issue. Canon Rice of Queenstown wrote to Butt in February:

the agitation of repeal at present would only alienate from Irish sympathies English Liberals and Radicals, and so indefinitely put off the overthrow of the establishment.[101]

People who were sincerely dedicated to the capturing of this, the one great concession which had been unequivocally offered to their generation by an English party leader, were not now to be diverted into what seemed to them the cloud-cuckoo land of a demand with such a long record of fruitless agitation under much more favourable circumstances, even though they might concede the ultimate desirability of 'a parliament in College Green'. There must have been many who reasoned in this way, as distinct from those to whom the liberal programme of disestablishment, denominational education, and land reform appeared adequate both for today and for tomor-

100 *Freeman's Journal*, 21 Oct. 1868.
Irishman, 24 Oct.
101 Canon Rice to Butt, 2 Feb. 1868, Butt MSS.

row. The practical dilemma of the theoretical repealer emerges very clearly from the friendly controversy which took place
at this time between John Martin and Dean O'Brien in the
columns of the *Nation*. Martin had written to the newspapers
in July offering himself as a candidate in any Irish constituency which was prepared to return him upon his own terms
and at its own expense. Repeal, he said, was being mistakenly
put aside by Irish patriots in and out of the English parliament, 'lest Messrs Gladstone and Bright should be embar-
rassed or offended, while they are exerting themselves to dis-
establish the English church in Ireland . . . I consider it to be
as little practical as it is dignified'. If returned, he says, he
would follow a completely independent course, would 'neither
vote for nor against their laws', but would use his return 'for
the purpose of telling the truth', and would 'do no act to
encourage the hateful fiction that Ireland enjoys constitutional rights and is a freely governed country'. 'I do not expect any constituency in Ireland to invite me seriously, upon
my own terms', he concluded sadly, 'and perhaps it will be so
best'. But it was characteristic of the nationalist movement in
this period that Martin's readiness to go to Westminster even
upon these novel terms drew down upon him the immediate
condemnation of his old friend and fellow convict, the exiled
John Mitchel.[102] Even Dean O'Brien deprecated any attempt
to revive the repeal agitation in this election as calculated to
divide the liberals, delight the tories, and fasten upon the
nationalists the blame for any failure to carry disestablishment.[103]

There were still those, nonetheless, to whom independence
and amnesty were all, and O'Brien's sweet reasoning so much
vain sedation. For them, the real battle erupted in the tiny
borough of Dungarvan; it was there that they shewed their
latent power. In possession of the seat was Serjeant C. R. Barry
who, as one of the crown prosecutors after the fenian rising,
had laid the charges against Kickham, O'Leary, and other
rebel leaders before the preliminary hearing in Dublin Castle.
It was Barry above all who had first drawn for press and pub-

102 *Tipperary Advocate*, 11 July, 29 Aug. 1868.
103 *Nation*, 20 Oct. 1868.

lic the official picture of fenianism as a conspiracy dedicated
to massacre and socialism. His subsequent protestations that
he had simply spoken from his brief, could not prevent his
becoming a symbol of oppression. In the election he was opposed by an English catholic liberal-conservative, Henry
Mathews, avowedly anti-whig, but pledged to the full three-
tiered Irish liberal programme. The personality of Mathews,
was, however, completely irrelevant; as he readily admitted
himself, 'I know that it is because I give Dungarvan an opportunity of rejecting Mr Barry that I am welcome amongst
you'.[104] The struggle produced a wonderfully vivid demar-
cation of the opposing sides. Among the press, all the leading
liberal papers supported Barry, the *Freeman's Journal, Cork
Examiner, Limerick Reporter,* and *Dublin Evening Post;*
even the *Nation,* while in principle hostile to whig office-
holders, reproved the 'scandalously unfair, false, and scurri-
lous manner' in which Barry was being attacked for having
performed the duties of his office.[105] Against Barry, on the
other hand, was all the 'advanced nationalist' press, the *Irishman, Flag of Ireland, Universal News, Dundalk Democrat,
Tipperary Advocate,* etc.[106] 'The catholic who votes for Mathews must be a renegade, an apostate', declared the *Freeman.*[107] 'A Tory before a traitor', pithily countered the *Universal News.*[108] The impecunious O'Donoghue, once the
young prince of repeal, but now the pensioner of Fortescue,[109]
came over from Tralee to sustain Barry; the procession con-
taining the two allies was greeted by counter-demonstrators
bearing banners inscribed with such slogans as 'down with
the moral assassin', and 'where is James O'Brien'?[110] Police
and soldiers were drafted in from the neighbourhood as the
rival forces clashed in the streets. While the O'Donoghue en-

104 *Irishman,* 14 Nov. 1868.
105 *Nation,* 19 Sept.
106 *Irishman,* 28 Nov.
107 *Freeman's Journal,* 16 Nov.
108 *Irishman,* 26 Sept.
109 O'Donoghue to Fortescue, 27 March 1868, Strachie MSS, Carlingford Political.
110 O'Brien was a young man from Dungarvan, tried at Cork Commission for fenianism, sentenced to death, but transported.

dorsed Barry's candidature, John Martin wrote denouncing him: 'I think it will be a scandal in Irish politics if any free constituency in Ireland will elect Mr Barry . . . There is a great opportunity for the free constituencies of Ireland at present', he adds, 'but the bishops and electoral politicians, unhappily for Ireland, are too *Liberal* to use the opportunity'.[111] Anonymous advertisements appeared in the *Irishman* denouncing Barry for his speeches against fenianism, and an outbreak of posters of the same nature spread from Dungarvan to Tralee with the intervention of the O'Donoghue.

Most significant of all was the fruitlessness of all the clerical influence which was exerted on Barry's behalf. Nationalist priests like Father Vaughan, of Barefield, Ennis, Father Lavelle, and Father Tom O'Shea of Mountrath, 'father of the Irish Tenant League', denounced Barry, and the head of the Augustinian House in Dungarvan, Father Anderson, was active in the cause of Mathews, but the full weight of official clerical influence was with the Serjeant. The bishop of Waterford, Dr O'Brien, endorsed him; Dean O'Brien wrote from Limerick attacking Mathews' intrusion; Dr Hally, the local parish priest, and his curates, campaigned for Barry with a vigour unmatched even in this election. At mass on Sunday, 16 September, before a congregation which included the objectionable interloper himself, Dr Hally 'made it tolerably plain that that gentleman had come over as the instrument of Disraeli, Stanley, and so to prevent the success of Gladstone in disendowing the church and doing justice to the Irish people'. 'The effect of the doctor's speech was what might have been expected', wrote the *Freeman* approvingly of one of these sermons; 'Oh God forgive him, this is awful', moaned one parishioner, according to the pro-Mathews *Waterford Citizen*. In the closing stages of the campaign the bishop wrote a letter which was read at all masses:

> I am surprised that any catholic, and much more a catholic professing devotion to St Augustine, should vote for Mathews . . . such a catholic I look upon as a favourer of heretics, and an advocate of no-popery doctrine and protestant ascendancy.

111 *Irishman*, 17 Oct.

The letter, and the comments upon it from the pulpit, 'made a profound impression, and one regarded as deciding the election against the tory candidate', wrote the correspondent of the *Freeman*.[112]

Nevertheless, despite these pronouncements, and despite the canvassing and speech-making of Dr Hally and his curates in company with their candidate, Barry was defeated by a quite substantial majority.

The fact of a candidate's defeat in a constituency of just over three hundred voters does not, by itself, provide much basis for generalised deductions. But the bitterness of the struggle, the passions it aroused, the divisions it revealed—above all, the spectacle of such vigorous and successful opposition to a candidate who had the backing of the church and of what purported to be the popular party—all these things together combine to make Dungarvan a key contest in this election. It demonstrated, in terms of physical conflict, what has been suggested here in the abstract, that is to say, the existence of a wide gulf between much of popular nationalist feeling on the one hand, and the clerical-liberal programme on the other. Dungarvan reminds us, in other words, of the essential impermanence of so much of the standard of values upon which the whole election was fought.

But that is not to contend that the influence of press or clergy unnaturally postponed the consideration of such issues as amnesty and repeal. Such a contention would ignore the rôle of Gladstone as catalyst. The boon which he offered in 1868 was disestablishment; it was logical that it should be seized upon by men for so long starved of concessions, and the election fought accordingly. If hindsight makes the debate of 1868 superficial, it reflected his values; it was his hand which chose one issue and lifted it from the well-stocked storehouse of Irish discontent. The election of 1868 was fought upon the level of understanding of Irish problems to which he had attained in that year. The long and uneven courtship of Gladstone and the Irish nation, which was to dominate the politics of these islands for more than two decades, had begun.

112 *Freeman's Journal*, 10 Sept., 18 Nov., *Irishman* 26 Sept.

CHAPTER II

Irish Public Opinion and the Liberal Administration, November 1868— February 1870

THE ELECTION resulted in a Liberal triumph in both islands, and Gladstone embarked upon his first administration with an overall majority of one hundred and fifteen. Of the one-hundred-and-five members whom Ireland despatched to Westminster, sixty-five pledged their loyalty to the English Liberal leader. It was a pledge marked, as we have seen, by few reservations. 'Since the days of O'Connell the public mind has not been so deeply stirred, nor has the people's fate been so trustingly given as it is now to you', wrote Dr Moriarty to Gladstone.[1]

Gladstone lost no time in honouring the first of his electoral commitments. The new session opened on 16 February 1869; the Established Church (Ireland) Bill was given its first reading on 1 March. The bill made no concessions to the Conservative plans of internal reform and concurrent endowment: the principle which Gladstone now put into operation was that which he had advocated in the election, the total separation of the state from the support of any religious denomination, and the perfect equality of all denominations before the law. This was the great Irish demand which had been expressed in the election in the cry of 'religious equality', and with relief the Irish representatives acknowledged Gladstone's complete satisfaction of it. Sir John Gray addressed Gladstone in the debate on the second reading of the bill as:

the leading statesman of the day—the man whom the world would recognise hereafter as the great statesman who gave peace

---

[1] Moriarty to Gladstone, 28 Nov. 1868, BM Add. MSS 44416 f 273.

and prosperity to Ireland and strength and liberty to the Empire by the just and wise Irish policy which he was originating —a policy which would identify his name with the first great effort during three centuries of English rule, to extend religious justice to the Irish people.[2]

The bill received an equally enthusiastic welcome from the Irish liberal press. Even the usually critical *Nation* could write that to later generations Gladstone would appear 'the happiest of English statesmen, as having led the party of progress in achieving the greatest victory ever won in the British Parliament'.[3] On behalf of the Catholic clergy Cardinal Cullen saluted the bill in comparably enthusiastic terms.[4]

Such criticism as the bill did arouse in Ireland was in relation to the secondary issue of the disposal of the surplus to be created by the disendowment proposals. Of the sixteen million pounds worth of property which the Irish church was estimated to possess, a surplus of approximately eight million was to remain after the payment of life interests, compensations of various kinds, and the lump payments to the catholic and presbyterian churches in compensation for the withdrawal of the Maynooth grant and the regium donum. The proceeds of this sum Gladstone proposed to use for the better maintenance of asylums, infirmaries, and other similar institutions until then inadequately supported by the county cess payments of the burdened smallholders. On the question of the disposal of this surplus a certain amount of controversy had taken place in Ireland during the period of the election, and suggestions had been made which ranged from its application to the relief of the poor rate to its expenditure upon arterial drainage, and reclamation of wastes and bogs, and even the establishment of a tenant proprietary. Gladstone's proposals were open to criticism upon two counts. The restoration of so large a sum as he proposed to the protestant church might be criticised as excessive generosity, or even as abandonment of the principle of disendowment; there were those,

2 op. cit., 1834-5.
3 *Nation,* 6 Mar. 1869.
4 Cullen to Gladstone, BM Add. MSS 44419 f 198.

also, who felt keen disappointment at the proposed application of such surplus as had been created by the disendowment
scheme. John Martin considered the devotion of £200,000 a
year to the 'keeping of poor lunatics' the height of extrava-
gance; O'Neill Daunt thought that the money should go to
relieve the rates.[5]

Whatever criticisms might be made, however, of this part
of Gladstone's scheme, it could not be denied that in regard
to the application of the surplus he had conceded the main
principle involved—that the money should be applied for exclusively Irish purposes. The *Nation* was expressing the
general attitude when it concluded:

> Mr Gladstone's measure, so far as it relates to disestablishment
> and disendowment, is a full, fair, and honest one. It comes
> thoroughly up to the expectations of the country; and for this
> Mr Gladstone is unquestionably entitled to the gratitude of the
> Irish people . . . As to the application of the church funds, that
> is really a minor question; but Mr Gladstone's proposal is cer-
> tainly not an un-national or a bad one. Taking the measure
> as a whole, we give it welcome, and our best wishes are for its
> speedy and successful passage through every stage until it be-
> comes an act of parliament and the law of the land.[6]

With the downfall of the establishment the bonds of the
liberal alliance could only seem stronger than ever. Ireland
had sought three great boons of Gladstone; the first, a bare five
months from the opening of parliament, was already on the
statute book. Irish hopes seemed even more justified, Irish
expectations even more likely to be realised, the talk of separation even less rational than in the height of the election itself. 'Believe me that disaffection is already in its agony',
wrote Dr Moriarty to William Monsell.[7] 'You have gained
the esteem and won the confidence of every honest and well-
disposed Irishman', wrote Dr Conaty to Gladstone, 'for we
are thoroughly convinced that since the Norman invasion no

5 *Nation*, 6, 20 Mar. 1869.
6 ibid., 6 Mar.
7 Moriarty to Monsell, 2 April, Strachie MSS, Carlingford Political.

statesman whether English or Irish ever entertained so sincere a desire or so honest a determination to do us justice '.[8]

Only in the columns of the advanced nationalist press was this happy unanimity broken. 'Rectors and vicars do not fling out poor families on the highway in winter' . . . wrote John Mitchel in the *Irishman*:

> nobody cares for them; but the landlords are an intolerable nuisance . . . ejecting landlords and agents in Ireland ought to be shot down like dogs. A few dozen of them justly executed at present would lend an additional interest to the debates which will shortly take place on disestablishment, to content the Irish people and make them " loyal ", and place them on an equality with their fellow subjects of England and so forth.[9]

'The fenian plough has upset the establishment', said an editorial in another issue of this journal; but ' look with watchfulness at those who follow in the furrow '.[10] Beneath the paeans of praise and gratitude, the basic divergence between much of Irish popular feeling and its liberal representation, already remarked in relation to the general election, again betrays its presence here. It was soon, through the medium of the amnesty agitation, to re-emerge into the open to challenge the validity of the alliance and the sincerity of its advocates.

It has been noted how the Amnesty Committee was formed in the closing weeks of the election campaign, too late to have its full influence upon the contests throughout the country. Throughout the spring of 1869 agitation for amnesty mounted. A petition was circulated for which 250,000 signatures were claimed, and in addition memorials were presented to the queen upon the subject of amnesty from most of the corporations and town councils in the southern part of the country. Funds were collected in all parts of the British Isles, ranging from some large subscriptions to a solid basis in the twopences, threepences, and sixpences of emigrant workmen in Britain. By March 1869 the average intake was £40 a week.

8 Conaty to Gladstone, 3 Aug., BM Add. MSS, 44421 f 230.
9 *Irishman*, 20 Feb.
10 ibid., 6 Mar.

C

but expenses—including aid to the prisoners and their de-
pendents—were high[11] A special St Patrick's day church collection produced varying returns, according to the degree of
co-operation extended by the local clergy; in Dublin diocese
any such co-operation was expressly forbidden by Cardinal
Cullen.[12] The committee also found itself hampered by the
confidence of the Irish members of parliament in Gladstone;
it was widely hoped that he would in fact urge clemency upon
the queen without any pressure from Ireland. But the Irish
officials were more hesitant than their leader,[13] and when, in
February 1869, the administration announced its intentions
with regard to the prisoners, they proved sadly disappointing
to Irish opinion. Of eighty-one prisoners only forty-nine were
to be released, and of this number only Kickham of the more
famous leaders was to be amnestied: Rossa, Devoy, and most
of the other principals were to remain in custody. From that
moment on a disappointed public opinion read with growing
anger the reports which appeared continually in the popular
press of prison harshness to the captives, of their shattered
physical, and in some cases mental, health. The Amnesty
Committee continued its activities throughout March, and
public meetings in support of the movement were held in
London and Manchester, but it was obvious that a stage in
the agitation had been reached, and that new and more vigorous efforts would be required in order to exact further concessions from the government. The more energetic section of
the committee, which included the secretary, John Nolan,
urged the organisation of a series of monster public demonstrations in the open air; the more cautious argued that such
a course would only antagonise the government and jeopar-
dise the prisoners' chances of ever obtaining clemency. The
division was a fundamental one, and the committee divided
in mutual recrimination and sporadic fisticuffs. Butt, as the
tacitly-accepted leader of the movement, had remained stud-

11 *Nation*, 13 Mar. 1869, et seq.
12 ibid., 20 Mar.; Cullen to Fortescue, 14 Mar., Strachie MSS, Carlingford Political.
13 e.g. Gladstone to Bright, 13 Oct. BM Add. MSS, 43385 f 46 Bright
MSS.

iously aloof from these dissensions, but when Nolan and his group formed the rival Amnesty Association at a public meeting in the Rotunda on 28 June, Butt was elected president. 'Bide your time', he told the meeting, 'the time is coming when we may have to say a great deal, and when, perhaps in this very room, we may re-enact scenes which, nearly a century ago, made this country famous'.[14]

The new association carried away all the popular support of the old. Its committee included, in addition to Butt and Nolan, Father Lavelle, John Martin, A. M. Sullivan, and Richard Pigott. A series of monster meetings was immediately inaugurated with a token protest on 29 June at Mallow, constituency of the attorney-general Edward Sullivan, who had inspired much resentment by his remark in the house of commons that the fenians had nothing to complain of about their trials except that they were tried at all. More than forty such meetings followed all over the country, culminating in October in a great demonstration at Cabra, at which, according to the association's estimate, two hundred thousand people were present to hear Butt, G. H. Moore, and other speakers. At this point the monster meetings were judiciously suspended by a leadership fearful of O'Connell's anticlimax of 1843.[15] Meanwhile Butt worked upon the presentation in pamphlet form of the case for amnesty. Writing of the period of the fenian trials, he summed up the attitude of the moderate sympathiser, whose feelings were emotional rather than revolutionary:

Gradually the conviction forced itself upon everyone, that the men whom they saw meet their fate with heroism and dignity, were not a mere band of assassins, actuated by base motives— but real and earnest patriots, moved by unselfish thoughts, and risking all in that which they believed to be their country's cause . . . " Speeches from the dock " became a portion of the national literature of Ireland . . . These I confess are the memories which haunted me, and which have stirred my heart,

14 *Nation*, 5, 12 June, 5 July, 13 November; *Freeman's Journal*, 31 May.
15 J. F. X. O'Brien to Butt, 28 Nov. 1869, Butt MSS.

when I thought that men like these were sent to herd with the vilest and meanest criminals.[16]

The influence of the Amnesty Association cannot simply be measured in terms of its effect upon the policy of the government. Its very failure was a political influence in its own right. The government of Gladstone was subjected to its second major test, and its reputation did not on this occasion survive untarnished. 'Justice for Ireland' was shown to be perhaps, after all, not a fundamentally novel approach to that country's grievances, but rather a variation upon the familiar theme of administering to Ireland the measures which English statesmen conceived to be good for her, rather than those which she might seem to desire for herself. In a positive sense, also, the association assisted the revival of an independent nationalist movement by providing a focus through which both advanced and constitutional nationalists could, for the first time, associate in constitutional action for a common object. The language used at the great amnesty meetings was often violent and inflammatory, and the response which they awoke in their audiences went much deeper than the simple desire for amnesty. From America John O'Mahony commented with more enthusiasm than discretion upon this aspect of the new movement:

> We regard these amnesty meetings with something beyond ordinary favour, we regard them as meaning more than the release of the fenian prisoners. We look upon them as the resurrection of a nation from its deathlike torpor. England is menaced by them and England knows it.[17]

The association also increased the stature of Butt as its president, and the respect for his person, if not necessarily for his ideas, which his work in the state trials had evoked among the fenians. Possibly most important of all, it indicated to the advanced party the power which they might generate if their energies were harnessed to a constitutional movement. This

---

16 Butt, *Ireland's appeal for amnesty*, Glasgow, pp. 14, 16, 1870.
17 *Nation*, 6 Nov. 1869.

most suggestive truth was to be spectacularly demonstrated in the Tipperary by-election in November.

Parallel with the amnesty agitation, the tenant right movement was reaching a new level of self-confidence. The preoccupation with the church issue in the election had not encouraged an inflexible expression of the tenant demand, still less the implementation of Butt's scheme of a tenant league. With the safe passage of disestablishment, however, the main barrier to an intense concentration upon the land issue was removed. The *Freeman's Journal* took it up as 'the question of the hour', and in a series of editorials on the subject urged without reservation the principle of fixity of tenure. The landlord, it declared,

> must be tied down only to such an increase of rent as he would be justly entitled to from the rise in agricultural prices, the improvement in property from railway communication or other circumstances of a similar nature.[18]

Meetings in support of this principle were organised by the tenant farmers all over the country. In September a combined meeting of the Munster Farmers' Clubs in Cork resolved upon the establishment of a national Tenant League. At a subsequent meeting of the representatives of the club of the southern counties in Tipperary this organisation was formally established, with Butt as its president. It was intended to contain 'as many of the tenant farmers of Ireland as possible', and it was to be conducted upon the model of the Catholic Association and the Repeal Association. Its aims were to be based upon principles laid down at the Cork meeting, that is to say, perpetuity of tenure, based upon an initial assessment of rent, and periodic revaluation, by a specially constituted board of agriculture; this valuation was to be based upon average market values over the past twenty-one years, excluding the value of any improvements created by the tenant. The league also expressed a general welcome for the proposals of John Bright upon the establishment of a tenant proprietary.[19]

18 *Freeman's Journal*, 2, 18 Nov. 1869.
19 *Nation*, 18 Scpt., 2 and 16 Oct.

Thus at the end of 1869 two great issues were the subjects of organised agitation in Ireland, land reform and amnesty. But it would be wrong to imply that there was any unanimity or co-operation between the protagonists of the two causes. Even within the land reform movement, there were significant divisions. The active popular movement was based upon the Farmers' Clubs, and organised in the Tenant League, under the leadership of men like Butt, William Bolster, and Dean O'Brien, with the *Nation* as its mouthpiece. Sir John Gray was at the same time conducting a parallel and scarcely less radical campaign in the *Freeman's Journal*, with the result that on this issue that normally muted organ found itself for once out of tune with the liberal chorus. A correspondent in the *Nation* expressed this divergence well, comparing Gray with another influential liberal member of parliament and newspaper proprietor, J. F. Maguire, member for Cork City and owner of the *Cork Examiner*. Gray, commented this observer, had been giving ' the utmost aid to the spread of tenant-right principles ', but Maguire, in the *Examiner*, had been continually suggesting that ' the great hero of the church measures may surely be with perfect safety left to his own unrestricted and unaided guidance on the land question '.[20]

In these circumstances, and given that so many of the tenant-right spokesmen had not shaken off their Gladstonian associations, it is less difficult to understand the distrust with which so many of the advanced nationalists regarded the entire agitation. In the first place, they objected to the mooting of irrelevancies while the political prisoners remained in English gaols; in the second place, while they respected Butt himself both for his work in the state trials and as the leader of the amnesty movement, they distrusted the whig associations of some of his allies.[21] Considerable tension was generated between the two movements throughout the country. When efforts were made to introduce the land issue into amnesty meetings, or to hold combined meetings on the two subjects, the advanced party retaliated by breaking up land

[20] ibid., 18 Sept.
[21] *Irishman*, 30 Oct. 1869. ' John Daly's recollections of fenianism ', in *Irish Freedom*, Oct. 1912.

reform demonstrations. In a joint meeting in Kanturk, sections of the crowd interrupted land reform speeches with demands for amnesty; in Limerick in November a tenant-right meeting was wrecked, and the platform broken down. The popular Father Quaid was given a hearing, but two other priests were ejected from the market-place by a band estimated at two hundred strong. The explanation given for this fracas was that the supporters of amnesty were exasperated by the bitter opposition of the bishop and clergy to the amnesty agitation in the teeth of which the St Patrick's day collection had been organised; the clergy were alleged to have denounced the opening meeting of the local Amnesty Association, only Father Quaid giving it his support.[22] Several more clashes of the same kind between amnesty and tenant-right supporters occurred in succeeding weeks.

From the unique position which he held as leader of both movements, Butt remonstrated with the advanced men:

> I believe the two objects, so far from being antagonistic, help each other . . . in the present circumstances of Ireland I can conceive no proceeding more mischievous than any attempt to sever the cause of the Irish tenantry from the cause of the Irish nation . . . I am sure that such a course would defeat our hopes of securing that united national party upon which the best hopes of Ireland depend.[23]

It was against the background of this conflict that the by-election in Tipperary was fought. It had been widely canvassed, when the vacancy was first created by the death of Charles Moore, that Butt himself should be put into nomination, and notices in support of his candidature were posted around the constituency:

> Butt for Tipperary, Butt for the release of the Political Prisoners. Butt for the Land Question. Butt for Education . . . Who defended the State Prisoners free of expense?—Butt. Who

22 *Irishman*, 6 Nov. 1869. This was John Daly's ' battle of the markets '. (Recollections of fenianism, *Irish Freedom*, Sept. and Oct. 1912).
23 *Nation*, 13 Nov.

wrote the best pamphlet on the Land Question?—Butt. Who
deserves the gratitude of Ireland most?—Butt.[24]

Butt, however, declined to accept nomination, declaring at a
dinner in Cork which followed the inaugural meeting of the
Tenant League that he believed himself to be of more use
outside 'an alien parliament'.[25] The adjourned county meeting at which Butt's name had been originally proposed met
again at the beginning of October. Butt's proposer having received, in the interval, formal notice of his refusal to accept
nomination, the meeting unanimously selected Denis Caulfield Heron, a distinguished catholic barrister, who addressed
the constituency in support of fixity of tenure, denominational
education, and amnesty. His candidature had the full support of the local tenant-right party, and of the *Freeman's
Journal*. But the advanced party were dissatisfied at the proposed return of 'the last law-adviser of Gladstone's government' as a companion for Barry, Dowse, and Sullivan 'the
viper', on a platform which placed tenant right first and amnesty third.[26] Almost at the last moment, the advanced section nominated in opposition to Heron, Jeremiah O'Donovan
Rossa, 'of Portland Prison, or Pentonville, England'. For
Rossa they could proclaim the simplest and most effective of
slogans: 'Remember the record of his unparalleled suffer-
ings—remember his thirty-five days torture with his hands
manacled behind his back.'[27] The Amnesty Association did
not officially endorse Rossa's candidature—with his associations in both parties Butt could scarcely have done so, although Nolan probably urged that he should, and J. F. X.
O'Brien wrote to Butt deploring the failure of the association
to support Rossa's candidature as a great amnesty demonstration.[28] But even without this endorsement, the election was
an unmistakeable struggle for predominance between the

[24] *Irishman*, 16 Oct.
[25] *Nation*, 25 Sept.
[26] *Irishman*, 30 Oct.
[27] ibid., 6 Nov.
[28] J. F. X. O'Brien to Butt, 28 Nov. 1869, Butt MSS. Butt had, in
fact, sponsored Heron. (Heron to Butt, 22 Oct. 1869, Butt Add. MSS,
10415).

fenian-amnesty and liberal-land reform parties. In a low poll, the fenian convict was elected.

The tremendous significance of this result was immediately recognised. 'Unquestionably the most remarkable event of the kind which has taken place in Ireland since the memorable contest for Clare in 1829', wrote the *Nation*[29] 'One of the most remarkable events of this the most critical period of our history', was the immediate comment of the *Freeman's Journal* upon the news of the result.[30] The following day the same organ attributed the result to the disappointed reaction of the Irish people to the denial of land reform, and their belief that Gladstone's government would not be permitted by the landed interest to introduce a genuine measure; it appealed to Gladstone and Bright to take the courageous step which lay in their power. In the meanwhile a further demonstration of Irish reaction against the liberal alliance was given in the Longford by-election immediately afterwards, where a hasty decision was taken to nominate John Martin, who was absent in America at the time, upon the battle-cry of 'The glorious example of Tipperary', in opposition to Reginald Greville-Nugent, son of the local liberal magnate Lord Greville, who had already been chosen by the local liberals and the clergy to fill the vacancy caused by the elevation to the peerage of his father. On this occasion Butt and the Amnesty Association openly endorsed Martin's candidature and his demand for Irish self-government. The clergy were exceptionally active and determined in opposition to Martin, and when in January 1870 polling took place, the liberal was returned by a large majority, only to be unseated on the grounds of bribery and clerical intimidation. The spectacle of determined independent nationalist opposition to the full force of clerical influence did not go unremarked.

While this evidence of a resurgence of independent nationalist action was becoming visible, an effort was being made to reconcile the two great forces of agitation. A special meeting of the Irish Tenant League was convened by Butt for the

---

[29] *Nation*, 27 Nov.
[30] *Freeman's Journal*, 26 Nov.

C*

afternoon of 14 December in the Rotunda, to be followed by
an open meeting in the evening, in the hope that it might be
possible to 'put an end to the unhappy dissensions which had
so long distracted the national party in Ireland'.[31] Dean
O'Brien wrote to Butt before the meeting:

> It is essential that *you* be at the great Dublin demonstration
> and per fas aut nefas (by which I mean wanted or not) you
> must make your own of it. Your presence there will knit the
> meeting to the League and give the League all its (the meet-
> ing's) power—it will make the League meeting popular—
> whereas if you do not carry that meeting we shall wither in its
> shadow.[32]

The afternoon meeting was largely concerned with the
technical aspects of land reform. The evening meeting was
obviously of a very different character, being opened to the
accompaniment of cheers for 'Tipperary and Rossa'. Butt
told this second meeting that the clergy were preparing to
take 'that bold step which is due to their position and their
flocks'. When a voice interjected 'they did not take it in
Tipperary', Butt urged the meeting to let bygones be bygones. He proposed a resolution to the effect that no reform
would satisfy the people so long as the political prisoners remained in custody. The meeting then proceeded to consider
another resolution in support of the Tenant League, but from
the floor of the hall C. R. Mahony of the Amnesty Association
tried to move an amendment:

> That we support the League only while under the presidency
> of Isaac Butt, who sacrifices his time and his talents for the
> people, without wishing to make any political capital for his
> labours.[33]

Meanwhile the land issue was approaching its climacteric
with the impending introduction of the government's land
bill. In January 1870 Gray and five other M.P.'s, together with
several prominent men outside parliament, circulated a re-

31 *Nation,* 18 Dec. 1869.
32 Dean O'Brien to Butt, Nov. 1869, Butt MSS.
33 *Nation,* 18 Dec.

quisition calling a land conference 'to confer as to the most effectual means of rooting the Irish people in the Irish soil.[34] The proposal was regarded with some suspicion by the members of the Tenant League; Richard Lalor of the Queen's County Independent Club replied that he would not sign the requisition because upon glancing down the list of its sponsors, many of whom had in the past opposed the principle of fixity of tenure, he did not believe that the conference would truly represent the tenant farmers, and also because the circular seemed to ignore the work already done and the stand taken by the public meetings of the Tenant League.[35] William Bolster also refused, declaring to Butt his determination to 'stick by the League '; he suggested, however, that Butt and Dean O'Brien should attend the conference to represent the views of the League:

> You would be powerful advocates of the right policy and a sprinkling of honest democracy in the body of the hall might be the means of keeping matters in proper trim.[36]

Butt attended the conference, which was held on 2 and 3 January in the Mansion House, and he was largely responsible for the framing of the resolutions which it considered. An eminently respectable and representative assembly heard him declare:

> They were done with delusions—they were done with compensation for improvements—they were done with the sale of right of occupancy—they were done with the Landlord's Ulster tenant right—they were done with everything that could leave a loop-hole for escape. and fixity of tenure, with fair rents, was now the rallying-cry of Ireland.

Resolutions were passed demanding continuous right of occupancy, subject only to eviction for non-payment of rent or for sub-letting without the consent of the landlord, and valua-

34 Bryan, Downing, Callan, D'Arcy, MacMahon; also the mayors of Dublin, Cork, Waterford, Wexford, Clonmel, Kilkenny and Drogheda, A. M. Sullivan, and P. P. McSwiney, chairman of the National Association. (Copy of requisition in Butt MSS, 1870).
35 Lalor to Michael Dwyer, Jan. 1870, Lalor MSS, 8566.
36 Bolster to Butt, 9 Jan. 1870, Butt MSS.

tion of rents, such valuation not to take into account the value of the tenant's right of occupancy. On the expiration of an existing lease, and in the event of disagreement as to the rent to be charged in future, independent valuation was to be arrived at by the local Land Tribunal.[37]

The decisions of this conference were of very considerable importance. They demonstrated the degree to which the land reform demand had advanced in clarity and in scope in the period between the election and the eve of the introduction of Gladstone's bill; they further demonstrated how the party of Gray and the *Freeman's Journal* had fallen in behind the radical proposals of fixity of tenure and valuation of rents. Lord Clanricarde wrote to G. H. Moore: ' I wonder no Tories or Nationalists have attacked the Freeman for the distrust of its pet, and be-praised administration, which the " conference" it is labouring to get up implies—or rather expresses'.[38] There was little chance that Gladstone could, even if he wished, grant such a sweeping measure of reform as the conference demanded. John Martin had opposed the course of the land movement for this reason as raising false hopes in the English parliament, and G. H. Moore had refused to attend the conference on the same grounds.[39] Looking back on the conference a month later, after the introduction of the land bill, J. A. Dease, an active pro-government liberal, wrote to William Monsell:

> The manner in which the Land Bill has been accepted is very much what I expected. Two years ago—as you may truly say— such a bill would have been hailed as the greatest boon Ireland ever received.

Public expectations, he said, had been excited ' to an extent that was quite beyond the bounds of possibility to satisfy '.

It is clear to anyone following the writings of the *Freeman's Journal* that Gray would of late have " backed " if he could.

[37] *Nation*, 5, 12 Feb.
[38] Clanricarde to Moore, 20 Jan. 1870, Moore MSS, Vol. VII.
[39] *Nation*, 11 Sept. 1869.
   Limerick Reporter, 5, 12 Apr. 1870; Moore to Hardiman,—Feb., 17 Feb., 1870, Moore MSS, Vol. VII.

This was clear enough at the Dublin Conference (which was a most truly melancholy exhibition of unreasoning violence) when Butt faced Gray and with the aid of men like Father Quaid made it plain to Gray that he would not be allowed to retreat from the extreme position he had led the country on to.[40]

But if Gray and his allies believed that they might, by countering in this way the pressure which the landed interest was believed to be continually exerting upon Gladstone, induce him to grant a radical measure, it seems unlikely that Butt had any such illusions. He told the Tenant League meeting in the Rotunda in December that ' he considered they would do as much service to Ireland by rejecting, in the name of the tenant farmers and people, an inefficient measure, as by accepting a good one ', and addressing the Amnesty Association at the end of October after Gladstone's negative reply to the address of the Cabra meeting, he had declared, in authorising a partial resumption of the agitation :

> I have a plan in my mind . . . Bide your time . . . Next session will prove the utter impotency of the English parliament to legislate for Ireland's people.[41]

The development of the amnesty and land reform movements had manoeuvred Gladstone into a position from which he could not extricate himself without either a decisive acceptance of the Irish popular demands or a dangerous disappointment of them. If he were to implement the principle of his ' justice for Ireland' policy in the sense in which the phrase was interpreted in that country—the government of Ireland in accordance with the desires of her inhabitants, he would have to grant an unqualified measure of amnesty and some form of fixity of tenure. Gladstone's understanding of Irish problems, much as it had increased in recent years, till it far exceeded that of any other English statesman of comparable stature, was not yet complete, and while he was statesmanlike

40 Dease to Monsell, 2 Mar. 1870, Monsell MSS, 8317.
41 *Nation,* 18 Dec. 1869.
 Irishman, 30 Oct.

enough to resist the pleas of his Irish officials for permission
to prosecute the *Irishman* for sedition and to proclaim several
Irish counties, he was quite unable to appreciate the absorption of Irish popular feeling in the amnesty and tenant-right
demands.[42] 'Gladstone is on his trial', declared Joseph Ronayne at an amnesty meeting in Queenstown.[43] The denial of
amnesty struck the first blow at the great position which Gladstone had built up in Ireland in the 1868 election: sympto-
matic of the reaction of the amnesty agitators was the resolution of the Limerick association in November, which called
upon Butt and G. H. Moore to convene a meeting in Dublin
to work out a policy for the obtaining of a national parliament as the only way of securing justice for Ireland in the
light of Gladstone's refusal to accede to the Cabra appeal.[44]
At the opening of 1870, with the culmination of the tenant
movement in the Tenant League meeting in the Rotunda
and the land conference in the Mansion House, the next great
challenge was thrown down before Gladstone. In the months
before the election of 1868, when Butt and Dean O'Brien and
others were working quietly in preparation for the time when
an opportunity would come to revive the demand for home
government, the Dean had written to Butt:

> In all cases it appears to me we ought to win; because the tend-
> ency to seek autonomy will grow equally by concession or dis-
> regard. It is wonderful that statesmen such as Gladstone and
> Bright think it possible by such things as disendowment to
> content the Irish people . . . Very likely we shall have to wait
> the reformed parliament—so much is promised which we can-
> not take the responsibility of jeopardising, however much we
> may disbelieve it will ever be granted . . . At any rate—every
> time—we are ready for our move. If we get too little we move;
> if we get much we move more strongly; if we get nothing we
> move instantly . . .[45]

[42] Gladstone to Fortescue, 11, 26 Oct. 1869; H. A. Bruce to Fortescue,
3 Dec.; C. R. Barry to Fortescue, 11 April 1870, Strachie MSS, Carlingford Political.
[43] *Irishman,* 23 Oct. 1869.
[44] ibid., 6 Nov.
[45] Dean O'Brien to Butt, 1868 (undated), Butt MSS.

Now a crucial test was approaching, and Dean O'Brien wrote again to Butt:

> It would be ruinous to speak of the Great Question now as *the* question. You would raise up all Ireland—unless one party—against you . . . It is clear that win or lose in the next session—our gain shoots up. A *settlement* of the Land Question unites all Ireland; a suspension of the settlement will unite the Democracy.[46]

On 15 February Gladstone introduced his land bill in the house of commons and showed his hand to all Ireland. In his introductory survey he specifically rejected the scheme of fixity of tenure as 'virtual expropriation' . . .

> the effect of that provision will be that the landlord will become a pensioner and rentcharger upon what is now his own estate.[47]

Instead, he proposed a scheme, or rather four parallel schemes, for securing existing customs of different kinds, and, where no custom existed, establishing a sliding scale of compensation for disturbance, based upon the rental of the holding; this, he hoped, would make capricious eviction so costly a process that the landlord would be effectively deterred from it. An important principle was accepted in the establishment of a court of arbitration with power to assess the damages to be paid for eviction, but the value of the scheme was largely negatived by its complexity, which offered endless opportunities for litigation and loopholes for escape, and by its specific exclusion of tenants evicted for non-payment of rent from the right to claim damages for disturbance.[48]

46 O'Brien to Butt, Nov. 1869, Butt MSS.
47 But a portent of the more drastic legislation he was later to introduce was contained in his admission that the state had a perfect right to do this if it wished, and his description of the evils of the present system as 'so great that I, for one, am prepared to say that I can hardly conceive of any alternative which would not be better than the continuance of the present state of things'.
48 Gladstone's speech is in *Hansard*, 3rd series, cxcix, 333-90; Butt's critique of the bill in *Freeman's Journal*, 22 Feb. 1870; Gray on the bill in *Hansard*, cxcix, 1681—1703.

The bill met with almost instant condemnation in Ireland. The *Nation* of 19 February, called it 'an elaborate and tremendous effort of tinkering'; the first comment of the *Freeman's Journal* of the same day was that the bill needed amendment—otherwise 'it will leave the old sore unhealed, the land question unsettled', but in the same issue the London correspondent of the paper wrote that 'the discontent is spreading rapidly and increasing as the bill is more closely examined'. On Monday 20th Fortescue's secretary reported: 'Sir J. G. had not yet broken ground from which I suppose we are to consider that unless driven on, he will support the bill'.[49] But that same day the editorial in the *Freeman* declared: 'the more we examine the bill the more we see the hopelessness of making it satisfactory'. Even a whig journal like the *Limerick Reporter* which had initially welcomed the bill, sneering at those who talked of 'improbabilities' such as 'perpetuity, pure and simple', was compelled, in the face of popular feeling, and in particular of the reaction of the *Freeman's Journal,* to make a complete volte-face and denounce it. The bill, it declared, 'has called forth an unmistakeable expression of dissatisfaction entirely unconnected with party spirit'. Listing the objections of the *Freeman's Journal,* one of which was that the power of the landlord capriciously to increase the rent remained unimpaired, it insisted upon the principle of periodic valuation, with security of tenure so long as the rent was paid: 'less than this will not, and ought not, to satisfy us'. In March it further commented that the passage of an unsatisfactory bill would inevitably strengthen the demand for a renewed repeal agitation.[50]

Faced by this hostile reaction a genuinely bewildered Gladstone turned for succour to Cardinal Cullen, and amid his conciliar deliberations in Rome the Cardinal found time to despatch a message of good cheer.[51] The Irish bishops at Rome were unanimous in commendation of the bill, wrote Mann-

[49] Coffey to Fortescue, 20 Feb., Strachie MSS, Carlingford Political.

[50] *Limerick Reporter,* 18, 22 Feb., 8 Mar. 1870.

[51] Gladstone to Cullen, 6 Mar. 1870, Cullen to Gladstone, 12 Mar., BM Add. MSS 44425 ff 192, 243; also Gladstone to Gray 28 Nov. 1869, BM Add. MSS, 44423 f 233.

ing, and prayed for Gladstone as 'the truest friend and benefactor of Ireland'.[52] In the commons the bulk of the Irish
liberals voted for the second reading, while expressing criticisms of it and reserving the right to seek its amendment in
committee. But Gray himself opposed the second reading, and
nine other Irish members followed him into the opposition
lobby. The public defection of Gray on the land issue was
undoubtedly the greatest single blow to the government in
Ireland.[53]

Gladstone nevertheless stood firm. A deputation of Irish
members and farmers' leaders led by Gray which called on
Gladstone on 5 March produced no concession, nor did a
memorandum communicated to the prime minister by Manning on behalf of the Irish bishops who were now having
second thoughts about the effectiveness of the measure.[54] The
cabinet was unanimous in its hostility to the valuation of
rents,[55] and such amendments as were accepted on the committee stage tended to the interest of the landlord rather than
the tenant. Gray's proposal to allow a landlord and tenant to
adopt by agreement the principle of valuation and non-dis-
turbance on payment of rent, which was the most important
of the Irish amendments, was defeated by 317 votes to 29.

The bill passed into law rejected by the Irish popular
leaders, not only by Butt and the Tenant League, but by
Gray and the *Freeman's Journal*. Dean O'Brien, whose views
on the importance of the impending land settlement in November 1869 have already been quoted, now wrote again to
Butt:

I have been disappointed by " the bill " and in it. The bill is
useless for any proximate good and too complicated to permit
any certainty of remote benefit. We have yet to look for a solution of the " Irish difficulty "—for we have not yet seen anything which will make Irishmen fight for Ireland. Of course
Mr Gladstone has closed the line of statesmen in whom I had

52 Manning to Gladstone, 24 Feb. 1870, BM Add. MSS, 44249 f 139.
53 Sir W. H. Gregory to Fortescue, undated, Strachie MSS, Carlingford Political.
54 Manning to Gladstone, 1 Mar., BM Add. MSS 44249 f 141.
55 Cabinet ' round robin ', BM Add. MSS 44638 f 40.

any hope—a hope which ought not perhaps have been inspired by his legislation of last year which lost his class so little. English wisdom has failed to see the nature of the crisis—and Irish warning has spoken in vain. We stand on the brink of the future which the " Limerick Declaration " two years ago shadowed forth. A new land bill is impossible—in this generation; and the present bill is useless for the end it should have contemplated. Landlords and statesmen have only one chance of saving us from coming confusion, and that is to permit us to make our own laws. I cannot go on with a sham-battle—I am sure that many of my class share my opinions—these battles have lasted long enough.[56]

O'Brien exaggerated the extent of his own disillusionment. The land bill was no moment of truth to him; long before it, his mind had been made up. In principle, though, he was right. There were those, like Cardinal Cullen, for whom confidence in Gladstone was only slightly shaken by a setback on an issue never closest to their hearts. But to many who had accepted Liberal leadership on sufferance the image of ' Justice for Ireland ' was heavily tarnished by the denial, firstly, of amnesty and, secondly, of tenant right within the space of little more than a year. The unanimity of 1868 was gone. The liberal alliance was by no means shattered, as the infant home rule movement was quickly to find to its cost. But it was remarkable that so great a breach in it had been so quickly made. Opposition to Gladstone could no longer be simply and lethally anathematised as treason to country and to faith.

---

[56] Dean O'Brien to Butt, 17 Feb. 1870, Butt MSS.

CHAPTER III

The Home Government Association

THE FAILURE of the land bill to satisfy the demands of the tenant leaders was the signal for Butt to launch the agitation for self-government which up to then he had cautiously deferred. The whole course of his conduct over the previous year—his systematic prosecution of the amnesty campaign, and the skill with which he committed Gray and the whole tenant party to a programme which he knew the government would never accept—reveals a deliberate plan to discredit the liberal alliance. In February 1870, immediately after the land bill debates, A. M. Sullivan wrote to O'Neill Daunt suggesting a meeting with John Martin and a few of the other leading repealers to discuss the launching of a new campaign. On 8 April Daunt suggested to P. J. Smyth that he and Sullivan should arrange with Butt and major Laurence Knox, proprietor and editor of the *Irish Times,* to call a meeting in the Rotunda. At the same time, Daunt began cautiously to sound his friends around the country on the subject.[1]

Butt and the other principals were determined above all that the new movement should be as broadly based as tact and persuasion could make it. Irish political sentiment fell, on the whole, into three categories, liberal, conservative, and fenian in sympathy. The effort to hold together elements from all these sections dominates the history of Butt's first three years as leader of home rule. It was an attempt faced, in each case, by considerable difficulties.

It has been argued above that the great achievement of the Amnesty Association and of the land agitation had been to

[1] Sullivan to Daunt, 22 Feb. 1870, Daunt MSS, 8048; Daunt to Smyth, 8 Apr., Gen. F. P. Dunne to Daunt, 11 Mar., MS 8045. J. Hodnett to Daunt, 10, 16 April, Maurice Lenihan to Daunt, 17 Feb., MS 8046.

dispel from the Liberal leader the aura of sanctity which had surrounded him in the election. But Gladstone was not yet to be abandoned by his Irish followers. Sir John Gray having spent his political daring in the land campaign reverted, with his paper, to his former caution, and declined to allow Butt to take him for a ride a second time; asked by Butt to join the leadership of the Home Government Association, he replied that he had only 'painfull recollections' of their earlier association.[2] As far as the catholic hierarchy was concerned, and with it that section of opinion most concerned with religious issues, confidence in Gladstone was not lightly to be withdrawn. In March 1870, in the middle of the land bill controversy, the pastoral letter of Cardinal Cullen rejoiced in the passage of disestablishment and expressed unbroken confidence that the donor of this boon would yet grant redress of every other Irish grievance.

Above all, there remained one perennial issue, that of education, upon which the administration had yet to make its policy plain. Until Gladstone committed himself in its regard, clerical approval would be given to no movement which sought to embarrass him. And in the long run, if home rule was to replace liberalism as the spokesman of Irish popular opinion, it could not itself remain untouched by the denominational controversy; no matter how deeply it might appeal to feelings of nationality among the masses, it could afford to ignore no aspect of Irish grievance. 'It is impossible to shut one's eyes to the fact that the feeling of Irish Nationality pervades the entire working class', wrote the liberal Bernal Osborne to Fortescue in November 1869:

> The farming class as a whole are not hot upon fixity of tenure, it is the cry of the artisans who are unconnected with agriculture. It strikes me that this amnesty question is the most difficult to meet, the feeling for it being most deep and sincere. The parish priests and bishops care most about denominational education; they are afraid of the Fenian organisation and know

---

[2] Gray to Butt, 27 Aug. 1870, Butt Add. MSS, 10415.

not where to turn as if they went directly contra to the movement their influence would vanish in the towns especially.[3]

If the liberals and the catholic clergy were subject to a mixture of motives, conservative support for home rule might well have seemed still more improbable. Yet it is to an upsurge of conservative nationalism that the origins of the Home Government Association are traditionally ascribed, 'It may be doubted that there ever was a time since 1800 when Irish Protestants as a body believed that Irish affairs could be better understood and cared for in a London legislature than in an Irish Parliament', wrote A. M. Sullivan in his historical bestseller, *New Ireland*. 'Concern for their rights, privileges, and possessions as a minority in the midst of a dangerous Catholic majority, was the real reason why they supported the Union system'.[4] It was the contention of Sullivan and other writers on the period that the disestablishment of their church and the invasion of their privileged position on the land by the reforming measures of the Liberal administration of 1868 destroyed the compact of mutual self-interest between Irish protestantism and the English legislature, and that the movement which Butt founded in 1870 owed much of its strength to a recrudescence of Irish protestant nationalism. This view has gained so much currency among later historians of the period that it will be necessary to give it some particular attention.

As has been stated before, the 1868 election resulted in the return of a body of Irish representatives the majority of whom were possibly more clearly pledged to support of the English Liberal party than at any time since before the famine. In the eyes of the Irish electorate these representatives were bound to a programme of disestablishment, tenant right, and denominational education. In the space of a few months the Liberal administration had fulfilled its promise of disestablishment. There seemed, at that time, to Irish opinion every reason to hope, or to fear, that the other reforms would follow with equal expedition.

[3] Osborne to Fortescue, 4 Nov. 1869, Strachie MSS, Carlingford Political.
[4] A. M. Sullivan, *New Ireland*, (14th ed., Glasgow, 1882) p. 328.

Among the Irish protestant conservatives, who had fought bitterly in the election against the threatened invasion of their hereditary privileges, resentment against Liberal policy took in some cases the extreme form of a sudden espousal of repeal principles. 'A Protestant clergyman of the County of Meath' wrote to the conservative *Daily Express* on 3 March 1869: 'Dissolve the Article of Union between Church and State, and you will see how few Protestants will be loyal to the connection between England and Ireland'.[5] 'A Protestant Repealer' wrote urging the formation of 'a united national party, composed of Orangemen and anti-Ultramontane Roman Catholics'.[6] A few days later another conservative journal, the *Dublin Evening Mail,* gave editorial expression to this new feeling:

> The value of the Union in Protestant eyes lay in the protection which it was supposed to afford to property, liberty, and life by the full extension to Ireland of the immunities and privileges of the British constitution. If the power of the Imperial Parliament be used only to suspend the Constitution in the whole of Ireland, it may very well be questioned whether the model of a free Legislature might not be advantageously borrowed, for Irish use, from Protestant Canada.[7]

At the same time, the third great conservative journal, the *Irish Times,* at this time possibly the leading Irish daily, made an even more unequivocal pronouncement of repeal sympathies:

> It is impossible to deny that daily and almost hourly the conviction is growing stronger and deeper in the minds of all thoughtful Irishmen that if they are ever to entertain a hope for the prosperity of their country, that hope lies only in a native legislature, meeting in the Irish metropolis, and disbursing Irish revenues upon Irish objects . . .[8]

Whatever the motives behind this attitude, its prevalence was beyond dispute. S. L. Anderson, of the Crown Solicitor's

5 *Daily Express,* 6 Mar. 1869.
6 ibid., 2 Mar.
7 *Dublin Evening Mail,* 11 Mar.
8 *Irish Times,* 10 Mar.

Office in Dublin Castle, noted in his diary in March: 'Repeal of the union commences to be agitated by conservatives and protestants'.[9] As the year drew on further expressions of quasi-nationalist sentiment were made by a number of leading protestant conservatives, including one Fellow of Trinity College, George F. Shaw, two conservative members of the Dublin Corporation, Major Knox of the *Irish Times,* and E. R. King Harman, a junior member of a leading protestant landowning family, who stood as a home rule candidate in the second Longford by-election in April 1870.

The attitude of the Gladstonian liberals to this new feeling was one of undisguised contempt. 'Tory Repeal', wrote the *Limerick Reporter,* 'is one of the most transparent of humbugs'.[10] The nationalists, on the other hand, less happy in the close-knit liberal alliance of 1868, viewed these converts with more sympathy. The *Nation* wrote:

> We are glad to hear the words of patriotism spoken by Irish Protestants, even though they are but hasty words, spoken in a fit of ill-humour. Who knows but some spark of the patriotic spirit contained in them may remain to less excited moments, and may spread, and glow, and kindle in the hearts of those men a flame of genuine and unselfish love for their native land.[11]

But a liberal who spurned Gladstone in the spring of 1870 was moved by the feeling that he reformed too little, a conservative by the conviction that he reformed too much. It remained to be seen if such conflicting motives could bring strength to one common movement.

The opposition of the fenians to constitutional activity of any kind was notorious, and the clashes between the rival agitators for amnesty and tenant right had shown that fenian susceptibilities had not been dulled by adversity. Butt must have viewed their reactions to the new venture with considerable trepidation. In later years fenians like Charles Doran and Denis Dowling Mulcahy insisted that the neutrality of the

9 Anderson Diary, 13 Mar., MS 5966.
10 *Limerick Reporter,* 12 Apr.
11 *Nation,* 13 Mar.

advanced party was secured upon the undertaking in writing by Butt that the home rule agitation should be allowed to operate for a trial period only, and then if unsuccessful abandoned. This alleged 'compact' is usually dated around 1873, but probably there was from the outset some such inference that the home rule movement was a last attempt at a peaceful solution. William O'Brien, himself, at the time, a member of the Irish Republican Brotherhood in Cork,[12] was present as a young reporter when Butt spoke at a banquet given in Dublin by the Amnesty Association to the first batch of liberated fenians:

> Butt's speech was almost wholly a plea to the released fenian leaders to give him a chance for trying other means. He was argumentative, pathetic, passionate by turns; but the passage that will always live in my memory was that in which, in language actually blazing with the divine fire of eloquence, he declared that, if the conciliatory methods he pleaded for failed, he would not only give way to those who would lead where all the nations of the earth had gone before them, but that, old as he was, his arm and his life would be at their service in the venture.[13]

Jeremiah Hodnett, an old ally of Butt's in his period as member for Youghal, wrote to O'Neill Daunt in March 1870: 'Mr Butt says he will have Repeal in five years, or, if not, separation'.[14]

The experience of the Amnesty Association had shown the willingness of the fenians in one case to lend their energy to a constitutional agitation. It had demonstrated to them the influence which they might wield through such a movement, and it had accustomed revolutionary and constitutional nationalists to work in association. The fenians were in no position to raise armed revolt in the near future; John Daly, who

---

[12] T. H. Ronayne to John Devoy, 24 Sept. 1881, *Devoy's Post Bag*, ed. O'Brien, W. & Ryan, D., vol. ii, p. 101.

[13] O'Brien, *Recollections*, (London 1905), p. 137. Unfortunately O'Brien destroyed his notes of this speech at Butt's request.

[14] Hodnett to Daunt, 16 Mar. 1870, Daunt MSS, 8046.

took up organisational work again on his return to Ireland in the summer of 1869, recalled years later:

It was thoroughly understood that the organisation was formed for no immediate effort at insurrection. The men in the movement at the time realised that the best thing to do was to arm and hold themselves in readiness for any opportunity that may present itself of England being engaged in a war.[15]

Furthermore, the two men who were popularly designated as the leaders of any revived parliamentary agitation, Isaac Butt and G. H. Moore, both had associations with the advanced party. The fenians were notoriously hostile to the majority of the constitutional leaders; Gray of the *Freeman* they dismissed as a whig, Sullivan of the *Nation* they detested, probably unjustifiably, as a felon-setter. Butt, however, as counsel for the fenian prisoners in the state trials had won their gratitude; as president of the Amnesty Association he had commanded their loyalty. Probably at no time did he inspire more respect among the advanced party than in the years 1869-73. Moore's position was at least as strong. A veteran of Gavan Duffy's party and one of the few who had adhered to its original principles, he commanded widespread respect for his integrity and his oratorical powers, but had made many enemies by his incautiously stinging tongue. Returning to politics in 1868 after a long retirement, his oratorical brilliance quickly established him as Butt's only potential rival for the leadership of the new movement. He was one of the principals in the negotiations of spring 1870, and planned a tour of the south to raise support for the cause.[16] In some ways he possessed the stronger claim to lead. He was already, unlike Butt, established in parliament, and possessed personal links with Disraeli, whom he seems to have hoped to interest in home rule.[17] In April 1870 he gave notice in the commons

15 *Irish Freedom,* September 1912.

16 M. Moore, *An Irish gentleman,* p. 382; M. F. Dwyer to C. S. Fortescue, 30 July 1869, Strachie MSS, Carlingford Political; Memorial address by Butt, 24 April 1870 (*Nation,* 30 April).

17 Moore to Disraeli, 7 Dec. 1869, 4 Mar. 1870: Rev. P. Conway P.P. to Disraeli, April 1870, Disraeli MSS.

of his intention to move a repeal resolution on 3 May; it was a call to action, the first serious repeal challenge at Westminster for many years. If friendly contact with the fenians were to be decisive, he had as great, if not greater, claims to precedence as Butt. According to John Daly, Moore was actually a member of the provisional council which was endeavouring to reorganise the Irish Republican Brotherhood, his fellow-members including John Nolan and Thomas Neilson Underwood, both associates of Butt's in the Amnesty Association, and John O'Connor Power and J. J. O'Kelly, both later home rule members of parliament. Such a council could well have been more favourable to parliamentary action than that which, a few years later, was dominated by Charles Kickham.

Daly's recollections are far from reliable. But Moore certainly seems to have taken the fenian oath around this time.[18] According to John Devoy, O'Donovan Rossa had wished to enrol Moore in 1864, but was thwarted by the hostility of James Stephens; Devoy recalled, however, being told by J. J. O'Kelly that after the failure of the rising Moore was consulted so frequently by the reorganised supreme council that he was virtually a member of it.[19] Another version credits O'Connor Power with persuading Moore to agree to an earlier 'new departure' in 1868-69.[20] And Moore's son Maurice

18 In his recollections, published in *Irish Freedom* forty years later, Daly is more than once mistaken about dates. He places Butt's election for Limerick City around the same time as his own return to Ireland and his clashes with the Tenant League, which in fact occurred two years earlier, and he ascribes to 1873 a meeting with Parnell which could not have taken place until 1874 or later. Furthermore, he admits that he did not himself know the result of an election for a Munster representative on the supreme council, ' as the greatest possible care was taken to preserve the identity of the men elected '. He was not himself elected to the supreme council until around 1873. His testimony cannot, therefore, be accepted unreservedly. But in this instance there is considerable corroborative evidence for the general assertion that Moore possessed close links with the Fenian leadership between the rising and his own death.

19 *Recollections of an Irish rebel*, 1929, p. 322.

20 M. MacDonagh, *The home rule movement*, 1920, pp. 115-6. MacDonagh gives no reference for this contention, but he was able to draw upon Power's papers, which have since disappeared.

had the word of his mother and of John O'Leary that the old parliamentarian had joined the I.R.B. by 1870:

> Though he had sympathised with the objects of the Fenians, he had formerly refused to join them in a hopeless rebellion, under leaders in whom he had no confidence, and whose actions he could not influence. Now the leaders were scattered and the rebellion suppressed, he hoped perhaps to guide the members in more reasonable ways.[21]

Perhaps he succeeded. Certainly, when Butt rose in Bilton's Hotel formally to propose the launching of home rule, he was able to say: 'As for the men whom misgovernment has driven into revolt, I say for them that if they cannot aid you they will not thwart your experiment'.[22] But if Moore's contacts had helped to make this pledge possible, they did not win him the leadership of the new movement, for this was the last service which he was to render to the cause of his country's freedom. He never moved the resolution he had placed for the English parliament, for on 19th April he collapsed and died at his estate in Mayo. The cause of his death was a heart attack. Relations between Moore and a section of his tenants had long been strained, and he had lately been plagued by sinister communications in which an untraceable 'Rory' threatened to take his life. Soon it was said that Rory had made good his threat—that it was the last of these letters which killed Moore, in a fit of that same ungovernable temper which in life had so often blighted the career of this remarkable man.

The death of Moore left Butt the uncontested leader of home rule. The initial steps which were taken in May 1870 were probably very largely the work of Butt with the assistance of Sullivan. There had possibly been only one comparable outburst of conservative nationalism in the century—that which had occurred between the famine and the 1848

21 M. Moore, op. cit., p. 350.
22 A. M. Sullivan, *New Ireland*, 14th ed., Glasgow, p. 344. One of R. B. O'Brien's anonymous fenians recollected promising Butt the benevolent neutrality of the advanced party at this time (*Life of C. S. Parnell*, 3rd ed., vol. i, p. 65, note 1).

rebellion. Butt, as the only notable survivor from the earlier movement, was particularly anxious to exploit to the full the opportunities offered by the second. John Martin wrote in the same strain to O'Neill Daunt in 1869: 'Of course we should gladly accept the help of the new repealers whom spite has converted. We don't want to banish these persons, or anybody, from Ireland if we had the country independent'.[23] Daunt himself had urged the circularisation of as many protestants as possible.[24] The meeting summoned for Bilton's Hotel in May was specifically orientated towards these new converts. Martin wrote to Butt that he believed that it was just as well that he was unable to get up to Dublin for the meeting, as his premature entry into the movement might frighten off 'many of the protestants now opening their minds to the consideration of the state of Ireland and of their own position in reference thereto'; instead he wrote to the *Nation* 'to cheer on the protestants to join in the movement'. To Daunt he described the movement in this initial phase as one of the protestant nationalists of Dublin. P. J. Smyth was also absent from the meeting, being omitted, allegedly by an oversight, from the list of those who received invitations; writing to him a few days later to apologise for this error, Butt described the meeting as having consisted of 'principally protestants and conservatives', and 'all men of some mark and station—many of them of consideration in the mercantile world'.[25]

Forty-nine people attended the Bilton's Hotel meeting; 12 additional names, including those of Smyth and Martin, were subsequently added to form a committee of 61, a list of which is preserved in A. M. Sullivan's *New Ireland*.[26] Of the 61 names listed, 28 were protestant conservatives, 10 were liberals, 17 were constitutional nationalists, and 6 were fenians or fenian associates. Politically, the group divided into 28 con-

[23] Martin to Daunt, 9 June 1870, Daunt MSS, 8047.

[24] Daunt to Smyth, 8 Apr., Daunt MSS, 8045.

[25] Martin to Butt, 26 May, Butt MSS. ibid., and *Nation*, 21 May. Daunt Journal, 13 June, MS 3041. Butt to Smyth, 23 May, Smyth MSS, 8215.

[26] 14th ed., Glasgow, pp. 339-41.

servatives and 33 liberals and nationalists, and by religion into 35 protestants and 25 catholics.[27] The conservative element was thus the largest single group, and although it did not actually predominate even at this early stage, it contained some significant adhesions to the home rule ranks. The proprietors of two influential conservative newspapers, Major Knox of the *Irish Times,* and Dr Maunsell of the *Dublin Evening Mail,* were among the number, which also included the Lord Mayor of Dublin, Alderman Purdon, a previous Lord Mayor—Sir John Barrington, an ex-high sheriff of Dublin, two fellows of Trinity College—Galbraith and Shaw, two members of the King Harman family, and Sir William Wilde. At the conclusion of Butt's address to the meeting, not one dissentient voice was raised to the proposition that the solution of Irish problems lay in the restoration of her domestic legislature, according to Sullivan.[28] But Galbraith recalled years later:

> A great many speeches were made—some of a very foolish character—some stating that a royal residence was needed, and that if the Duke of Connaught were made a sort of perpetual viceroy or resident, all the evils of which they complained in Ireland would be removed.[29]

The sincerity, the proportionate influence, and the permanence of conservative participation in the home rule movement deserves closer examination than it has hitherto received.

In the first place, the proportions of the Bilton's Hotel meeting inevitably were not long maintained. The meeting resolved itself into a committee and arranged to assemble again the following Thursday. Captain John Dunne, an old friend of Butt's and a kindred spirit, who had joined him in many a bottle of wine and many an unpaid debt, was appointed acting secretary.[30] After several meetings the committee

27 Sullivan's classification of these people is, so far as I can ascertain, correct as to religion; his political classification I have amended in five cases.

28 *New Ireland,* 14th ed., p. 344.

29 *Nation,* 10 Feb. 1877.

30 Butt to Smyth, 23 May, Smyth MSS, 8215. Dunne to Daunt, 4, 7 July, Daunt MSS, 8045.

had grown to number 359 members, and the first public move of the new association was taken in July with the publication of the full list of these members, together with the request that sympathisers should allow their names to be added.[31] The original list of sixty-one had already included such leading figures of liberal and nationalist politics as Smyth, Martin, Butt, Sullivan, and William Shaw, liberal member of parliament for Bandon, together with such noted fenian sympathisers as John 'Amnesty' Nolan. Now to this nucleus were added nearly all the leading exponents of the liberal nationalist tradition; repeal priests in Dean O'Brien of Limerick, Father Lavelle of Partry, and Father Quaid of O'Callaghan's Mills; W. J. O'Neill Daunt, Richard Pigott of the *Irishman*, John George MacCarthy, A. J. Kettle—a tenant-right agitator now making his first notable essay into nationalist politics; such advanced nationalists at Patrick Egan, John Denvir, and Joseph Ronayne; together with two more liberal nationalist members of parliament, Philip Callan, member for Dundalk, and George Ekins Browne, who had been elected for Mayo upon the death of G. H. Moore. With this broadening of the movement, and the entry into it of those who had possibly been deliberately held back in the early stages for fear of frightening the conservatives, the importance of the original conservative element, which remained more or less static in number, began correspondingly to decline. William Shaw had written to Butt in April:

> The National Movement in its new shape must be launched and handled with great judgment. As regards the great body of the people I have no doubt of them going with the movement, but it will be essential to get the better class well into it.[32]

But the support of influential aristocratic conservatives was never really secured, and Shaw himself in June opposed the publication of the list of Committee-members as giving the association 'too much the appearance of a Dublin shop-keeping movement'.[33]

31 *Nation,* 20 Aug. 1870.
32 Shaw to Butt, 23 Apr. Butt MSS.
33 Shaw to Butt, 6 June, Butt MSS.

As early as October 1870, at the first monthly meeting of the Home Government Association, Butt admitted that in point of religion the catholics had a small majority on the committee and that politically the liberals outnumbered the conservatives by three to two.[34] This shift in the composition of the association had its effect even in these early months; the *Daily Express,* which had welcomed the 'newborn feeling' in May as evidence that the power of the priests was on the wane, withdrew all its approval from the movement and called instead for the formation of an anti-ultramontane Irish party. Of the first public meeting of the association in September it commented that most of the protestants held aloof, and 'the audience was, for the most part, made up of the persons who on divers occasions, such as funeral processions and amnesty meetings, are wont to appear in the character of "the people of Ireland".'[35] Even the *Irish Times,* despite the fact that its editor was a founder member of the association, remained kind but non-committal, so much so that Butt wrote personally to Knox in November asking him to induce his newspaper to treat the association with greater cordiality.[36]

The enthusiastic publicity which the nationalists gave to the presence in the association of a conservative clement did, however, as will be seen, have one considerable result in the field of practical politics—it provided the Gladstonian liberals with a strong pretext for declining to support it. In this context there are some basic facts as to the role of the association which must always be borne in mind. The new body was never much more than a Dublin pressure group; it did not put forward candidates in by-elections, nor did it undertake any form of local organisation. Butt urged the formation of local home rule associations, but they were not formally affiliated to the original body and owed it no obedience other than deference to its seniority and to its federal programme. Looking back on the progress of the movement in October 1871,

---

[34] *Dublin Evening Mail,* 6, 7 Oct.
[35] *Daily Express,* 18 May, 12 Aug.
[36] Knox to Butt, 5 Nov., Butt MSS.

Butt declared:

> It would be a mistake to think that the movement was intended
> to form a great popular organisation. What they intended to
> do was to bring the question before the public mind . . . They
> never contemplated the raising of a great fund; their expenses
> were all defrayed by the ordinary one pound subscriptions of
> the members, and they had succeeded in bringing together
> more than eight hundred Irish gentlemen of different religious
> and political persuasions.[37]

These points must be emphasised because they illustrate
how in practice from the very outset the Home Government
Association was divorced from the main sources of Irish political energy; through its orange reputation, which discouraged the liberals and the catholic clergy from joining it,
through its refusal to affiliate local branches, and through its
reluctance to endorse parliamentary candidates, it left the
practical advancement of the cause to the work of local agen-
cies and in particular of local by-election struggles. It was
through these that the character of the movement became
significantly altered from that which its original protagonists
had envisaged.

The new movement had one particular characteristic
which Butt never tired of stressing—it was aimed exclusively
at the attainment of home rule. In May 1871 he urged the
local associations which had by then been formed upon the
model of the parent body 'not to mix up abstract topics with
the question',[38] and it was for fear of such excesses that he
avoided any form of affiliation with them. By these tactics he
hoped to win for home rule the support of men who totally
differed upon every other subject of political controversy. In
practice, this formula of Butt's for national unity was never
feasible. Whig catholic papers such as the *Dublin Evening
Post* and the *Limerick Reporter* were openly hostile to the
new movement from its inception—'a vile sham—a stalking
horse to conceal Orange and Tory manoeuvres', wrote the

37 *Nation,* 18 Oct. 1871.
38 ibid., 27 May.

THE HOME GOVERNMENT ASSOCIATION

Limerick Reporter, in what was taken to be clerically-inspired comment.[39] Conservative participation in the home rule movement was never, even at the outset, as great as later historians have appeared to assume; it certainly did not represent the new departure which Butt had hoped to achieve. But it was sufficient to make the home government association permanently suspect in the eyes of the clergy and of the liberals.

The reconciliation of conservatism and home rule was not by any means the only problem which faced the association in these opening months. After the inaugural meeting of the new body in the Rotunda on 1 September, rooms were taken in Grafton Street, and a series of monthly meetings was begun. In November an address was circulated, stating the basic aims of the association and appealing for support. It was signed by the Reverend J. A. Galbraith, F.T.C.D., George Browne, M.P., and Laurence Waldron, as secretaries.[40] The recipient was asked to co-operate in the demand for 'the restoration to Ireland of that right of domestic legislation, without which Ireland can never enjoy real prosperity or peace'. But going further, the address declared:

> We have also resolved to accompany this with a proposal of such a Federal Union between the three portions of the United Kingdom as may still combine them into one great Imperial State . . .

It was the adoption of this federal programme which was the principle innovation of the revived agitation. It was not achieved without considerable heart-searching and misgiving among the older nationalists.

The opening pronouncement of the association did not elaborate upon the federal proposals which it envisaged.

> This is not the time for offering the complete plan of such a federal union. That must come with the authority of a united Ireland. At present we invite the adhesion of all who are willing to co-operate in the general object of obtaining for Ireland a parliament of her own. When our association becomes strong

[39] *Limerick Reporter,* 15 Apr. 1870; J. Hodnett to Daunt, 16 Apr., Daunt MSS, 8046.
[40] November 1870, Butt MSS.

D

enough to recommend such a step, we propose to invite our countrymen to meet in a general conference finally to settle on the details of a plan such as Ireland may present for acceptance to the English parliament and ministers.

But in the same year Butt himself produced a pamphlet upon the subject of Irish federalism, and since this became at once generally accepted as the basis for the home rule demand, it is appropriate that some analysis of its proposals should be made at this point.[41]

'The outline I suggest is intended rather as a framework for suggestion and deliberation than as a complete plan', wrote Butt in introducing his proposals, and throughout the whole of his career as home rule leader he was to be adamant in his opposition to repeated suggestions that he should commit the home rule plan to the precise form of a parliamentary bill. He feared that if he did so he would be compelled to defend not the principle of home rule but the minutiae of its administration.

It is enough to say that I intend to propose a system under which England, Scotland, and Ireland, united as they are under one sovereign, should have a common executive and a common national council for all purposes necessary to constitute them, to other nations, as one state, while each of them should have its own domestic parliament for its internal affairs. I say each of them, because, although my immediate concern is only with Ireland, I do not suppose that if Irishmen obtain the separate management of Irish affairs it is at all likely that Englishmen or Scotchmen would consent to the management of their domestic concerns by a Parliament in which Irish members still had a voice. Whether England or Scotland would still desire to have the internal affairs of Great Britain managed by one common Parliament is a matter entirely for themselves to decide.

Here at once one of the basic difficulties of the home rule proposal was already exposed—the question of the retention

41 Butt, *Home government for Ireland, Irish federalism: its meaning, its objects, and its hopes,* Dublin 1870. References are to its fourth edition, Dublin 1875.

or non-retention of the Irish representatives in a British as
opposed to an 'Imperial' parliament. Butt's proposal is typic-
ally on the grand scale: far more than simply an Anglo-Irish
settlement, it looked ahead to an entire system of imperial devolution.

> The Imperial Parliament ought plainly to be the great Council
> of the Empire, with which should rest the constitutional right
> of advising the sovereign on all questions of peace and war,
> and of the foreign relations of the country. It ought also to
> possess, in relation to these matters, all the constitutional checks
> which in practice Parliament possesses over the crown. There
> should be an Imperial Ministry responsible to the Imperial
> Parliament, and that Parliament should have the power of con-
> trolling the expenditure and supplies for Imperial purposes.

This was one way, argued Butt, in which Ireland would be in
a notably stronger position than before the act of union, when
she possessed no representative influence whatever in imperial policy. The imperial crown should retain the great
officers of state—the Secretaries for War, India, the Colonies,
and Foreign Affairs, together with a Chancellor to hold the
great seal of the United Kingdom and a Home Secretary, 'to
manage the communications between the central authority
and the national administrations'. These, together with a
Treasurer and a Chancellor of the Exchequer should form an
imperial cabinet.

The imperial parliament would vote men, money, and arms
for defence. The money would be raised either by imperial
taxation or by a national quota system for the army and navy.
Ireland as a member of the imperial parliament would naturally have to bear her burden of imperial expenses.

> The Federal arrangement which I contemplate is one which
> would preserve the Imperial Parliament in its present form. It
> would leave to that Parliament all its present control over
> everything that affected the Imperial Crown—its dominions,
> its colonies, and its dependencies—over the foreign relations of
> the Empire, and all questions of peace and war. It would leave
> it still the power of preventing any tampering with the per-

manent taxation, which is the security for the payment of the
interest on the national debt, and the other charges on the
revenue to which the faith of Crown and Parliament is pledged.
It would leave it still the power of providing by Imperial taxation for Imperial necessities, including an Army and a navy
such as it judged necessary for the safety of the country, either
in peace or war—imposing only a guarantee in the nature of
the taxation that the levy should be one to which each member
of the United Kingdom should contribute in proportion to its
ability and its means.

The reconstitution of the Irish parliament presented slightly more difficulty. It would be impossible, argued Butt, to
restore it exactly as it was; many of the closed boroughs of the
earlier period no longer existed, and many of the corporations and honorary bodies which formerly held voting rights
were similarly defunct. His own preference was for the summoning of an Irish assembly, elected upon the basis of household suffrage, to settle the constitution of the new parliament,
but fearing this to be 'visionary' and impracticable, he would
accept that the local parliament should be established by an
act of the imperial body.

Members of the Irish House of Commons, to number from
two hundred and fifty to three hundred, should be chosen in
a completely separate election from that for representatives in
the imperial parliament. Butt suggested representation for
the counties and for every town with a population of over
three thousand. An immediate redistribution of seats would
be necessary, but the question of franchise reform, though
equally pressing, should not be made part of a home rule
settlement—it could be dealt with later. An impartial commission could fix the constituency boundaries and resolve
similar problems of detail.

Despite strong and persistent opposition from many of his
followers, Butt was adamant in demanding the restoration of
the Irish House of Lords as an integral part of the new parliament. He did this partly out of his desire to reproduce
faithfully the tested institutions of Westminster, but also in
order to reassure the Irish aristocracy against any fear of

spoliation and to retain their loyalty and their services for a self-governing Ireland. 'There is no people on earth', he reminded them, 'less disposed to democracy than the Irish'. He agreed, however, that there were many Irish peers who had earned no right to act as legislators in their native country. Absentee peers, and those whose titles had long since lost any connection with Ireland, and whose ancestors had never taken their seats in the Irish House of Lords, should be excluded. The additional creations by the crown over future years should augment the number of those remaining; but in addition to this he suggested, again with remarkable foresight, the creation of life peers from among such men 'distinguished in any field of intellectual achievement, as the Sovereign might think fit to associate with our hereditary nobility in the Upper House'.

As to the powers of the new parliament:—

> The Irish Parliament, consisting, be it always remembered, of the Queen, Lords, and Commons of Ireland, would have supreme control in Ireland, except in those matters which the Federal Constitution might specifically reserve to the Imperial Assembly.

The queen would retain all her prerogatives; the Lord Lieutenant would remain as her representative, responsible to the imperial parliament, but acting through Irish ministers responsible to the Irish parliament in the same way as those of Canada and Australia, two examples frequently cited by Butt and his followers. Under these provisions, Butt reminded the inveterate repealers, Ireland would enjoy responsible cabinet government for the first time. Legislation would have to be passed by both houses of the Irish parliament and receive the royal assent just as at present in the imperial parliament.

The imperial parliament would continue to assemble in annual session, but could take its reduced volume of business in a leisurely and painstaking fashion.

> In England—if the plan I propose were adopted in its integrity —the English members and the English peers would assemble in a separate Parliament for the transaction of all purely

English affairs. Whether they would still form one Parliament with the Scotch members is a question with which Ireland would have nothing to do . . .

That which is important is that Ireland would send, as we do now, 105 representatives to vote in an Imperial Parliament on all questions of Imperial concern, and in return we would submit, as we do now, to be taxed, but only for certain definite purposes and in a certain definite manner.

At home in Ireland we would have our own Parliament controlling all the affairs of our internal administration.

Butt's scheme was obviously one of immense grandeur and imagination. Some of its drawbacks were no less obvious. It provided an excellent basis for a modernised and federated Empire, but it was less immediately suitable for resolving the relationship between Britain and Ireland, assuming the different parts of the United Kingdom to have no desire to be separated from each other. Were the Irish representatives to be allowed to continue to exercise that influence in English and Scottish affairs which they refused to permit reciprocally over their own? Or was the parliament at Westminster to assemble each year as a different body in two separate sessions simply for the convenience of the Irish? The question of police and legal administration in Ireland also presented difficulties. Such questions, said Butt, could be resolved by discussion and agreement; he suggested tentatively the adoption of the procedure followed in the United States of America in regard to the separate judicial powers of the states and the federal authority. But what course was to be adopted in relation to the indigenous Irish crime of treason against the imperial constitution?

For the moment, however, Butt was less concerned with hostile English reaction than with the winning over of the repealers and the advanced nationalists. To these he offered three main arguments. The federal arrangement would give Ireland a voice in imperial matters, and responsible cabinet government, neither of which she had possessed before 1800. It did not impair her separate existence, but at the same time it offered a solution which England might grant with honour, whereas she would never yield repeal, equated by many Englishmen with separation. Finally, and not least among his arguments, he reminded the nationalists that no man could legislate for eternity. Parliamentary and other reforms could follow upon the attainment of his constitution. Still more important, he conceded that separation from England might ultimately be the course which the Irish people would choose to take. Under a home rule settlement such a destiny could arrive peacefully which at present could be attained only by war and revolution.

The federal scheme was nevertheless greeted with a considerable amount of hostility by the old repealers when it was first placed before them by the Home Government Association. When a revived agitation had been canvassed in 1869-70, it had generally been assumed that it would follow upon the O'Connellite plan. Gradually in 1870 disquieting reports reached men like Martin and Daunt. Daunt recorded in his journal in June:

> Martin says the protestant nationalists who for some weeks have been assembling in unreported meetings in Dublin, must intend something seriously good, as they have invited him to join their councils. I urged him— needlessly I am sure—to keep them up to the level of 1782. Less will not satisfy.[42]

When the federal programme of the association became public a controversy immediately started in the *Nation* upon the issue of federalism versus simple repeal. Martin wrote several times to Dublin urging the members of the new group to adhere to simple repeal and not to confound and complicate the national question; only an Irish parliament, he argued, had the right to enter into a federal arrangement on behalf of the Irish people. Notified in June of his election to the committee of the association, without his consent, he replied to King Harman, one of the secretaries, that he had always sought repeal, and urged that the home rule demand should be left as wide as possible to include nationalists of all shades without tying them down too closely. To Daunt he wrote of

42 Daunt Journal, 13 June 1870, MS 3041.

his misgivings :

> I observe, in the list received this morning, the names of several repealers as prononcés as myself—such as P. J. Smyth, A. M. Sullivan, Alderman Plunkett. Also at least two names of vehement Fenian sympathisers and confidants. But I understand Federalism to be the present creed of the majority.

In July he wrote to Daunt again in the same critical strain:

> I am afraid we repealers are permitting this committee for a time to misrepresent the nationalist feeling of the country. Many of the names upon their list of members (yours, mine, and a dozen others, I could pick out) are of men who would not give the English on any pretence, federalist or other, the smallest control over our affairs.[43]

As late as the end of August, when the assocation planned to launch its campaign with its first public meeting at the beginning of September, Martin wrote: ' I am not well inclined to go, being bothered by their federalist scheme. But I have not determined to stay away '.[44]

But a great victory for the new proposals was gained with the adherence to them at the beginning of July of Daunt himself, probably the most widely respected survivor of the O'Connellite agitation. Admittedly he joined with certain reservations:

> July 4. The Home Government Association have sent me a circular letter and prospectus. Sent them my subscription and a letter saying that I joined their movement on the clear understanding that I looked on their federal scheme as a provisional rather than a final arrangement of our relations with England, and that, if attained, it would help us to work out the rest. Nothing short of 1782 can or ought to satisfy Ireland.[45]

This interpretation was quite adequate for the association's purpose. ' It would be impossible to get together any large number of individuals holding hard and fast and iden-

---

43 Martin to Daunt, 16 June, 26 July, Daunt MSS, 8047.
44 Martin to Daunt, 28 Aug. 1870, Daunt MSS, 8047.
45 4 July, Daunt Journal, MS 3041.

tical opinions', replied the acting-secretary, Captain Dunne, thanking him for his adherence to the movement.[46] Other leading repealers joined with the same proviso. Father Quaid wrote to Butt in June:

> I had some hesitation about joining at present as I am an advocate of an independent parliament such as we had in '82 however I have come to the resolve to join the present movement hoping it will lead to our ultimately obtaining an independent parliament.[47]

The difference between home rule and repeal was not in fact so great as to cause serious misgivings to the average person who was sympathetic towards the idea of a revived repeal agitation. Such people were for the most part willing to accept Butt's assurance that the home rule demand had greater possibilities of being accepted by the English and by the Irish protestants. P. J. Smyth's version of his own adherence to the movement, written in later years when it had become a matter of controversy, is of some interest. On his return from the Waterford City by-election in February 1870, he says, he began to work up a new repeal association:

> Then I heard of a private meeting of federalists. Seeing that amongst those who took part in it were people heretofore conspicuous for their hostility to the Irish cause in every shape and form, and not without hope of their radical conversion, I deemed it my duty to put my own plan aside, and give to this movement what encouragement I could . . .[48]

Repeal remained the first love of many active home rulers, and catholic liberals like Alderman P. P. McSwiney could argue that in abandoning it the Home Government Association had given yet another proof of the spuriousness of its kinship to the ancient tradition of O'Connell. But Smyth alone caused serious embarrassment to the association by his reversion to repeal. Martin was finally induced to give his

[46] Dunne to Daunt, 4 July, Daunt MSS, 8045.
[47] Father Quaid to Butt, 27 July, Butt MSS.
[48] 12 Nov. 1875, Hickey MSS, National Library.

D*

loyalty to the association by the example of his friends and by the possibility of winning the conservatives over to any kind of nationalist endeavour. In September he came up on a visit to Dublin and subjected the association and its leading personalities to a first-hand scrutiny at the end of which he was completely won over to their experiment. He wrote to Daunt a long letter giving his impressions of what he had seen, and this picture of the new group in its first months of existence, sketched with insight by a veteran repealer, makes an appropriate postcript to the launching of the Home Government Association.

I want to tell you my impressions about the men and the affair. I have had conversations with Dr Shaw and Dr Galbraith, Fellows of Trinity College, and members of the committee of 61. I have seen also, at the rooms of the association, Captain Dunne the secretary, Messrs Erson, Graham, Lemon, Vokes Mackey, Manning, and some others, and had chats with them. Besides, I was introduced to Mr Edward King Harman (recently candidate for Dublin), Dr Grattan, and several others. I sat through a committee meeting of over three hours, all occupied with mere committee details about appointment of honorary treasurers, honorary secretaries, sub-committees on organisation, of publication of finance, etc. etc. It was irksome to me to see the men spend so much time and earnestness upon the petty formalities of agitation, while so little is done to really agitate the country. But it was very gratifying to see the men *earnest* in anything towards nationality and to think that nearly all these men—all persons of social importance in Ireland— were till lately enemies of nationality. I suppose you have got the list of the elected 61 of the first General Committee, and have remarked that not only yourself and myself but several more of the old notorious repeal nationalists are among the elected. P. J. Smyth, Father Quaid, Father Lavelle, A. M. and T. D. Sullivan are there. Also Thomas Ryan and James Cantwell and John Nolan and Thomas Begg, men understood to have strong pro-Fenian sympathies. In short the committee of 61 pretty fairly represents all sections of the nationalists, old

and new. Mr Butt was present at the meeting and took the lead
in the business. Mr Waldron, also, took a considerable part. It
was settled that, till further notice, the association should hold
regular meetings on the first Thursday of each month, open to
the public. Mr Butt wants to speak at the meeting next month
and to get some prominent Catholic priests to speak. I observed
that all the members present who were formerly attributed to
the ascendancy faction were *anxious* to have a public (and real)
union with the Catholics. Father Lavelle (who, like myself,
attended for the first time) was quite affectionately greeted by
each person.

The dispositions of the new association are good—genuine
feeling of the need of home government both on moral and
material grounds, longing desire for concord of sects and
classes, spirit of resentment against the nation which has made
us subject, patriotic and prudent anxiety to avert revolution
and anarchy. I am not sure that any men of great and striking
ability have yet been produced in the new movement. Certainly
Mr Butt is a man of very high ability, and of qualities and
accomplishments even more valuable for propagandism of our
cause than even his ability. But his influence is much marred,
when he is personally known, by his incorrigible habits of
looseness about money matters. He seems to have grown callous
to the shame of having bailiffs in his house. He makes arrangements with his creditors and breaks them wantonly. He keeps
himself continually in trouble and want, through his extrava-
gance and negligence. I am very fond of the man, else I might
not speak so angrily of the defects of his character. I wonder
have you seen his pamphlet on *federalism*. Probably not; and I
shall therefore send you a copy by post. You will find it a treat
to read. In knowledge of his subject, clearness and fullness of
statement, elegance and easy dignity and style, persuasiveness
of manner, kindliness, and generous earnestness of spirit, he is
unsurpassed. But this seems to me the best thing he has done—
or rather the thing he has done best. As to the question itself I
am still of the opinion that the proper and desirable course for
Ireland is simple repeal and subsequently such federal arrangements as our parliament, self-reformed under the influence of
free Irish opinion, may consent to make. And in my mind *the*

less connection of a political (or of any other) kind between our country and England the better.[49]

In this summary may be detected suggestions of some of the underlying weaknesses of the new movement which were to come to the surface in the future. It appears a little pretentious and pompous, over-preoccupied with the running of its little Dublin club. Butt has not so far attracted enough men of real fire and ability into the movement, and already he is waking up to the need to woo the catholic clergy into the association. His own notoriously improvident reputation weakens the authority to which his talents entitle him, and if he has managed to secure the support and the affection of men like Martin for him and his federal compromise, he has imparted to them none of his own enthusiasm for it as an imperial experiment in its own right. But these were weaknesses which were latent as yet, and as, after a summer of preparation, the association began to address itself to the general public, Butt could afford to congratulate himself cautiously upon the extent of his own and his colleagues' achievement. The bulk of the conservatives might remain aloof, but remarkable acquisitions had been made from the ranks of those formerly completely hostile to the demand for self-government. The *Daily Express* might be hostile, but the *Irish Times* and the *Dublin Evening Mail* were not unsympathetic. Expanding from the basis of the Bilton's Hotel meeting, the association had succeeded in securing for the federal demand the support of the veteran nationalists whose aid it had not dared to solicit at the outset for fear of alienating the new supporters; now for the first time Smyth, Daunt, Martin, Father Lavelle, Father Quaid, Dean O'Brien, the Sullivans, were joined together with some of the leading protestant conservatives of

---

[49] Martin to Daunt 23 Sept. 1870, Daunt MSS, 8047. Erson, Lemon, Vokes Mackey, and Manning, were all prominent in Dublin municipal life, and former conservatives. Dr Grattan was a descendant of Henry Grattan; very elderly and eccentric, he made repeated trouble at successive meetings, including the home rule conference of 1873, with his views upon repeal and the precise definition of home rule. Waldron was a former liberal candidate for Tipperary with slight conservative tendencies.

Dublin in a movement for home rule. The naturality of the advanced party, and the loyalty of some of its most prominent supporters, had also been gained.

These were in themselves notable achievements. But as yet the influence of the movement was still largely confined to the city of Dublin. If Butt was to arrive at his goal of a united nationalist party, he would have to show not only that he could retain the support which he had so far won, but also that at the same time he could make such a public appeal to the ordinary liberal voters of the country and to the catholic clergy as would secure for the new movement the national support which was essential for its success.

Unfortunately for the growth of the new movement, the strenuous efforts which it had made to conciliate the protestant conservatives very quickly began to recoil upon it. The superficially impressive list of 359 supporters which was published by the association in August had two notable deficiencies. While it included the names of 21 clergymen of the Church of Ireland, it contained only 12 catholic priests. 4 of these were well-known nationalists, and one, the Reverend Dr Rice of Queenstown was a personal friend of Butt. Of the remaining 7, 4 came from Mayo, in the diocese of Archbishop MacHale, scarcely the most typical of the Irish prelates of the period, and one from Liverpool. Upon the great body of the catholic clergy the movement had as yet made no impression, nor had it won the approval of the leading Irish spokesmen in parliament such as Gray and J. F. Maguire. The other notable defect in the list was that preponderance of Dublin middle-class names upon which Shaw had remarked.

The association held its first public meeting in the Rotunda on 1 September. Shaw, Galbraith, Laurence Waldron, and George Browne, M.P., were the principal speakers. At no stage did any sitting conservative member of parliament join the association. Butt approached Sir Arthur Guinness, the conservative member for Dublin City, and David Plunket, his colleague as candidate in 1868, without success.[50] On 6 October the first monthly meeting of the association was held

50 Plunket to Butt, 11 July 1870.

ation:

in its rooms in Grafton Street. A council of sixty-one was elected; Butt and Lord Mayor Purdon headed the poll, closely followed by A. M. Sullivan, Dean O'Brien, and Galbraith.[51]

In May, before the association had commenced its operations, the principle of home rule was subjected to a preliminary electoral test when E. R. King Harman, a founder member of the association and a protestant conservative by background, who was very typical of this phase of the movement, opposed the liberal George Greville-Nugent in Longford. This was the second by-election to be held in that county within a few months. It was caused, it will be recalled, by the unseating, on the grounds of improper clerical influence, of George's younger brother Reginald, who had defeated John Martin in January. Once again, though not quite so blatantly, the clergy were active in support of the Greville interest, and upon this occasion their opponent was one the sincerity of whose nationalism was much more suspect than that of John Martin. Harman stood with the approval of the *Nation* and of the *Dublin Evening Mail,* and P. J. Smyth went down to Longford to campaign for him, but the *Freeman* declared: 'We should hold fast to Mr Gladstone, and not furnish followers to Mr Disraeli', and urged the electors to repudiate 'the insidious attempt made to seduce them from their allegiance to their country and drag them into the mire of Toryism'.[52] The new protestant conservative home rule feeling sustained its first reverse at the poll by 1217 votes to 932, and the *Dublin Evening Mail* accused the nationalist press of having given it only half-hearted support.[53]

In August, after the launching of the Home Government Association and the publication of the federal programme, King Harman stood again on home rule principles in Dublin City, in opposition to the liberal candidate Sir Dominic Corrigan. Corrigan had stood for the city in 1868 when the pro-

51 *Nation,* 15 Oct.
52 *Freeman's Journal,* 5, 12 May 1870.
53 *Dublin Evening Mail,* 14 May. A few days earlier in Mallow Major Knox was defeated on a programme even more equivocal than Harman's. The contest in this small and not notably spotless borough aroused less interest.

disestablishment forces were united in his behalf, and the situation was complicated in this by-election by the survival of old loyalties to him among the liberal nationalists. Addressing the electors in favour of a catholic university, denominational education, and the ballot Corrigan condemned the federalist movement as premature, and calculated to divert public attention from more immediately practicable reforms. Harman was nominated by a veteran catholic repealer, Alderman Plunket, and seconded by a lifelong conservative, now a member of the Home Government Association, Alderman James Vokes Mackey, both of whom had taken part in the Bilton's Hotel discussions. But once again the liberal candidate had the support of the catholic clergy and of the liberal press, and the conservative home ruler was defeated.[54] The liberals distrusted him as a conservative; the conservatives looked upon him as a renegade. The nationalists of the Home Government Association were steadily urged towards the conclusion that the mixture of conservatism and liberalism which was Butt's formula for a united nationalist party contained too many parts of the first and too few of the second, and that the association's approach would have to be reorientated towards the catholic liberal position. As early as July 1870 T. D. Sullivan wrote to Daunt expressing concern at the small number of priests who had so far joined the association.

> I fancied they were keeping out of it for a while lest their presence in large numbers might frighten off the somewhat timid newcomers, most of whom have a certain amount of fear of " Catholic ascendancy ". But the idea of *their* being frightened from it by the number of protestants who have joined it— I had almost said preposterous.[55]

But preposterous or not, Daunt, who was the most distinguished and unexceptionable catholic in the association, and

---

[54] Corrigan 4468, Harman 3444. It is only fair to add that when Harman was finally elected to parliament in 1877 his subservience to the conservative whip did much to justify the forebodings of his liberal opponents in 1870.

[55] Sullivan to Daunt, 13 July 1870, Hickey MSS.

its chief intermediary in this period with the catholic hierarchy, confirmed this judgment.

> I suspect that the priests are kept back, as a certain parish priest tells me that *he* is, by the number of Tory names on the committee.[56]

In an effort to retrieve their position in relation to catholic opinion, Butt and Martin wrote to Daunt, making the first of what were subsequently continually repeated appeals that he should come up to Dublin and assume the secretaryship of the association.[57] When Daunt, a rustic valetudinarian, declined to leave his small estate in county Cork, Captain Dunne wrote to him with the request that he should get in touch with as many members of the hierarchy as he knew personally to solicit their support for the movement; only two had signified their approval so far.[58] Daunt wrote to Dr O'Hea, bishop of Ross, and to Dr Leahy, Archbishop of Cashel. He received from both courteous replies, holding out some hope of their eventual adhesion to the movement, but at the same time expressing a complete lack of confidence in its present leaders.[59] Dr O'Hea expressed his reluctance

> unaccompanied and unsustained by my brother prelates, to throw myself into the ranks of those who never manifested towards poor Ireland but slight and contempt.[60]

Of Dr Leahy, Daunt noted in his journal:

> April 3rd. Letter from the archbishop of Cashel, assigning as a reason why some prelates are slow in joining the home rule movement, their want of confidence in the motives of some of the protestant leaders, who, his grace says, *look on the movement as identical with a movement against Rome rule* . . . it is

56 Daunt Journal, 15 July, MS 3041.
57 ibid., 3 Oct.
58 ibid., 14, 15 Nov. The two bishops were probably Dr MacHale and Dr Conaty, Bishop of Kilmore. (Conaty to Butt, 7 Sept. 1870, Butt MSS).
59 Leahy to Daunt, 7, 20 Dec. 1870, 14 Feb., 1 Apr. 1871, 3 Aug. 1872, Daunt MSS, 8046; O'Hea to Daunt, 18 Nov. 1870, Daunt MSS, 8047.
60 O'Hea to Daunt, 18 Nov. 1870, Daunt MSS, 8047.

curious that while the orange party oppose home rule as being identical with Rome rule, the protestant Home Rulers are accused by certain stupid catholics as intending by their movement to upset Rome.[61]

The realists in the Home Government Association were not slow to perceive this reluctance and to urge that some concessions should be made to it. Father Lavelle wrote to Daunt in July that many catholics would shrink with 'not quite unnatural repugnance from immediately close contact, political or otherwise, with the orange faction ',[62] and Dean O'Brien wrote to Butt in November questioning the wisdom of having put King Harman in the chair at the last public meeting of the association

> in a case where the mass of the Irish nation, as yet, think the H.G.A. only a Tory dodge to break the ranks of the Liberals, and we want to show it is not *such a dodge*.[63]

If the lesson of these first months, that a greater identification of home rule with popular liberal attitudes, and a purging of conservative taints, would be necessary before any national success could be won, was not sufficiently clear, the course of the by-elections which were fought in the following year made such a reorientation inevitable. Home rule candidates contested fourteen by-elections between the beginning of 1870 and the middle of 1873; of these they won nine, of which five were uncontested, and lost five. In each of the by-elections fought in 1870, the same trend was maintained: the contest was between a clerically-supported liberal candidate and a home ruler of conservative origins; in both cases the liberal was successful.

The by-elections which were fought in 1871 followed a significantly different course. The first of them occurred in Meath, where the nationalists took advantage of the vacancy created by the death of M. E. Corbally to put forward for a second time the veteran repealer John Martin. The liberal

---

[61] 15 Nov. 1870, Daunt Journal, MS 3041.
[62] Lavelle to Daunt, 27 July 1870, Daunt MSS, 8046.
[63] O'Brien to Butt, 23 Nov. 1870, Butt MSS.

candidate was the Honourable George Plunkett, a member of the ancient catholic family of Fingall. His candidature had been approved by the local clergy before the entry of Martin, but the clerical attitude on this occasion was notably different from that of the two Longford contests, for while they preferred Plunkett, they exerted no such intense influence against Martin as they had done against the home rule candidate on those two occasions. The *Freeman's Journal* opposed Martin, on the grounds that no one knew what was best for the home rule cause as well as it did;

> As advocates of home rule, we protest against such abortive efforts as Dublin and Longford; being hastily got up without organisation or public concert. Three defeats have already been courted for the people. A fourth is now challenged. The principles of local government will not be advanced by improvised raids against such men as the son of a Fingall—a Plunkett in whose veins flows the blood of martyrs in the cause of catholicity.[64]

But the candidature of a man like Martin, with the additional factor of clerical neutrality, provided no such an easy target for liberal polemic as that of a King Harman. An energetic campaign resulted in the return of Martin by 1028 votes to his opponent's 642.

The Meath result was the first indication that the new movement would have to be taken seriously. It came as a complete surprise to the liberals. 'An event full of instruction', commented the English *Daily News*: 'the nationalists are more powerful than the ultramontanes'.[65] The result induced the *Freeman* to offer by far the most sympathetic comment upon the new movement that had yet appeared in its columns. Mr Martin's victory, it said, was contrary to all expectations:

> It can be accounted for in one way only. Mr Martin is a sincere nationalist, an earnest repealer, and the Irish people have arrived at the conclusion that the policy of all English parties

64 *Freeman's Journal,* 2 Jan. 1871.
65 *Daily News,* 9 Jan. 1871.

is to make such concessions only as may conduce to party power
—to make none to the nation in deference to its will, and to
stamp out the last vestiges of nationality. The Meath election is
a great fact. It may eventuate in nothing important, but even
should it be so, it is still a great fact. It may, however, prove to
be the beginning of the end.[66]

The *Nation* expressed the same truth more brutally: 'Henceforth the spell-word of self-rule must be the open Sesame to
the constituencies'.[67]

All these comments were fully justified. The Meath result
had two lessons to offer. It had been possible to win it, while
it had not been possible to win before, because the candidate
was no new and suspect convert to nationality, but a respected
repealer, holding opinions from which he had never deviated
in a long career. Furthermore, it showed that however sceptical the liberals might be of the sincerity of the orange nationalists of the Home Government Association, the home rule
demand as such was fully capable of capturing the imagination of the electorate. The first lesson suggested that the home
rulers might be well advised to adopt a new approach to their
choice of candidates; the second suggested to ambitious liberals and to priests fearful of losing all influence in their constituencies, that it might be necessary to adopt a more friendly
attitude to home rule. Both conclusions pointed to a greater
orientation of the movement towards the liberals.

Further evidence of the growing popularity of the home
rule demand was soon forthcoming. In January the Farmers'
Clubs of Munster declared for home rule, and the Queen's
County Independent Club, after a long debate, followed suit,
Father O'Keeffe and Father O'Shea speaking for the move-
ment despite the opposition of the Reverend Dr Magee, P.P.
Stradbally. In February the aged archbishop of Tuam, Dr
MacHale, publicly welcomed the Meath result.[68]

But all this support was for the principle of home rule, not
for the Home Government Association. Kenelm Digby, M.P.

[66] *Freeman's Journal*, 6 Jan.
[67] *Nation*, 14 Jan.
[68] *Nation*, 21 Jan., 4 Feb. 1871.

for Queen's County, wrote to Richard Lalor, president of the Independent Club, concurring in the club's approval of home rule, but expressing at the same time his lack of confidence in the Home Government Association. Lalor agreed:

> We had five or six C.C.'s but they took no very prominent part. As to the catholic clergy in this county, I think the case stands thus. The bishop and most of the parish priests of Kildare and Leighlin are not in favour of the agitation—but those of Ossory are—and the former must follow, not lead, their flocks in this matter. Your opinion of the " Home Rule Association " appears to agree with the majority of the people in this county—There is no confidence in many of its most prominent members.[69]

He went on to suggest the abandonment of the association and the establishment of a new body led by Digby, George Bryan, M.P. for Kilkenny County, Edmund Dease, M.P. for Queen's County, Lord Bellew, John Martin, Philip Callan, and others who might be able to command more general approval. In June a public controversy between Butt and P. J. Smyth developed on this theme. Smyth called for the abandonment of federalism in favour of a simple demand for legislative independence, and the establishment of a popular movement to which all who were prepared to pay the subscription would be admitted, without, as was necessary in the Home Government Association, the prior approval of the governing executive. Butt replied that the association had never been intended to take the place of a popular organisation, the establishment of which it was premature to consider:

> If the public voice or the exigencies of the national cause require, sooner or later, a reconstruction of the Home Government Association, there is not, I am sure, among its members a single one who will not cheerfully assent . . .[70]

This ambivalence between popular support for home rule and popular distrust for the reputed toryism of the association was to endure for the remainder of that body's life. But the liberalisation of the popular movement continued with

[69] Digby to Lalor, 14 Jan., Lalor to Digby, 19 Jan., Lalor MSS, 8566.
[70] *Nation*, 10 June 1871.

each successive by-election. In February Mitchell Henry was returned unopposed for Galway County. The choice had lain between three candidates, Captain J. P. Nolan, Hyacinth D'Arcy, and Henry, all of whom had included some kind of endorsement of home rule in their election addresses. The other two were catholics, and of them Nolan had the greater degree of clerical support. Henry, however, had unrivalled claims as the economic benefactor of the whole Connemara region, where he had built Kylemore Castle, spent vast amounts on land reclamation, schools, etc., and given employment and security to the local peasantry, while Nolan's record as an evicting landlord weighed heavily against him. The fruits of home rule's increasing popularity were evident in this election; it was the first in which the contest was between candidates of other wise orthodox liberality all of whom had found it necessary to incorporate home rule in their platforms. Henry, a former Liberal candidate for Manchester whose candidature actually possessed the benevolent interest of William Monsell,[71] announced he was 'of liberal politics', and addressed the electors in support of denominational education, the maintenance inviolate of 'the dignity and independence of the Pope', and home legislation. The *Freeman's Journal* preferred Nolan, who demanded a charter for a catholic university and whose views on the Papal question were more decidedly for restoration; the *Irish Times* preferred Henry, no doubt for the same reason. The *Dublin Evening Mail*, significantly, disliked both candidates, not for their acceptance of home rule, but for the unmistakeably liberal character of their other pronouncements. In the end it welcomed the return of Henry as opposed to 'the ultramontane candidate'.[72]

If the Galway County election demonstrated how popular feeling was compelling an amalgamation of liberal policies with home rule on the hustings, the Westmeath contest in June showed how the same pressure was compelling the clergy similarly to rethink their position. Two principal candidates competed for the seat, P. J. Smyth and J. A. Dease.

71 Dr McEvilly to Monsell, 1 Mar. 1871, Monsell MSS, 8318.
72 *Dublin Evening Mail,* 22 Feb.

The nationalist was presented with a tremendous asset with the passage just before the election of a coercion act with special provisions for the pacification of Westmeath. The bishop, Dr Nulty, and the clergy resolved to examine the prospective candidates and to select one of them for approval, in order to avoid the turmoil of a contest. Dease arrived in the county early in June, and immediately wrote to William Monsell that he had not 'a ghost of a chance', as 'the fenian element' had decided to start P. J. Smyth; as for the clergy, his own parish priest told him that they would be 'afraid not to go with the popular demand'.[73] The clergy held their examination on 13 June in Mullingar. Dease described the meeting to Monsell:

> I was put through my catechism by Dr Nulty in the presence of some 40 " sacreds " . . . I have reason to know that the Bishop was personally strongly in my favour, as were the real sympathies of all the P.P.'s and several of the C.C.'s as well. " Home Rule " was the sole difficulty. Great efforts were made to induce me to swallow that pledge and I have some curious letters (that I may show you some time or other) from priests and from others in the clerical influence, urging me to declare for " Home Rule " (with any kind of mental reservation I pleased and preferring as a reason for so doing that " the whole thing was a mere *cry of the moment* and would be *forgotten before the next* election " . . .
>
> Nothing could exceed the personal courtesy I met with from the whole meeting—but the result was a declaration that they would support Smyth. One thing I am sure of—that Dr. Nulty and many of the priests—tho' they concur in this course, do so with bitter shame. The bishop told me privately in so many words that " *they were afraid to oppose the popular feeling that would be evoked* " . . . " That in those parishes in Meath where the priests worked hard (and very few they were, by the way) for George Plunkett, an antagonism has arisen between the . . . [priests and people].[74]

73 Dease to Monsell, 9 June 1871, Monsell MSS, 8317.
74 The manuscript is incomplete. Dease to Monsell, 14 June 1871, and Dease to E. Dease, 15 June 1871, Monsell MSS, 8317. Also undated statement by J. A. Dease in Strachie MSS, Carlingford Political.

Allowing for Dease's probable desire to find excuses for his failure, his account of the clerical attitude in this election is still full of significance. In Longford and in Dublin they had been prepared to oppose the nationalist demand and sustain the liberal; in Meath they had remained neutral; in Galway they had accepted one liberal home ruler more or less reluctantly over another; in Westmeath they endorsed the popular candidate. As Smyth had addressed the electors for denominational education and home rule the *Freeman's Journal* too, renounced Dease and gave its support to the home ruler. The changing character of the movement was obvious, and although the *Irish Times* and the *Mail* welcomed the return of Smyth over the liberal as a man 'at all events, Irish and honest', the position of the conservative 'anti-ultramontane' home ruler was becoming increasingly anomalous.

But if the reputation of Smyth as a '48 man and as a staunch defender of catholic claims made it difficult for the liberal clergy and the *Freeman's Journal* to oppose him, the Monaghan by-election immediately afterwards demonstrated that their hostility to the conservative home ruler was unabated. This contest fell into three stages, each of which illustrated strikingly the divided loyalties of the movement. On the death of the conservative C. P. Leslie, who had represented the county for twenty-nine years, the suggestion that Butt himself should go forward was widely canvassed in the popular press. 'The claims of every candidate must stand second to Mr Butt', wrote the *Freeman*.[75] On 10 July, however, the *Mail* carried the address of John Madden on home rule principles; appended to it was an appeal signed by Martin, Sullivan, and Galbraith, and a number of other home rulers, calling upon the protestants not to vote for the conservative candidate John Leslie, younger brother of the late member, and on the catholics not to vote for the liberal H. Owen Lewis, who had already addressed the constituency for the ballot, denominational education, and the defence of the Pope.

The refusal of Butt to stand, and the emergence of Madden, Leslie, and Lewis as the rival candidates, produced an im-

---

[75] *Freeman's Journal*, 30 June.

mediate realignment of interests. Madden, although, unlike either Henry or Smyth, already a member of the Home Government Association, was a well-known orangeman, and his candidature revived all the catholic liberal hostility which had marked the first home rule contests. The *Mail* called for the return of either Madden or Leslie; the *Irish Times* was prepared to give the home ruler enthusiastic support against both the other candidates; the *Freeman,* however, while declaring its support for the principle of home rule and its readiness to sustain the candidature of Butt, could not bring itself to endorse Madden 'Pending the achievement of home rule', it wrote, 'he goes into parliament, or we are deceived, as a full-blooded Orangeman'.[76] Faced with the coldness of the local conservatives, and the hostility of the catholics, Madden withdrew.

On the withdrawal of Madden, and rather than allow the election to go uncontested, Butt at the last minute allowed his name to be put forward, and thus caused a final reshuffle of the different home rule elements. The clergy, the liberals, and the *Freeman* dropped Lewis and supported Butt; the *Mail,* on the other hand, declined to take Butt's last-minute intervention seriously. The conservative home rulers rebuffed by the abandonment of Madden, noted with disapproval that in what seemed to them defiance of his own maxim that home rule should not be associated with other controversies, Butt chose to fight the election mainly upon the issue of tenant-right.[77] In the poll Leslie was victorious by 2538 votes to 1451. The result was not in the circumstances a severe setback for home rule, but the contest itself had shown up all too clearly the internal contradictions in the movement.

But if the conservatives were becoming more sceptical, the liberals continued to become less reluctant. In July the Dublin Corporation agreed to receive a deputation from the Home Government Association to explain its principles to a special meeting of the corporation. The council of the association chose the deputation with a special eye to the importance of

[76] *Dublin Evening Mail,* 10 July, *Irish Times,* 13 July, *Freeman's Journal,* 11 July.
[77] *Irish Times,* 5 Sept.

the occasion. Martin suggested the selection of one protestant and two catholics—one a priest. But in the end a 'religious shamrock'[78] was decided upon; Martin, as the representative of presbyterian nationalism, Daunt, as the most em-
inent catholic survivor from the Repeal Association, and Galbraith, as one of the former conservatives in the association.
At this special meeting Alderman Peter Paul McSwiney, as
a diehard catholic liberal, moved that the corporation should
postpone taking any decision upon the question for six
months; the new agitation, he said, fell short of O'Connellite
repeal, and at the present time could only have the effect of
deferring the settlement of the education question. But by a
large majority the corporation voted for immediate endorsement of the home rule demand. The *Irish Times* was approving but cautious; home rule, it said, would also have to gain
the support of the landlords by proving that it was not subversive of property. The *Freeman's Journal,* on the other
hand, was now full of praise, and while understanding
McSwiney's motives, rejoiced that his motion had gained no
support whatsoever. In August another great liberal newspaper threw in its lot with the movement when J. F. Maguire,
M.P. for Cork City and proprietor and editor of the *Cork
Examiner,* one of the most influential of the catholic liberal
members of parliament, abandoned his early suspicion of the
association and was admitted to membership.

The growing disquiet of the conservatives at these developments was enhanced by the circumstances in which the home
rule leader himself was finally returned to parliament for
Limerick City in September 1871. Butt, who agreed to stand
on the invitation of Callan, took little part in the campaign,
remaining most of the time in Blackheath suffering, he explained, from 'nervous exhaustion, and quite unable to go to
Limerick'; rumour ascribed his disappearance to the activity
of his creditors.[79] The campaign was conducted in his absence by his son Robert. The detachment of the Dublin association from these by-election contests is strikingly illustrated

---

[78] Martin to Daunt, 3 July, Daunt MSS, 8047.
[79] Butt to Sullivan, undated, Butt MSS, Vol. II, MS 831. *Freeman's
Journal,* 8 Sept.

by the fact that not even here, where its own leader was standing, was the support of the association given to his candidature. Butt had strongly disapproved of the council's endorsement of Smyth in Westmeath in June; and now he wrote to Sullivan:

> I have as you know a very strong feeling that the Home Rule Association as a body ought not to interfere at present in any election. *I would not wish them to do it for me.* But an independent committee would I think be of use as showing an interest in the election . . . if John Martin went down spontaneously or as if by accident his presence for one evening would be of use . . .[80]

No doubt by this advice, as by the refusal to affiliate local associations, Butt hoped to maintain the programme of the association distinct from the views of its supporters as individuals. In practice it simply meant that the movement took its character from the hustings declarations of its members.

The Limerick election was the most decisive in this regard. Butt's candidature aroused great popular enthusiasm; John Daly recalls refusing to aid it, but the popular nationalist sentiment was with Butt. W. H. O'Sullivan was one notable figure from the advanced party who worked on Butt's election committee, and in the opinion of one catholic liberal observer, the fenians put in Butt against the priests.[81] Torchlight meetings were held nightly outside his committee rooms, and the efforts of William Monsell and the bishop of Limerick, Dr Butler, to start a government candidate foundered upon the rock of overwhelming popular sentiment. Charles Barry, the Solicitor-General, whose absence from parliament was sorely felt by the administration, nevertheless flatly refused to stand; 'no man not putting "Home Rule" forward as the strength of his programme would be listened to', he told Gladstone, 'and I fear that it will be the same in every constituency'.[82]

---

[80] Alfred Webb to Butt, 14 June, Butt MSS. Butt to Sullivan, undated, Butt MSS, Vol. II, MS 831.

[81] J. A. Dease to Monsell, 29 Sept. 1871, Monsell MSS, 8317.

[82] Barry to Gladstone, 6 Sept., BM Add. MSS 44431 f 233.

But it was the programme under which Butt chose to appeal to the electors of Limerick which above all increased the disquiet of the conservative home rulers. At a meeting in Limerick which formally adopted him he called for the establishment of a catholic university, religious equality, and denominational education, in addition to restating his well-known radical views on tenant-right. The *Irish Times* accused him of neglecting home rule for other issues again as in Monaghan, and suggested that 'the most conspicuous member of the Home Rule Association distrusts that principle as a popular card to play'. Butt's promise to vote for a charter for a catholic university, wrote the *Cork Constitution,* 'a declaration which Mr Gladstone himself is afraid to make, has produced the desired effect. The priests will rush to his standard, and he will remain their very obedient servant.'[83]

The circumstances of Butt's return, as leader of the original movement, brought into the open at last the issues which had been latent in the preceding by-elcctions, and for the first time conservative home rulers openly accused the leadership of the movement of having abandoned the pure home rule principles upon which it had been launched. Urging the creation of an Irish Imperial party, the *Mail* criticised 'the proclamation of ultramontane views in conjunction with home rule on the Limerick hustings':

> Must every Irish candidate henceforth be an ultramontane; or like Mr. Butt, if a home ruler, a home ruler pledged specifically to every dogma of the ultramontane creed? Must home rule itself be, as a principle, adulterated and destroyed, here by an ultramontane, there by a fenian ally?[84]

Meanwhile further affronts were offered to the conservatives. In Galway County a second by-election was impending; the priests and the home rulers combined on this occasion to support Captain Nolan, who since the previous election had accepted an arbitration award restoring a number of his evicted tenants to their holdings. He was regarded by the

83 *Irish Times,* 5 Sept. 1871.
84 Quoted in *Dublin Evening Mail,* 9, 12 Sept.

landlords as a symbol of agrarian revolution, and the struggle which followed was as much upon the issue of the application of the compensation principles of the land act as upon the subject of home rule. Whig and tory landlords, the Clanricardes and the Clancartys, combined to oppose the clerical, tenant-right—and home rule—candidate. Lord Westmeath, one of the leading catholic peers in Ireland, wrote to Lord Creville:

> Mr Trench has been almost unanimously selected by the gentlemen, as we would rather see the Queen and Mr Gladstone at the head of affairs than Odger, or Butt, or Martin.[85]

And in October, the *Nation,* which at this time was regarded as almost the official home rule journal, formally endorsed the declaration of the catholic hierarchy pledging themselves to oppose any candidate in future elections who would not promise to support the demand for denominational education.

Conservative hostility to these developments was carried an important stage further with the defection from the movement in October 1871 of the *Irish Times,* whose proprietor, Major Knox, it will be remembered, had been one of the founders of the association, and in whose columns the new conservative nationalism had found its most coherent expression. Pointing to the remoteness of the association from the country it wrote:

> It may seem like a paradox, but the fact is plain and palpable, that while home rule is in everybody's mouth, and while thinking men and sincere patriots in every part of the country are casting about in all directions to try and discover such a reconstitution of Ireland's relations with England as may be compatible with the welfare of both, that same Irish public takes hardly the most languid interest in the sayings and doings of the little home rule conclave in Great Brunswick Street. The subscriptions of its members hardly amount, we believe, to some £4 or £5 a week . . . its funds are so ill-replenished that it cannot afford to hire a good-sized room for its public meetings.

[85] Westmeath to Creville, 23 Dec. 1871, Creville-Nugent MSS, 8239. Odger was a well-known trade unionist and member of the First International.

The explanation which the *Irish Times* gave for this state of affairs was quite simple; the movement had been 'appropriated by persons who for one reason or another were unable to command public confidence'.

> We gladly admit that the original list of members contained a certain number of respectable names, but it is a matter of common observation that the attendance of these gentlemen on the public and committee meetings has always been small, and has steadily declined . . .[86]

Butt replied vigorously to the charge that the association was declining. But the conservative critics were right on one essential point: the character of the movement had radically changed in the eighteen months since it was first launched. It was not true that the movement had been appropriated by persons unable to command the confidence of the country— if anything the reverse was the case: they were better able to command it than the conservative home rulers. But the idea of a united non-party home rule demand, completely dissociated from every other popular aspiration, was collapsing under the pressure of practical politics, and home rulers throughout the country were increasingly also the spokesmen of tenant-right and denominational education. Sir John Barrington was one of the conservative founders of the association who withdrew from it about this time, and in later years he recalled his motives for doing so in language that betrays the shallowness of much of that conservative nationalism:—

> They, as honest Irishmen, and wishing for the benefit of the city of Dublin, and Ireland generally, thought that if there was a combined movement made at the time—combining parties of all politics, going for one common object—to check the great expenditure of money that took place in London, dragging their aristocracy over there, and their lawyers over there to carry bills, and, as it were, dragging the vitals out of the country and if they could manage by any effort of theirs to induce any representative of the royal family to come over, and occupy a residence in Ireland, they thought they would be achieving a

86 *Irish Times*, 31 Oct. 1871; also 17 Oct., 6 Nov.

great object. He was thoroughly loyal in that, and adhered to those principles still. But what was the consequence? As soon as the Repeal party and the agitating party found that this question was taken up by a body of gentlemen, they said, " We will league ourselves with them and make capital out of it for our own ends ". He watched the ship as it rocked upon the waves of fortune, and the principles of home rule of that day lasted one year and six months. After that he saw the element of discord coming in. He saw principles inculcated and disseminated at these meetings that no loyal man could subscribe to, and he at once, with a number of other gentlemen who had joined with him in supporting what they considered a moderate system, when they found that this was emasculated and turned into another system, they withdrew from it, and now there was not a single conservative but his honest friend, Mr Galbraith, who belonged to that home rule.[87]

The following year saw the continuance of these trends, with home rule drawing further away from the conservative position, but gaining steadily in popular support. Six by-elections were fought by home rule candidates, in Kerry, Galway County, Wexford Borough, Mallow, Londonderry City, and Cork City. Of these the Wexford election, in which W. A. Redmond was returned in place of R. J. Devereux, was the only one in which no contest took place. In each of the others there was a vigorous struggle, and each in its different way throws light upon the strength and the weaknesses of the home rule agitation.

The Kerry and Galway elections both took place in February of 1872, and these two bitterly fought home rule victories are usually classed together as signs of the progress of the movement. But while this similarity they certainly shared, and although the Home Government Association upon this occasion called upon both counties to sustain the home rule candidates, the two contests in reality represented totally different phases of the home rule struggle.

In Kerry the home rule candidate was a young protestant fresh from Oxford, Rowland Ponsonby Blennerhassett. Blen-

87 *Nation*, 9 Sept. 1876.

nerhassett's candidature was bitterly denounced by the local bishop, Dr Moriarty, who supported his catholic liberal opponent J. A. Dease, the same who had been rejected in Westmeath the previous June. In a letter published early in January, Dr Moriarty condemned the home rule agitation as 'in the present circumstances of the country, one of the most mischievous movements to which you have been ever urged or excited'. The most convinced unionist among the hierarchy, he appealed to the electors to adhere to Gladstone and to reject the leaders of the Home Government Association.

Amongst them are some of those who, a few years ago, sought to plunge you into a rebellion, which ended in shame before it had time to end in slaughter. They are the men who would have become what the commune in Paris became . . . They are now acting under cover—under the disguise of a constitutional agitation. Do not trust them.

A few of the leaders are favouring this agitation in order to embarrass the present government. They wish to take revenge for the disestablishment of the protestant church—for the equality to which Mr Gladstone's government has raised you. As soon as a Tory government comes in there will be an end of " Home Rule " for them . . .

After going wrong for seven hundred years in its rule of Ireland, the imperial government for the first time goes right; and, no sooner does it begin to serve you with a will and a power, which without it you could not command, than you rise up and bid it stop, that you will have no more of it.

We would humbly pray you to wait a little—let us have a few more good measures from the imperial parliament before we part with it; before we try this future parliament of yours, of which we know neither the constitution nor the spirit.

He also expresses the specific fear which underlay much of the catholic liberal opposition to the home rule agitation that Gladstone might feel released by it from his responsibilities in reference to education.[88] The utmost exertions were made on both sides in the contest which followed. Dr Mori-

[88] *Dublin Evening Mail*, 11 Jan. 1872.

arty put heavy pressure on the priests to sustain Dease's candidature, and the majority of the landlords were also active on his behalf, his chief financial backer, the Earl of Kenmare, spending in the region of £6000 on the contest.[89] Blennerhassett, for his part, described his outlay as 'enormous',[90] and Sullivan, Galbraith, and John Blunden came down from Dublin to stump the county for home rule.

In Kerry the issue was that of the first contests in 1870—catholic whiggery versus home rule, or as one priest put it, 'A Catholic and no souper for north Kerry'.[91] Cardinal Cullen wrote to Moriarty endorsing his support for Dease.[92] The intervention of Moriarty also revived many of the qualms of the liberal home rulers. The *Nation* of course supported Blennerhassett, and the *Irish Times* and the *Mail* were sympathetic; the *Freeman*, however, rediscovered the unwisdom of opposing the clergy. There was no doubt that

> the document expresses the sentiments of the vast body of the Irish prelates and clergy—nay, more, that it also embodies the views of a large and influential section of the Irish laity; a section which up to this has been the strength of Irish liberalism and to whose public spirit and energy Ireland owes many a much-needed reform.[93]

But the most striking thing about Dr Moriarty's intervention in the Kerry contest was its failure not only to influence the result but even to carry with him the rest of the clergy. Dr McEvilly, bishop of Galway, declined to intervene in the contest:

> We have so much hard work on hands to keep out a tory of the deepest dye . . . that nothing can induce me to write a word or do an act politically that has not reference to the Galway election in which we must not be beaten.[94]

[89] S. de Vere to Monsell, 22 Feb. 1872, Monsell MSS, 8317.
[90] Blennerhassett to Butt, 18 Jan. 1873, Butt MSS. It cost him £5,000 according to *Nation*, 1 Feb. 1873.
[91] Canon McDonnell to Moriarty, 7 Jan. 1872, Monsell MSS, 8629.
[92] Cullen to Moriarty, 5 Jan., Monsell MSS, 8629.
[93] *Freeman's Journal*, 12 Jan.
[94] McEvilly to Moriarty, 19 Jan., Monsell MSS, 8319.

Dr Delany, bishop of Cork, could not accept Moriarty's view of the home rule movement:

> The object of the present agitation differs from fenianism, it is not criminal in the eyes of religion as to its object or means ... I would not wonder if we obtained something, such as a national grand jury for Irish affairs. Mr Gladstone seemed to me to intimate obscurely such a thing in his Glasgow speech. As far as I can understand the rational portion of the present nationalist men don't contemplate much more. We need not have or fear serious impiety.[95]

Even among the parish clergy of Kerry, the episcopal condemnation of home rule was by no means universally accepted. Father Bourke, P.P. Murher and Knockanure, wrote to Canon McDonnell, P.P. Listowel, one of the most active of the pro-Dease priests, declining to allow his name to be put on Dease's committee, 'as I could not go against the people here, who are all the other way'. His curate, Father Harrington, also refused.[96] 'If the Devil from Hell were to publish Blenner-hassett's address he would adopt him', declared another priest.[97] Father McCarthy of Ballyheigue was reported as having told his parishioners 'that where a vote was concerned they were not to mind "landlord, priest, bishop, or even the Pope himself".'[98] At the nomination Blennerhassett was proposed by the Reverend Father O'Donoghue, P.P. Ardfert, an act of defiance for which that priest was subsequently 'disciplined' by Dr Moriarty. The election was bitterly and violently fought; Dease was compelled to retire to bed for some days in the middle of the campaign to nurse the wounds inflicted upon him by the electors of Castleisland. In the poll Blennerhassett was victorious by 2237 votes to 1398 for Dease. 'The revolutionists aided with most shameful activity by the Priests have scourged the party of order along the whole line in Kerry', wrote Canon McDonnell to Moriarty.[99]

95 Delany to Moriarty, 10 Jan., Monsell MSS, 8319.
96 Bourke to MacDonnell, 6 Jan. 1872, Monsell MSS, 8319.
97 McDonnell to Moriarty, 7 Jan., Monsell MSS, 8319.
98 James Cr ... to Moriarty, 24 Jan., Monsell MSS, 8319.
99 McDonnell to Moriarty, 15 Feb., Monsell MSS, 8319.

E

The Kerry victory, more than any of the other by-elections, revealed the strength of the popular desire for home rule, and forecast many more triumphs for home rule candidates, wrote the *Irish Times*:

> The general election which must ensue on the ballot becoming law will certainly issue in the return of a number of home rulers sufficient, very possibly, to hold the balance of power in the house of commons . . .[100]

'The most singular triumph yet achieved by the national cause', exclaimed the *Freeman's Journal*, hurriedly scrambling back on to the bandwaggon;

> In Kerry, as in Galway, an unholy alliance was consummated between the liberal and tory landlords, which, we regret to say, received the sanction and active support of the venerable bishop of the diocese of Kerry . . . Galway, we always felt, would return Captain Nolan, the Home Ruler who fought under the banner inscribed "Restoration". But Kerry we trembled for, feared for, and hardly dared to hope for.[101]

The *Freeman* was never notable for its courage, but the accuracy of its observation in this instance cannot be faulted. Kerry was essentially the home rule victory, the greatest which the movement had yet won, Blennerhassett, young, protestant, untried and not particularly remarkable, had triumphed over a massive clerical-liberal alliance by the simple fact of popular feeling for home rule.

In Galway, on the other hand, Nolan was as much the symbol of tenant-right as of home rule, and he had for his opponent a conservative, E. le Poer Trench, instead of a catholic liberal. Clerical support in this contest was even more energetically and unanimously exerted on behalf of Nolan than it was for Dease in Kerry. The victory added little to home rule as such. But if Kerry was the more striking home rule victory Galway had an individual significance of its own. The very success of Blennerhassett made the repetition of such head-on conflicts with the church increasingly unlikely,

100 *Irish Times,* 10 Feb. 1872.
101 *Freeman's Journal,* 10 Feb.

and Nolan is much more typical of the home rule member of the future. The association of home rule with victories such as that in Galway further widened the rift between the movement and the conservatives and identified it with the tenant and education parties. The result was followed by an immediate petition on the grounds of improper clerical influence, and at the end of May, after a lengthy trial, Judge Keogh in a celebrated judgment declared Nolan unseated. The conservatives were jubilant, and the justice of the decision was admitted by many liberal catholics. Unfortunately Keogh took the opportunity to deliver an attack upon the catholic clergy, their manners, education, and morality, couched in language of such personal viciousness as to cast serious doubts upon the sanity of its author. Furious popular feeling forgot the merits of the election petition; the judge was burnt in effigy throughout Ireland, and local home rule branches joined in passing resolutions of condemnation. The O'Donoghue and other liberals gave notice of their intention to pursue the question in the house of commons, and rather than be swept aside by the popular feeling, Butt was compelled, somewhat reluctantly, to undertake the leadership of the campaign in parliament.[102] When the judgment further resulted in the prosecution by the state of one bishop, Dr Duggan of Clonfert, and twenty-three priests, Butt accepted the brief for the defence. The Keogh controversy aroused old religious animosities to a higher pitch of excitement than at any time since the disestablishment campaign. Lord Claude John Hamilton, on behalf of the Irish conservatives, appealed to Disraeli to defend Keogh in the debate, and upon the issue of the home rulers' participation in the attack, Laurence King Harman, another of the conservative founders of the movement, resigned from the Home Government Association.[103]

Home rule candidates had now contested eight by-elections since the beginning of 1871, and had won six of them.[104] But

102 Henry to Butt, 7, 20 June 1872, Butt MSS.

103 *Nation*, 10 Aug; Hamilton to Disraeli, 12 June, Disraeli MSS.

104 But of these Nolan was unseated, and by a subsequent decision of the Court of common pleas, his opponent Trench was given the seat, although beaten by 2823 votes to 658.

by its very success the movement had outgrown the organisational framework of the old association. Before considering
this problem, however, some reference must be made to the
three further by-elections which were contested by the home
rulers in 1872. None of these contests was as spectacular as
those in Galway and Kerry, but each was of considerable importance within the association itself.

In the first of these by-elections, in Mallow in June, the
home rule candidate, J. G. MacCarthy, was defeated by his
wealthy liberal opponent, W. F. Munster, by a margin of 91
votes 78. The actual result in this tiny borough was not of any
great significance, but the contest showed up once again the
futility and disunion of the Home Government Association.
MacCarthy was a Cork solicitor who had written an able
pamphlet in favour of home rule, and who was warmly supported in Mallow by the local parish priest. He was, however,
intensely unpopular with the advanced party, among whom
he had the reputation, apparently undeserved, of having
given information against O'Donovan Rossa. The Home
Government Association had still not arrived at any permanent policy in regard to by-election contests. At first it endorsed MacCarthy's candidature and arranged to send a deputation to Mallow to support him.[105] Butt, however, was
still reluctant to take part in such contests, and receiving reports of MacCarthy's unpopularity with the advanced party
from his close friend D. A. Nagle, editor of the *Cork Herald,*
a fierce critic of MacCarthy, he appears to have reopened the
question in the association. The council decided not to carry
out its original resolution. Galbraith, Martin, and Sullivan
appear to have supported MacCarthy, but reports of a deputation being sent from Cork to break up his meetings confirmed Butt in his reluctance to intervene. Daunt supported
MacCarthy's candidature in a letter to the press; Martin,
Maguire, and Sullivan went down to Mallow to canvass for
him; the *Nation* and the *Freeman's Journal* also wrote on his
behalf. But Nagle wrote to Butt agreeing that the association

105 MacCarthy to Daunt, 24 May, Daunt MSS, 8047.

had acted prematurely in the first instance, and that a reorganisation of it was overdue.[106]

If MacCarthy had the support of the middle-class home
rulers and the hostility of the advanced party, the candidates
in the other two by-elections which were fought later in the
year represented precisely the opposite case. Yet each contest
pointed to the same conclusion—the need for a more consistent and active central direction of the movement. These
two by-elections, which occurred in Londonderry City and
in Cork City, were remarkable in the first place as the first
contests in Ireland conducted by secret ballot, and they were
watched with especial interest on account of this novelty. The
ballot had been variously estimated as likely to ensure the
triumph of the nationalists by ending the power of the landlords, and, conversely, as likely to ensure the triumph of conservatism by ending the rule of the priests and of the mob. In
both constituencies home rule candidates were immediately
put forward. In Londonderry J. G. Biggar, then president of
the Belfast Home Rule Association, was early in the field, and
secured the support of the local home rulers, who formally
launched their own home rule organisation in September at
a large meeting which was addressed by Martin, Galbraith,
and Sullivan. Conservative hopes were centred upon C. E.
Lewis, a London lawyer, who was not himself a strong candidate, but who could count on the full influence of the
powerful Hamilton family, eager to reverse the defeat which
they had so unexpectedly sustained in the general election.
The vacancy had been created by the elevation to the bench
of the attorney-general, Richard Dowse, and the liberal candidate was Dowse's newly appointed successor in that office,
Christopher Palles. Upon Palles, himself a catholic, now devolved the duty of conducting the long-deferred clerical prosecutions consequent upon the Galway petition judgment, a
circumstance which the nationalists exploited to the full in
an effort to win catholic support away from the government.
The advanced party were naturally particularly active in the

106 Nagle to Butt 19, 20 May, Butt MSS; Galbraith to Daunt, 31 May,
Butt MSS, vol. iii, MS 832; MacCarthy to Daunt, 1 Mar., 20, 24 May,
Daunt MSS, 8047.

cause of Biggar; John Ferguson, one of their most vigorous
spokesmen in the home rule movement, and a member of the
council of the Home Government Association, came over
from Glasgow specially to organise his campaign. He appealed to Butt to throw in his weight: 'You know the association in Dublin is doing nothing and people begin to see it'.
Butt's answer was to explain, not for the last time, the difficulty which he found in devoting himself to home rule owing
to the necessity to earn his living at the bar, and to threaten
to withdraw from the leadership. In October Ferguson again
urged that the Home Government Association should take a
more active part in constituency politics, and with the entry
of Palles into the contest the appeals from Derry to Dublin
became frantic, Ferguson expressing the belief that an address
from Butt could ensure victory. The determination of Palles
to contest the vote altered the complexion of the contest:

> We cannot win if he goes to the poll! Our hope is that as he
> has not the ghost of a chance he will retire . . . We will fight
> hard but we must have some help from Dublin. The *entire*
> people are with us and a letter from you or from the Associa-
> tion would do good.[107]

Any possibility of a home rule victory was finally destroyed
in the last week of the campaign, when the bishop and clergy,
who up to that time had remained neutral, threw their influence behind Palles. Catholic distrust of the Home Government Association, and fears for the fate of the education question, remained unallayed. In Dublin Cardinal Cullen was
rumoured to be floating the idea of a Catholic Association as
a rival to home rule; asked at the outset of the campaign for
his views on the education question, Biggar replied: 'The
primary question at present is home rule. If you had home
rule, Irishmen would then decide the question'.[108] The
clergy swallowed their distaste for the prosecutor of the bishop of Clonfert and rallied round the government candidate,
while Butt, for his part, shunned the whole desperate

107 Ferguson to Butt, 14, 23 Aug., 2 Oct., 3, 12 Nov.; Biggar to Butt,
26, 30 Oct.; Butt MSS.
108 *Nation*, 31 Aug., 28 Sept.

enterprise. The poll resulted in the conservative victory anticipated even by Gladstone,[109] but the defeat for home rule was unexpectedly humiliating; Lewis gained 696 votes, Palles 522, and Biggar 89. The home rulers were widely blamed for the conservative victory, and Ferguson urged Butt vainly to persuade the Home Government Association to dissociate itself from this reaction by passing a vote of thanks to the eager vanguard of Derry.[110]

The Derry defeat left considerable dissatisfaction behind it among all parties in the movement. 'The Londonderry *fiasco* has had an injurious effect here', wrote Philip Callan, who had been watching events from the detachment of the Reform Club.[111] The *Freeman*, which had remained carefully aloof from the contest, reserved its main censure for the presbyterians who had refused to support a catholic liberal in Palles: Biggar's hopeless candidature had only inflicted 'humiliation and injury' on the home rule cause.[112] The *Dublin Evening Mail,* probably with some justice, ascribed Palles's defeat to the refusal of the presbyterians to be associated with denominational education; it might also have drawn a more significant conclusion from this contest—that home rule would achieve no success in Ulster except where it possessed a large body of catholic support.[113] The presbyterians might vote liberal; they would not be induced to vote for home rule. Again the futility of Butt's efforts to woo protestant opinion seemed apparent. As for the advanced party, the election left them with a feeling of having been let down, and long irritated by the eternal hesitancy of the Dublin association, they redoubled their demands for a thorough reorganisation of the movement.

But if the energy of the advanced men recoiled upon their heads in Derry in November, they were able to carry all before them in the contest which took place in Cork City im-

---

[109] Gladstone to Fortescue, 31 Dec. 1869, Strachie MSS, Carlingford Political.

[110] Ferguson to Butt, 25 Nov. 1872, Butt MSS.

[111] Callan to Butt, 12 Dec., Butt MSS.

[112] *Freeman's Journal*, 25 Nov.

[113] *Dublin Evening Mail,* 25 Nov.

mediately afterwards. The vacancy here was created by the
death of J. F. Maguire, who, it will be recalled, had joined
the Home Government Association in August of the previous
year. A home rule victory was much more likely on paper
than in Derry but the situation was complicated by the participation not only of a catholic liberal, J. C. Mathew, nephew
of the famous temperance crusader, but also of two rival home
rule candidates, the mayor of Cork John Daly, who addressed
the electors for home rule, denominational education, and
amnesty, and Joseph Ronayne, 'the well-known nationalist,
who makes no political professions, except that he is a beli-
ever in the undying right of Ireland to govern herself'.[114]
Ronayne was a man of great ability and integrity, a distinguished engineer and the proprietor of the Cork-Macroom
railway, a separatist rather than a federalist by instinct, who
had championed amnesty against the whig programme in the
1868 election, and who possessed the enthusiastic support of
the advanced party. Daly was a liberal by background, and
a more recent exponent of home rule principles, but he enjoyed the patronage of the clerical and liberal middle-class
home rulers as against Ronayne's more popular following.
The *Nation* supported Ronayne, but for men like whom, it
reminded the electors, there would have been no nationalist
movement for Daly to join; the *Freeman* favoured Daly.[115]
Daly was first in the field, and had strong claims for support,
but it was remembered against him that he had declined to
attend the amnesty demonstrations because he said, 'he
thought that these assemblies were calculated to do more
harm than good'.[116] The farmers' clubs and the artisans declared for Ronayne, and Daly was compelled to withdraw.
Mathew having also withdrawn, the liberal home rulers and
the clergy, faced with the alternative of a conservative victory,
had to endorse Ronayne, a course in which they were followed by N. D. Murphy, the other sitting member for the city,
who now for the first time gave his support to home rule.
Ronayne in return attested his loyalty to the principle of de-

114 *Nation,* 9 Nov.
115 *Nation,* 16 Nov., *Freeman's Journal,* 7 ,12, 18 Nov.
116 ibid., 14 Nov.

nominational education. In the poll he defeated the conservative, J. E. Pim, by 1883 votes to 1110. Butt himself seems to have favoured Ronayne, with whom he was in constant communication, but the latter, unlike Ferguson in Derry, was sufficiently confident of his position not to seek any public intervention by the association.[117] Mitchell Henry and Martin also welcomed Ronayne's return enthusiastically.[118] But the division in the home rule camp left its share of bitterness behind it, a bitterness which was enhanced by a minor incident which followed upon the result. A banquet was arranged by Ronayne's committee in celebration of the victory, at which Butt was to have been the principal guest. Butt, however, was advised of the possibility that disorders might break out, and requested the cancellation of the function. The project was abandoned, but the advanced party resented yet another apparent slight upon their loyalty.[119]

[117] Ronayne to Butt, 8 Nov. 1872, Butt MSS.
[118] Henry to Butt, 9 Dec., Butt MSS; Martin to Daunt, 16 Dec., Daunt MSS, 8047.
[119] MacCarthy to Daunt, 23 Nov., Daunt MSS, 8047. J. Horgan to Butt, 16, 17, 19 Dec., Butt MSS.

E*

CHAPTER IV

The Founding of the Home Rule League

THE SUCCESSIVE by-election victories which were won by the home rule candidates in the years 1871 and 1872 were striking assertions of the popularity of the home rule demand in the constituencies. But they demonstrated equally clearly the separation of the Home Government Association in Dublin from the spontaneous enthusiasm of the constituencies. The home rule members who were returned in these by-elections went forward, canvassed, spoke, and were elected, as individuals. If they possessed the support of the home rule leaders, it too was given as the goodwill of individuals, and not, as a rule, as endorsement by a formal organisation with the right to speak for the movement. Not all the candidates returned were even members of the association, and its attitude to the endorsement of candidates was incomprehensible even to its own supporters.[1] Home rule associations were formed only where local initiative undertook the task; there was no effort at national organisation until 1873. In Butt's own constituency of Limerick a home rule association was not founded until September 1872. 'The Dublin Home Rule Association claims no authority, no precedence whatever, over the numerous Home Rule Associations which have sprung up in Ireland, England, and Scotland', insisted its secretary, Galbraith, 'The only precedence we ask for is that which naturally belongs to us—namely, that of seniority'.[2]

This caution stemmed, of course, from the desire of Butt to preserve the home rule demand from contamination by popular excesses, and in this way to keep the support of sections of opinion, especially the landed aristocracy, who might be in

---

[1] A. Webb to Butt, 14 June 1871. H. B. de Molines to Butt, 1 July 1872, Butt MSS.
[2] *Nation*, 21 Sept. 1872.

violent opposition to the majority on every other political issue besides home rule. But in practice, as we have seen, this ideal was never really achieved. Conservative participation in the movement, large at the outset only in proportion to the tiny scope of the association, not merely declined proportionately with the expansion of the movement, but was actually to a great extent withdrawn as the individual home rulers showed themselves even more dedicated than the original ogre of English Liberalism to the causes of land and educational reform. The main contribution of conservatism to home rule in this period seemed to many to be the alienation of the catholic majority.

It was in the light of this realisation that demands for the reorganisation of the association were strongly put forward as early as 1871. The lack of publicity and the parsimony of the association were criticised;[3] 'the smallness of support we are receiving is very discouraging', wrote Alfred Webb to Daunt, 'but we must only hold on and not let the people know we are discouraged. People will agree with us to any extent but they do not appear to care to join'. . . .[4] The distrust of the hierarchy remarked on before had not yet abated, however the lower ranks of the clergy may have felt. Daunt renewed his pleas to Dr Leahy, bishop of Cashel, to join the association in 1871, and received the usual reply. In April he told Daunt that he had, as requested, sounded his colleagues upon the question: they too shared his distrust of the protestant leaders of the association.[5] In August 1872 he again refused to be moved:

> I cannot now, any more than months ago, see my way to the open advocacy of home rule by joining your association. I am a repealer—always have been since O'Connell's agitation for repeal. But I am not willing to join the Home Rule Association.[6]

3 J. Ingoldsby to Butt, 4 Oct. 1871, Butt MSS.
4 Webb to Daunt, 12 Apr. 1871, Daunt MSS, 8048.
5 Leahy to Daunt, 1 Apr. 1871, Daunt MSS, 8046.
6 Leahy to Daunt, 3 Aug, 1872, ibid.

John Martin and T. D. Sullivan were particularly anxious that the association should accept a wider responsibility towards the people who shared Dr Leahy's attitude. Sullivan wrote to Daunt:

It has been proposed in the Council of the Home Government Association that we should get up a requisition—largely and influentially signed—calling a conference of the friends of home rule, to be held in Dublin. There are in the country a large number of gentlemen who claim to be the friends of the movement, but who do not choose to join the existing association, because it is a self-formed one, because it is composed, for the most part, of conservative gentlemen who are newcomers to the national ranks, and whose sincerity, they think, is not to be depended on. Many of these men say they would join an association founded by a public meeting in response to a call coming from representative men of all creeds and classes, but they will not step in and join our little body. Now as the association must do something to extend itself and push on the agitation, do you think we should try to get up such a requisition for such a conference? Can you ascertain for us whether any of the southern bishops would attach their names to such a requisition? I wrote to Father Ulick Bourke, secretary to his grace the archbishop of Tuam on the subject, and I have learned from him that his grace highly approves of the idea of a conference, but would not attach his name to the requisition because he would not wish to take any part in calling a meeting to be held in a place under the jurisdiction of another bishop. Father Bourke says of his grace: —' He heart and soul joins in the movement; still he must work as one approving and counselling rather than as one in the ranks ' ...

I may add that Mr Butt does not favour the idea of such a conference. He thinks it would be a failure and that we could not get up, at present, such a requisition as we ought to have. He would prefer that the association should ' go to the country ' and hold a series of great public meetings in the chief towns in Ireland. This would be an excellent—it would probably be the *best* plan, but the association cannot carry it out for want of men and money. What is to be done under these circumstances? The association must do something, or it will die of inanition, and so dying will do great injury to the cause.[7]

Lack of funds was the greatest barrier to such a reorganisation. Martin wrote to Daunt also favouring such a national conference, and the appointment of a paid organising secretary.

But in the actual state of the association, I am afraid it has no funds to pay a proper salary. I *know* nothing about the financial affairs of the association. But there has been no good accession of members of late. And how can it have funds?[8]

The expansion of the home rule movement into England added a new and particularly vocal group to the critics of the association. The English wing of the movement, which drew its support largely from immigrant labouring Irish, was notable from the first for its energy and its advanced sympathies. By the end of 1872 home rule associations had been set up in most of the principal English industrial towns, and the English home rulers were convinced of the necessity for a nationally unified organisation long before it became apparent to the Home Government Association. In October 1872 the Leeds association urged the holding of an annual meeting of the English home rulers, to be presided over by Butt, and in December 1872 the Manchester association invited delegates from other branches to a joint conference to consider the future of the movement. The chief spokesmen of the English movement in its dealings with the Dublin association, John Ferguson of the Glasgow branch and John Barry of Manchester, were both drawn from the fenian element. Ferguson, who became a member of the council of the Home Government Association in August 1872, was a publisher whose business took him frequently to Ireland, especially to Ulster. His criticisms of the inaction of the Home Government Association in connection with the Derry election have already been quoted; in October 1872 he appealed again to Butt to lead the association into the constituency struggle.[9] But such criticisms appear

7 T. D. Sullivan to Daunt, 6 May 1871, Hickey MSS.
8 Martin to Daunt, 19 Feb. 1871, Daunt MSS, 8047.
9 Ferguson to Butt, 2 Oct. 1872, Butt MSS.

only to have depressed and dispirited the home rule leader. He opened the year 'in splendid health and spirits', but by the autumn he was 'desponding', and threatening to retire from the leadership owing to the pressure of his own professional work.[10]

In 1872 the criticisms of the clergy, the liberals, and the advanced men were all combining to force a reorganisation. The final compulsion which made it a matter of immediate urgency was the sudden disintegration of Gladstone's secure majority. The belief in an imminent settlement of the education issue had been perhaps the chief inhibition to Irish catholics, and in particular the hierarchy, from any countenancing of the home rule movement. As time went on without any overt move upon Gladstone's part to deal with this most complicated of Irish grievances, the security of his hold upon the loyalty of Irish catholics had progressively weakened, and the anti-denominational speeches of some of his ministers, notably that of Hartington at Knighton in 1872, had done much to undermine their hopes of a settlement favourable to their interests. In April 1872 the support of sections of the Conservatives and of the Liberals for Henry Fawcett's university bill, which aimed chiefly at the abolition of religious tests in Trinity College and the reconstruction of its governing body, almost brought about the downfall of the ministry: Gladstone was able to avert disaster only by the publication of a semi-official 'manifesto' in the Daily News making it quite clear that the government intended to treat its opposition to certain provisions of the bill as a matter of confidence.[11] By the end of 1872 Gladstone's administration had held office for four years; a general election could not be very far off, and judging by the increasing unpopularity of the government in Ireland, and the ominous pronouncements of the Liberal ministry upon the subject of denominational education, such an election would scarcely be fought upon the terms of that of 1868.

[10] J. Martin to Daunt, 1 Jan. 1872, Daunt MSS, 8047; Ferguson to Butt, 23 Aug., M. Barnett to Butt, 11 Sept., Butt MSS.
[11] Daily News, 22 April 1872.

As the year drew on this circumstance had two principal effects. In the first place, it threw into ever sharper relief the glaring inability of the Home Government Association to undertake the responsibility of influencing the course of a general election. As early as December 1871 Butt had called for the return of eighty home rule members in the next election, and his entire policy turned upon the achievement of some such electoral success. But little was done in 1872 in preparation for such a task, and in November Ferguson was still strenuously urging the holding of a national convention to raise funds to organise the registry all over Ireland.[12]

The progressive disintegration of Gladstone's position offered a second and no less pressing challenge to the Home Government Association. Always, as we have remarked, there had been those liberals who were turning more and more to home rule but who could not be prevailed upon to enter the ranks of the association. It will be recalled that in January 1871 Richard Lalor and Kenelm Digby, M.P., had urged the abandonment of the association and its replacement by one which would command the support of the liberals and the clergy, and that T. D. Sullivan, Martin, and even Butt himself had been prepared to make concessions to this attitude. In September 1872 yet another liberal M.P., McCarthy Downing, called for the dissolution of the Home Government Association and the establishment of a new organisation in which members of the original body would be invited to participate. Significantly, the *Nation,* almost the official journal of the association, now not merely published Downing's plea, but endorsed it.[13]

By the end of 1872 it was, therefore, obvious even to Butt that an advance from the initial bridgehead could no longer be deferred. On 13 December a special meeting of the council of the Home Government Association was held 'to consider what steps the Association might take to provide for the home rule interest in the next General Election'. A. M. Sullivan, who was present at this meeting, wrote 'a glowing account'

12 Ferguson to Butt, 12 Nov. Butt MSS.
13 *Nation,* 21 Sept.1872.

of it to Martin, who in turn described it to W. J. O'Neill
Daunt: —

A sum of £1000 was voted to the council for use in the next
twelve months in providing for registration, etc. And, though
nobody was warned that a subscription might be entered into,
£500 was put down on the spot. Mr. Sullivan adds that the
spirit and practical earnestness were such that it was agreed to
try again to persuade *you* to come to Dublin and undertake
the work of first minister of the association. He thinks that in
a single year wonders may be done for the cause if the *man*
can be got to direct and do it: and you are the *man*. He begs
me to write to you . . . it would be but right to make sure, before accepting office, of such payment as would enable you to
leave Kilcascan—if it be practicable for you to leave it, even
for a year.[14]

'I am too old to retain much mental and physical energy',
wrote Daunt in his journal; 'I should not like to leave
home'.[15] In January he received letters from Martin, Galbraith, A. M. Sullivan and Butt renewing their appeals.[16]
The pleas of his friends overcame his reluctance. In January
1873 W. J. O'Neill Daunt was appointed secretary to the
association at a salary of £400 a year. At the same time the
association took 'really handsome and central offices in West-
moreland Street', and, in addition to the permanent assistant secretary J. McAlister, who had already held office for
some time, it appointed a new travelling secretary, Hugh
Heinrick, formerly a commission agent and leader-writer of
the *Nation*, who was immediately despatched on an organisational tour, first of the industrial towns of Britain, and then
around Ireland.[17]

The appointment of Daunt as secretary of the association
was a decisive step forward in the development of the movement. It was not so much that he was an exceptionally vigor-

14 Martin to Daunt, 16 Dec. Daunt MSS, 8047.

15 Daunt Journal, 22 Dec. 1872, MS 3041.

16 ibid., 12 Jan. 1873.

17 Martin to Daunt, 29 Jan. Daunt MSS, 8047, Sullivan to Daunt, undated, ibid., 8048.

ous organiser; an amiable hypochondriac in his sixty-sixth year, he was if anything scarcely suited to the more active duties of an organising secretary. Nor did he induce the association, by the power of his personality, radically to modify its programme. His significance was more as a symbol; just at the time when the association was being compelled to recognise the necessity of making a new approach to the liberals and the clergy, and just when events were moving towards a situation in which home rule would have a better chance than ever before of succeeding in such an approach, Daunt, symbolic of Irish catholic nationalism, succumbed to the pleas of the home rule leaders to lend the authority of his name to just such a new offer. At once he commenced the attack. In January he proposed the idea of a circular to the catholic clergy;[18] in February he drafted an address to the people of Ireland which was approved by the council of the association with some minor alterations. But he devoted much of his energy to the making of personal contacts with the clergy, whose lukewarmness he bitterly reprobated in his diary. Cardinal Cullen, he wrote,

> not only does not help, but actually thwarts the home rulers. Not a priest in his diocese except two has ventured to join our association up to this time; and of these two, one has withdrawn his adhesion.

On 1 March he met the bishop of Clonfert, Dr Duggan; on 4 March he wrote to the bishop of Cloyne, Dr Keane, and several priests, on behalf of the movement; on 10 March he wrote to the bishop of Meath, Dr Nulty, to the same effect.[19] At the same time the association began to make some effort to get down to what Martin regarded as the most urgent task before it, the organising of the constituencies with a view to the next general election, and in January Butt, speaking at Manchester, forecast the return of eighty home rule M.P.'s.[20] But the council was not always unanimous upon the extent to which it should widen its responsibilities; in February Daunt was

18 Martin to Daunt, 16 Jan. 1873, Daunt MSS, 8047.
19 Daunt Journal, 13, 17 Feb., 1, 4, 10 Mar., 28 July, MS 3041.
20 Martin to Daunt, 14 Feb. 1873, Daunt MSS, 8047. *Nation*, 11 Jan.

involved in differences with A. M. Sullivan, and in April was expressing himself to Martin as thoroughly discontented with his position on the council.[21]

But if there were some in the association who were still reluctant to commit themselves to a full-scale reorganisation of the movement, the political crisis which was produced in February and March of that year by the introduction of Gladstone's university bill precipitated them willy-nilly into action. Looking back upon the education struggle in 1877, after reading Pope Pius IX's letter to the French bishops upon the same subject, the bishop of Limerick, Dr Butler, reflected:

> had he written so to *us*, we could have acted differently from what we have done in our struggle for catholic education. But the Holy Father would not make concessions to us which the 'hardness of our hearts' did not seem to require. He thought that under the principles of our constitution, we—the vast majority of the Irish people, could claim and obtain something better than the French people looked for, or the French legislature of that day would think of conceding.[22]

But the Irish catholics were not conceded the right of a majority upon this question; their claims had to be balanced against English Liberal and above all nonconformist opinion, and in retrospect it seems obvious that any attempt by Gladstone to endow sectarian education in Ireland would have shattered the English Liberal party.

Gladstone appears to have made no effort to ascertain the feelings of the bishops in regard to his proposals before publishing them, although the wisdom of such a course had been pointed out to Monsell.[23] Cardinal Cullen sent the premier a 'little book' on Irish education in 1872; subsequent events do not suggest that he found time to read it.[24] In his dealings with the English Liberals Gladstone rather seems to have

---

21 Martin to Daunt, 21 Feb., 7 Apr., Daunt MSS, 8047.
22 Butler to Monsell, 2 Nov. 1877, Monsell MSS, 8317.
23 P J. Keenan to Monsell, 25 Dec. 1872, Monsell MSS, 8317.
24 Cullen to Gladstone, 25 Feb. 1872, BM Add. MSS, 44433 f 237.

boasted of his neglect of the hierarchy's views.[25] In August 1870 he wrote to Fortescue:

It occurs to me that while information as to the views of the Roman Hierarchy on education, especially on the higher education, cannot but be useful, yet in the present state of jealousy about them we cannot use too much caution as to any direct communication or proceeding which might be used. It seems to me that in the main we know what we ought to give them whether they will take it or not.[26]

In December 1870 the chances of a settlement of the education question were reduced still further by the replacement of Fortescue as Chief Secretary by the Marquess of Hartington. Fortescue was not the most efficient of administrators, and his readiness to succumb to the insistence of his wife, the beautiful Frances Waldegrave, that the family should annually defer taking up residence in Ireland until the end of the London season, had drawn upon him the gibes of Hartington and the reproofs of Gladstone.[27] But he was at least experienced in handling the Irish representatives, in whose eyes he shared some of the glory of the years of Gladstonian fulfilment. Hartington accepted the transfer to Dublin with extreme reluctance; he believed the education question to be insoluble, and found the persistence of the Irish members in its regard highly distasteful. 'The management of that body', he told Gladstone, when offered the appointment, 'is a task for which I do not feel any aptitude or inclination'.[28] In November 1871 J. A. Dease conveyed to the viceroy, Lord Spencer, as the very least that the bishops would accept, a draft scheme originated by Monsell himself and approved by 'episcopal authority',[29] but the following January, when Monsell had occasion to take Hartington to task for his anti-denominational pronouncements, the latter had replied: —

25 *Standard,* 31 Dec. 1873.

26 Gladstone to Fortescue, 19 Aug. 1870, Strachie MSS, Carlingford Political.

27 Gladstone to Fortescue, 24 Dec. 1868, ibid., Hartington to Gladstone, 26 Dec. 1870, BM Add. MSS, 44143 f 44.

28 Hartington to Gladstone, 24 Dec. 1870, ibid., 44143 f 40.

29 J. A. Dease to Monsell, 29 Nov. 1871, Monsell MSS, 8317.

I must confess that the speeches which have lately been delivered at public meetings on this question, and the require-
ments of the Roman Catholic bishops (as I understand them)
do appear to me to demand an amount of control on their part
over the system of state education which I do not think the
government or parliament would be justified in conceding.[30]

Spencer himself was not empowered to make direct contact
with the Cardinal until the Liberal proposals had been published and the clerical reaction crystallised.[31]

In February 1873, three years after the introduction of the
land bill, Gladstone finally made clear his intentions upon
the subject of education. It is not within the scope of this book
to penetrate deeply the tangled history of the Irish university
question. Gladstone's bill provided, amongst other things, for
the establishment of a national university, to consist of five
constituent colleges—Trinity College, Dublin, Queen's College, Cork, Queen's College, Belfast, Magee University College, Londonderry, and the Catholic University of Dublin.
The council of the new university was to be nominated in the
first instance by the crown, and thereafter to be chosen by the
constituent colleges. It was to have no chair of theology, philosophy or modern history; these subjects were to form no part
of the compulsory curriculum, nor were they to be eligible
for study for prizes or emoluments. Trinity College was to lose
its status as a university, and its privilege of returning two
members to parliament, which was to be transferred to the
new university; its religious tests were to be abolished, and its
divinity school was to be detached from it and transferred to
the Representative Church Body.

Lectures were not to be compulsory in the new university,
and its teaching duties were to be limited. It was to be endowed by the sum of £500,000 taken from Trinity College;
the cost of providing buildings would be subsidised out of the
church surplus. The constituent colleges were to continue, ex-

[30] Hartington to Monsell, 11 Jan. 1872, ibid, 8319. Also Hartington
to Gladstone, 12 Jan., BM Add. MSS, 44143 f 131.
[31] Memorandum by Spencer of conversations with Cardinal Cullen,
25 Feb. 1873, BM Add. MSS, 44307 f 161.

cept as above mentioned, to manage their own affairs as before. Anticipating the criticism that this would leave Trinity College still in a much stronger position than the other constituent colleges, Gladstone reminded the House that it alone had

> voluntarily renounced its denominational safeguards, and which proposes to make the whole of its emoluments and offices accessible to all Irishmen who may be its members, entirely irrespective of religious distinctions. Parliament has adopted for many years in its policy the principle that these are the colleges to which alone endowments shall be given.[32]

The bill was essentially an uneasy compromise. Hartington disliked it so much that he had threatened to resign the Chief Secretaryship.[33] Yet in Ireland it was not at once received unfavourably. The *Dublin Evening Post* remarked on 14 February that it could place the Catholic University in a position of equality with the other colleges, 'and with this advantage, to begin with, we should be able to accomplish a great deal more for ourselves'. 'For myself, I would accept it for England', wrote Cardinal Manning to Gladstone, promising to use his influence in its favour.[34] But soon it became evident that the catholic bishops were bitterly disappointed. P. J. Keenan, commissioner of National Education, wrote to Monsell on 15 February in reply to his request for news of the Irish reaction to the bill: —

> (1) Bishops and clergy. I have as yet met only Dr Butler, Dr Woodlock, and a few priests.
>   You know, I suppose, Dr Butler's opinion already—great disappointment, a conviction that there is no *equality* in the measure etc., but at the same time a resolve to accept the bill . . .

[32] Hansard, 3rd series, cciv, 378-426. See also T. W. Moody, The Irish university question of the nineteenth century, in *History*, vol. XLIII, No. 148, June 1958.
[33] Hartington to Gladstone, 30 Nov. 1872, Gladstone to Hartington, 1 Dec., BM Add. MSS 44143 ff 208, 210.
[34] Manning to Gladstone, 14, 15 Feb. 1873, BM Add. MSS 44249 ff 83, 85.

The few priests I have met are dead against the bill—the want of grist to the mill in Stephen's Green being the great defect . . .

Acceptance I think is on the tongue of nearly every catholic layman.[35]

Very Reverend C. W. Russell of Maynooth commended the bill as 'a most able and ingenious one', which seemed to provide every possible safeguard against unsound teaching.[36]

On 15 February Dr Woodlock went down to Meath to see Cardinal Cullen, who declined to express any opinion on the bill until he had time to consider all its aspects and to consult with the bishops and other interested parties.[37] Immediately he summoned a meeting of the hierarchy for 27 February.[38] From Queen's County Edmund Dease reported that it was only 'the personal confidence the bishops and clergy have in Mr Gladstone' which had prevented an outburst of public opinion against the bill.[39] But as early as 15 February the *Dublin Evening Post* had drawn critical attention to the disparity between the resources of the constituent colleges, and in the week which followed it repeated its criticisms.[40] 'I see that the *Evening Post*—which I suppose is the organ of the priests and the Cardinal—is down upon the proposals', wrote Mitchell Henry to Butt; 'John of Tuam furious at the education bill and preparing a pastoral', he added on 22 February[41] Dr MacHale did not even wait for the decision of the hierarchy before publishing his condemnation.

The bishops met on 27 February, but their verdict was never in much doubt. The day before the meeting took place Cardinal Cullen told Monsell of his disappointment at the bill, which left the Catholic University without endowment or

[35] Keenan to Monsell, 15 Feb. 1873, Monsell MSS, 8317. Dr Woodlock was rector of the Catholic University.
[36] Russell to Monsell, 15 Feb., Monsell MSS, 8317.
[37] John Canon Farrell, P.P., to J. A. Dease, 20 Feb., Monsell MSS, 8318.
[38] Cullen to Moriarty 23 Feb., ibid., 8629.
[39] E. Dease to J. A. Dease, 22 Feb, ibid., 8318.
[40] *Dublin Evening Post*, 16, 21 Feb.
[41] Henry to Butt, 17, 22 Feb. Butt MSS.

subsidy to oppose the entrenched battalions of mixed education.[42] The hierarchical meeting resulted in a series of resolutions condemning the measure as 'being framed on the principle of mixed and purely secular education'.[43] The hard-
pressed Monsell asked P. J. Keenan to explain the wishes of
the bishops.

(a) Endowment of their college in Stephen's Green . . .
     Endowment is their sine qua non . . .
(b) Trinity College *not* to be opened . . .
(c) The professional part of the University is also an object
     of their execration—simply on the ground that it favours
     'mixed education'.[44]

But the proclamation of the bishops went much further
than simple disapproval of the bill; it called on 'the catholic
clergy and laity of Ireland'

> to use all constitutional means to oppose the passing of this
> bill in its present form, and to call on their parliamentary re-
> presentatives to give it their most energetic opposition.[45]

This summons to the attack was the final and most decisive
blow delivered upon the liberal alliance of 1868. The English
Liberals were furious. The *Spectator* was prepared to admit
that every concession, and every act of conciliation by Gladstone, had been directed towards the radical critics of the bill
in England, but to the majority of the Liberals, who had detested the bill from the outset as a totally unwarranted concession to ultramontanism, the conduct of the hierarchy was
inexplicable.[46] To the *Times* Gladstone was 'the very Lear
of statesmen, turned out of doors by his favourite children, the
Irish priest and tenant'.[47]

There were also some among the Irish catholic laity who
deplored the attitude of the hierarchy. 'The bishops want a
seminary or rather a number of diocesan seminaries under

42 Cullen to Monsell, 26 Feb., Monsell MSS, 8317.
43 *Nation*, 1 Mar.
44 Keenan to Monsell, 2 Mar., Monsell MSS, 8317.
45 *Nation*, 1 Mar.
46 *Spectator*, 15 Mar. 1873.
47 *Times*, 18 Mar.

their absolute control', wrote Professor Sullivan of the Catholic University.[48] But the nationalists were jubilant for the first time for many years over the political conduct of their pastors. 'A thrill of joy and thankfulness will run through the hearts of the catholics of Ireland on reading the series of resolutions adopted by the bishops at their recent meeting', wrote the *Nation*.[49] They appreciated the political significance of the decision. 'Gladstone's education bill unsatisfactory to the bishops "Serve 'em right",' wrote Daunt in his diary.[50] 'A fine reward' . . . said Martin, 'for giving their political support to Mr Gladstone & Co.'[51] In the crisis the home rulers threw all their forces behind rejection of the bill. Butt prepared a memorandum which materially aided the bishops in reaching their decision, and for which he was offered an honorarium which he declined to accept.[52] J. G. MacCarthy wrote to Daunt that he hoped the bill would 'throw the clergy frankly into our ranks'.[53] Others to whom this prospect was less welcome were equally as quick to recognise it. As early as 22 February Edmund Dease prophesied to his cousin that the fiasco would throw the prelates into home rule.[54] 'I foresee uneasy times before us and a melancholy strengthening of the hands of the home rulers', lamented J. A. Dease in turn to Monsell;[55] what was to become of the catholic members of the government, asked Dr Delany, of St Stanislaus College, Tullamore: 'Against priests and Home Rulers they would have little chance indeed of re-election. As it is, if there were a dissolution it would need every effort to hold the seats of many'.[56]

But worse was to follow. The directive of the bishops was highly embarrassing to the Irish liberal members, most of whom Speaker Brand believed to be friendly 'both to the bill

48 W. K. Sullivan to Monsell, 15 May, Monsell MSS, 8318.
49 *Nation*, 1 Mar.
50 Daunt Journal, 15 Feb., MS 3041.
51 Martin to Daunt, 21 Feb., Daunt MSS, 8047.
52 Dr Woodlock to Butt, 1 and 3 Mar., Butt MSS; *Nation*, 8 Mar.
53 MacCarthy to Daunt, 1 Mar., Daunt MSS, 8047.
54 E. Dease to J. A. Dease, 22 Feb. 1873, Monsell MSS, 8318.
55 J. A. Dease to Monsell, 2 Mar. 1873, Monsell MSS, 8317.
56 Delany to Dease, 1 Mar. 1873, Monsell MSS, 8317.

and to the government '.[57] A meeting of thirty-two Irish liberal members was called by requisition and decided inevitably to oppose the bill. The division on the second reading took place on 11 March. Of the Irish liberals and home rulers, twelve protestants and five catholics followed the government whip; twelve protestants and twenty-seven catholics went into the opposition lobbies. Nine home rulers voted against the bill and none for it, unless an exception is made of Sir Rowland Blennerhassett, always a doubtful home ruler, who voted with the government.[58] The thirty-five Irish conservatives who voted naturally opposed the bill. But at the same time a large number of English Liberals who could not tolerate what seemed to them so large a concession to denominationalism, notably H. Fawcett, E. P. Bouverie and McCullagh Torrens ignored their own whip. The government was defeated by 287 votes to 284.

The ministerial defeat produced a parliamentary crisis. Gladstone's resignation was believed to be imminent, but the conservatives were reluctant to undertake minority government. After several days' confusion Gladstone resumed office and abandoned the bill. He had suffered 'all the disaster of a moral as well as a political check', wrote the *Spectator*, and must dissolve parliament upon his very next defeat. At the latest a dissolution was expected in the autumn.[59] To Manning Gladstone wrote, with understandable bitterness, but prophetic inaccuracy, of 'the vision of my liberty dawning from beyond the hills. For when this offer has been made, and every effort of patience employed to make it a reality, my contract with the country is fulfilled, and I am free to take my own course '.[60] In August William Monsell, efficient as a weathervane, if not as Postmaster-General, asked Gladstone for a peer-

57 Brand Diary, 10 Mar.
58 Two home rulers were absent, Butt himself, and Martin, who made a point of not voting except on home rule.
59 *Spectator*, 22 Mar. *Freeman's Journal*, 18 Mar. Henry to Butt, 15 Mar., Butt MSS.
60 Gladstone to Manning, 8 Mar., BM Add. MSS, 44250 f 115.

age. He anticipated his dismissal by twenty-four hours.[61] The premium upon eager Irish agents was sadly depreciated.

It was against this background of disillusionment that the national conference was held and the Home Rule League founded. It was clearly a situation full of opportunities for home rule. The 'obvious inference' of the university fiasco, declared Dr Donnelly, bishop of Clogher, in his Lenten pastoral, was that

> it is time to proclaim that we have had enough of legislation from a parliament that cares neither to understand nor remedy our grievances, a parliament that confessedly loathes our religion and loathes ourselves because of our religion.[62]

'The bishops will come in, in good time' . . . wrote Father R. O'Reilly, P.P. Kingscourt, to Daunt: 'if they are not satisfied now that there is no hope from an English parliament, then I say, they *are alone in Ireland*'.[63]

But if the university bill fiasco was home rule's opportunity, it was also for the movement a challenge full of peril. It has already been remarked that in 1872 there were many prominent liberals, both inside and outside parliament, who were turning towards the principle of home rule, but who were not members of the Home Government Association. The fiasco of the university bill, the ministerial crisis, and the prospect of an imminent general election, multiplied the number of these people many times over. Many took the course of a belated entry into the Home Government Association. In April the clergy of the Clifden deanery sent in their support to the association; in May the deaneries of Castlebar and Achonry followed suit; in June thirteen catholic clergymen were admitted to membership.[64] In September Sir Joseph McKenna, Former M.P. for Youghal, joined the association. But others were still reluctant to join a small group which they had condemned at the outset as conservative and in which they would

---

[61] Gladstone to Monsell, 5 Aug. (marked 'Cancelled'), Monsell to Gladstone, 6 Aug., BM Add. MSS 44152 ff 221, 225.

[62] *Nation,* 8 Mar.

[63] O'Reilly to Daunt, 6 May, 1873, Daunt MSS, 8047.

[64] *Nation,* 26 April, 10 May, 7 June.

have to take a very junior position. Sir John Gray, for example, still declined to come in 'till the bishops would
lead'.[65] As late as 12 November Dr Duggan, bishop of Clonfert, would not accede to the requests of Butt and Daunt that
he should make public his support for the association.[66] The
Dublin Evening Post was appealing to the Irish catholics not to
abandon a leader who had given them so much, because of a
single reverse.[67] J. G. MacCarthy wrote to Daunt in April:

> Why don't the priests join? Because the bishops don't begin.
> And why don't the bishops? Because they are always cauti-
> ous, and because they don't trust B, and because they think the
> Fenians dominate you, and that the Internationalists are allied
> to you . . .[68]

But the most immediate problem was that of the liberal
members of parliament, facing a general election without
either a leader or a raison d'etre of any kind. As early as the
beginning of March the *Saturday Review* had prophesied that
with the failure of the university bill many Irish Catholics
who then sat as liberals would come back to parliament as
home rulers.[69] There were two possible attitudes which the
association could adopt towards such people. The *Nation* represented one. There were, it remarked in March, five classes
of sitting M.P.'s: —

> 1. Declared Home Rulers; men who have given service to the
> cause.
> 2. Men who are probably Home Rulers, but who have made
> no sign of the faith that is in them.
> 3. Whigs who will 'swallow' Home Rule in the hope of be-
> ing re-elected.
> 4. Whigs, who will try to get elected *without* swallowing it,
> by saying they 'go farther', or 'don't go so far', or that they
> 'don't understand it', or that it has not been 'defined', or by
> being seized with a sudden spasm of gushing love for our holy

---

[65] Heinrick to Butt, 25, 27 June, Butt MSS.
[66] Duggan to Butt, 12 Nov., Butt MSS.
[67] *Dublin Evening Post*, 11, 12 Mar.
[68] MacCarthy to Daunt, 4 Apr., Daunt MSS, 8047.
[69] *Saturday Review*, 8 Mar.

religion, or for the Pope, or for our persecuted nuns, or for the
Fenian prisoners, or for anything else in the wide earth that
they think will help them to bamboozle the ' free and independent ' electors.

5. Tories . . .[70]

And again in July it warned the electors to be on their guard
against ' sham ' home rulers, prophesying at best the return of
a home rule party of 50-60 of whom half would be genuine.[71]

But that was essentially the attitude of the ideological nationalist, who had been almost suffocated by the liberal alliance in 1868 and who had little time now for its former cham-
pions. There were many who looked with more sympathy
upon the liberal position. Shaw wrote to Daunt in September:

> I still think that in the early winter as soon as any government
> announcement comes out somewhere in October, we should
> have some representative gathering in Dublin to allow those
> who are outside to have a fair public opportunity of joining the
> movement. We must in such a moment as this make allowance
> for the weakness of human nature of men who while they are
> as sincere home rulers as ourselves are influenced by pride,
> vanity, and selfishness. We must work them into the cause—
> better have them for than against us. Our cause must be pre-
> sented to the constituencies not as a small association in Dub-
> lin but if possible as a great national movement. If we go to a
> general election without in some way uniting all sections of the
> national liberal party and without stirring up the enthusiasm
> of the people we cannot succeed.[72]

The conference idea had, as we have seen, long been urged
by many sincere nationalists in the association who were tired
of its futility and vacillation. As late as July the inconsistency
of the association's attitude to by-election candidates monotonously reproduced another home rule fiasco in Waterford
County, where H. W. Villiers Stuart, son of Lord Decies, was
permitted by Butt, amid a welter of conflicting advice, to pass
uncontested into parliament upon the flimsiest of home rule

[70] *Nation,* 22 Mar.
[71] ibid., 26 July.
[72] Shaw to Daunt, 2 Sept. 1873, Daunt MSS, 8047.

innuendoes. His landed connections earned him this easy triumph; elected, he repudiated his nationalist utterances, and was introduced into the house of commons by Hartington.[73] In the same month Mitchel Henry drew up a draft plan for a home rule conference.[74] The advanced nationalists in the movement, especially those of Great Britain, were also pressing hard for reorganisation, and in January, at a conference in Manchester under the chairmanship of Butt, plans were initiated for a national English home rule organisation. A second conference was held in Birmingham, and finally in Newcastle in August the reorganisation of the Irish movement was anticipated with the ratification of the decision of these previous conferences, and the formal election of a national executive for the Home Rule Confederation of Great Britain, with John Barry as its secretary.[75]

The reluctant acceptance by the association of the conference project was above all else a triumph for the liberal interest and a final defeat for the inbred conservatism of the original movement. The association had long been debating the proposal, when what was probably the decisive influence was exerted upon them in September. Dr Keane, bishop of Cloyne, and the clergy of his diocese, in this month publicly announced their adhesion to the programme of the association, but at the same time called for

> the holding of an aggregate meeting in Dublin of the representatives of all interested in this great question—and they are the entire people, without distinction of creed or class—for the purpose of placing, by constitutional means, on a broad and definite basis, the nation's demand for the restoration of its plundered rights.[76]

In the same issue of the *Nation* in which this address was published, the editorial described it with understandable hyperbole as ' by far the most important event in Irish politics since

---

[73] J. A. Blake to Butt, 30 June, 7 July; J. Fisher to Butt, 2, 3, and 5 July; H. J. Slattery to Butt, 4 July; Butt MSS. *Nation*, 5, 12 July.
[74] Butt to Callan, 12 July, Butt MSS, vol. ii, MS 831.
[75] *Nation*, 11 Jan., 30 Aug., 27 Sept.
[76] *Nation*, 20 Sept.

the close of the repeal agitation'. As for the plan it proposed : —

> Even before that recommendation came before them the leaders
> of the Home Government Association had recognised the ad-
> vantages which such a step would confer, and had themselves
> which such a step would confer, and had themselves suggested
> the necessity of enlisting in the Home Rule cause the whole
> strength of the country through the medium of a grand nation
> al conference. The time has come when the people in one grand
> combination must take up the work heretofore carried out by
> the Home Government Association. That body has never
> claimed for itself the character or powers of a great national
> organisation. It was established by a number of patriotic gentle-
> men to disseminate and support the doctrines and principles
> of Home Rule, but it eschewed anything like a representative
> character, and it recognised from the outset the fact that it was
> nothing more than a precursor society . . . Let us not be mis-
> taken. We believe that no political body was ever more success-
> ful in propagating its principles, in sowing the seeds of action,
> in kindling the energies and uniting the hearts of a nation than
> the Home Government Association . . . but it is not, and it was
> never intended to be, such an association as is called for by the
> circumstances of the present time. We want something broader,
> larger, stronger, and greater. We want an organisation which
> will embrace the whole manhood and intellect of the home
> ruler within its fold, and which will strike its roots deep in the
> population of every barony and every parish. The time is come
> for it. The imminence of the general election throws a responsi-
> bility and an amount of work upon the country which can only
> be satisfactorily dealt with through some such gigantic agency.[77]

Butt took great pains to deny the suggestion of the London
Standard that these proposals involved his being 'laid aside'.[78]
Yet in private he expressed misgivings.[79] No doubt he feared
an effort on the part of the liberals to ignore the existing home

[77] *Nation*, 20 Sept. 1873.
[78] ibid., 27 Sept.
[79] Butt to Daunt, 18 Oct. Butt MSS, vol ii, MS 831. Butt to Henry,
1 Dec. Butt MSS, vol. iii, MS 832.

rule leadership. William Shaw wrote to Henry at the beginning of November: 'You may be quite sure the Irish M.P.'s will not give Butt any leadership on general questions in the House, whilst they may be quite willing to follow his lead on the Irish question',[80] and the *Roscommon Messenger* remarked ominously that while Butt was at present the leader of the home rule movement, it was quite sure he would return to the ranks if he felt it was better for the unanimity of the movement.[81]

But the apparent imminence of a general election forced Butt to risk the consequences of an appeal to the country. It was decided to issue a requisition calling for a conference to discuss the best means of forwarding the home rule demand, since it was obvious that a simple invitation from the existing association would prejudice the success of the plan from the outset.[82] The circular asking for support was prepared at the end of September, and issued on 11 October, bearing the signatures of Shaw, King Harman, Callan, and Daunt. At the same time an intensive campaign was undertaken to secure the signatures of as many representatives as possible of the catholic hierarchy. Dr MacHale was at first reluctant to anticipate his colleagues by signing such a proposal, sending instead a letter of support for publication in the press, but with the public launching of the requisition plan his signature and that of Dr O'Hea, bishop of Ross, were the first to be secured[83] Following upon this, Butt wrote to Dr Duggan, bishop of Clonfert, and Dr Dorrian, bishop of Down and Connor, A. M. Sullivan to Dr Keane, bishop of Cloyne, Callan to Dr Donnelly, bishop of Clogher, and Daunt to the primate, Dr McGettigan, Dr McEvilly, bishop of Galway, Dr Conroy, bishop of Ardagh, Dr Butler, bishop of Limerick, Dr Conaty, bishop of Kilmore, and Dr Nulty, bishop of Meath.[84] Of these ten, Dr Donnelly declined to sign, though friendly to the cause, as did

80 Shaw to Henry, 2 Nov. Butt MSS, vol. iii, MS 832.
81 Quoted in *Nation*, 27 Sept. 1873.
82 ibid., 27 Sept., 4 Oct.
83 Daunt Journal, 7, 25 Sept., MS 3041; *Nation* 15 Nov.
84 Butt to Daunt, 5 Nov. 1873, Butt MSS, vol. ii, MS 832; Daunt to Butt, 11 Nov., Butt MSS.

Dr Dorrian, and Dr Duggan. The replies of the others have not survived, but Dr Keane's signature was attached to the requisition.[85]

The conference, which met in the Rotunda on 18, 19, 20, and 21 November 1873, was the most important event which had yet taken place in the agitation. In it the movement was established in the form in which it is generally remembered, and many of the characteristics and deficiencies which marked it in later years owed their origin to the decisions of this assembly.

The requisition for the conference expressed the conviction of the signatories of the necessity for the restoration of a domestic parliament. It further pledged them to the adoption of a federal arrangement. Some 18,000 signatures were obtained, but William Shaw as chairman of the conference stressed that the requisition had not been canvassed among the general public.[86] Twenty-five liberal or home rule M.P.'s held tickets for the conference and give to its programme a varying degree of loyalty.[87] Nearly fifty catholic priests and some ten protestant clergymen were also among the ticket-holders. The neutrality of the advanced men seems to have been secured, as in 1870, before the opening of the public proceedings. William O'Brien subsequently recalled being present upon the night before the conference at a private consultation on the subject between the leaders of the advanced party, who had come up from the country to deliberate whether there ought to be any truce with parliamentary agitation.

---

85 Butt to Daunt, 5 Nov., Dorian to Butt, 8 Oct. Duggan to Butt, 12 Nov., Butt MSS; *Nation*, 15 Nov.

86 *Proceedings of the Home Rule conference*, Dublin, 1874, pp. 69-70. The ensuing analysis is based partly upon the reports of the conference in the press, and partly upon this report, published by the Home Rule League, and hereafter referred to as *Conference Proceedings*.

87 The Members of parliament who held tickets were:—Butt, Bryan, Browne, Blennerhassett, Brady, Callan, Downing, D'Arcy, Dease, Digby, Delahunty, French, Gray, Henry, Martin, Murphy, O'Reilly, D. M. O'Conor, O'Conor Don, O'Brien, Redmond, Ronayne, Synan, Smyth and Shaw. H. Mathews signed the requisition but did not attend the conference (*Nation*, 27 Dec. 1873).

There can be no harm in saying now that the most influential men among them were Mr Joe Ronayne (the never-to-be-forgotten member for Cork); Mr C. G. Doran, of Queenstown; Mr Mat. Harris, of Ballinasloe; Mr O'Connor Power, and Mr John Walsh, of Middlesboro. I cannot at this moment recall whether Mr J. F. X. O'Brien was of the party on that particular occasion, although I am quite sure that he was one of the most determined that, within certain limits, Mr Butt's projects should have fair play . . . Mr Butt assented readily to the qualifications with which his movement was to have free fling, and when Mr O'Connor Power got up in Mr Butt's support the next day from the midst of the little group who represented the Extreme Left of the conference, a sigh of relief went through the ' cognoscenti ', who knew what a cloud hung over the birth of the movement.[88]

He does not, unfortunately, specify the nature of the 'qualifications', but in later years certain of the fenians who abandoned Butt insisted that he had been permitted to go ahead with the agitation only upon the guarantee that if unsuccessful after three years he would retire and make way for less constitutional methods.

There is no proof that this compact was ever made, but too many references to it survive for it to have been a complete fabrication. According to John Daly's recollections Butt was informed just before the conference that Barry of Manchester and other delegates from Northern England ' had a set of resolutions to propose which were so strong as to embarrass him or compel him to resign '. Butt and these men had a consultation:

' the result of which was that in order to buy them off, Butt entered into an agreement that they should withdraw their resolutions from the Convention, and he signed a paper pledging himself that if the English parliament did not grant him a Home Rule Bill inside of 3 years—that was by the year 1876— he would come back to Dublin and submit himself to the Fenian Party—Charles Doran, of the Cove of Cork, told me since

[88] O'Brien, Personal Reminiscences of Isaac Butt, in Butt MSS, vol. i, MS 830.

F

I came out of prison that he had that paper signed " Isaac
Butt ". Where it is, or what became of it, God knows '.[89]

It is hard to believe that so astute a lawyer as Butt would
have signed so unequivocal a pledge; perhaps he bound himself to place his policy before the decision of a second and
thoroughly popular national conference. At any rate the three-
year period does seem to have had some especial significance.
In 1876 Doran, Daly, Denis Dowling Mulcahy, and their followers, hitherto quiescent, began to break up and interrupt
home rule meetings, especially those of their former associate
O'Connor Power. Doran wrote to P. J. Smyth in January 1877
enclosing some document which 'could be used with advantage' soon against the home rulers.[90] Was this perhaps the
famous pledge? We may never know. But Ronayne in the conference said that the Irish people had reserved the right 'to
seek redress by other means' if home rule was not honestly
carried out by its leaders and fairly granted by England, and
Mitchel Henry told Alfred Webb that home rule would be
carried in three years or not at all.[91]

The great Rotunda conference of the home rule movement
lasted from 18 to 21 November 1873. Resolution after resolution saw the first principles of the movement stirringly affirmed, from the inalienable right of Ireland to the restoration of
her self-government, to the inalienable right of the Irish
House of Lords to be restored at the same time. But there
was one issue above all which, cutting across the patriotic
oratory, provoked genuine dissension, and, across the lapse of
time, most clearly reveals the internal weaknesses of the movement. Twenty-six members of parliament had given some
kind of support to the requisition by which the conference
had been called; only eight of these had been elected on the
home rule platform. The great majority were offspring of the
Gladstonian honeymoon of 1868. How much loyalty would
such precipitate converts be prepared to concede to home rule,
to Butt, and to each other?

---

89 *Irish Freedom*, April 1913.
90 Doran to Smyth, 24 Jan. 1877, Smyth MSS, 8215.
91 Webb to Henry, 6 Dec. 1873, Butt MSS, vol. iii, MS 832.

The first hint of the answer to this question was given at the conference, in the debates upon the fourth and ninth resolutions. The fourth, and in A. M. Sullivan's words the crucial resolution, defined the national demands in the federalist terms already stated by the Home Government Association. Major O'Reilly, liberal M.P. for Longford, replied with a plea for an avoidance of any rigid commitment on 'details'. The O'Conor Don, member for Roscommon, who had recently achieved the feat of speaking for two hours at a home rule meeting in Roscommon without telling his audience if he was a home ruler,[92] thought the resolution too precise:

> There are some of them, perhaps, drawn up in a form which if submitted to me for my individual signature for approval I could not be able to give it. But am I on that account to get up and raise dissension here? No, certainly not. I look beyond the mere form and terms that appear in the resolution. They will be forgotten in a very short time; but the principle that this great national conference met here today to affirm—the principle that some form of self-government for Ireland is demanded—that principle will remain . . . I am in favour of any scheme which will secure to my countrymen a more extended power over the laws which regulate their own affairs, any system that will secure that further control—consistently, of course, as we all here admit, with the preservation of law and order, the rights and security of property.

Sullivan at least was quick to perceive the dangers inherent in this attitude: —

> let no man in this hall think that it is permitted to him, after this resolution passes without his honest, outspoken, manly dissent, to think that he has reserved to himself, by any ambiguous speech, the right to go outside this meeting and take up a dubious attitude towards the national aim of the country.

Doubtful representatives should make way for those who would reflect popular feeling, said Ferguson more bluntly on behalf of the advanced party: 'The people's day had come, and they would find the people's men'. If some binding

[92] *Nation,* 18 Oct. 1873.

pledge had been exacted at this point, much later dissension might have been avoided. But there were enough liberals and repealers present to make such a step dangerously controversial; Martin found the O'Conor Don's explanation 'entirely satisfactory' and Smyth also opposed the imposition of a rigid pledge on federalism. Butt personally strongly deprecated the O'Conor Don's ambiguity, but after the entire day had been devoted to the issue the discussion was allowed to drop, and the resolution to pass without any official ruling upon its implied responsibilities.

A third session proving necessary, the chairman William Shaw reopened the conference the following morning with a request to the delegates to endeavour to conclude its business that day. The fifth resolution, which stressed the moderation of the home rule proposal, was moved by Sir Joseph McKenna, M.P., and seconded by McCarthy Downing, M.P., who took advantage of this opportunity to defend the attitude of the O'Conor Don on the previous day. At this point John Ferguson endeavoured to introduce a motion upon the subject of parliamentary action but was ruled out of order by Shaw, who admitted the importance of the issue, but urged that it be left to the new league. These were apparently Butt's wishes.[93] But after the passage of the 6th, 7th, and 8th resolutions, which called for responsible cabinet government, expressed the belief that a federal arrangement would strengthen the empire, and declared a willingness to incorporate guarantees against religious ascendancy into any such settlement, the issue arose four-square upon the ninth resolution, which was proposed by Doran and seconded by O'Connor Power:

> That this conference cannot separate without calling on the Irish constituencies at the next general election to return men earnestly and truly devoted to the great cause which this conference has been called on to promote, and who, in any emer-

93 According to the *Irishman* a resolution had been in contemplation binding the Irish members to withdraw from Parliament in the event of the refusal of Home Rule. (*Irishman*, 22 Nov 1873). Perhaps this was the one which Ferguson sought to introduce or possibly it was one of those withdrawn by the advanced men in response to Butt's pleading.

gency that may arise, will be ready to take counsel with a great National Conference to be called in such a manner as to represent the opinions and feelings of the Irish nation, and that with a view to rendering members of parliament and their constituencies more in accord on all questions affecting the welfare of their country, it is recommended by this conference that at the close of each session of parliament the representatives should render to their constituents an account of their stewardship.

O'Connor Power, in seconding this resolution, admitted that it might not go far enough to satisfy everyone in binding the members of parliament; nor did it. Michael Cahill of the Queen's County Independent Club proposed, and Joseph Biggar seconded, an amendment:

That, to render the Irish vote effective, we recommend that the Irish members shall form themselves into a permanent committee for the discussion of every ministerial and other proposal which affects the interests of Ireland, that no individual shall introduce any bill, or give notice of any motion of importance, unless his proceeding shall be sanctioned and supported by such committee; and finally, that the Irish members shall always vote in a body, or abstain from voting on all party questions, as the majority may decide.

At this point the hour of 5.30 p.m. was reached, and the conference adjourned. A fourth and final day would be needed to debate this crucial issue.

At 11.30 a.m. on Friday, 21 November, the conference reassembled and Cahill rose to propose his amendment, which he said would merely involve the adoption of the majority rule already followed in the English parties. But it was Biggar who stated the case for the amendment most strongly:

the most important part of the business of the Conference had now been reached . . . he considered the amendment preferable to the resolution. The only objection he had to it was that it did not go far enough, and that there should have been a clause introduced calling upon candidates for parliamentary honours to give written pledges . . . It recommended organised action on the part of the home rule members, and if there was that organisation they could carry whatever they pleased in the British house of commons. It also recommended voting and abstaining from voting on party divisions. What did they care about whig or tory, or whether Gladstone or Disraeli was in power if they could only get accomplished the object they had in view for the benefit of the country? One great objection raised at the conference was that the land question and the education question were not to be brought before them. These things had been kept very fairly in the background. Their one great object was to gain home rule for Ireland, and the only way to get home rule from the English Parliament was for the Irish members to keep compactly and honestly together.

This attitude was completely opposed to Butt's method of seeking interim concessions, in addition to his view of the individual freedom necessary for members of parliament. Even John Ferguson preferred the original resolution as 'more in accord with the spirit of their leaders—Messrs Butt, Martin, and others'. King Harman attacked the amendment even more vigorously, denouncing it in terms intended to be satirical but, in fact, ironically prophetic of Parnellite discipline:

Let them give their members but one pledge; that pledge should be Home Rule, and nothing but Home Rule. Let them vote freely and in accordance with their conscience on every question, but let the constituents see before they send them in that their common sense and conscience point to Home Rule. If they bind their members more he would say—'Establish a fund; pay your representatives and dismiss them after a week's warning as you would any other servant ' . . .

The point that Butt's pledge bound a member only to vote for an annual home rule motion and otherwise to act exactly as he pleased no doubt occurred to Biggar; he got little opportunity to raise it. One after another the sitting members ridiculed the amendment. Martin would not enter parliament under such a pledge; Synan thought the 1852 pledge 'was intended as a substitute for character and produced the perjury'; he also considered the pledge of a conference in the original resolution absurd. To Downing, the amendment was 'perfectly monstrous'; send men of strength and character to parliament, said Gray, and all will be well.

But the decisive intervention was that of Butt, who in a long and vigorous speech 'strongly opposed' the amendment. As this was, in effect, the first statement of the parliamentary policy which he was to follow in the next five years, it merits some detailed consideration. He supported the resolution on the assumption that it simply meant 'that when any great emergency arose the men elected should be willing to take counsel with a conference like this of the Irish nation'. The time was not ripe to 'lay down by hard and fast lines any plan to which they should expect the representatives in the house of commons to adhere'. If independent opposition meant:

> a system of indiscriminate voting against every ministry upon every occasion that could turn them out . . . then that policy was one which he could not adopt, and if he were asked to pledge himself to vote on every occasion against every ministry which did not make home rule a cabinet question, he would not accept a seat in parliament on condition of accepting such a pledge. To bind himself to such a pledge would destroy every particle of moral influence which any action of his would have in the house of commons . . .

So the vision of 'moral influence' at Westminster was first revealed. Butt made quite clear his reverence for the institution of parliament:

> Extreme cases might justify a policy of obstruction. If they ever did, the obstruction would probably be carried on in other and more decisive ways than that of voting on all mere party questions with the opposition. But if such a policy were adopted and avowed as the ordinary purpose and policy of any party in the House of Commons it would fail. The truth was, it was opposed to all free parliamentary action. If eighty men by such means could carry home rule, eighty men could carry the Permissive Bill or the Inspection of Nunneries, or any other measure which they would conspire to force upon parliament in the same way.

Mr Cahill asked him, by the amendment, to surrender his convictions and his judgment into the hands of a number of

men who were not yet elected, of whom he knew nothing . . .
He believed that he would betray his own principles, his dignity, his personal honour and personal honesty, if he now gave
a pledge that he would submit his future conduct to the absolute control of any tribunal on earth, except his own conscience, and that higher tribunal, his responsibility to God.
However desirable it might be that the members should act
together, however valuable it might be to lay down a distinct
and plain line of conduct, from which no one could deviate
without dishonour, he thought they would find every high-
minded man would shrink from pledging himself to act in
accordance with the decision of a majority, no matter what that
decision might be.

What Butt did concede, in a passage which was remembered against him in later years, was that it might be wise 'to
lay down a rule that henceforth they would have no political
intercourse with ministers or ministerial officials except across
the table of the house of commons'. But a pledge such as
Cahill's would 'put up the Irish representation to a sort of
competition by auction, in which the hardest swearer will be
the highest bidder . . .

Were he himself as an elector to choose a man to represent a
constituency of which he was a member, he would prefer a
thousand times the honest and manly hesitation of the O'Con
or Don to the strongest pledge ever swallowed, and yet to be
swallowed by many a political trafficker who would seek to dis-
place him.

Cahill's amendment was withdrawn and Doran's resolution
passed unanimously, and the shade of Burke no doubt applauded, perhaps for the last time in British parliamentary history.
In the story of home rule, the importance of this debate can
scarcely be over-estimated. It is clear that the great majority of
those at the conference were not ready to accept a firm pledge,
and consequently the defeat of the proposal can scarcely be regarded as a decisive event in the home rule movement. But
the exhibition which it provoked of the parliamentary policy
envisaged by the movement's leaders was in a sense a turning-
point in its history. Many of the catastrophes which followed

originated in the fatal weakness which it revealed. Already, in 1873, the implacable realism of Biggar stood in stark contrast to the gentlemanly deportment of the parliamentary leaders.

The conference reassembled for the last time in the afternoon. All the resolutions on policy had now been passed, and in quick succession the conference passed a second series dealing with organisation. On the motion of George Bryan, M.P., seconded by Callan, a new association was set up, to be known as the 'Irish Home Rule League', and to have as its aims the resolutions of the conference. A special fund, in addition to the regular income of the league from subscriptions, was established to promote the organisation in Great Britain and Ireland. It was also resolved that an appeal should be made to Irishmen all over the world; this resolution was proposed by O'Connor Power, who looked forward especially to the despatching of home rule deputations to America. The thirteenth resolution fixed the annual subscription of the association at £1, but recommended that 'steps should also be taken to enrol the great mass of the people in the league'. The membership of the league was to consist in the first place of all members of the old association together with such of those present and those who had signed the requisition for the conference who might pay their subscriptions before 1 December, after which date admission to membership was to be regulated by the rules of the league, to be drawn up by a committee of sixteen which was then appointed, and to be submitted to a meeting of the league on 2 December which would also elect the first officers. A vote of thanks to Shaw as chairman was then passed, and the conference was closed by Butt and Martin.

The conference had had all the external signs of success. The *Irishman* commended it warmly; the *Irish Times* admitted its representative character and the 'dignity, moderation, and . . . rare ability' with which its principles had been expressed. The *Dublin Evening Post* welcomed the abandonment of the old body:

> eclectic in party colour, mixed in creed, varied in race, and holding but one article of faith or union—namely, home rule

F*

. . . we have no doubt that the catholic episcopacy and clergy, the liberal gentry, and the masses of the people, will now look, without apprehension, on the future, whether they formally join the new league or not.[94]

But this same liberalisation of the movement which gave so much pleasure to the *Post* was equally obvious to the conservatives. The *Mail* commended Butt for having kept the clerical programme in the background. But it professed to have no illusions over the sincerity of the liberal members of parliament: 'There will be a large demand for Federal rhetoric on the hustings in 1874, and it will not fail of its effect—in returning Liberal Members to Parliament'. The *Daily Express* wrote of the new converts: —

They have not the least intention of going into opposition unless Mr Gladstone alters his policy, and Mr Butt is far too wise to ask them to do so. On a direct vote for home rule most of them would walk into the same lobby with Mr Butt, and the rest would absent themselves; but with this act, and possibly a tiresome speech, their advocacy of federalism will begin and end.[95]

The league, however, faced still more immediate problems. So far, its organisation existed only on paper. Johnston Russell, an active Limerick home ruler and tenant right agitator, summed up the situation concisely in a letter to Butt:

The Home Rule Association which I think you yourself describe as 'a private Association of Gentlemen', has been changed into 'a League of the People', as far as merely passing a resolution at the Conference could effect the change.

But how, he asks, is this to be done in practice, by separate branches or by a monolithic organisation. He suggests the branch officers should be ex-officio members of the Dublin Council; he further objects to the old rule of the association which made one member who paid a pound equal to twenty associates who paid a shilling each; if the subscription is kept

---

[94] *Irishman*, 22, 29 Nov., *Irish Times*, 22 Nov., *Dublin Evening Post*, 21 Nov.
[95] *Dublin Evening post*, 22 Nov., *Daily Express*, 19 Nov.

at a pound the league will remain a private body like the association:

> Which would be best for Home Rule, 10,000 leaguers at £1 each, or 200,000 at 1s each . . . *unless we have 200,000 Leaguers Home Rule will never be obtained,* and unless the subscription is small we shall not get the people to join it.[96]

The committee which was appointed by the fifteenth resolution of the conference to draw up rules and by-laws for the new organisation did nothing to meet these representations[97] The laws which it adopted deserve some attention, as they were to be of some importance in less fraternal times. The annual subscription was fixed at one pound, although members might give more. No person could be proposed for membership at a meeting of the league until after his name had been approved by the council and his subscription paid. Members could be expelled from the league on the recommendation of the council.

The council was to consist of fifty members elected by postal ballot in January each year, together with fifty more elected at the first meeting of the council in February. In addition to this total of one hundred members, the council might co-opt any peer or member of parliament who was a member of the league. The council elected the executive committee of twenty-one, but the honorary secretaries and the treasurer were to be appointed by the annual general meeting of the league. The council was empowered to make its own rules, fix its own quorum, and to appoint all committees and paid officials.

The council was to meet once in every month, or the executive might call a meeting of it at three days' notice. In between council meetings, the management of the league was vested in the executive, which could incur expenses on behalf of the league, but which had to submit its expenditure to the approval of the council. All acts of both bodies were subject to the ultimate control of the league as a whole, which was

[96] Russell to Butt, 1 Dec. 1873, Butt MSS.
[97] A report on the foundation of the League is bound into *Conference proceedings.*

also to meet once in every month, and which was to hold its annual general meeting on the first Tuesday in February. Its meetings were to be open only to members; the press might be admitted or excluded according to the wish of the meeting. A league meeting could also be convened at any time upon three days' notice in the Dublin dailies. No motion, if objected to, could be moved unless notice had been given at the previous meeting, and the laws of the league could be altered only at monthly meetings on notice given at the previous meeting.

From the recital of these rules and regulations a number of salient points emerge. The league had plumped for the single, monolithic method of organisation; the local branches continued and might increase, and even enjoy representative status at national conferences such as that envisaged in the ninth resolution of the Rotunda conference, but they enjoyed no representation in the league. The league consisted of a body of people who were able to pay a subscription of at least one pound a year, and its monthly management furthermore devolved upon those who were able to attend in Dublin. The provision for the addition of fifty members of the council to those elected by ballot ensured total supremacy for the party elected to even the barest authority. Divisions such as these lay in the future, but it was questionable whether the league at any time represented a sufficient step away from the old association and towards a national movement.

In December 1873 the association held its last meeting and was formally wound up. Immediately after the conference Daunt retired to his beloved Kilcascan, and no inducements being able to prevail upon him to return to Dublin, the new organisation found itself at the outset without a secretary. For a time the council debated the merits of twenty applicants for the position, but in January 1874 Butt wrote to Henry: 'You have heard I suppose that John Martin has expressed a wish for the secretaryship. All here are agreed we must take him . . .'[98] The choice thus made was probably not the best; Mar-

[98] Webb to Henry, 19 Dec. Fottrell to Henry, 29 Dec. Butt to Henry, 13 Jan. 1874, Butt MSS, vol. iii, MS 832.

tin was neither a young man nor in good health, and his parliamentary duties interfered with his organisational work for the league. With characteristic scrupulousness he refused to accept more than two-thirds of the appointed salary in 1874, and at the beginning of 1875 resigned the office altogether.[99] But the most pressing need was for a thorough organisation of the country. 'We must lose no time in looking at the constituencies', wrote Shaw to Henry; 'I suppose a General Election is certain next year'. Henry foresaw an election in May, and urged Butt to hurry on his plans for widening the basis of the league.[100] Following on the generally-held expectation that the dissolution would take place in the summer, Butt produced an elaborate plan of campaign which was circulated among the leading parliamentary representatives of the movement in December 1873. The conference, he wrote, had achieved a tremendous amount;

> But it has done little in the way either of placing funds at our disposal or adding to our numerical strength. These things can only be done by attracting public attention to our proceedings and keeping that attention fixed.

To do this would require constant public meetings and efficient staff and organisation:

> We may take two dates as landmarks—the first meeting of the league is fixed for the 13th of January: Its annual meeting for the third of February. Before the 13th January the council will have commenced weekly meetings on each Friday . . . On the 13th I have undertaken to propose the enrollment (sic) of all home rulers on a National Roll—each paying a shilling for enrollment . . . I entertain the most confident expectation that this will, if properly and vigorously managed, give us in a very short time 100,000 men and £5,000 . . . no pains ought to be spared . . . It ought to emanate from a very influential meeting, at which men of rank and station should sign the roll and pay down their shilling. After this the plan could be managed from the office in Dublin . . .

99 Martin to Daunt, 21 Feb. 1875, Daunt MSS, 8047.
100 Shaw to Henry, 20 Dec., Butt MSS, vol. iii MS 832. Henry to Butt, 12 Jan. 1874, Butt MSS.

Side by side with this plan, Butt held that a programme of parliamentary activity would be necessary to maintain the morale of the country. He suggested that the home rule members should sponsor a list of measures which included bills to restore to Ireland, possibly in Kingstown and Queenstown, the two seats lost in the disfranchisement of Cashel and Sligo, to assimilate the borough and municipal franchises of Ireland to those of England, to give Irish municipal corporations the privileges of their English counterparts, to establish representative county councils to undertake the fiscal responsibilities of the grand juries, to establish a fishery board on the Scottish model, 'to secure the Ulster Tenant Right and generally to amend the Land Act', and finally 'Mr Smyth's bill' to repeal the convention act. The land question he regarded as the most important; the Ulster tenant right proposal he hoped would have the effect of winning the support of the Ulster tenant associations which were due to meet in conference in the near future. It was also, he believed, essential that a motion should be brought in early in the session condemning the whole system of Irish government. 'There is also the risk of the session coming abruptly to an end. I do not anticipate this, but we ought to secure such a discussion before the dissolution'. To effect this, he proposed a meeting of home rule members on 3 February 1874.[101]

This was, on the face of it, bold and comprehensive planning. But meanwhile, three letters written to Mitchel Henry between December 1873 and January 1874 by Alfred Webb, treasurer of the new body as he had been of the old, painted a most gloomy picture of the actual position of the league:

(6 December 1873) Subscriptions are coming in *miserably*. We have only about £130 for league and £520 special fund—besides £160 to be paid over by the old association. Our liabilities are about £350—chiefly advertising. I made out a list of our liabilities today. I have been deterred from advertising our subscription list for very shame on account of its small amount. (19 December 1873). If you are rather in despair about our prospects; I am about completely in despair. (Bear in mind,

101 Dec. 1873, Butt MSS, vol. i, MS 830 (2 copies).

however, that I generally look at the black side of things). On the trust fund, we have £753 in bank. On the league funds, we are, counting all our engagements, about £400 in debt. The funds are coming in miserably; and unless there is some turn in things in the course of a fortnight, I will insist upon our not going further into debt . . . We are sending out circulars to people asking them to join and subscribe, but the responses are wretched.

As to branch and local associations, I don't see how the league can galvanise the country into action unless there is some spontaneity throughout the country. I hoped that the conference would have roused the country to some spontaneity of effort. I see none of it.

(1 January 1874). Mr Butt is building the most brilliant castles in the air—I do trust they are not castles in the air—but I fear they are . . .[102]

Even allowing for a recurrent streak of pessimism in Webb's character, one point emerges beyond all doubt: a new national organisation for home rule had indeed been founded, but at the beginning of 1874 it existed only on paper, and the practical state of the movement throughout the country was still as it had been under the old Home Government Association. Butt was enthusiastic about his plan of a 'National Roll'; perhaps in time it might have given the movement the popular support it had always as yet lacked. But no such opportunity was to be granted to home rule. Scarcely had the league been founded, when in the midst of the confusion which surrounded its birth, it was immediately called upon to face the challenge for which it was only then planning to prepare itself. On 24 January 1874 Gladstone announced that parliament was to be dissolved at once and a general election held in less than three week's time. So the six years of Liberal promise came to an abrupt and discreditable end. For home rule they had been good years, years of preparation and of mounting hope. The years that followed upon them were to bring only disillusionment and anticlimax.

[102] Butt MSS, vol. iii, MS 832.

CHAPTER V

The General Election of 1874

A: THE CONTEST

IN TRADITIONAL histories, 1874 is the year in which home rule routs liberalism once for all upon the Irish hustings. In any comparison with the election of 1868 the most striking change is certainly the return of constitutional nationalism to the centre of the political stage. 1874 saw the first of a series of historic Irish contests of which home rule was the theme; of the election addresses published in 1874 by candidates other than conservatives, no less than ninety per cent made reference to home rule, and some sixty per cent gave it pride of place. Denominational education, the only issue from the programme to 1868 to survive unchanged, held the next place in the majority of popular addresses, with amnesty and land reform not far behind. Among the peripheral issues, pride of place went to the reform of the grand jury system and the defence of the papal states.

But the primacy of home rule as an issue by no means guaranteed the success of the movement as a political party. The dissolution came only two months after the conclusion of the conference; it gave the Home Rule League, which still existed largely on paper, less than three weeks in which at least eighty candidates were to be found if its earlier hopes for the election were to be realised. The importance of this one fact can scarcely be exaggerated. More than from any other single cause, the futility of the first home rule party stemmed from the haste and disorganisation of those three hectic weeks, in which the proponents of home rule were compelled to scramble together as their representatives a job lot in which the genuine was scarcely to be distinguished from the opportunist. In a rallying address, published by the league, Butt warned the

176

constituencies: 'the work of years is compressed for you into the next two weeks'.[1] He was in his sixty-first year, and he was only too unhappily right.

In appraising the traditional picture of a home rule landslide it will, then, be necessary, at the end of this chapter, to examine the credentials of the victors. For the moment it may be remarked that only a fraction of the 'home rule' candidates in this election had been previously tested as members of the league. The candidates can be divided into four categories: members of the outgoing parliament who had been elected as home rulers or had given the movement longstanding support; new men of proven loyalty in the association or the league; outgoing members of parliament, elected as liberals in 1868 and but recent converts to home rule; and, finally, newcomers of more or less obscure antecedents. There were, in general, very few who cannot be classified in one of these categories. Conservative home rule candidates were virtually unknown. P. Hynes in King's County and General Francis Plunkett Dunne in Queen's County might be thus broadly described; neither pressed the contest to the poll. In Tralee Johnston Russell, a loyal home ruler of conservative background, was unable to win the confidence of the popular party and retired in favour of the liberal home ruler John Daly, ex-mayor of Cork. In Westmeath the former Conservative member Lord Robert Montagu, as a catholic, was in no sense representative of the early conservatism of the movement. Of those who had carried the conservative home rule banner in the struggles of the old association, only John Madden stood again in Monaghan; he was again defeated, a defeat which he ascribed to the disunity of the catholic voters, the bulk of whom seem to have favoured the catholic liberal home ruler P. McMahon.[2] King Harman, the most prominent conservative among the founder members of the association, protested in vain to Butt at the influx of 'whig trimmers'; his

---

[1] *Nation*, 31 Jan. 1874.
[2] Madden to Butt, 6 Mar. 1874, Butt MSS.

own name was put forward in several constituencies but in each case he had to give way to rivals of a more liberal complexion.[3]

The vital conflict which faced home rule in 1874 was, then, with the entrenched battalions of Irish liberalism. But it was neither as frontal in its character nor as one-sided in its outcome as might at first appear. The resistance of liberalism to home rule expressed itself upon two different levels, in the open opposition of unionist liberal candidates to home rule nominees, and in the endorsement of liberal home rulers over nationalist candidates of a more singleminded variety. The latter was by far the more common and the more important; it was here, moreover, that the influence of the catholic clergy most made itself felt. Nowhere in 1874 was the participation of the clergy as striking a feature of political activity as it had been in 1868. But if catholic priests were seldom found in direct opposition to the movement which so many of them had once viewed with disquiet—if, indeed, they were much more frequently in sympathetic association with home rule candidates—it would nevertheless be wrong to dismiss their contribution as uninfluential. In participating in the campaign for home rule they made a significant contribution to the form in which it developed.

It is a striking testimony to the power of the home rule demand that only rarely were liberal candidates found in firm and open opposition to it. Of the thirty-eight sitting liberal members of parliament who sought re-election, only twelve did so without some kind of general endorsement of the programme of the home rule conference, and of this twelve, only Jonathan Pim in Dublin and the O'Donoghue in Tralee made their opposition to the programme of the league unmistake-

---

[3] *Nation,* 13 Jan. 1877. Bowyer (Wexford Co.) and Morris (Galway City) had both flirted with Disraeli in the 1860's and in the liberal climate of the 1868 contest had been denounced as conservatives, but as catholics and supporters of denominational education they can scarcely be classed as conservatives in the sense applied above to some of the founders of the Home Government Association.

able.[4] All of them, even chief secretary Chichester Fortescue in Louth, gratefully adopted the formula of Gladstone in his address to the electors of Greenwich and pronounced portentously in favour of the establishment of local boards to relieve, in some unspecified way, the pressure of business in the imperial assembly. Only five sitting liberals withdrew rather than gamble with home rule opinion; one of them, John Bagwell, wrote bitterly of the conduct of his less fastidious colleagues: 'it is plain that nothing can be expected from Irish gentlemen who are ready to take that pledge or any other'.[5]

Coming, as it did, little over five years after Gladstone's proclamation to Ireland of the unionist millennium, the total rout of liberal unionism as a marketable political philosophy is undoubtedly the most immediately striking feature of the 1874 election, and incomparably the most remarkable achievement of Butt's home rule movement. In 1874 home rule destroyed liberal unionism as a political force in Ireland, and ensured that the Irish electorate would never again accept anything less than some form of nationalist party to represent it at Westminster. Some of the first conflicts between home rule and liberalism stand out as particularly noteworthy. The defeat of Agar Ellis in Kilkenny County, where his family was universally respected, was especially acclaimed by the nationalist press.[6] The defeat of the sitting member, Pim, in Dublin City by the Lord Mayor Maurice Brooks was also a signal triumph for the movement, since Brooks himself, a protestant who in spite of his public statements was alleged by some of the liberals to be a member of an Orange lodge and a freemason, was unable to command the unanimous support

---

4 Cogan and Fitzgerald (Kildare), O'Reilly Dease (Louth), Agar Ellis (Kilkenny Co.), Fitzwilliam (Wicklow), Fortescue (Louth), Greville (Westmeath), Herbert (Kerry) O'Donoghue (Tralee), Pim (Dublin City), Power (Wexford Co.) and McClure (Belfast). McClure, endeavouring to retain his seat in the face of a conservative revival in Belfast, may fairly be excluded from this analysis. (*Nation*, 31 Jan. 1874, *Irishman*, 31 Jan., *Freeman's Journal*, 28, 30 Jan., 2, 4, and 9 Feb.

5 Bagwell, to Fortescue, 21 Feb., Strachie MSS, Carlingford Political.

6 *Irishman*, 14 Feb. 1874.

of the clergy of Dublin diocese.[7] But by far the most striking of these direct home rule victories was that which took place in Louth, for in Louth alone, where the sitting liberal members, Chichester Fortescue and Matthew O'Reilly Dease, were opposed by Philip Callan and A. M. Sullivan, was the full force of episcopal condemnation turned upon the home rule candidates as it had been in the first contests of the movement. At the very outset of the campaign, the County Louth Independent Club had been formed, to campaign for home rule 'as laid down by the national home rule conference', denominational education 'as demanded by the catholic bishops of Ireland', and fixity of tenure. At the same time the clergy of the diocese met and resolved not to support any candidate in any constituency in their area who would not bind himself to the home rule programme.[8] Fortescue's pledge to work for 'the improvement and strengthening of local administration, and to the provision of greater facilities for the despatch of overgrown Parliamentary business',[9] scarcely passed muster, but he was the very symbol of Gladstone's Irish policy. The aid of Cardinal Manning was enlisted, and both he and Cullen wrote to the primate, Dr McGettigan, urging him to exert all his influence upon Fortescue's behalf. William Monsell, still, as Lord Emly, assiduously lobbying for the liberals, heard of these preparations from P. J. Keenan, the Irish commissioner for education:

> The primate *will* write and this day too. *The letter* of course. Mr. F. should get it posted on every gate and wall in the country. I had a long letter from his grace today. He arrives in Dundalk, as I suggested, to do duty as sentinel and oracle pending the contest—He says that even in Dundalk Callan is sure to be defeated, a certain forerunner of defeat in the county. Fiat, he adds, and a second time, Fiat.[10]

---

7 Woodlock Diary, 15 Feb., MSS 4498-5011. *Freeman's Journal*, 6 Feb., etc.

8 *Nation*, 31 Jan. *Freeman's Journal*, 10 Feb.

9 *Irishman*, 31 Jan.

10 P. J. Keenan to Lord Emly, 2 Feb., Monsell MSS, 8317.

Ten to one might be laid on Fortescue, added Keenan, and the same on Charles Russell in Dundalk.

Fortescue, as a practising politician, knew the form better; even before the poll was taken he was canvassing Gladstone for a peerage.[11] Dr McGettigan's letter was not even read in all the chapels of the diocese; in those in which it was read, the congregation, according to the *Nation*, rose and left.[12] The clergy met in Dundalk on 8 February; the primate repeated his arguments for Fortescue, but the assembled priests resolved to adhere to their original resolution. Four priests accompanied Fortescue on his canvass of Dundalk, but the great majority in the diocese adhered to Callan and Sullivan in the county, Callan in Dundalk, and O'Leary in Drogheda. Callan subsequently claimed fifty out of fifty-five priests for home rule. In direct opposition to their bishop the priests of the diocese accompanied home rule candidates on their canvass and introduced them at after-mass meetings. In all three constituencies home rule was victorious. In Dundalk Callan defeated Charles Russell, later Lord Russell of Killowen; in Drogheda Dr O'Leary won a victory over the wealthy merchant Benjamin Whitworth which surprised even his own supporters; and Callan and Sullivan left Fortescue and Dease ignominiously defeated in the county.[13]

The Louth contest was in many respects the most remarkable in the entire election. Not only was Gladstone's chief minister in Ireland symbolically routed; the church, making its only frontal onslaught upon home rule, was repudiated even by its own parish clergy. The movement had indeed come far since 1870.

From what has been said above it is obvious that clerical influence held no such commanding position in 1874 as in 1868. But if it exerted a less direct and monolithic pressure upon national policies, it did nevertheless significantly in-

11 Gladstone to Fortescue, 11 Feb., Strachie MSS, Carlingford Political.

12 *Nation*, 14 Feb.

13 *Freeman's Journal*, 9, 14, 20 Feb. *Drogheda Argus*, 30 Jan., 7 Feb. *Nation*, 14 Feb., The figures were: Sullivan 1,250, Callan. 1.202. Fortescue 607, Dease 265.

fluence the course of a number of important contests. Throughout southern Ireland in this election the priests as a rule
either held themselves aloof from the struggle or exerted their
influence on behalf of those liberal home rulers who were
most loyal to the Church's educational policy. It was here that
the clergy made their most important contribution; there
were candidates like Shaw, Henry, and Butt himself, who
could sincerely combine the advocacy of other reforms with
that of home rule, but enthusiasm for denominational education was in 1874 all too often the subterfuge of the liberal,
eager to divert the attention of his constituents from any
analysis of his pledges in relation to home rule. In such a contest, clerical sympathy generally went with the liberal in possession rather than with an invading nationalist. In Ennis, for
example, the sitting member, William Stacpoole, was a typical example of the 1868 liberal, seeking re-election on the
basis of a last-minute espousal of home rule; he had not even
attended the conference in the previous November. Both the
Nation and the *Irishman* were united for once in suspicion of
his motives; the latter ridiculed the home rule utterances of a
member who had voted for coercion. The eccentric Donal C.
O'Brien first took the field against him, but a stronger candidate being found necessary, the league for once decided to
intervene directly, and upon the motion of Martin and Galbraith the council requested the veteran O'Gorman Mahon
to undertake the advocacy of home rule. The clergy, however, remained faithful to Stacpoole; he was accompanied on
canvass by the Reverend R. Fitzgerald, C.C., and in the nomination, at which Mahon was proposed by the local home
rulers, Stacpoole was nominated by the Very Reverend Thomas
John MacRedmond, D.D., president of Killaloe diocesan college.[14] At the poll the sitting member was returned.

There were several similar cases of clerical partiality for
sitting liberals of dubious nationalist zeal. In county Clare the
contest was conducted upon a peculiar three-cornered basis.
The sitting members were the liberal Sir Colman O'Loghlen,
who had not attended the conference in November but who

---

[14] *Nation,* 31 Jan. *Irishman,* 31 Jan., 7 Feb., *Clare Journal,* 2 Feb.

now resurrected the nationalist principles of his youth for the benefit of a new generation, and the conservative C. M. Vandaleur, who had voted for disestablishment. The third candidate was Lord Francis Conyngham, second son of the Marquess of Conyngham, one of the largest landowners in Ireland; Conyngham was an active home ruler who enjoyed the full confidence of the league. The three candidates were at great pains from the outset to make clear their total dissociation from each other. The clergy worked and spoke from the pulpit for O'Loghlen, who had also the enthusiastic support of the *Freeman's Journal;* the bishop was reported as favouring Vandaleur as his colleague; the home rulers worked for Conyngham and distrusted O'Loghlen. But the liberal conservatism of Vandaleur was an anachronism in the 1870's; Conyngham was adopted by the farmers' clubs and at the nomination was proposed by the redoubtable Father Quaid. At the last minute priests, liberals, and home rulers united to return their respective candidates.[15]

In the single-seat constituency of Athlone, traditionally the carpetbagger's prey, no such compromise was possible. The sitting liberal, J. J. Ennis, had formerly enjoyed the confidence of the clergy, but as an unashamed camp-follower of Gladstone he was repudiated by the nationalists. Several candidates entered the field against him, including the persistent D. J. Reardon, former member for the borough, Edward Sheil, son of General Sir Justin Sheil and nephew of Richard Lalor Sheil, and E. R. King Harman. The *Nation* and the *Irishman* both supported Harman against Sheil, but the clergy retained their old distrust of King Harman; a clerical meeting under the chairmanship of Dr Gillooly, bishop of Elphin, endorsed Sheil, who was returned.[16]

In Mayo the sitting home rule member, George Ekins Browne, who held George Henry Moore's old seat, was secure, but the contest for the second seat produced a direct if impermanent clerical victory. Here John O'Connor Power, a lecturer in St Jarlath's College, Tuam, who had made a

---

[15] *Clare Journal,* 25 Feb.; *Freeman's Journal,* 27 Jan., 2, 5, 9, Feb.; *Irishman,* 7 Feb.; *Nation,* 21 Feb.

[16] By the lowest possible margin, one vote, after a disputed result.

marked impression at the home rule conference entered the field with the backing of the *Irishman*, letters of support from Martin and Henry, and claiming the personal approval of Butt himself. The clergy, however, distrusted Power; even the fiercely nationalist Father Lavelle could not be charitable in his regard.[17] A meeting of the clergy of Tuam, Killala, and Achonry, presided over by Dr MacHale himself, appears to have ignored Power's claims; Thomas Tighe, a young catholic landowner, was invited to stand as Browne's colleague. Power withdrew in deference to the wishes of the clergy, but his supporters, and the advanced party in the home rule movement, bitterly resented the slight upon their most fluent spokesman, and Tighe's election being invalidated upon a technicality, they were able in the subsequent by-election to reverse the result.[18]

In King's County, on the other hand, the coalition of clergy and liberals was overpowering. Here the two sitting members were blatant examples of the liberal timeserver. Sir Patrick O'Brien had attended the conference, and joined the league in January 1874, endorsing its programme before the electorate;[19] David Sherlock condescended merely to incorporate a vague endorsement of the home rule demand in his election address.[20] At the outset of the campaign the *Nation* demanded the replacement of Sherlock at the very least; neither candidate, it held, was worthy in ideal circumstances to be a nation-

17 ' My Dear Mr Butt ', he wrote; ' You may have often heard the question put—" Who is this Mr O'Connor Power "? I often did but never could get an answer. I am, however, now in a position to tell you that he is the bastard son of a policeman named Fleming from Co. Cavan, and a house painter by trade, who has managed to live on his wits and the gullibility of others and myself for years—! ! ! ' (Lavelle to Butt, 12 Mar. 1874, Butt MSS).

18 *Freeman's Journal*, 6 Feb., *Irishman*, 7 Feb., *Nation*, 14 Feb.; John Ferguson to Butt, 21 Feb., Butt MSS.

19 *Nation*, 31 Jan.; *Irishman*, 31 Jan.

20 ' It is obvious that the House of Commons cannot satisfactorily dispose of the accumulated business of the United Kingdom, and, being convinced that the people of Ireland are competent to manage their own affairs, and feeling that a large and influential portion of my constituents desire a domestic government, I am prepared to vote for " Home Rule " in Ireland '. *(Nation, 31 Jan.)*

al representative.[21] Bernard C. Molloy, a former papal soldier whose membership of the league had the merit of some antiquity, was the candidate most favoured by the home rule organisation. But the *Freeman's Journal* was wholeheartedly in favour of the sitting members. Sherlock canvassed Banagher with two of the local clergy; the parish priest and curates of Parsonstown conducted him through their town; he was similarly escorted in Tullamore, where he addressed the electors from the chapel yard. Molloy reminded them of his opponents' inconsistency on the principal issue of the hour, but on the last Sunday before the poll the clergy throughout the whole county called upon the people to vote for O'Brien and Sherlock. The two liberal home rulers were elected.[22]

Kildare was the scene of a very similar division. The sitting members, the Right Honourable W. H. F. Cogan and Lord Otho Fitzgerald, were dismissed as whigs by the *Nation* from the outset.[23] A county meeting called by the local tenants' defence association adopted C. H. Meldon, a Dublin barrister and a small landlord, and Captain H. F. Morgan as the home rule candidates. Cogan was refused a hearing. In the days which followed Meldon seems to have won considerable liberal support, including that of the farmers and of the *Freeman's Journal*. A clerical meeting presided over by the Reverend Dr Kehoe, P.P., adopted Meldon and Fitzgerald as candidates, the latter on the ground that he was a popular landlord. As for Captain Morgan, said Dr Kehoe, he agreed with Father Nolan, another cleric present, who had remarked that he was not the worse for being a protestant, but he thought that:

> A great Irish catholic constituency might get a better candidate than an English protestant soldier, and at this crisis it was of special importance that catholics should be sent to parliament to watch the interests of catholic education.

At the poll Cogan was returned with Meldon.[24]

21 ibid., and 7 Feb.
22 *Freeman's Journal*, 4, 10 Feb., *Nation*, 31 Jan., 7 Feb., *Irishman*, 7 Feb.
23 *Nation*, 31 Jan.
24 *Freeman's Journal*, 30 Jan., 2 Feb.; *Nation*, 7 Feb.

A sufficient number of cases have been cited to allow the deduction that in those instances, and they were quite frequent, in which a liberal candidate who endorsed home rule was opposed by a nationalist of the new order, the *Freeman* and the clergy were generally willing to accept as adequate the pronouncements of the liberal, the *Nation* and the home rule organisation quicker to question his sincerity. In Waterford County Sir John Esmonde declared himself in favour of 'any well-defined system which shall (without endangering the integrity of the empire) transfer to Irishmen the management of purely Irish affairs'. The *Nation* called for his rejection as a 'pure and simple ministerialist'; but the *Freeman* thought his reservation might be regarded as 'supererogatory', and urged his re-election. Not even their aversion to the liberal, however, could enable the home rulers to swallow his only rival, Pearson Longbottom, an English carpetbagger of dubious origin and wonderfully comprehensive principles, and Esmonde was re-elected *faute de mieux*.[25] In Tipperary the sitting liberal, Captain White, was joined by the Honourable Wilfred O'Callaghan, son of Lord Lismore, whose home rule declarations were scarcely more explicit than those of Esmonde.[26] But here as in Waterford no suitable opponent could be found by the local organisation in the short time available. Kickham and his associates nominated John Mitchel, but the advanced vote was divided by the intrusion of Peter Gill of the *Advocate*, and the nationalist contribution was largely negative. White was shouted down in Thurles, but the clergy, meeting in Killaloe, adopted him with O'Callaghan, and the two were returned.[27] A similar division took place in Cork City, where Mitchel was also unsuccessfully nominated by the advanced party. The liberals worked for their sitting representative N. D. Murphy, whose espousal of

[25] *Freeman's Journal*, 5, 6 Feb., *Nation*, 7 Feb.

[26] 'The British parliament is admittedly overweighted and unable to discharge the very important functions entrusted to it by the nation, and self-government for Ireland, and the exclusive management of her own affairs, so far as it will not be inconsistent with the integrity of the United Kingdom, shall have my warm support'. (*Nation*, 31 Jan.)

[27] *Freeman's Journal*, 5, 6 Feb.

home rule was little more than a year old, and the home rulers for Joseph Ronayne. Ronayne would not coalesce with the Mitchel party, but he was careful to dissociate himself from Murphy. Ronayne and Murphy were elected. In Wexford County, on the other hand, the two sitting ministerialists had few adherents; interest centred upon the choice of a colleague to accompany Sir George Bowyer, returning to politics in the home rule interest. The *Nation* and the *Irishman* urged the claims of George Delany, a consistent and active member of the league who had been invited to stand by the local farmers' club. But the clergy chose the chevalier Keyes O'Clery in his place, a choice ascribed sarcastically by the *Irishman* to the latter's expressed determination 'to restore the pope to his temporal authority as soon as he gets inside the hall of St Stephen's.' Bowyer and O'Clery were adopted by a county meeting as the popular candidates and elected.[28]

There were, of course, several cases in which the clergy were totally identified with the aims of their home rule constituents. J. G. Biggar and W. G. Fay in Cavan, George Bryan and P. Martin in Kilkenny County, M. W. O'Reilly and George Errington in Longford, Mitchel Henry and Captain Nolan in Galway County, R. P. Blennerhassett in Kerry, P. J. Smyth and Lord Robert Montagu in Westmeath, were all swept into parliament with enthusiastic clerical and in some cases outspoken episcopal support, and the work of the parish clergy in defiance of their bishop in Louth, Drogheda, and Dundalk has already been mentioned. But even in some of these cases the clergy showed a preference for a certain type of candidate. In Galway, it will be recalled, Nolan rather than Henry had always enjoyed clerical support. After the election Henry wrote to Butt:

> A few days before the polling a vast number of priests instigated I think by all three of the bishops went round and begged the voters to plump for Nolan—fearing he might be left out. Darcy plumped 495, Nolan 385, and I had only 67.[29]

[28] *Irishman*, 31 Jan., 7, 14 Feb., *Freeman's Journal*, 4 Feb., *Nation* 31 Jan.
[29] Henry to Butt, 20 Feb. 1874, Butt MSS.

In Kilkenny and Longford Bryan and O'Reilly had been
elected as liberals in 1868; O'Reilly declared his life to be
devoted to the cause of catholic education.[30] Errington, his
colleague in Longford, was a distinguished catholic layman
and honorary secretary of the Catholic Union; Martin in Kilkenny was a barrister of uncertain origins. None seem to have
been members of the Home Rule League; Bryan and O'Reilly
had attended the conference. The address of the Bishop of
Ossory, Dr Moran, in support of Martin in Kilkenny, made
no mention of home rule; at this crisis, it declared,

> it is most important that our catholic people should have as
> their representatives in parliament men able and willing to de-
> fend our religious as well as our national interest. Your address,
> like that of Mr Bryan, is most catholic, and sets forth, in no un-
> certain terms, the popular principles of this country.[31]

This ambivalence between the claims of denominational
education and of home rule expresses much that was latent in
the conflict between liberal and nationalist home rulers.
Home rule was 'the one great object to which all our energies should be directed', declared Isaac Butt in his address to
the electors of Limerick City;[32] 'the Irish platform is home
rule and denominational education', announced the *Freeman*: 'Let no one get a vote who is not in favour of these two
principles'.[33] It is appropriate that Butt's own constituency
should provide a final illustration of this tacit distinction.
Never again did Butt enjoy as enthusiastic support from the
advanced party as in this election. John Daly, 'leader of the
nationalists', and later to become a bitter critic of the home
rule party, spoke and worked for Butt throughout the campaign:

> he defended the prisoners without fee or reward. He took the
> parts of the priests of Galway when they were assailed by

30 *Freeman's Journal*, 27 Jan.
31 ibid., 4 Feb.
32 *Irishman*, 31 Jan. He did, however, promise to agitate also for
franchise and grand jury reform, industrialisation, repeal of the coercion acts, tenant right, denominational education, and amnesty.
33 *Freeman's Journal*, 3 Feb.

Keogh, and he conducted the home rule conference with an ability which any prime minister might envy. The other candidates promised everything which Ireland wanted—if necessary, they would bleed for their country. But after the election they would probably forget all their promises.

At another meeting Daly declared:

> He was a man of peace, and would willingly lead them in the fight for home rule, as he had led them before in time of trouble and danger (cheers).[34]

W. H. O'Sullivan, Daly, and others of the same persuasion took part in monster torchlight processions and demonstrations in Butt's interest; thousands of people marched in trade organisations and bands. The clergy and the liberals did not, of course, oppose Butt: they appear, however, to have taken little part in his campaign, devoting themselves to the cause of Richard O'Shaughnessy, a catholic barrister who had made a special study of the education question, whose claim to the second seat was challenged by several other candidates, including the conservative home ruler Sir Peter Tait. O'Shaughnessy found no favour among the advanced party, and the rival parties clashed violently one Saturday night; but at the poll he was returned with Butt and both factions were satisfied.[35]

So far in this section two general principles have been advanced. Rarely, in 1874, did the catholic church in Ireland put itself forward as the opponent of the home rule movement. In the one notable instance where a catholic bishop did thus intervene directly, in Louth, he found himself repudiated, not only by the electors, but by the majority of his own parochial clergy. On the other hand, the clergy could frequently exert a less direct influence: where two or more home rulers were in opposition, or where a sitting liberal member who had lately endorsed home rule was opposed by another home ruler, the clergy in a considerable number of

---

[34] *Limerick Reporter,* 3 Feb. Also *Irishman,* 14 Feb., *Freeman's Journal,* 30 Jan., 2, 4, and 5 Feb.
[35] *Irishman,* 7 Feb., *Limerick Reporter,* 30 Jan., 3 Feb.

instances threw their weight decisively upon the side of the
liberal. In this way they added the power of clerical opinion
to the forces making for the preservation, under a new guise,
of the liberal character of the Irish representation.

Mention must, however, be made in conclusion of some
notable exceptions to this rule. In some cases the wishes of the
clergy were ignored, and alternative candidates, usually of
more advanced views, were elected. In Meath, where Edward
McEvoy had retired from the representation because of his
inability to accept the home rule plan, the majority of the
clergy seem to have favoured, as the colleague of John Martin,
Alderman P. P. McSwiney, who addressed the electors as a
'lifelong repealer', prepared now to accept the home rule
plan as a substitute. The *Freeman* also acclaimed McSwiney
the 'popular' candidate; his success, it commented, would be
'hailed by the catholic party as a valuable accession to their
parliamentary force'. But Nicholas Ennis, a tenant farmer of
the county, was the choice both of his class and of the local
home rule association. McSwiney had to retire, recognising
'the danger to nationality and conscience by having four liberals in the field', and the clergy, realising that Martin and
Ennis 'would be regarded by the vast majority of the electors
as the most suitable and eligible men', waived all personal
inclinations and endorsed their candidature.[36] In Galway
City the clergy were able to compel the retirement of Sir Rowland Blennerhassett, not on account of his views upon self-
government, which were somewhat indeterminate, but because of his approval of and unrepentant support for Gladstone's university bill.[37] They were unable, however, to secure the election of the candidate whom they favoured as his
successor, Frank Hugh O'Donnell. This young lawyer, returning from London to attend the home rule conference the previous November, had antagonised many at that gathering by
his outspoken reverence for the imperialist tradition. At this
stage of his career, however, O'Donnell depended rather
upon his reputation as an advocate of denominational educa-

36 *Freeman's Journal,* 28 Jan., 2, 3, 4, 7 Feb.; *Nation* 7 Feb.
37 ibid., 29 Jan., 2 Feb.

tion than as a home ruler, and he arrived in Galway armed with a testimonial from Cardinal Manning. 'A clever young ultramontane', wrote Lord George Hamilton to Disraeli's secretary: 'a pet of Cullen's and Manning's'.[38] But the former member for Galway, George Morris, a classic casualty of 1868, returned to the field as an advocate of home rule and denominational education, and in the less enthusiastically pro-liberal context of this election won back his seat. The other sitting liberal, Viscount St Lawrence, was re-elected, but the death of his father, the Earl of Howth, on polling day, brought St Lawrence to the peerage and O'Donnell to the vacant seat.[39]

But by far the most remarkable of these exceptional cases was that of Limerick County. Here the elevation of William Monsell to the peerage as Lord Emly in December 1873 caused a by-election which was run off as part of the general contest. The campaign, however, naturally commenced a full month before Gladstone's decision to dissolve parliament. First in the field was James Kelly, son of John J. Kelly, a one-time member of the Repeal Association.[40] But his candidature was unacceptable both to the tenant farmers and to the nationalists. The former recalled his father's record as an evictor,[41] the latter were doubtful of the sincerity of his home rule pledges. He had only lately joined the Home Rule League, and, wrote John Ellard, one of Butt's most loyal supporter's in Limerick, possessed the support both of all Monsell's 'little whigs and satellites' and of the *Dublin Evening Post,* 'enough to damn him in my estimation as a politician';

> The opinion here is that he is a mere nominee of Monsell's and the bishop, and that he has been allowed to come forward for home rule, which he makes a secondary question to education in his address.[42]

[38] ibid., 31 Jan.; Hamilton to Corry, 4 May, Disraeli MSS.
[39] From which he was, in turn, unseated on the ground of clerical intimidation. He did not re-enter parliament until his election for Dungarvan in 1877.
[40] Ellard to Butt, 23 Dec. 1873, Butt MSS.
[41] W. H. O'Sullivan to Butt, 24 Dec. 1873, ibid.
[42] Ellard to Butt, 25 Dec. 1873, ibid.

The Limerick Farmers' Club met on 31 December, and on
the proposal of Johnston Russell and Michael Ryan of Bruree,
two more of Butt's most active supporters in the county, resolved to return W. H. O'Sullivan of Kilmallock free of expense.[43] O'Sullivan was a prosperous tenant-farmer and hotel
proprietor, and an exceptionally strong candidate insofar as
he possessed the affection of both the main popular groups,
not normally noted for their co-operation, the farmers, to
whose class he belonged, and the advanced nationalists, with
whom he had close ties, not least through the long imprison-
ment of his son as a suspected fenian in 1867. This familial
honour, however, made him anathema to clerical authority.
Butt himself seems to have first suggested to O'Sullivan that
he should stand, and in private the home rule leader certainly favoured him more than Kelly, and was confident of his
success.[44] But the selection of O'Sullivan was met with unexpected resolve by the clergy. A meeting of eighty priests,
under the presidency of Dr Butler, bishop of Limerick, adopted, with only five dissentients, a manifesto in favour of Kelly;
the return of O'Sullivan, it declared, would be a disaster for
home rule which would confirm the worst fears of those who
already suspected the movement to be no more than a cloak
for separatism.[45] The clerical pronunciamento precipitated a
struggle of extraordinary bitterness, in which rival mobs frequently clashed and one of O'Sullivan's supporters was shot
dead. Both sides appealed repeatedly to Butt for some public
declaration of his support; such appeals were transmitted to
the home rule leader, busily canvassing in the north and mid-
lands of England, by his son Robert, with accompanying advice to stay out of a dangerous controversy. This was the kind
of advice which Butt was by nature delighted to follow; to the
request of Kelly's agent, Jonas Blackall, for a statement he

[43] O'Sullivan to Butt, 3 Jan. 1874, Butt MSS.
[44] O'Sullivan to Butt, 24 Dec. 1873, Butt MSS. Butt to Henry, 3, 13
Jan., 1874, Butt MSS, vol. iii, MS 832.
[45] *Nation*, 17 Jan. O'Sullivan, writing in this issue, denied that the
minority at this meeting was as small as the figure quoted in the press
and above.

replied declining to be drawn into correspondence concerning the contest; to Ellard he sent a copy of Blackall's letter.[46]

As their campaign gathered way, however, the supporters of O'Sullivan became confident that Butt's intervention would be superfluous. Ellard wrote:

> You will not be asked again to interfere in our election and you should not do so, we can win in a canter without you, the bishop's manifesto notwithstanding.

The Limerick priests, he asserted, were not in fact unanimously in favour of Kelly, while the Cashel priests supported O'Sullivan.[47] Protests had stopped the reading of the manifesto in some churches, and the archbishop of Cashel, while declining to intervene on the ground that he could not oppose Dr Butler, had admitted that out of thirteen parishes in the Limerick part of his diocese, twelve were for O'Sullivan, the odd one being Kelly's own parish priest.[48] The farmers' club met again and reaffirmed its support for O'Sullivan; by a majority of 28 to 17 it decided to leave the issue as between Kelly and Synan, the sitting member, to the electors.[49]

With O'Sullivan obviously gaining ground, the clergy began to look for a way of retreat. Synan telegraphed to Butt asking him to receive a deputation from the bishop and clergy to appeal to him to stand as a compromise candidate;

> The parties who accepted a candidate without consultation with the people regret what they have done . . . The advanced section of the home rulers having proposed Mr O'Sullivan I believe as a protest against dictation may be induced by you and the council of the league to withdraw him in your favour. If matters proceed as at present, all moderate men and all ecclesiastics tell me they will despair of any good from home rule.

[46] J. Russell to Butt, 30 Dec. 1873; O'Sullivan to Butt, 4, 6 Jan. 1874; H. O'Shea to Butt (with signatures of John Daly and others) 7 Jan.; J. F. X. O'Brien to Butt, 8, 12 Jan.; and for Kelly, J. Blackall to Butt, 7 Jan. R. Butt to I. Butt, 30 Dec. 1873, 5 Jan. 1874. Butt to Blackall, 9 Jan.; Ellard to Butt, undated; Butt MSS.

[47] Ellard to Butt, undated, Butt MSS.

[48] Ellard to Butt, 8, 12 Jan. 1874, Butt MSS. *Irishman,* 21 Feb.

[49] *Freeman's Journal,* 2 Feb.

G

As to Kelly he would be abandoned by the priests at a moment's notice. In fact he is a mere puppet and you must regard him as nothing more . . . The contest here had assumed two aspects, one of division between home rulers—the other of a fight of class against class, and both are equally fatal to the cause.[50]

Butt, however, while unwilling to come out openly on O'Sullivan's side, was not so gullible as to allow himself to be used to extricate the whigs from an untenable position, and in the process of so doing to leave his own seat in the city open to a similar conflict. The three candidates went to the poll amid tremendous excitement, and the result was a crushing defeat for the clerical nominee, O'Sullivan taking first place with 3521 votes, Synan following with 2856, and Kelly trailing with 995.

The contest in Limerick County, however, was in no sense typical of the 1874 election: it was rather the exception that proves the rule already stated—that a candidate of liberal background, and clerical support, who was prepared to make some concession to home rule feeling in his public statements, was usually able to overcome the opposition of a possibly more genuine home rule candidate who had little more than his nationalism to recommend him, even where the latter had the more or less official support of the home rule organisation. The liberal home ruler represented in a sense an effort to prolong pre-1870 political techniques into a new era; the advanced home ruler like O'Sullivan, on the other hand, was entirely the product of the nationalist conflict. The latter was to triumph under Parnell; for the moment the former was able to preserve a semblance of his political oligarchy. Limerick County showed the power of arbitration which an active home rule organisation could hold throughout the constituencies, but its current national leader would not, as he considered, stoop to exert that latent strength. O'Sullivan's victory, the exception in 1874, looks forward to Parnell's historic intervention in Ennis in 1879.

[50] Synan to Butt, 6, 9, 10 Jan., Butt MSS.

B : THE HOME RULE VICTORY

The result of the 1874 election was, at first sight, a sweeping victory for home rule and a total reversal of the political balance of 1868. R. B. O'Brien, in his life of Parnell, follows the majority of the nationalist press at the time in claiming fifty-nine victories for home rule.[51] 'Ireland had revolted against whiggery and refused to return members just to swell liberal lobbies', declares a more recent study of the election.[52] If this was, in fact, the case, how then was Butt able to make so little tactical use of the massive party which had been returned to follow him at Westminster?

The answer to this enigma, and the key to many of Butt's subsequent difficulties, is found upon closer examination of the so-called home rule triumph. How genuine was this upsurge of nationalist zeal among the very men who, six short years before, had stumped the country upon the Gladstonian platform?

In endeavouring to answer this question, it is necessary first to establish one point. At no time in the election was there in existence any such thing as a formal 'Home Rule Party'. Even if Butt had wished to create a fully-fledged electoral machine, and there is every reason to think that he did not, the precipitancy of Gladstone's dissolution of parliament, coming so soon after the founding of the League, would have made it impossible. Few candidates possessed even the official backing of the League, and its endorsement was in no way essential as a prerequisite for acceptance in the constituencies. To apply the description 'Home Rule Party' to the fifty-nine candidates who were elected after some kind of home rule declaration is, then, in one sense, to use a misleadingly suggestive term.

Ten of this fifty-nine were sitting members who had already demonstrated their loyalty to the movement; eight of these had been returned in by-elections between 1868 and

[51] *Life of C. S. Parnell* (3rd ed., 1899) vol. i, p. 69. *Nation*, 14 Feb. 1874.

[52] L. J. McCaffrey, Home Rule and the general election of 1874, in *Irish Historical Studies,* vol. ix, no. 34, Sept. 1954.

1874.[53] Ten more who were not outgoing members had given service of one kind or another to the Home Government Association or the League.[54] The party thus had at most a nucleus of twenty members of theoretically proven loyalty. Even amongst these, however, there was room for insincerity. Sir George Bowyer, for example, had first lost his seat to a liberal in 1868; he was a relatively early adherent to the home rule cause, but on his return to parliament in 1874 he sat on the government benches and habitually took the government whip. In 1877 he wrote to Disraeli:

> I knew that unless I accepted the 'shibbolet' (sic) of Home Rule I must retire forever from public life. And many of my colleagues feel the same. It did not necessarily imply anything calculated to injure the integrity of the empire.[55]

Of the remainder of the members claimed for home rule, eighteen had originally been elected as liberals, seventeen in 1868 and one, E. G. Dease, in 1870.[56] Six of these had not attended or even held tickets for the conference at which, less than three months previously, the League had been founded.[57] Of these, one, W. Stacpoole, had held Ennis against one of the few home rule candidates to possess Butt's official endorsement. Two more of these alleged recruits to the movement, David Sherlock and Sir John Esmonde, had, it will be recalled, been described, by the *Nation* as, respectively, un-

53 R. P. Blennerhassett, G. E. Browne, Butt, P. Callan, M. Henry, J. Martin, W. A. Redmond, J. P. Ronayne, W. Shaw, and P. J. Smyth. The last-named, although elected as a home ruler, had already made public his reservations about the feasibility of Butt's federal plan. Callan and Shaw were the two elected in 1868.

54 J. G. Biggar, Sir G. Bowyer, Lord F. Conyngham, N. Ennis, J. G. MacCarthy, Sir J. N. McKenna, J. P. Nolan, W. H. O'Leary, W. H. O'Sullivan, and A. M. Sullivan.

55 Bowyer to Disraeli, 6 Nov. 1877, Disraeli MSS, General Correspondence.

56 J. Brady, G. Bryan, E. G. Dease, K. Digby, M. Downing, Sir J. Esmonde, Sir J. Gray, N. D. Murphy, Sir P. O'Brien, O'Conor Don, D. M. O'Conor, Sir C. O'Loghlen, M. W. O'Reilly, Lord St. Lawrence, D. Sherlock, W. Stacpoole, E. J. Synan, Capt. C. W. White.

57 Esmonde, O'Loghlen, St. Lawrence, Sherlock, Stacpoole, and White.

worthy 'to get a vote from any patriotic elector '[58] and 'a pure
and simple ministerialist'.[59] On the eve of the election Esmonde had begged Gladstone for a peerage, pointing to 'the
unflinching services of my family to the liberal party ever
since Catholic Emancipation'.[60] 'The taint of whiggery'
clung to another, wrote the *Irishman*[61] while yet another,
Viscount St Lawrence (Galway City), did not even go so far
as to give a token endorsement to the programme of the
League, of which he was not a member, adopting, instead, a
form of words of his own.[62]

Of these eighteen liberals, the other twelve had either attended or at least held tickets for the national conference in
the preceding November. But even amongst these no absolute
loyalty to the League programme, let alone to its leadership,
can be assumed. N. D. Murphy had been forced to express
sympathy with the movement by the election of the fenian J.
P. Ronayne as his colleague in Cork City in the by-election of
November 1872; but he had dissociated himself from the amnesty movement at the end of the previous decade and was
disliked as a whig both by the nationalists of Cork and by his
own colleagues.[63] He had declined to sign the requisition for
the home rule conference because of his doubts as to the feasibility of the federal scheme, and at the conference had urged
as an alternative programme the adjustment of the union to
incorporate the best points of federalism.[64] His career as a
'home rule' member was fully to justify the misgivings of the
nationalists. McCarthy Downing (Cork County) had made an
enthusiastic declaration in favour of home rule at the conference, but he was suspected by Butt and his intimates of hav-

58 *Nation,* 7 Feb. 1874.
59 ibid.
60 Esmonde to Gladstone, 28 Jan., BM Add. MSS 44442 f 119.
61 *Irishman,* 7 Feb.
62 'I advocate that Irish affairs, as apart from those of imperial interest, should be managed by the Irish people themselves, through their
chosen representatives in their own country'. (*Freeman's Journal,* 2
Feb.)
63 *Nation,* 31 Jan.; Ronayne to Butt, 27 Nov. 1872, Butt MSS.
64 *Proceedings of the Home Rule Conference,* Dublin, 1874, pp.
111-13.

ing endeavoured to use his clerical connections in an effort to take over the leadership of both the home rule and tenant-right movements.[65] He had opposed not only the imposition of a parliamentary pledge upon the home rulers but even the proposals for the holding of periodic national conferences and for the prior consultation of home rule members of parliament before the introduction of a bill by any one of their number, and he had urged that they should be bound to vote together only 'when it shall appear to them calculated to advance the cause of home rule and the general interests of Ireland'.[66] Sir P. O'Brien had only joined the Home Rule League in the month preceding the election.[67] E. J. Synan was another who had bitterly opposed the idea of a parliamentary pledge. J. A. Brady had not spoken at all at the conference; the sole reference to the topic of home rule in his address to the electors of Leitrim was his observation that their new power, if used with judgment and discretion, would lead to their future progress and social advancement—even to home rule. The protests of his constituents compelled him to add a more formal endorsement of home rule by telegraph.[68] Mr. W. O'Reilly, who was a prominent member of the Catholic Union, an organisation regarded by many of the home rulers as a device to subvert the movement for independence, had also shown no previous interest in home rule and does not seem at any stage to have been a member of the League; in 1868 Gladstone had contemplated offering him a Lordship of the Treasury.[69] Most of his political interests were involved in the question of education; at the conference he supported the plea of the O'Conor Don that the maximum amount of latitude should be allowed to the home rule representatives[70] In the opinion of W. H. O'Sullivan, M.P. for Lim-

[65] J. Russell to Butt, J. B. Kennedy to Butt, 14 Apr. 1873, Butt MSS: Butt to Callan, 16 Sept. 1873, Butt MSS, vol. ii, MS 831.
[66] *Conference proceedings*, pp. 182-3.
[67] *Nation*, 31 Jan. 1874.
[68] *Freeman's Journal*, 2, 13 Feb.
[69] Gladstone to O'Reilly, 12, 18 Dec. 1868, BM Add. MSS 44416 f 349, 44417 f 106, both marked 'Cancelled'.
[70] *Conference proceedings*, p. 92.

erick County, he was only a 'mock home ruler'.[71] Of the two
O'Conors, the younger, Denis, member for Sligo County, had
given a 'cordial adherence' at the conference to the full federal programme,[72] but his elder brother had been the chief
spokesman of those liberal critics of federalism who sought
complete freedom of interpretation for each protagonist of the
home rule demand; his speech at the conference had brought
down upon him the disapproval of Butt and A. M. Sullivan,
and it will be recalled that their exchanges were reckoned
among the most crucial in that assembly.[73] Even the *Freeman's Journal* had described as 'guarded' and 'not easy to
paraphrase' O'Conor's promised resolve:

> to support any scheme which would, consistently with the pre-
> servation of all justly recognised rights, confer on my country
> the inestimable benefits of real self-government.[74]

Of the two representatives of Queen's County, Kenelm Digby
and E. G. Dease, Digby had distinguished himself at the conference by his carpings at the projected revival of the Irish
House of Lords; in the past he had supported Downing's move
to replace the old Home Government Association with a body
of a more liberal complexion.[75] Dease had expressed himself
at the conference with much more enthusiasm, but his support was subject to a qualification of another kind. At the dissolution of parliament he had been extremely anxious to retire from public life, and had gone so far as to draw up his
farewell address. It was only the pleading of the local Independent Club, unable to find a substitute at such short notice,
which prevailed upon him to change his mind, on the understanding that he would not be able to give his full time to his
parliamentary duties.[76] His constituents appear to have been
uneasy about the sincerity of his home rule principles, a dis-

---

[71] O'Sullivan to Butt, 24 Dec. 1873, Butt MSS.

[72] *Conference proceedings,* p. 124.

[73] ibid., pp. 81-91, 94-9.

[74] *Freeman's Journal,* 30 Jan. 1874; *Nation,* 31 Jan.

[75] *Proceedings of the Home Rule Conference,* Dublin, 1874, p. 61.
Digby to Lalor, 14 Jan., Lalor to Digby, 19 Jan. 1871, Lalor MSS, 8566.

[76] M. Cahill to R. Lalor, 21 Jan. 1878; R. Lalor to E. Dease, 24 Jan.
1878, Lalor MSS, 8566.

quiet which would have mounted had they known the version of his relations to them given by his cousin, J. A. Dease, the liberal candidate whom P. J. Smyth had defeated in the Westmeath by-election of 1871.[77]

It is, naturally, often much more difficult to ascertain the political antecedents and attitudes of those twenty representatives who had not been members for Irish constituencies in the outgoing parliament.[78] Two of them possessed parliamentary experience, Lord Robert Montagu (Westmeath), and George Morris (Galway City). Montagu was a younger son of the Duke of Manchester; he had represented Huntingdon as an English Conservative, voting, as late as 1869, against the disestablishment of the Irish church. His sudden conversion to catholicism put paid to his career as a member of the English Conservative party, which formally expelled him in 1873. In 1872 he approached Butt in search of an alternative political venture:

> I have spoken to our archbishop on the subject, and he expresses himself as very favourable to my project for standing for a seat in Ireland on the home rule platform (but remaining, in other respects, a conservative).

[77] In 1871 J. A. Dease had rejected the idea, apparently put forward by his cousin, that he should 'nibble' at home rule; of E. G. Dease he wrote to Monsell: 'I know not what his friends will expect of him in Queen's Co. nor how far he will be prepared to go when the time comes' . . . (J. A. Dease to E. G. Dease, 15 June 1871, J. A. Dease to Monsell, undated, 1871, Monsell MSS, 8317). J. A. Dease had also felt it necessary to apologise to Monsell on his cousin's behalf for the latter's vote against the land bill (22 Mar. 1870, Monsell MSS, 8317).

[78] These were: Brooks (Dublin City), Collins (Kinsale), Dunbar (New Ross), Errington (Longford), Fay (Cavan), Lewis (Carlow Boro), Martin, P. (Kilkenny Co.) Meldon (Kildare), Montagu (Westmeath) Moore (Clonmel), Morris (Galway City), O'Byrne (Wicklow), O'Callaghan (Tipperary), O'Clery (Wexford Co.), O'Gorman (Waterford City), O'Keeffe (Dungarvan), O'Shaughnessy (Limerick City), Power, R. (Waterford City), Sheil (Athlone), Tighe (Mayo), plus French (Roscommon) who had been elected on a nebulous programme in a by-election in 1873, but perhaps falls most fittingly into this 'unknown' category. This, with 20 members 'of proven loyalty' and 18 liberals makes 59.

How would Montagu reconcile these dual loyalties? In April 1873 he expressed the belief that the home rule members should act ‘in strictest discipline’ on all questions under Butt; when asked the following autumn to sign the requisition for a national home rule conference he stipulated however, that his name should be published separately from those of the other signatories, together with a statement of his conservative reservations. When Butt objected to the making of this exception, he insisted upon writing himself to the press.[79] On this evidence alone, Montagu was an eccentric recruit. His motives, however, become clearer on examination of his relations with Disraeli. Before announcing even this highly qualified adhesion to home rule he wrote to the conservative leader for permission, reminding him that Colonel Taylor, the Conservative whip, had concurred in the view that no seat could be gained without some expression of home rule principles. In later years he asserted that Colonel Taylor had promised in Disraeli's name that if he would endorse home rule he would be rewarded, immediately upon his election, with either high cabinet office or the audit office with a salary increased to £3000 per year.[80] So much for one of the two former M.P.'s in this section. The other, George Morris, does not appear at any time to have been a member of either the Association or the League, and his return was claimed as a victory, with equal enthusiasm, by the conservatives.[81]

Finally, in the case of the eighteen members in this section who had never before sat in parliament, one is faced with an obscurity only partially penetrable. None seem to have been a member of the League. George Errington (Longford) was secretary of the Catholic Union, to which reference has already been made.[82] H. O. Lewis (Carlow Borough) had stood

[79] Montagu to Butt, 9 Mar. 1872, 1 Mar., 24 Apr., 30 Sept. 1873; and Butt to Montagu (copy), 1 Nov. or Dec. 1873, Butt MSS.

[80] Montagu to Disraeli, 29 April 1872, and undated, Disraeli MSS, General Correspondence.

[81] *Nation*, 14 Feb. 1874.

[82] See above, p. 198. In later years Errington justified his membership of the home rule party solely on Gladstone's failure to settle the university question (Errington to Gladstone, 11th Aug. 1877, BM Add. MSS, 44455 f 39.

in the Monaghan by-election of 1871 as a liberal candidate in opposition to the home rule nominee, John Madden, despite the direct endorsement of Madden by the Home Government Association.[83] Arthur Moore (Clonmel) was the son of Charles Moore who had represented Tipperary as a liberal from 1865 until 1869; he declared explicitly for home rule, but his election was secured mainly on the issue of education, concerning which his opponent had taken the Gladstonian viewpoint.[84] W. O'Callaghan (Tipperary) on the other hand earned distinction by the classic ambiguity of his statement on home rule quoted above.[85] The only previous political activity in the young life of Keyes O'Clery, member for Wexford County, had been as a soldier in the Papal army, for his services in which the knighthood of the Order of St Gregory had been conferred upon him.[86] John O'Keeffe (Dungarvan) was known as 'a consistent and steadfast nationalist';[87] Richard O'Shaughnessy (Limerick City) had acquired some reputation as an educationalist. Concerning the rest, little can be discerned which is politically illuminating.

The loyalty of these recruits was soon to be tested, and many of them to be found wanting. But on the basis of this analysis alone some obvious conclusions can already be drawn. Fifty-nine members, representing sixty seats, were, as we have seen, claimed for home rule by the *Nation,* and in this estimate it was followed at the time more or less exactly by the leaders of the nationalist movement and the home rule press, and, in later years, by the historians of the period. The analytical consideration of these fifty-nine members, their political origins, their published statements, and the circumstances of their selection and return can only serve to demonstrate the unreality of this estimate. Valid, perhaps, as a piece of political propaganda, its acceptance by later writers as a basis upon which to assess the potential power of the party, and a yardstick against which to measure its failure, has served only to

83 *Freeman's Journal,* 6 July 1871.
84 ibid., 2 Feb. 1874.
85 See page 186, n.1.
86 *Dod's Parliamentary Companion,* 1876.
87 *Nation,* 14 Feb. 1874.

distort the historical evaluation of the first home rule movement.

The *Nation,* before the election, had given warning of the scope for the opportunist and the carpetbagger on the one hand, and the deliverance for the liberal in retreat on the other, which were offered by Gladstone's precipitate dissolution of parliament; Butt himself had doubted that he could secure the return of a party one half in size the force which he had once hoped to command.[88] The contest fought, home rule claimed a sweeping victory; but it claimed it as a political movement, playing the game of politics in an effort to impress English opinion with the depth of Irish discontent. The elements whose return Butt and the *Nation* had feared had seized their opportunity with thankfulness; the time-servers were only too numerous in the ranks of the fifty-nine. Perhaps one third genuinely regarded themselves as elected to a new party discipline; one third were unknown; one third represented the dead hand of Irish liberalism. It was a triumph to have compelled the majority of the Irish representatives to accept the principle of home rule, but it was only the first step in a long process of political realignment. The calamities which followed can only be understood if a basic principle be conceded. The 1874 election was a victory for the home rule programme; it was, if anything a defeat for the home rule movement, the defeat and the disappointment which Butt foresaw when the news of the dissolution first leaped to the headlines of the United Kingdom at the end of January 1874.

John Cashel Hoey wrote to William Monsell during the election prophesying that the majority of Butt's party would be 'though home rule in the carnal part still good liberals at the heart'.[89] The fenian John Barry wrote to Butt from Newcastle immediately after the election:

There is no use disguising the fact that honest earnest Irishmen both at home and abroad are bitterly disappointed at the calibre of the majority of the men returned; the history of the next

[88] ibid, 31 Jan.
[89] Hoey to Monsell, 4 Feb. 1874, Monsell MSS, 8317.

few years will endorse the correctness of their political foresight. It is said on all sides that you have not around you a sufficient number of the right stamp to keep the others in a straight
line.[90]

'The victories we have just won are a great advancement to
our national cause', concluded the *Nation* in a moment of
candour, 'but we shall have to win them again, and to add to
their number, before we reach the final settlement of the
Irish question'.[91]

90 Barry to Butt, 27 Feb., Butt MSS.
91 *Nation*, 14 Feb.

CHAPTER VI

Home Rule, Class, and the Ballot

IT HAS been remarked at the outset of this study, that the majority of nineteenth-century measures for the reform of the franchise were extended to Ireland only in part, and that the important measure introduced by Disraeli in 1867 touched scarcely at all upon the Irish representation. The period between the two elections so far discussed, those of 1868 and 1874, did, however, see the application of one tremendous innovation, the ballot, to Irish politics. In the early 1870's the consequences to be expected from the introduction of the ballot were the subject of the most conflicting predictions. Some prophesied an end to the political power of the clergy; some the exclusion from politics of the landlords; some, perhaps wisest of all, expected matters to remain much as they were before.[1] But even without the passing of the ballot, it would still be of moment to ask whether the character of the Irish representation altered at all in this period, if the launching of the home rule movement brought into politics a new and more plebeian type of representative. The fact that the first of these two elections was conducted with the ancient formality of the open hustings, and the second under the secrecy of the modern system, makes such a comparison obligatory.

In the table below a statistical analysis of the members elected in 1868 and in 1874 has been made.[2] In this analysis the members are classified in three groups, which might be loosely described as the landed interest, middle class and lower middle class. In each case the occupation of a member has been defined as the means from which he drew his main financial support; for example, although Sir John Gray was a

---

[1] T. M. Ray to O'Neill Daunt, 25 Feb. 1873, Hickey MSS.
[2] See p. 207.

qualified medical practitioner, it is obviously more correct to classify him as a newspaper proprietor. In the case of the landed interest, Dr Conor Cruise O'Brien's definition of a landowner has been adopted,[3] i.e. the possession of a landed property valued at at least £1000. Some of those who fall into this category possessed professional qualifications; in such cases the criterion I have adopted has been their employment in practice. Charles Meldon, for example, had landed property, although somewhat less than the standard adopted here; he practised as a barrister, and has been listed as such. McCarthy Downing, on the other hand, a qualified and practising solicitor, is listed as a landowner, since his possession of over 4000 acres in Cork and Kerry valued at £1413 seems to argue not only his deriving a considerable income from the land but also his identification with its interests.[4] It is this question of identification of interest which has above all dictated the classifications. It led me to include as separate subsections of class one the elder and younger sons of landowners, the former because obviously their interests would be in all likelihood those of the class to which they would inevitably belong, the latter because of the presumption of a similar identification, though here, the link being more tenuous, I have taken care to exclude those like Sheil in Athlone who had been put to some profession. The sum of these three

---

3 Conor Cruise O'Brien, *Parnell and his party*, 1957, p. 18.

4 The sources for my information have been the *Return of owners of land in Ireland*, (c.1492), H.C. 1876, LXXX, 61, and U. H. de Burgh: *The landowners of Ireland*, 1878. For other occupations I have consulted the relevant volumes of *Dod's Parliamentary Companion, Thom's Directory, Complete Peerage* (G.E.C.), *Debrett's House of Commons Annual*, Boase: *Modern English Biography,* and the *DNB;* the occasional item of information is given in the contemporary newspapers. For the educational backgrounds of members I have consulted the same reference works; also: Burtchaell, G.D. and Sadleir, T.U.; *Alumni Dublinienses* 2nd ed., 1935; the Senior Lecturer's entrance matriculation lists, Trinity College, Dublin (MSS), and the relevant volumes of the *Catholic Directory.* In two cases where I was unable to obtain other information, those of E. G. Dease and G. Errington, I have followed their classification as landowners in *Return of the persons holding the commission of the peace in Ireland,* pp. 62 & 74, H.C. 1884 (13) lxiii, 331.

groups I have taken as representing, within class one, the landed interest.

The second group is self-explanatory, except in the case of the 'rentiers'; I have placed in this category those members who appear to have followed no paid occupation but the source of whose means cannot be traced. The third class, that of farmers and shopkeepers, represents a lower stratum of society which is only beginning to gain its first representation in 1874.

	1868			1874				1874—new M.P's			
	Con	Lib	TOT	Con	Lib	HR	TOT	Con	Lib	HR	TOT
Landowners	26	28	54	21	3	18	42	6	—	6	12
Eld. sons of Landowners	5	7	12	4	—	1	5	—	—	—	—
Younger sons of Landowners	5	2	7	1	—	4	5	—	—	1	1
TOTAL	36	37	73	26	3	23	52	6	—	7	13
Rentiers and land agents	—	4	4	1	1	7	9	—	1	3	4
Merchants, financiers, newspaper props., etc.	3	14	17	3	4	8	15	1	4	4	9
Professions	1	10	11	3	2	19	24	—	2	8	10
TOTAL	4	28	32	7	7	34	48	1	7	15	23
Farmers, shopkeepers						2	2			2	2

With these terms defined, it is possible to answer some of the questions posed at the beginning of the chapter. The first and most obvious conclusion is the tremendous political importance of the landlords. Out of 105 seats in 1868, 54 were held by landowners, and 73 by representatives of the landed interest. Merchants, financiers, and newspaper owners supply the next highest total with 17 representatives; only 11 professional men are returned. The strength of this landlord representation had survived the forty years since emancipation

and the first reform act, and it would not be overturned at a
blow by the introduction of the ballot; the Irish elector in
1868 was only too glad to find a spokesman from the ranks of
his social superiors; of the 65 liberal members returned, no
less than 37 were drawn from the landed class. This was by
modern standards a striking preponderance, but it is still
more striking that of 40 conservative members 36 belonged
to the landed interest. Commerce supplied 3 conservatives
and 17 liberals, the professions 1 conservative and 10 liberals.
The more popular cause had the more plebeian representatives.

If this is an important conclusion, it is still more under-
lined in 1874. Between these dates two fundamental political
upheavals had taken place. Not merely had the ballot replaced the open vote, but a new constitutional national movement had given some expression to the pent-up nationalism
of the people. The introduction of the ballot could not immediately overturn the landed representation; but the combination of these two forces none the less had its effect. 73
out of 105 representatives were grouped in class one in 1868,
but only 52 out of 102 came from the landowning class in
1874.[5] The representation of the commercial classes remained
steady, but the number of professional men rose from 11 to
24, and two tenant-farmers became the first representatives of
their class to be elected.

Striking as these comparisons are, they can be pressed further with even more notable results. It was hardly to be expected that the combination of the ballot and home rule
would produce an immediate purging of the representation;
in the previous two chapters I have emphasised the number
of liberals who were able to preserve their seats for the moment as home rulers. 64 of the members elected in 1874 had sat
in the outgoing or previous parliaments; only two of them,
Ronayne, an engineer, and C. E. Lewis, a solicitor, had been
elected under the ballot. The separate classification in our
table of the 38 who now entered parliament for the first time

[5] Cashel and Sligo Borough had been disfranchised, and Philip Callan held two seats.

produces most significant results. Only 13 of this number came from the landed class; 23 came from group two, and 2 were tenant-farmers. In other words the proportion of representatives from group one had dropped from almost 70 per cent of the total in 1868 to 51 per cent in 1874, and of the newly elected representatives only 32 per cent came from this group.

It is clearly, then, possible to deduce that the ballot produced an immediate effect upon the calibre of the representation. But it is questionable whether the ballot alone, without the further democratising influence of the home rule movement, could have produced such swift results. Much has been written concerning the aristocratic and conservative nature of Butt's home rule party, and undoubtedly it numbered in its ranks a higher proportion of wealthy men than was to be found in the party of Parnell. But this view of the first home rule party is one which I have been compelled frequently to criticise above, and it must now again be qualified. Of the 52 representatives of the landed interest returned in 1874, no less than half were conservatives; only 23 out of 59 home rulers came from the landed class, and 19 were from the professions, a higher total than the entire professional contribution in 1868. Moreover, it was in the home rule ranks that the two tenant-farmers made their historic appearance.

Were the home rule members, then, drawn from origins more plebeian than those of their political opponents? Such a conclusion is at complete variance with the normal picture of Butt's party. On further analysis, the two views can, however, be quite simply reconciled. Those liberal survivals who littered the right wing of the party were, broadly speaking, the same who gave it its traditionally aristocratic complexion. Of the 35 home rulers elected before 1874, 16 came from group one, the landed class, 19 from group two; of the 24 new members 7 came from group one, 15 belonged to the second group, and 2 to the third. In other words, only 29 per cent of the new home rulers came from the landed class, compared with 46 per cent of those previously elected, and 51 per cent of the entire representation in 1874.

It is, of course, folly to argue from the particular to the general; only two elections are here considered, and the influence of the ballot act upon the representation can scarcely be deduced from the results of the 1874 contest alone. But certain conclusions can undoubtedly be drawn from the evidence.

In 1874, there was an immediate and sharp decline in the representation of the landlords. Yet despite the appearance of two representatives of the tenant class, one cannot yet go so far as to argue a general democratisation. The landlord representation remained high, and the class which benefited most from its decline was so far the middle class, the professional men from whom career politicians were traditionally sprung. The representation of this class more than doubled between 1868 and 1874.

This conclusion is supported by a study of the educational backgrounds of the new members: the proportion of university graduates remained constant at around 50 per cent of the representation in 1868 and 1874, and amongst the new members. The army, traditionally the career of aristocratic younger sons, supplied no new members in 1874. The denominational balance, on the other hand, was noticeably altered. Of the 105 members elected in 1868, 68 had been protestants and 37 catholics; these proportions were now altered to 54 protestants and 48 catholics. Only 2 of these catholics were to be found outside the home rule party. Inside the home rule party Catholics were in a majority of 46 to 13.

In this context it is important to remember that the ballot had not merely diminished the opportunities for corruption and intimidation. Accurate figures are not obtainable, but there can be little doubt that the introduction of the secret vote greatly decreased the cost of political campaigning which faced a prospective candidate and at once reduced the disadvantage at which a candidate of slender means had been placed in competition with a wealthy man. Again, the professional classes would be naturally the first to benefit from this change.

Despite the traditional picture of Butt's party, it is then, clear that its parliamentary representatives were, in fact, drawn from a lower social scale than their predecessors or their rivals. Landowners were to be found within its ranks, but they were mostly men who had been elected in previous contests, and whose political careers had survived into a new period. The new members were on average from a lower social stratum; one third of them were professional men, and two, O'Sullivan and Ennis, were tenant-farmers.

In sum, there was an alteration in the representation between 1868 and 1874, perceptible but not catastrophic. The ballot, then, did have an immediate effect, but it is questionable if this alteration can be ascribed to it alone. The relatively much greater change in the class structure among the home rule members than amongst the rest of the representation argues that the new nationalist movement played a complementary part in producing the change; subverting the liberal order, it lowered also the social standard of the national representation. The survival of so many landlords, even in the home rule party, warns us against exaggerating the extent of this change. But the entry of Ennis and O'Sullivan, the increase in the representation of the professional classes, and, on the whole, the comparatively much swifter reaction of these forces upon the nationalist representation, compel us to conclude that the nostalgia of Frank Hugh O'Donnell in later years for the aristocratic golden age of Butt[6] has a questionable basis in fact, and that the leavening of the representation which he ascribes to the influence of Parnell was in fact the acceleration of a process already obvious in 1874.

[6] F. H. O'Donnell, *History of the Irish parliamentary party*, 1910, vol. i, p. 467.

CHAPTER VII

The New Party and its Leader

ON 16 FEBRUARY 1874 a circular was dispatched, over the names of Butt, Henry, Martin, Kenelm Digby, and W. A. Redmond, calling together the fifty-nine members which the cause of home rule claimed for its own.[1] On 3 March forty-six of them arrived in the City Hall in Dublin to concert their tactics for the coming session of the new parliament. Eight sent letters of apology for their absence;[2] four made no acknowledgment of the summons.[3] Out of these twelve, one, Sir John Esmonde, refused pointblank to join the party and never supported it in parliament,[4] while neither George Morris nor Colonel White ever became a member.[5] P. J. Smyth, who attended this meeting, had defected openly from the party by the following April. The O'Conor Don, now judiciously absent, subsequently objected to the resolutions passed at this conference and refused to join.[6] N. D. Murphy, whose loyalty had always been suspect, after a long career of backsliding formally dissociated himself from the party in January 1876.[7] The initial membership of the party was thus fifty-three, including for the moment Smyth and Murphy. The addition of G. H. Kirk and Dr M Ward who filled the vacancies in Louth and Galway City brought the number to fifty-five.

At this meeting a number of resolutions were passed. As they were to be frequently recalled and the obligations which

[1] Butt MSS, vol. ii, MS 831 (letters to P. Callan, 16 Feb. 1874).

[2] Bowyer, Conyngham, French, Montagu, O'Byrne, O'Conor Don, O'Conor, and White.

[3] Esmonde, Moore, Morris, and O'Callaghan, The total had been reduced to 58 by the Galway vacancy.

[4] O'Shaughnessy to Butt, 17 Sept. 1874, Butt MSS.

[5] *Nation,* 21 Mar., 2 May 1874.

[6] ibid., 21 Nov.

[7] ibid., 8 Jan. 1876.

they carried as often disputed, the texts of the most important are given here in full:

> That in the opinion of this conference the time has arrived when the Irish members who have been elected to represent the national demand for home rule ought to form a separate and distinct party in the house of commons, united on the principle of obtaining self-government for Ireland, as defined in the resolutions of the conference held in Dublin last November.
>
> That while our future action must depend upon the course of events, and the occasions that may arise, it is essential to the due discharge of our duties to our constituents and the country that we should collectively and individually hold ourselves aloof from, and independent of, all party combinations, whether of the ministerialists or of the opposition.
>
> That, deeply impressed with the importance of unity of action upon all matters that can affect the parliamentary position of the Home Rule party, or the interests of the Home Rule cause, we engage to each other and to the country that we will use our best endeavours to obtain that unity by taking counsel together, by making all reasonable concessions to the opinions of each other, by avoiding as far as possible isolated action, and by sustaining and supporting each other in the course which may be deemed best calculated to promote the grand object of national self-government which the Irish nation has committed to our care.
>
> That nine gentlemen, three of whom shall be a quorum, be appointed, and requested to act as a parliamentary committee to the Irish Home Rule party during the ensuing session. That the committee be provided with funds to meet all requisite expenditure by a subscription of two guineas each from each member of the party. That the committee, or their honorary secretary, shall at any time summon a meeting of the party on requisition signed by any ten of its members; the requisition to state the object of such proposed meeting.

Shaw, Butt, Henry, Downing, D. M. O'Conor, Gray, Callan, Browne and Redmond were at once elected to form the first parliamentary committee. It was finally resolved that copies of these resolutions should be sent to the absent members with a request that they should reply adhering to them.[8]

On the whole, the home rule leaders seem as yet to have been satisfied with the achievements of the conference. 'It was a great and blessed day's work that laid finally and securely the foundations of an Irish national party in the house of commons', wrote the *Nation*.[9] 'I hope you approve of what we did at the conference of Irish members', wrote Butt to Daunt: 'We have, I hope, formed a compact party and I feel confident we will act up to our resolutions'.[10] To a later age it must seem incredible that the home rule members should emerge from this conference pledged only to 'take counsel' with each other and to make 'all reasonable concessions' to each other's opinions. Without any really authoritative executive, it was scarcely at all a party in the modern sense of the word. Yet these decisions were no more than the logical consequence not merely of the diversity of its membership but of the clear disavowal of parliamentary pledges by the conference the preceding November. At a league meeting a few days later, Butt asserted his willingness to justify all that was done at the conference: he did not believe that a single member could possibly desert the cause. Henry also defended the meeting on the ground that it would be impolitic for the movement to reveal its plans to the enemy. Even O'Connor Power believed the conference had gone just as far as discretion demanded. The members of the league unanimously approved its decisions. But at the same meeting they resolved to contest the impending by-election in Dublin County, and chose as their candidate a young man named Charles Stewart Parnell, who was to develop rather different ideas on party discipline.[11]

In London the party took offices at King Street, Westminster. Whips were appointed, first O'Shaughnessy and Nolan, and later, on O'Shaughnessy's resignation owing to ill-health, Conyngham and Nolan. Butt was chosen as leader, and Hugh Heinrick, former travelling-secretary of the league, was ap-

8 *Irishman,* 28 Feb.
9 *Nation,* 7 Mar.
10 Butt to Daunt, 7 Mar., Hickey MSS.
11 *Irishman,* 14 Mar.

pointed secretary to the Irish home rule members. Most typi-
cally, a fortnightly home-rule dinner was arranged, 'with songs
and all that', wrote John Martin, ' the only objection to which
is that it is a little too expensive '.[12]

But despite these manifestations of unity, there was little
real authority in the party at any stage. The committee summoned meetings of the members intermittently, but attendance was not obligatory, and even at the outset rarely exceeded twenty or thirty. The attendance of the members in
parliament was equally spasmodic; as early as April 1874 the
parliamentary committee was deploring the absence of twenty-
one home rule members from the division in which Butt's
Municipal Franchise (Ireland) Bill was defeated by less than
forty votes.[13] This neglect was to grow steadily worse. From
the outset there was little co-ordination of the party's activities; members spoke and voted as they pleased with an eye to
their constituents rather than to any common party line.[14]
With Butt's first home rule motion tabled for 30 June, Martin wrote to Daunt on 8 June that its terms were not yet
settled, nor had there been any meeting of the home rule
members to discuss them or the procedure of the debate.[15]
After the debate a sympathetic correspondent noted : —

> The home rule party exhibited neither direction nor discipline
> . . . Mr Butt appeared to be content with making his speech.
> He then seemed practically to abandon the field, and to let the
> rank and file of his party scramble into action in any way they
> could. There was not a vestige of plan or arrangement; no
> direction; no discipline; nothing of that generalship which, in
> a great debate, is so essential. The result was confusion.[16]

After the debate Butt conceded the justice of these criticisms,
and expressed the hope that they would encourage the members of the party to allow him a little more authority. Arrange-

[12] Martin to Daunt, 24 May, Daunt MSS, 8047.
[13] *Nation*, 25 Apr.
[14] ibid, 11 July.
[15] Daunt Journal, 6 June 1874, MS 3041; Martin to Daunt, 8 June,
Daunt MSS, 8047.
[16] *Nation*, 11 July.

ments were at once initiated to appoint sub-committees for
the consideration of particular bills, and to assign certain
subjects to individual members,[17] but the decision of the
national conference not to limit the right of members to introduce private bills bore its inevitable fruit in lost measures and
embittered minority votes. The whips for crucial divisions
were phrased in the form of appeals;[18] disobedience to them
was subject to no other sanction than popular disapproval.
Members of the party sat wherever they chose in the House;
Bowyer, Montagu and later King Harman sat on the government benches, the ex-liberals upon the opposite side. Butt
himself and his closest allies appear to have sat below the
gangway on the opposition side, which became traditionally
Irish in later years, but their colleagues were not bound to
join them. John Martin wrote to Daunt before the 1875 session:

> I don't expect ever to see such perfect discipline and union
> among the home rule representatives as to cause them all to
> vote on one side. In fact I myself would be exceedingly reluc-
> tant to hold my vote at the disposal of the leader of my party
> or of a majority of my party. Only one question commands the
> votes of us all—home rule.[19]

Not unnaturally, the backsliders habitually absented themselves, and in desperate efforts to arrest the steady decline of
the party vote in the divisions upon its measures, the force of
public opinion was deliberately enlisted by the home rule
leaders through the publication of the attendance records of
party members, first in the *Nation,* and later in the *Parliamentary Green Book* of the party.

Among the home rulers, the former liberals were not sur-
prisingly the most consistent offenders. In the summer of 1874
a new liberal Club, the Cavendish, was formed. The Irish
members were repeatedly circularised and asked to join; Butt,
however, wrote refusing to do so on the grounds that it would

[17] ibid., 1 Aug. 1874, 13 Feb. 1875.
[18] Butt to Callan, 29 Mar. 1875, 5 Aug. 1878, etc., Butt MSS, vol. i,
MS 830.
[19] Martin to Daunt, 2 Feb. 1875, Daunt MSS, 8047.

be incompatible with his position as a home rule member, and Power replied to the same effect. 'Mr Butt's letter may be taken as a type of the majority of the nationalists' rejoinders', reported the *Irish Times,* and the *Nation* commented that any other course would be a breach of the home rule pledge.[20] Many of the home rulers, however, such as Callan, Bowyer, and O'Loghlen, saw no inconsistency in retaining the Reform Club as their political head-quarters, until some were expelled from it for their frequent voting against 'the party'[21] In 1875 Gladstone announced his 'fixed and irrevocable' decision, at the age of sixty-five, to retire from the Liberal leadership.[22] Forster, Goschen, and Hartington were all named as likely to succeed him, and considerable interest attended the deliberations of the party meeting which was called in the beginning of February to elect a new leader. On 30 January a circular letter, signed by Browne and O'Shaughnessy as party secretaries, was dispatched to the home rule members, apprising them that at an informal meeting of the available members of the party, fifteen in all, held in Dublin on 21 January, it had been unanimously resolved:

> that in the opinion of those present it would be inexpedient and inconsistent with the position we have taken as home rulers that any of us should attend the meeting about to be convened in London to elect a successor to Mr Gladstone.
>
> We have been requested to communicate to you this expression of their opinion in the hope that it may meet with your approval and concurrence.[23]

This circular produced an immediate response to Butt from Sir Colman O'Loghlen:

> My dear Butt,
> I was sorry to receive this morning a circular, signed by Browne and O'Shaughnessy, about the proposed meeting of the Liberal party at the Reform Club on Wednesday next. I write

---

20 *Nation,* 1 Aug. 1874.
21 Rev. T. Morley, *Reminiscences,* (1882), vol. ii, pp. 231-5.
22 *Nation,* 23 Jan. 1875.
23 30 Jan. 1875, Butt MSS.

to you on the subject as I see you were present at the ' caucus ' from which this circular emanated.

It seems to me altogether beyond the ordinary practice of parliamentary parties that the ' whips ' should write to individual members telling them that they should not—or rather *ought* not—to attend this meeting or that meeting . . . They might as well tell me with whom I should dine—what club I should have—or what club I should not join—as call on me not to attend a meeting as ' inconsistent ' with my actions as a Home Rule member.

Every member must judge for himself what is ' inconsistent ' with his political avowals . . . I am not to be, or rather I should not be ' denounced ' by official whips if I take different views from you and act differently.

I am not going to attend the meeting of the Reform Club on Wednesday—because I will not be in London on that day— But the fact of my being a member of the Home Rule party would neither prevent me from attending, nor voting, if I felt inclined to do so at the proposed meeting.

I cordially approve of the principle of being attached to the Home Rule party in the House of Commons—but the fact of being a Home Ruler does not make me indifferent to the distinction between the Conservatives and the Liberals.

I have been, and am, and always will be, a Liberal in politics; and when consistent with my duty to Home Rule I shall always vote with the Liberals and not with the Conservatives, and I never can or will consider anything that concerns the Liberal party in the House of Commons foreign to me.[24]

O'Loghlen was not an untypical representative of the followers whom Butt now led forward to do battle for nationality. One endeavours with difficulty to image the dispatch of such a letter to his leader by one of the members of the home rule party of Parnell. Butt, however, was in no position to en-

[24] O'Loghlen to Butt, 31 Jan. 1875, Butt MSS. Of the question of the new liberal club, referred to above, he remarked : ' Last July I saw that you declined to join the Cavendish Club—if I could afford it I would have joined it—I could not afford it so I did not join it. But why should you and I fall out, or resort to " Whip " circulars because I should join a club which you should refuse to join '?

force his personal authority. Now sixty-one years old, naturally indolent and haphazard, and not over-endowed with
moral courage or the capacity for ruthless decision, he returned to Westminster as home rule leader just at a time
when he was becoming subject to increasingly frequent fits of
despondency about the difficulties of his own situation, in
particular those of his financial position.

Butt's long career of dissipation in London, his notorious
improvidence, and his professional devotion to the fenian prisoners, had left him with a crushing burden of debt. Endless
stories abound of his lifelong battle with the bailiff; in precise
terms his debts were estimated in 1871 at ten thousand
pounds.[25] So far as the home rule movement was concerned,
this situation had one damaging result: the necessity to avoid
a second appearance before the courts as a debtor compelled Butt to pursue his professional practice, leaving only
a part of his time for political leadership. These twin obligations inevitably produced failure at both; he never cleared
himself from debt, and the party suffered badly, particularly
in the sessions of 1876 and 1877, from his intermittent attendance at Westminster. In 1872 began the first of his many requests to be allowed to withdraw from the leadership.[26] As
Butt wrote to Henry in December 1873:

> When I am asked to continue to take the part I do in the
> movement—it is exactly the same thing as if I asked you or Mr
> Shaw to do something to serve the cause which would at once
> cut down the profits of your mercantile business by *at least* one
> half.
>
> It requires familiarity with four courts life to realize this
> fully—it is not the time that is abstracted from professional
> pursuits that does the mischief so much as the impression that
> I cannot be depended upon to be present in a case when I
> may most be wanted.[27]

25 M. Barnett to Butt, 1 Feb. 1871, Butt MSS.
26 Ferguson to Butt, 23 Aug. 1872, Butt MSS.
27 Butt to Henry, 8 Dec. 1873, Butt MSS, vol. iii, MS 832.

Perhaps most important of all, Butt's health and powers of concentration in the years from 1876 onwards began to succumb to the strain of his dual task.

For a long time Butt considered various devices to enable him to free himself from debt. An American lecture tour, ever the standby of impoverished Irish genius and patriotism, an elaborate scheme of life insurance which would have reduced his yearly payments to his creditors to £1,440, and the organisation of a national tribute to him on the lines of that which had been so successfully raised for O'Connell, were the most-discussed expedients.[28]

Around the beginning of November 1873, as the association was giving way to the league and a general election loomed near, Shaw, Henry, Sullivan, and one or two others met in Morrison's Hotel to consider how Butt might be set free to undertake the responsibilities of parliamentary leadership. The meeting authorised Shaw and Sullivan to approach Butt with the proposal that a certain sum of money should be guaranteed to him by a number of individuals to relieve his immediate difficulties; in return he would bind himself to undertake a lecture tour of the United States in order to raise funds both to recompense them and to establish his finances upon a permanently healthy footing.[29] Butt at first concurred in the proposal, of which it is extremely probable he had previous knowledge. He confided to Henry:

> If a sum of £2000 is provided it will be ample for all the purposes we wish.
>
> £500 ought to be placed at my disposal *now*.
>
> £500 more at the meeting of parliament.
>
> £500 placed at the disposal of Mrs Butt for home expenses.
>
> £500 to provide for any deficiency or unexpected need.
>
> I can hand over two policies of £1000 each but a premium of £125 is to be paid.

28 M. Barnett to Butt, 1 Feb. 1871, 26 Aug., 11 Sept. 1872; J. Ellard to Butt, 4 Sept. 1871; M. Hewson to Butt, 11 Dec. 1872; Butt MSS.
29 J. A. Blake to M. Henry, 24 Dec. 1873, Butt MSS, vol. iii, MS 832; Butt to Henry, draft letter, 24 Dec., Butt MSS.

I must engage to provide for the repayment of the money at the end of a year. If I could not do it any other way I would feel bound to go to America in the autumn.

Independently of this I have made up my mind to do so.[30]

Not wishing to take a prominent part in the financial negotiations, Butt appointed J. A. Blake, former member for Waterford City, to act for him. Blake approached Callan, Harman, Bryan, and McKenna, and by the end of November a sum of £1500 had been provisionally guaranteed, apparently consisting of £500 each from Shaw, Henry, and McKenna.[31]

From the outset, however, there were severe handicaps to the plan. Shaw, accustomed as a banker to the calculation of risks, thought Butt a poor one. In particular he was sceptical of his leader's dollar-earning potential as collateral for the investment. To Henry the merchant he voiced his professional misgivings:

I don't think till after the general election there is any great point in Butt's spending the whole time of the session in London. You may be quite sure the Irish M.P's. will not give Butt any leadership on general questions in the house, whilst they may be quite willing to follow his lead on the Irish question. Then being in London with very little to do he would be sure to fall into mischief of some sort that would be damaging to himself and to the cause. Then are you quite sure if we guarantee the money to a bank, that it is not already used, that we won't be only securing a debt already incurred. I have a strong suspicion from some matter that came to my own knowledge that he and another of our men are deeply in with Power's Bank . . . It will give me pleasure to join in the matter (not to the same extent as you) and so will Ronayne, but we should like to know who are the others that you think likely. They should all be men who would not do it with the object of having a grip on Butt and some day throwing it in his face or using it in any shape as a means to some personal ends . . .

---

[30] Butt to Henry, undated, Butt MSS, vol. iii, MS 832.
[31] Blake to Butt, 18 Nov., Butt MSS; Blake to Henry, 29 Nov., Butt MSS, vol. iii, MS 832.

'Whatever I put my name down for', he concluded grimly, 'I feel certain of having to pay'.[32]

Meanwhile, unknown to Shaw, Butt was also having second thoughts. The American expedition was a prospect which he had resisted for several years; it appealed to him no more now. To Henry he argued that it would defeat the purpose of the whole scheme by compelling his withdrawal from Ireland, and he suggested a 'modification' of it, apparently to the effect that the guarantors should be recouped from the proceeds of a national tribute to the home rule leader.[33]

For the hard-headed Shaw, this was the last straw. Together with Henry he drew up and conveyed to Butt via Blake as conditions for the continuance of the project, firstly, that Butt should bind himself to go to America as originally planned, and secondly, that he should give fuller details of his indebtedness.[34] To this Butt replied by cutting off the negotiations and reiterating his decision to retire.[35] But the old threat had been used too often, and from Henry it drew only the sympathetic rejoinder that he also contemplated withdrawing from politics—'it would not break my heart'.[36]

On receipt of this rebuff from his colleague, Butt sat down to the production of a lengthy and much re-drafted apologia. Beneath the rhetoric and the frustration this document, written at the turning-point in his leadership, looks back without affectation to the triumphs behind and without self-deception to the pitfalls ahead.

> I have been thrown by circumstances not of my own seeking into a position of great honour, but one, the exigencies of which I am not prepared to meet. I am quite sure that any man to guide the home rule movement as it ought to be guided must be able to devote to it the main portion of his energies and thoughts.

32 Shaw to Henry, 2 Nov. 1873, Butt MSS, vol. iii, MS 832.

33 Butt to Henry, 24 Dec. Butt MSS.

34 Blake to Henry, 1 Dec., Butt MSS; and 2 Dec., Butt MSS, vol. iii, MS 832.

35 Butt to Henry, 1 Dec., Butt MSS, vol. iii, MS 832; Henry to Butt, 2 Dec., Butt MSS.

36 Henry to Butt, 2 Dec., Butt MSS.

The time has come when the conduct of it must engage the attention of the world, when at the same time the demands upon the thoughts and energies of its leader will be immensely increased. And when a very deep responsibility will rest upon the man who leads the people to believe in its success.

I have thought deeply and earnestly upon the subject, and I believe that, if I were able to guide it as it ought to be guided for three years, it would succeed.

But, apart from all under or over-appreciation of myself, unless I do so guide it I have no confidence that it will.

And more than this; I mean by guiding it to be able to *plan*, to think over, to execute, *in many instances personally* what I plan and think.

No one knows how much of our past success has depended on this. You will not accuse me of self-conceit if I say that much of our present success depends on my having done so—on the result of combinations which I planned and carried out *alone*, and of which in the beginning no one saw the meaning.

The present position of the movement requires all this more than ever. I could occupy a long day's thoughts over and over again in devising plans of action which in time would have their effect. Even to guide and direct the mechanical part of the movement here—the meetings of the Council and of the League—would make vast demands upon my time and energies. It cannot be done without incessant watchfulness and labour. Even the correspondence my position involves would occupy, if attended to, some hours a day. It will every day increase.

It is not easy for anyone who has not tried it to judge of all this. You know something of what I have done, but no one knows how much I have left undone—how many plans I have abandoned because I could not find time to execute them—how much and how often the cause has lost by this.

I believe that such omissions now would tell with far more injurious effect. I believe the next year will be one that will tax all the resources and all the energies of home rule. I do not think the next session of parliament will be an uneventful one to that cause. I do not believe it can be so. I am sure that a well-directed plan of parliamentary action would do an immensity to serve the cause—the want of it great harm. But I am sure that you cannot avoid a number of parliamentary skirmishes in which repeated small defeats will be great disasters, and repeated small successes be great triumphs, and in which the conduct of the Irish members may cover our cause with honour or with shame. How often have you told me that my presence in the House of Commons was essential? In matters like this *I believe it is.*

I want you to judge me fairly and *you must read over and weigh every word I have written,* and say if I have one particle exaggerated the demands the cause must make upon its leader.

I need not tell you that for me to meet them *is a physical impossibility.* You might as well put a man who was working 12 hours a day in some absorbing occupation to fulfil the duties of Prime Minister in the snatches of his leisure hours, or call on him to be general of an army in the field. And now I ask you as *my friend*—anxious for my character now—anxious for my place in history—ought I to continue to seem to fill a place the duties of which I cannot discharge?—Is it fair to myself?—Is it just to a great cause?—Is it honest to my countrymen—many of whom have joined it on the faith of my leading, when, in any true sense, I am not leading and cannot lead?

Can I with honour and truthfulness tell the people to have faith in its early success when in my inmost soul I know that the conditions upon which I believe success depends cannot be fulfilled? . . .

Will I stand higher as the inefficient leader of an ignoble failure, or as one who gave up regretfully but honourably the place he could not fill?[37]

' If the Irish nation want you they must secure you ', replied Henry: in the meantime, Butt's duty was clear—to organise the league for an election. If he was prepared to accept the American project the guarantee could be revived.[38] Shaw wrote in the same terms to Butt and Henry; he was still pre-

37 Butt to Henry, 3 Dec. 1873, Butt MSS, vol. iii, MS 832. There is also a copy in the general body of the Butt MSS.
38 Henry to Butt, 6, 10 Dec., Butt MSS.

pared to participate provided only the most intimate friends
of Butt were involved.[39]

Blake resumed negotiations with Henry. The final arrangements hinged upon the agreement of Shaw.[40] But this was
not forthcoming. Suddenly Shaw announced that he would
not be associated with Sir Joseph McKenna in the guarantee;
Ronayne concurred in this attitude.[41] Their aversion to
McKenna was based partly upon his doubtful reputation as a
financier, partly upon the current rumour that he had gained
an ascendancy over Butt.[42] But Shaw, one feels, seized thankfully the opportunity to get his money out of harm's way. In
America, he warned Henry, Butt would

> stump it about as the great Irish orator . . . then as to the
> national tribute on which from his letter to you he has evi-
> dently set his mind I don't think neither does Ronayne that it
> will ever produce much . . . No large sum can be got without
> the active aid of the priests and if you subtract a half-dozen of
> them who are his personal friends the great body of them are
> indifferent, and many of them look on him with absolute dis-
> trust . . . Something should be done. I think Mr Butt should
> be placed in a position to reckon with certainty on £1000 or
> £1200 a year while the agitation lasts. An arrangement should
> be made with a bank that his cheque for £100 say should be
> honoured on the first of every month.
>
> Butt should be able easily to earn eough at his profession with
> this to keep himself free from all entanglements . . . If we
> guarantee now £2000 we must reckon with certainty on having
> to pay it. I don't believe he will ever be able to repay us from
> any source. Instead of this I would propose that we should get
> a private subscription spreading over this year. I am ready to
> join in this so is Ronayne or if you don't think this can be done

[39] Shaw to Butt, 5 Dec., Butt MSS; Shaw to Henry, 5 Dec., Butt MSS,
vol. iii, MS 832.

[40] Blake to Henry, 17 Dec., Butt MSS, vol. iii, MS 832.

[41] Shaw to Henry, 16, 20, 31 Dec., Butt MSS, vol. iii, MS 832; Blake to
Butt, 19 Dec., Henry to Butt, 4 Jan. 1874, Butt MSS.

[42] Shaw to Henry, 20 Dec. 1873, Butt MSS, vol. iii, MS 832.

H

both of us will join in the guarantee you formerly proposed provided other unobjectionable parties come forward . . .[43]

The fact that Blake had already invited McKenna to participate, however, caused Ronayne to withdraw altogether.[44] He and Shaw demanded a postponement of the project; it was never revived.[45] The plan of a national tribute was to be attempted in 1875 with results as gloomy as Shaw had foretold.[46]

The year 1873 drew to a close. Gladstone announced the dissolution of parliament. In Dublin the tortuous financial negotiations came to an abrupt end. Nothing had been achieved beyond the humiliation before his principal colleagues of the national leader. The new year brought a demand from Butt's landlords for the arrears of rent which he owed them upon his home in Eccles Street.[47] It brought him to the ultimate responsibility of party leadership; it left his time and his vital powers burdened as heavily as before by a dual obligation, the dangers of which to the successful conduct of the parliamentary movement he had so ominously predicted.

43 Shaw to Henry, 24 Dec., ibid.
44 Shaw to Henry, 31 Dec., ibid.
45 Henry to Butt, 4 Jan. 1874, Butt MSS.
46 See below, pp. 262-5.
47 Messrs. Battersby to Butt, 10 Jan., Butt MSS.

CHAPTER VIII

Two Sessions of Argument

A: THE SESSION OF 1874

PARLIAMENT OPENED in March with the home rulers in a characteristic state of unpreparedness. When the customary motion of an address in reply to the queen's speech was moved by the new conservative administration, Butt, in accordance with a decision which he admitted had been taken only the previous night, rose to propose an amendment calling for a parliamentary investigation into the dissatisfaction of the Irish people with their system of government. The debate occasioned only a brief preliminary skirmish. 'He did not at present ask the house to concede home rule to Ireland. That question remained to be discussed, and perhaps to be discussed for many years'. But even so soon as this first debate the party demonstrated its damning lack of cohesion. When Gladstone questioned the wisdom of Butt's immediate challenge, Lord Robert Montagu, technically a home ruler, hastened to concur; he would not, he said, have supported the proposal of an amendment to the address if he had been consulted in advance. He further agreed with Gladstone that it would be illogical to retain the Irish representation at Westminster after the concession of a separate legislature. 'What the Irish members demanded existed in Ireland until 1800', he declared: his leader had done 'an unwise thing' in coining the new expression—home rule.[1]

The amendment was defeated by 314 votes to 50. Defeat had been inevitable, and the *Nation* expressed itself more than satisfied with the debate.[2] But the outcome was not altogether happy. In addition to Montagu's peculiar contri-

[1] *Hansard,* 3rd series, ccxvii, 110-71.
[2] *Nation,* 28 Mar. 1874.

bution, the division lists had provided an unexpected result. Much emphasis had been laid by Butt during the election upon the necessity to conciliate the English democracy; it was in pursuit of this aim that he himself had devoted almost the whole of his energies in the campaign to the canvassing of the northern English industrial towns. As a result of the promises exacted by the Irish voters in the election, no less than twenty-nine English and Scottish liberals had been claimed by Butt as pledged to support the demand for a parliamentary inquiry into the home rule proposal.[3] But only four of these in fact supported the amendment, while of the Irish home rulers, only forty-six and the two tellers were in evidence. The exposure of these figures, wrote the *Irishman*, had been one beneficial result of the debate:

> That is the winnowing of the corn heap, and about one sixth of it has turned out to be mere chaff.[4]

The debate was followed by an immediate conference of the party in the Westminster Palace Hotel, at which an attendance of thirty-nine was mustered. It was agreed that the home rule demand should be brought formally before parliament during the session. The form in which this should be done was not as yet decided. The *Nation* added threateningly:

> a game of obstruction is one at which two can play, and the home rulers, although they are a minority of the whole, may, if they are put to it, be able to find means of making themselves troublesome at unexpected times.[5]

Butt put down his name for a day upon which to discuss home rule; at first he was allotted 23 June, but later his motion was deferred by the government until 30 June.[6] In the meanwhile home rule members gave notice of bills to assimilate the borough franchise of Ireland to that of England, and to assimilate the municipal franchise and privileges of the two islands, together with motions calling for the state purchase

3 ibid., 21 Feb.
4 *Irishman*, 28 Mar.
5 *Nation*, 28 Mar.
6 *Daunt Journal*, 25 May, 6 June, MS 3041.

of Irish railways and for immediate state action to revive the Irish fishing industry. Two of these had a certain amount of success. The fisheries motion was carried unexpectedly by 95 votes to 93, the home rulers enjoying the support of a number of Irish and English liberal and conservative members.[7] The second reading of the Municipal Privileges (Ireland) Bill, which sought to obtain for the Irish corporations the rights of their English counterparts, was permitted to pass by the government.[8] The nationalist press heralded these minor triumphs as the first victory of the Irish party. But the municipal privileges bill, after passing through its committee stage in the commons, was rejected by the lords.[9] The second reading of the Municipal Franchise (Ireland) Bill, a far more important measure which would have greatly increased the Irish municipal electorate, was defeated by 125 votes to 88. The meeting of the party committee which followed deplored the absence of no less than twenty-one home rule members from this midnight division.[10] The railways motion was rejected by 235 votes to 59. of whom only twenty-five were home rulers.[11] In this division Major P. O'Gorman (Waterford City) voted with the government on the ground that he was opposed to any extension to the power in Ireland of the ancient enemy. The Borough Franchise (Ireland) Bill, which sought to equalise the urban franchise in the two islands, did not come up for discussion until the end of the session, when it was withdrawn by Butt without a division after a short debate.[12]

Undeterred by such reverses, Butt transferred his attack to what was, after home rule, the most important of the popular issues, that of the land. On 5 May he introduced his land bill or Ulster Tenant Right Bill, so called because it sought as its main aim to extend to the rest of Ireland the protection afforded by the Ulster custom in relation to compensation for

7 *Hansard,* 3rd series, ccxviii, 1498-1530.
8 ibid., 945-56.
9 *Nation,* 25 July.
10 *Hansard,* 3rd series, ccxviii, 784; *Nation,* 25 Apr.
11 *Hansard,* 3rd series, ccxviii, 1263-1335.
12 *Hansard,* 3rd series, ccxxi, 1262-4.

eviction.[13] Butt's speech in moving the bill was praised as an exceptionally fine effort; the proposal possessed, moreover, the support of the Ulster presbyterian Richard Smyth (Londonderry County) in addition to that of the home rule members. After this auspicious introduction, however, the fortunes of the bill languished under the pressure of government business, and in August it was finally withdrawn.[14]

All these were only preliminary skirmishes to the two main battles of the session. On 30 June Butt introduced his home rule motion. Martin and Daunt had been invited by him to co-operate in drafting the terms of the proposition to be laid before the house, but insufficient planning seems from the outset to have attended this vital debate.[15] Defeat was of course expected; but the disposition of the Irish members had already become a grave issue, and a special urgent whip was prepared by the parliamentary committee. The form finally taken by the motion was to propose in the first instance:

> That this house resolve itself into a committee of the whole house to consider the present parliamentary relations between England and Ireland.

If this motion were accepted, Butt proposed to move in committee:

> That it is expedient and just to restore to the Irish nation the right and power of managing all exclusively Irish affairs in an Irish parliament.
>
> That provision should be made at the same time for maintaining the integrity of the empire and the connection between the countries by reserving to the imperial parliament full and exclusive control over imperial affairs.

The terms of the motion were agreed at a meeting of the party which was attended by thirty-two members.[16] The only amendment placed upon the table of the house of commons was in the name of Richard Smyth; it deprecated any such change in the constitution of the United Kingdom as 'pre-

13 ibid., ccxviii, 1699-1705.
14 ibid., ccxxi, 1256.
15 Daunt Journal, 25 May, MS, 3041.
16 *Nation*, 27 June.

judicial and dangerous to the peace and independence of the Irish nation '.

The house and the galleries were full for this first formal introduction of the home rule demand; amongst those in the gallery was Sir Charles Gavan Duffy, temporarily returned from Australia, who was frequently surrounded by home rule members. The prime minister was present; Gladstone was judiciously absent. Butt, in introducing the motion, spoke for one and a half hours in what all the political correspondents seem to have concurred in regarding as a masterpiece of persuasive eloquence. He outlined the history of the Irish parliament and its fall under the union; he went on to explain the federal proposal. He concluded:

> Give us a new participation in a new compact, carried not by fraud and coercion, but founded on the free sanction of the Irish people. Backed as I am now by sixty representatives of the Irish people, in their name I offer you this compact, and I believe if it is accepted, it will be, humanly speaking, eternal.

His plea fell, of course, upon deaf ears. By what was conceded to be a piece of parliamentary bad manners, the Irish attorney-general, J. T. Ball, the latest contribution of the Dublin University constituency to the legal advisers of the conservative party, interposed himself between Butt and his seconder. The ' mischievous agitation' for home rule, he declared, should be abandoned immediately. By adopting federalism Butt had cut himself off from O'Connell, whose abilities and representative position the attorney-general thus it seemed posthumously conceded. He denied the inability of the imperial parliament to legislate adequately for Ireland— the poor law act had ' given independence and strength to the people of Ireland (laughter) '. The notion had got abroad that it was only necessary to ask to obtain, he concluded: let them be firm, and the agitation would die.

Richard Smyth, as an Ulsterman, took care to dissociate himself from the jibes of Ball:

I feel for an Irishman the exigencies of whose office compel him to speak with official contempt of a large proportion of his countrymen.

But his opposition was as hostile if more rational. The land reform measures of Gladstone, he maintained, had given to the Irish tenant an unprecedented sense of security; there was no justification for the sweeping changes demanded by the home rulers. Pithily he concluded:

> I do think my honourable and learned friend credits the united legislature with too much childlike simplicity when he asks it to constitute an Irish legislature for the avowed object of doing things which it does not think ought to be done at all.

The subsequent Irish contributions added little to the debate. Colonel Charles White, allegedly home rule member for Tipperary, thought Gladstone's Greenwich address judged nicely the degree of local devolution which might safely be conceded to Ireland. He realised that he might 'be told that many Irish representatives went further than he did, but he was responsible only for his own opinions'. Only Sullivan spoke with real fire:

> It is very necessary to remember that in this debate the Irish members are not pleading before a tribunal the judgment of which can be held to be independent, or the decisions of which can be fairly accepted upon the merits of their case. To accuse a man to himself, to ask of him a verdict upon his own actions, is hardly to constitute an impartial authority . . . I want it understood that I address myself not to my judges, but that I accuse my wrongers; glad, indeed, to let their reply and my accusation be weighed by public opinion—the public opinion of the world; but quite refusing to let the decision of the accused, judge the merits of the case I plead . . .
> Ours is the ancient constitutional and indefeasible claim of a nation to their birthright—a right which they never surrendered—a right wrested from them by terrorism and intimidation the most brutal, and by corruption the most flagitious—a right the illegal overthrow of which they have never sanctioned

or condoned, and with which they are today equitably and morally as fully endowed as before that crime had been done.

This, however, was scarcely the language of persuasion, and the O'Conor Don, in particular, was careful to dissociate himself from it when he spoke on the second day of the debate. He did not think that home rule would restore 'a great and glorious nationality'; he was also ready to admit the drawbacks in the proposal, notably the hostility to it of almost all the northern counties, an admission which drew protests from his colleagues. Far from being vague, the scheme, he thought, 'erred in being too minute'. He was prepared, however, to vote for the proposal to go into committee.

The other speakers for the motion were Power, O'Clery, Henry, O'Connor Power, MacCarthy, O'Loghlen, Nolan, Downing, and O'Brien. The last three spoke at the end of the second day's debate, to the accompaniment of impatient cries of 'divide'. Major O'Brien brought the home rule case to an embarrassing conclusion by speaking in a state of intoxication, and Butt ,'much annoyed', declined to reply.[17] No English member spoke in support of the motion; Hartington for the liberals deprecated the dangerous mildness of the amendment. The house, he said, must tell Ireland that 'they could never give their assent to the proposal'; any flirtation with it would lose more support in England than it could ever gain in Ireland. For the government, the prime minister wound up the debate in his most satirical style with an airy *pas seul* across the surface of the Irish case. The house retired to the lobbies in high good humour and voted down the proposal by 458 votes to 61.[18]

Limited as Irish expectations can have been, the debate scarcely fulfilled them. Defeat itself was taken lightly for the moment:

We are barely on the threshold of the home rule campaign. The first portion of our task was to demonstrate by formal and constitutional evidence, not once or thrice, but with an itera-

[17] Brand Diary, 3 July 1874.
[18] *Hansard,* 3rd series, ccxx, 700-91, 874-969; Nation, 4, 11 July.

H*

tion that will bring the fact home to the mind and conscience of Christendom, that English rule is judged and condemned by the vote of Ireland; that England holds our country under the present system by force alone. This position made good, we shall in due time advance upon another. Courage, men of Ireland! Courage and perseverance!—we have struck the road that leads to liberty.[19]

But the lack of organisation in the debate, and the contributions made by some who chose to speak, drew unfavourable comment. John Martin wrote to Daunt:

> I might sooner have written you a word after our debate, had I been able to give you a comfortable account of it. I must with shame and sorrow confess that when it closed I felt that our side had not had the honours of it.[20]

An analysis of the division lists proved still more disheartening. The English vote confirmed the impression given by the division on the home rule amendment to the address. Only ten English members were prepared even to go so far as to support the proposal to give the home rule demand a hearing in committee;[21] eight of the twenty-nine members claimed by the nationalists at the end of the election as pledged to support such a motion of inquiry actually voted against it. The total Irish vote in favour of the proposal to go into committee was fifty-three, including the O'Conor Don, who had made quite plain the uncertainty of his support for the second part of the motion. Brooks, Callan, White, and O'Reilly paired for the motion; Montagu and Murphy neither paired nor voted.[22] 'It is clear', wrote Brand, 'that the Home Rulers are divided amongst themselves and that they mistrust their leader, Butt. Some are for federation only, others for separation also'.[23]

19 *Nation,* 11 July.
20 Martin to Daunt, 7 July, Daunt MSS, 8047.
21 They included Sir Charles Dilke, T. Burt, one of the two working-class representatives in the house, and Joseph Cowen (Newcastle) who was to be a consistent friend to Irish interests.
22 *Nation,* 11, 18 July.
23 Brand Diary, 30 June.

That there were amongst the home rule members some to whom the policy of 'iteration' was already becoming a source of frustration was strikingly demonstrated even before the end of this first session of the new parliament. The second reading of the Expiring Laws Continuance Bill, which provided, amongst other things, for the retention of the existing special powers of the Irish executive, was greeted on 25 July by stern opposition on the part of the home rulers. Sullivan at once moved the adjournment on the ground that a measure of which importance should not be sandwiched into the Saturday morning of a long and busy week; Butt supported him —'against that system of dealing with Ireland he, for one, was determined to set his face and to offer every resistance that the forms of the house allowed'. With the full concurrence and leadership of Butt, the home rule members fought the second reading with successive motions of adjournment, being defeated on each occasion with minorities of from thirty-three to thirty-five. The Chancellor of the Exchequer, Sir Stafford Northcote, tried to placate the Irish members with the offer of a day for the committee stage of the bill; Butt, however, demanded that the consideration of the coercion code should be deferred altogether until the next session. The second reading was finally carried and the house adjourned at 7.15 p.m., after a seven hour debate. The committee stage on Thursday promised a further struggle; Disraeli now refused to be bound by the original offer of a full day—if the premier did not concede it, replied Butt, 'although they were a small they were a strong minority, and they would resolutely obstruct his measures'.[24] A home rule party meeting was held, and a special whip was issued for the anticipated struggle.[25]

But Thursday brought confusion and disunity. Butt moved an amendment upon the motion to go into committee; amongst those who supported it was J. G. Biggar, who gave evidence of being in hostile mood by his dogged persistence in reading extracts from previous acts of parliament, until he was finally compelled to desist by the speaker.[26] The amend-

[24] *Hansard*, 3rd series, ccxxi, 713-46.
[25] *Nation*, 1 Aug.
[26] *Hansard*, 3rd series, ccxxi, 987-1027.

ment was defeated by 156 votes to 83, Butt having the support of 43 English members.[27] Satisfied with this moral achievement, Butt decided to allow the committee stage of the
bill to proceed, without endeavouring deliberately to block
its passage, as 'he had no wish to protract the discussion un-
reasonably'. In adopting this course he had apparently the
support of the bulk of his party.[28] A few of his followers, however, not sharing his enthusiasm for moral victory, were loth
to abandon his earlier resolve of obstruction. Prominent
among them was Biggar, who, in association with an unnamed
colleague had, in Disraeli's words, 'introduced a new style into parliamentary proceedings' by putting down over a week
ago a vast list of amendments to the bill. Captain Nolan, for
the party, moved a first token amendment; ruled out of order
on a technicality he retaliated by moving the adjournment of
the committee. When this motion was beaten by 204 votes to
50, O'Clery reintroduced it in his name. It was beaten this
time by 199 votes to 31. At once Biggar moved it a third time.

At this Butt felt compelled to assert his leadership. He had
voted with the minority until now, he said, but he hoped that
Biggar would not persevere in his intention.

> It would not only impede the business of the house, but would
> bring discredit and disgrace upon the proceedings which some
> Irish members thought it their duty to take. He was always pre-
> pared to resist any attempt on the part of the majority to over-
> bear the rights of the minority, and to use the privileges of the
> house for that purpose; but he thought that was the only case
> in which a minority was justified in resisting the majority of the
> house. He believed that the Irish people would endorse what
> he said (Major O'Gorman: No, No!). They would, he believed,
> better consult the dignity of the house and the interests of Ire-
> land by proceeding with the bill—a course which would give
> him an opportunity of moving his amendments—than by fur-
> ther seeking to impede the progress of the bill.

'The honourable member has spoken like one who is proud,
and justly proud, of being a member of this house', exclaimed

27 ibid., 1008-10.
28 ibid., 1011, *Nation*, 8 Aug.

Disraeli. But Biggar, unmoved, pressed his motion, and found thirteen members prepared to enter the lobby with him despite their leader's wishes, against a government vote of 206[29]

A lull followed in which Butt was able to introduce a second amendment. On its defeat, however, by 169 votes to 40, O'Gorman again moved the adjournment. Beaten by 167 votes to 34, Callan at once moved it again, on the ground that the prime minister was 'in a state of somnolence'. Sullivan dissociated himself from this introduction of personalities. The motion to adjourn was defeated by 157 votes to 16, and promptly reintroduced by Biggar. The bill was finally reported at 3.45 a.m. on Friday.[30]

Butt and those who shared his distaste for these tactics appear to have left the house before this time. Sullivan noted:

Close of coercion bill debate—last scene in house—apparent disruption of party—Butt denounced Biggar—several cross divisions—and break up of discipline.[31]

In the morning, however, he was instrumental in calling a meeting of the party to consider the disagreement:

—had everything reconstructed most happily—we went over to the house in force, delivered our final blow as a compact body, and 'left the field with colours flying'.[32]

When the house met again on the following, or more correctly, the same day, an arrangement had in fact been arrived at. The Irish members met in the party offices in King Street and agreed that the government's offer to reduce the operation of the bill from one year to three months justified their

29 *Hansard*, 3rd series, 979-1025.

30 ibid., 1026-7. The members who most consistently followed Biggar were Callan, Dunbar, Fay, Gray, Kirk, Martin, Nolan, O'Clery, Ronayne, and O'Gorman. On one of his motions to adjourn fourteen home rulers voted with the majority: Blennerhassett, Brady, Butt, Collins, Conyngham, Errington, Henry, McKenna, O'Byrne, O'Leary, Sheil, Sherlock, Stacpoole, and Ward. (*Nation*, 15 Aug.).

31 Butt to Sullivan, undated (footnote appended and dated by Sullivan), Butt MSS, vol. iii, MS 832.

32 ibid.

ceasing to resist it. It was decided, apparently without opposition, that Butt should record their formal protest against
the measure, contest a final division, and then press the matter
no further.[33] When the bill was reported the same night Butt
accordingly rose and announced his intention. Disraeli praised
his 'fair and moderate speech'; the house divided; the amendment was defeated by 137 votes to 56, and the incident was
closed.[34] Butt wrote the next morning to Sullivan:

> Reading the *Times* I feel that we have accomplished all we
> desired.
> We left the field victorious and with colours flying.
> How can we ever thank you for your thought of the meeting
> and the course we took.
> It was an inspiration of genius.
> That we made a triumph of disaster is all due to that inspir-
> ation. All I did was to control its spirit and carry it out.[35]

The following week parliament was prorogued.

So ended the session of 1874, with an ominous and hastily
healed division in the ranks of the party. But contemporary
observers do not as yet seem to have drawn any very serious
conclusions from these disagreements. The national press took
Butt's side, but without heat; Biggar's tactics were gently deprecated by the *Nation* as unwise.[36] If the session had shewn
signs of disorganisation and lack of preparation, most of the
supporters of the movement seem to have been prepared for
the moment to make allowances for the circumstances under
which the party had been brought together, and the unfami-
liarity of its members with their task and with each other.

Nevertheless it had already become obvious that the number of reliable and active home rule members was smaller
than had been thought, and that the number of sympathisers
among the English members of the present house was negli-
gible. In view of the size of the conservative majority, it was

---

33 *Nation,* 8 Aug. Butt to Sullivan, undated, Butt MSS, vol. iii, MS
832.
34 *Hansard,* 3rd series, ccxxi, 1071-80.
35 Butt to Sullivan, undated, Butt MSS, vol. iii, MS 832.
36 *Nation,* 8 Aug.

clear not only that home rule could not be carried in the lifetime of this parliament, but that it might never be carried
unless a substantial shift in English opinion could be induced
either by persuasion or by extra-parliamentary pressure. Butt
promised that the next session would see better organisation,
more unremitting persistence, but he was quick to point out
that such efforts could achieve nothing unaccompanied by
outside influence. As early as April, in the meeting of the
Home Rule League which followed the rejection of his first
parliamentary effort, the amendment to the address, Butt
sounded this warning:

> They should not exaggerate the importance of parliamentary
> votes. Again and again he said that the parliamentary repre-
> sentation was only a part, and he believed a subordinate part,
> of the means by which Irish self-government would be achieved,
> Home rule was to be won first of all by the Irish people show-
> ing that they were in earnest in seeking for it, it was also to be
> won by appealing to the public opinion of England and of the
> whole world, and to every one of those things their represen-
> tatives in parliament could very slightly contribute. What they
> could do was this: they could, by their presence, proclaim the
> solemn protest of Ireland against the system under which it is
> governed; they could place their views fairly and distinctly be-
> fore the British house of commons, and leave to them the res-
> ponsibility of rejecting the demands of the Irish people; they
> could destroy misrepresentation by making a statement of what
> Ireland really seeks; and, above all—and he was sure they would
> do her a most important service—they could expose the system
> of coercive oppression, and unconstitutional tyranny, by which
> England alone maintained her present system of government.
> By that means the Irish members could exert an important in-
> fluence on public opinion. Beyond that they could do nothing
> —beyond that everything rested with the people . . . When,
> however, Ireland returned eighty members to the British par-
> liament, the day of a parliament in College Green was near at
> hand.

The present parliament, he added, was not in his opinion likely to endure longer than three years.[37]

It is obvious from this speech that Butt had already abandoned any hope of victory, at least upon the issue of home rule, within the lifetime of the existing parliament, and looked instead to a determined onslaught upon the public opinion of both islands preparatory to the next general election. In an editorial in August entitled 'work for the winter' the *Nation* urged the parliamentary leaders of the movement to take full advantage of the parliamentary recess. Poor law boards and town councils as well as the parliamentary representation should all be captured for home rule, and the registration of voters should be closely watched. The young men of every town in Ireland should meet once a week, hire a room, collect a small library, and organise lectures and other functions. But in addition to this work 'a series of great public demonstrations' should be organised during the recess, to remind the English parliament of the recurring danger to them of an unsatisfied Irish feeling.[38] W. H. O'Sullivan and Richard O'Shaughnessy wrote in the same strain to Butt, urging the holding of a monster meeting in Dublin in October, to be followed by similar meetings throughout the country.[39]

It has already been remarked that the organisation of the league established by the national conference was not perhaps ideally qualified to undertake this kind of campaign. Its subscription, at one pound a year, was still, like that of the old association, relatively high; it remained a single unified organisation for the entire country, which did not formally affiliate local branches; its monthly meetings were held in Dublin and were not easily accessible to country members; it tended to work largely through its council, which, from the election, and still more the deliberate co-option to it of members of parliament and persons of social eminence, was not the most spirited of assemblies. Council meetings, even more

[37] *Nation,* 11 Apr.
[38] *Nation,* 15 Aug.
[39] O'Shaughnessy to Butt and O'Sullivan to Butt, both 6 Sept., Butt MSS.

than those of the league, were naturally largely controlled by those of its members who, as resident in Dublin, could habitually attend them.

Butt was not unaware of the necessity to bridge this gap between the league and the people. It will be recalled that the thirteenth resolution passed by the Conference had declared:

> That the annual subscription of each member of the Irish Home Rule League should be £1, and that steps should also be taken to enrol the great mass of the people in the league.[40]

At the first meeting of the provisional council of the new organisation in December 1873, Butt had promised to introduce a plan for a national roll at the first meeting of the league on 23 January 1874, and on 16 January he formally moved the adoption of the scheme in the council.[41] Everyone in the country who sympathised with the home rule movement was to be enrolled, on payment of one shilling, upon a grand national roll of home rule supporters. 'I entertain the most confident expectation that this will, if properly and vigorously managed, give us in a very short time 100,000 men and £5000', wrote Butt in a confidential memorandum upon the future of the movement.[42]

But the number of signatures which were gained never came anywhere near these expectations. At no time does anyone else in the league seem to have shared Butt's enthusiasm for the project. In particular, Martin, as organising secretary, was sceptical as to its value. It has already been remarked that he was not, perhaps, the ideal occupant of the post which he filled. He was neither young nor strong; part of his time was necessarily occupied with his attendance at parliament, and for that part which he was able to devote to league affairs he appears to have had what he considered better uses than the prosecution of enrolment, in particular the launching of an independent home rule periodical.[43] But this project proved

40 *Conference proceedings,* p. 194.
41 *Nation,* 20 Dec. 1873, 17 Jan. 1874.
42 Dec. 1873, Butt MSS, vol. i, MS 830.
43 Martin to Daunt, 23 Feb. 1874, Daunt MSS, 8047.

equally abortive, and by March 1874 Martin was lamenting
that the funds available to the league were being swallowed
up by the publication of the proceedings of the conference
and by the arrangements for the national roll.[44] In April he
was complaining of Butt's complete absorption in the roll;
additional staff and rooms had been taken for it 'quite need-
lessly', and in face of his protests:

> Mr Butt had wildly sanguine ideas about the raising, and at
> once, of a huge money income by the scheme. And so, to do the
> work fast and well, he insisted upon a special committee . . . a
> separate staff and separate rooms and an expensive machinery
> —and most provoking of all that I as prime minister should
> superintend and control and be responsible for all. I could
> only protest and warn . . .

The number enrolled in these first months was only a little
over three thousand, and the income thus gained merely
covered the expenditure to date.[45]

Inevitably, retrenchment was forced upon the league. In
May it was compelled to give up the rooms in Upper Sackville Street which had been taken as headquarters for the new
campaign.[46] The national roll scheme was retained, but drew
increasing criticism, and Butt had to defend it against the
objections of Sullivan as well as Martin.[47] Gradually hope in
it seems to have been abandoned.

In August an effort was begun to organise the 'autumnal
campaign' projected by the *Nation*. A series of public meetings addressed by Butt, Martin, Galbraith, Biggar, and O'Connor Power were held in Ulster. Constituency meetings were
also called by the more active home rule members of parliament. In Cork, Shaw, MacCarthy, McKenna, Murphy, Downing, Galbraith, Daunt, and several priests attended a home
rule assembly in the courthouse presided over by the mayor;
unfortunately the lack of prior negotiation between Ronayne
and the advanced party caused the latter to take up a hostile

---

44 Martin to Daunt, 21 Mar., ibid.
45 Martin to Daunt, 15 Apr., ibid.
46 Martin to Butt, 30 May, Butt MSS.
47 Butt to Sullivan, undated, Butt MSS, vol. ii, MS 831.

attitude, and hecklers interrupted the meeting to demand that it should be transferred to the open air and held on a Sunday, in order that working men might be able to attend it. Ronayne received 'a tremendous ovation', but the motion of confidence in the sitting members provoked abuse of 'shoneen whigs' and a cry of 'what about Nicholas Dan Murphy'?[48] Limerick was the scene of similar conflicts. The proposal of the Farmers' Club to call a home rule meeting aroused the ire of John Daly and his friends who, claiming the credit for having returned Butt and O'Sullivan in the first place, felt the convening of such a gathering to be their right rather than that of the farmers. Daly said:

> I make no objection, as I stated before, that the home rule plat-
> form should be accepted as a compromise . . . But we must be
> told when it is going to be finished, for I don't want, and I will
> not be a party to seeing, the ambition of a certain class of
> people satisfied while hunger exists in the land and the emig-
> rant ships take our best men away to be slaves of other
> nations . . .

Daly and his supporters invaded a meeting of the Farmers' Club and threatened them with a re-enactment of the cele-brated 'First of November' when two hundred amnesty men routed the farmers in the market-place of Limerick. The *Nation* attributed this dispute to the rumour that the far-mers were anxious to 'shunt' the home rule issue in favour of tenant right.[49] The dilemma was resolved by the holding of two meetings. One in Limerick, organised by 'the democ-racy', was attended by Butt and O'Shaughnessy; the mayor presided, but only six priests were on the platform, of whom four were members of orders and only two parochial clergy. O'Sullivan was with Butt earlier in the day but stayed away from the meeting. Daly, in proposing a vote of thanks to the chairman issued a warning to the home rule leader:

> He never would appear on a public platform were it not the
> fact that Mr Butt offered compromise between the Irish people

---

[48] *Nation,* 17 Oct. Daunt Journal, 12 Oct., MS 3041; Captain Dunne to Butt, 15 Oct., Butt MSS.
[49] *Nation,* 24 Oct.

and the English government, and he accepted that compromise on behalf of the democracy so long as consistent. But the moment representatives degenerated to whiggery or toryism, that moment they would unfurl the banner they struck under before.[50]

A few days later another home rule meeting was held at Kilmallock, O'Sullivan's home town, attended by Butt, O'Shaughnessy, O'Sullivan, Synan, Martin, and large numbers of priests, under the auspices of the Farmers' Club.[51]

Meetings were also held in other constituencies. A large convention in Maryborough was attended by Sullivan, Meldon, and O'Shaughnessy as delegates from the league, but not by the sitting members for the county, Digby and Dease.[52] The O'Conor Don and Charles French attended a Roscommon meeting at which the former at last elucidated his attitude to the home rule party. He had been physically unable to attend the party conference in March, he explained; afterwards, he found himself intellectually unable to accept the resolutions which it had passed in his absence. Pledges to united action were useless as the members did not know to what they were pledging themselves. He, for example, had assumed that the pledge bound members to avoid all English party associations, and to consider themselves 'neither liberals nor conservatives, but simply members of the Irish party'; however:

> Subsequent events very soon proved that this was not a correct interpretation, for shortly after one of the most prominent and able members who took part in the meeting, and who subscribed to those resolutions, was to be found organising and starting in conjunction with an English party a new entirely political and party club, and on the list of the provisional committee formed for the purpose of establishing this club his name can be found.

For his part, the member for Roscommon had no criticism for such a course:

50 ibid., 31 Oct.
51 ibid., 7 Nov.
52 *Nation,* 10 Oct.

I have not, then, gentlemen, accepted these pledges, but at the same time I have ever been ready, since you first returned me as your representative, to meet my Irish colleagues and to discuss with them all matters of public interest whenever so doing seemed to me to be likely to be of any service.

French, on the other hand, unhesitatingly aligned himself with the party. The meeting expressed satisfaction with the conduct of both members.

Constituency meetings of the same kind were also held in Cavan, Galway, Mayo, Wexford, and Carlow. The series was concluded in November by a packed gathering in the Rotunda at which William Shaw presided and seven home rule members of parliament attended.

With the exception of the Ulster series referred to at the outset, these were not, however, essentially recruiting meetings. The league never went to the people with the kind of popular appeal which had been suggested by the *Nation* and by O'Sullivan; its main effort to gain popular support, the national roll scheme, evoked a disappointing response. Efforts had been made to set up local home rule associations in different parts of the country through the agency of the travelling secretary of the league, Hugh Heinrick, a pompous individual whose appointment was attributed, probably correctly, by the fenian element to the influence of his former employer in the *Nation*.[53] In December, however, the poverty of the league compelled it to discharge Heinrick, and to rely solely upon the assistant secretary, J. P. McAlister; at the same time Martin announced his determination to give up the paid secretaryship if the financial position of the league did not improve.[54] In February 1875 Martin did in fact resign and was elected an honorary secretary;[55] no successor was appointed to the paid position. Thus at the end of little over

53 J. Nolan to Butt, R. Pigott to Butt, 5 Mar. 1873, Butt MSS. Also numerous letters from Heinrick to Butt in the same collection, June, September, and October 1873.
54 Martin to Daunt, 12 Dec. 1874, Daunt MSS, 8047.
55 Martin to Daunt, 25 Feb. 1875, ibid.

a year of existence the league had one paid official in place of
the three which it had initially engaged.

The year 1874, then, saw a sudden and in some respects
disastrous election, an unimpressive parliamentary session,
and a relative failure on the part of the league to broaden its
influence throughout the country. It saw, in addition, some
threatening divisions within the ranks of the movement. The
election was followed almost immediately by the defection
from the party of P. J. Smyth, who at once initiated a bitter
controversy with the home rule leaders as to the relative merits of O'Connellite repeal and the federal programme. In his
campaign Smyth possessed the valuable support of the eccentric Marchioness of Queensberry, support valuable not so
much from her powers as a controversialist, which were in
some doubt, as for her financial assistance, which enabled him
to make an arrangement with Richard Pigott under which
the latter, in return for a cash payment of two hundred pounds,
agreed to place three columns of the *Irishman* every week at
the disposal of Smyth's '82 clubs.[56] These bodies never won
much public support, but the goodwill of the *Irishman* gave
Smyth additional publicity for his anti-home rule campaign,
which, reaching its apogee in the debate on the home rule
motion of 1876, seriously compromised the representative
character of the home rule party in the eyes of English critics.
Already in 1874 enthusiastically hostile papers were spreading
rumours of the impending disintegration of the party. It cannot have been difficult to believe such reports of an organisation so notoriously unwilling to accept discipline even upon
the conduct of the one issue which was its *raison d'être*. Besides the open disagreements at Westminster, another dispute
inside the party was permitted to become public. It will be
recalled that in the by-election which followed the invalida-
tion of the Mayo result, O'Connor Power, who had been compelled by clerical disapproval to withdraw from nomination
in the general election, now contested the issue with the two
previously elected members, George Browne and Thomas

---

[56] Pigott to Smyth, 18 July 1874; Pigott to M. of Queensberry, 28
Sept. 1875, 27 Jan., 10 Feb. 1876; Smyth MSS, 8216.

Tighe. The majority in the party favoured their erstwhile colleagues, but John Blunden, one of the honorary secretaries of the league, and a close friend of Butt, went down to Mayo to work for the candidate of the advanced wing. An irate meeting of the party, called upon the requisition of Bryan, O'Callaghan, Digby, Sheil, O'Loghlen, Bowyer, and Blennerhassett, all of the right wing of the party, was only prevented from censuring Blunden by the promise of Butt that the league council would publicly disclaim all responsibility for his action. 'In liberal political circles' all opinions, wrote the *Nation,* were unanimously in favour of Browne and Tighe. It was Power, however, who returned with Browne to Westminster.[57]

As the year drew to a close, the issue of the land was moving once again into the forefront of Irish politics. So long as home rule seemed an immediately practicable objective, there was a possibility that the agitation for it might consume popular interest to the exclusion of other issues. But now, with hope apparently deferred until another general election might increase the power of the home rule representation, minds were turning once again to older grievances. In October the chairman of the Limerick and Clare Farmers' Club found it necessary to arrange a county meeting with the parliamentary representatives in order to

> remove from their constituents, the farming class, the impression which he should say was gaining ground, that tenant right had been left in the background in consequence of the great question of home rule.

Home rule meetings, during the recess, continued, as always, to pass resolutions calling for land reform, but the resentment of the farmers at the alleged neglect of their interests was unappeased.[58] To resolve these differences, and to plan more positive parliamentary action on the land issue in the 1875 session, it was decided to summon a land conference.

[57] *Nation,* 16 May 1874.
[58] *Nation,* 10, 24 Oct., 21 Nov.

Butt's Tenant League had lapsed upon the passage of Gladstone's land act, and the tenant farmers had been left for a time without any national organisation, although the local farmers' clubs had remained in existence. As the shortcomings of the act became, however, increasingly apparent, the need for such organisation returned. Landlords granted or redrafted leases so as to compel their tenants in many cases to opt out of the act; the employment of this device by the Duke of Leinster in the 'Leinster lease' led to the establishment of the first 'tenants defence association'.[59] Other parts of the country were quick to follow suit.

It was upon the county Dublin association that the organisation of the impending conference mainly devolved. Its secretary, A. J. Kettle, was an enthusiastic home ruler and a loyal follower of Butt. To Butt he explained his intention to establish the conference upon a firm basis by the cultivation from the outset of close relations with the parliamentary party. He proposed not merely to persuade the delegates of the different clubs to invite the co-operation of selected members of parliament, notably Butt, Gray, Sullivan, and Meldon, and in their joint names to assemble the conference but also to hold, on the day previous to the conference, a private meeting of these members and of the 'more thoughtful' club spokesmen to draft a bill for submission to it. Kettle warned Butt, however, of two difficulties. The leaders of the Ulster farmers had prepared a bill of their own which they had not shown to their southern counterparts, and they appeared to be going to ask the government to settle their problems on a party basis. The farmers of the south, on the other hand, were, he believed, only lukewarm on the home rule issue, because they suspected a similar indifference towards their problems on the part of the home rule members. The conference would have to resolve these differences.[60]

[59] A. J. Kettle, *Material for victory*, Dublin, 1958, p. 14. One of the chief aims of Butt's 1874 land bill had been the repeal of those clauses of the 1870 act which made possible this 'contracting-out' of its provisions.

[60] Kettle to Butt, 19 Dec. 1874, Butt MSS.

Butt approved of all these plans. But Kettle's worst fears were borne out. The Ulster members of parliament refused altogether to attend the conference or to co-operate in drafting a joint bill. A section of the farmers, incensed by what they considered Butt's neglect of their interests in the last session, insisted upon confining the preparatory meeting of 19 February to their own delegates, and upon drafting their own bill without any consultation with the parliamentary representatives prior to the actual conference on the following day. Kettle strongly disapproved of this attitude, and to circumvent it proposed to hold a private meeting with the leading members of parliament, including Butt, together with such veteran tenant-right agitators outside parliament as Fathers O'Shea and O'Keeffe, Richard Lalor, Mulhallen Marum, William Bolster, and E. McElroy of Ballymoney. To Butt he expressed his deep concern at these dissensions:

> I am delighted to hear that you will be able to gain a good deal of attention to this question, before the conference . . . Your bill of last session did not meet the views of the southern clubs by any means, nay I heard it stated that part of it was contradictory of your own resolutions.[61]

The conference assembled on 20 February 1875 in the Rotunda. Sixteen members of parliament, all home rulers, were present, including Butt,[62] but the chair was taken by one of the handful of Ulster delegates, W. D. Henderson of Belfast. Thirty organisations were represented, mostly farmers' clubs or tenant defence associations; only four were located in Ulster. Resolutions were passed protesting against arbitrary evictions and increases of rent, and calling for security of tenure, 'the acknowledgment of the tenant's property in the value created by his improvements, and the free and unrestricted right of sale of his interest in his holding'. The Ulster

---

[61] Kettle to Butt, 5 Jan. 1875, Butt MSS. Most of the preceding paragraph is based upon this letter.

[62] They were Meldon, Collins, MacCarthy, Browne, Sullivan, Fay, Martin, O'Shaughnessy, Nolan, O'Sullivan, O'Brien, and Ronayne, all of whom spoke, and Butt, Shaw, O'Clery, and O'Byrne, who also attended. Also present was Charles Stewart Parnell.

tenant right, 'where observed in its integrity', satisfied these demands, and its extension to the south would be welcomed. The conference called for the introduction of a bill to meet its resolutions in the coming session; it also agreed upon the inclusion of a clause making some provision for the housing of agricultural labourers. A parliamentary committee was appointed to draft the bill and to help to promote the cause in the next session.[63] It was subsequently agreed that in order to take full advantage of the Ulster custom, the northern representatives on this committee should be asked to draft a bill based upon the usage of their province, to which Marum undertook to add southern clauses; both were then to be laid before a legal committee consisting of Meldon, Martin, Marum, and some northerners, for final approval. Kettle had fully concurred in the appointment of this committee, he told Butt:

> Why your name was omitted can only be explained by your own expressed wish that no members of parliament should have anything to do with drafting the bill—but now that other M.P's. have been appointed to act I think it right to let you know the circumstances hoping that you may be able to give them some assistance.
>
> The enclosed is the northern draft which only came to hand on the 19th inst. I expect that Mr Marum's work will be done in a few days, so that by the end of next week we should have the matter in shape.[64]

But in their lack of deference to the experience and authority of Butt, the farmers had erected a barrier between themselves and the political movement which was to deny them parliamentary expression in the session which now opened.

63 *Nation*, 23, 30 Jan.
64 Kettle to Butt, 21 Feb., Butt MSS.

CHAPTER IX
_____

Two Sessions of Argument (contd.)

B: THE SESSION OF 1875

AT THE opening of the parliamentary session of 1875, the land question was not the only difficulty which faced the home rule leaders. In January Captain White, the home rule member for Tipperary, retired from the representation. The name of John Mitchel was at once put forward by the fenian element. On his last visit to Ireland in the previous summer, Mitchel by keeping clear of politics, had escaped the prosecution as an undischarged felon to which his return had laid him open.[1] He had, however, made little secret of his dislike for the home rule movement and his determination to avoid contact with its leaders other than Martin. To Smyth he wrote in September 1874 that he had declined an invitation to stay with Sullivan.

> I will be the guest of no ' home-ruler ' in Dublin, not even with John Martin. In fact I am savage against that helpless driftless concern called ' home rule ', and nearly as vicious against your simple repeal. But if I were under any obligation (which I am not) to put in my oar at all into the puddle of Irish politics I would rather—as I have told John Martin—pull in your boat than in Butt's.[1]

But he had let Martin know that he would be willing to stand if a by-election should occur in a constituency which was prepared to elect him on his own terms, and expressly that he would accept nomination in Tipperary, which he had contested unsuccessfully in the general election.[2] Invited to

[1] Mitchel to Smyth, 3 Sept. 1874, Smyth MSS, 8215, also Mitchel to Smyth, Aug.-Sept. 1874, Young Ireland MSS, 3226.
[2] Martin to Daunt, 20 Aug. 1874, Daunt MSS, 8047. Martin to John O'Leary, 19 Aug., O'Leary MSS, 5926.

stand on White's retirement, he at once took ship from New York.

The nomination of Mitchel placed the home rule leaders in a dilemma. To endorse him was to endorse an open critic of the party, and Dr McCarthy, bishop of Cloyne, one of the few bishops who openly supported the home rule movement, urged Butt to dissociate the league publicly from Mitchel's candidature.[3] But to take this alternative would be to offer a direct affront to the advanced nationalists. With characteristic discretion the league therefore chose officially to ignore the existence of the contest. But John Martin probably expressed the sympathies of most nationalists when he wrote publicly to Kickham deprecating Mitchel's attitude to home rule as 'neither impartial nor friendly', but urging the voters to elect him as a reward for his services to Ireland and to 'trust him to do what he may deem right for the cause of Ireland'. O'Connor Power, and several branches of the English Home Rule Confederation followed Martin's lead in openly supporting Mitchel.[4]

Meanwhile the new session opened in February. At the first meeting of the home rule members O'Shaughnessy resigned as whip on the grounds of ill-health and was appointed honorary secretary to the party; his place was taken by Lord Francis Conyngham. A new parliamentary committee of eleven was elected, consisting of Butt, Shaw, Henry, Gray, Downing, Redmond, O'Connor Power, Blennerhassett, Sullivan, O'Shaughnessy, and John Martin as secretary of the league. The education question was entrusted to Butt's care, that of the political prisoners to O'Connor Power, and that of tenant right to Sullivan.[5]

Hopes that the session of 1875 would see all that resolution and organisation which had been lacking in the party in 1874, were however, soon disappointed. Owing to ill-health and the pressure of his legal practice, Butt found attendance at Westminster even more difficult than before, and he was unable

3 McCarthy to Butt, 12 Feb. 1875, Butt MSS.
4 *Nation*, 6, 13 Feb.
5 *Nation*, 13 Feb.

constantly to direct the tactics of the party.[6] Another absentee from amongst the most useful members of the party was
Mitchell Henry, grief-stricken after the death of his young
wife while on holiday with him in Egypt.

The address in reply to the Queen's speech passed upon
this occasion without any formal home rule amendment, although O'Connor Power, Ronayne, and Martin spoke in the
debate. Irish interest was centred at once upon the victory of
Mitchel in Tipperary. On Mitchel's election, Hart Dyke on
behalf of the government immediately moved for the placing
before the house of the papers relating to his trial, conviction,
and escape, with a view to his disqualification as an undischarged felon. Nolan, as the only home rule member present,
protested, and in the time gained other members of the party
were assembled. The motion was carried, however, by 174
votes to 131[7] Disraeli at once gave notice of his intention to
move the issue of a fresh writ. When this motion came before
the house on the Thursday following, O'Shaughnessy, for the
home rule party, opposed it on two grounds. The first was the
failure of the government to give the electors any previous
warning of Mitchel's incapacity to sit; secondly, he argued
that Mitchel, condemned, unlike Rossa, to transportation, had
in fact discharged his sentence by remaining outside the
United Kingdom for its term. The attorney-general conceded
that Mitchel was not liable to re-arrest, but contended that
as an undischarged felon he was nevertheless incapable of
taking his seat. Hartington, for the opposition, went so far as
to demand a committee on the question. The government
motion was carried by 269 votes to 102. A considerable number of English members voted with O'Shaughnessy; Butt himself, however, was absent from both the debate and the division, while Montagu and O'Callaghan, both technically home
rulers, voted with the government.[8] Vainly the indignant

6 Martin to Daunt, 10 Mar., Daunt MSS, 8047.

7 *Hansard*, 3rd series, ccxxii, 416-22, Joseph Cowen (Newcastle) was
the only English member to vote in the minority. (*Nation*, 20 Feb.)

8 *Hansard*, 3rd series, ccxxii, 490-539.

nationalists of Tipperary called for O'Callaghan's resignation.[9]

The Mitchel affair brought little credit upon the influence of the party either in Ireland or at Westminster; its aftermath was no more fortunate. Disqualified once, Mitchel stood again as a challenge to the decision of the government. Upon this basis Butt now felt able to endorse his candidature, and after an energetic campaign organised by young John Dillon, lately auditor of the Literary and Historical Society of the Catholic University, Mitchel was again returned.[10] At once the seat was awarded to the conservative candidate, Stephen Moore, whom Mitchel had defeated by 3,114 votes to 746. The exertions of the campaign proved too great a strain upon the ailing Mitchel; less than a fortnight later he was dead, to be followed in as little time by John Martin, who caught a chill while attending the funeral of his old friend and brother-in-law. 'Poor Mitchel's last legacy to Ireland is a tory misrepresentation of Tipperary', wrote O'Neill Daunt in his diary.[11]

Meanwhile at Westminster the old arguments ground on in the watches of the night. McKenna and Butt moved for an inquiry into the imperial taxation of Ireland; after a short debate their motion was withdrawn.[12] O'Connor Power similarly moved and withdrew a resolution urging the release of the remaining political prisoners.[13] P. J. Smyth's perennial bill for the repeal of the convention act was defeated by 110 votes to 38.[14]

On 22 March the annual struggle on coercion opened in an atmosphere of quiet formality with the second reading of the Peace Preservation (Ireland) Bill. Montagu, proposing its rejection, was followed by several other Irish members. O'Leary

[9] *Nation*, 27 Feb.
[10] *Nation*, 6, 13 Mar.
[11] Daunt Journal, 28 May, MS 3041. The home rule strength was further depleted by the death in April of Sir John Gray. Martin's seat in Meath was held by Parnell, who thus entered Parliament for the first time; those of Gray and Captain White were lost. This brought the theoretical membership of the party to fifty-four.
[12] *Hansard*, 3rd series, ccxxii, 1703-27.
[13] ibid., 1759-69.
[14] ibid., 1957-61.

at one stage sought to move the adjournment, but was restrained by Sullivan. The debate spread into a second day, in which Butt, attending consistently for the first time in this session, was one of the speakers. The second reading was carried by 264 votes to 69.[15] The bill, wrote the *Nation* grimly, should not be allowed to become law 'until it has been made very much more of a scandal and a trouble to the English parliament',[16] and Butt wrote:

> We believe we can promise that the Irish party will in this matter, at least, exhaust all the forms of the house to attain their just and righteous object.[17]

The committee stage was taken exactly a month later. In the interval Butt's Municipal Corporation Bill had been adjourned to death, and only with difficulty had the home rule leader dissuaded Nolan and Meldon from moving a retaliatory adjournment upon the next piece of English business.[18] As a special urgent whip summoned the party to the battle on coercion, its more active members were thus already in a mood for reprisal. As soon as the debate opened, Biggar showed that he at least was prepared to carry out to the letter Butt's warnings to the government. On the motion to go into committee he proposed an amendment calling for the rejection of the bill. For four hours he continued to speak, reading extracts from newspapers 'in a manner which made it impossible to follow the application', and illustrating his argument with a mass of statistics which were 'almost inaudible'. The house, its forbearance 'sorely tried', emptied. A count was taken, and Biggar resumed, reading extracts from the evidence before the Westmeath commission 'in a manner which rendered him totally unintelligible'. Reproved for his inaudibility by the speaker, Biggar took his papers and a supply of water, and moving into the front opposition ben-

---

[15] *Hansard,* 3rd series, ccxxiii, 148-219, 232-92.
[16] *Nation,* 27 Mar.
[17] Home rule party circular, ibid., 10 April.
[18] *Hansard,* 3rd series, ccxxiii, 295-6. Shortly afterwards Butt withdrew both this and his municipal franchise bill, apparently despairing of their progress in that session. (*Nation,* 24 April).

ches, which had been vacant throughout, resumed his speech. Finally inspiration failed him, and being 'unwilling to detain the house any longer', he sat down.[19]

Biggar was followed by McKenna, O'Clery, O'Conor, MacCarthy, Downing, Fay, and Nolan, who, with the ministerial speakers, in the words of the *Nation,* 'protracted the debate for two or three days longer'.[20] But although none of the other Irish members chose to follow Biggar's tactics, neither did they condemn him openly. O'Connor Power and O'Gorman defended him against the sarcasm of Disraeli; Sullivan, on the other hand,

> assured the house that the honourable member for Cavan had spoken as he did, not from any prearrangement with the other Irish members, but totally on his own responsibility, and without having given them any previous intimation that he intended to address the house at any such length.

The adjournment was moved by O'Leary, supported by Butt. Defeated by 245 votes to 63, it was at once moved again by Major O'Gorman, a patriot the fire of whose eloquence was in direct ratio to his degree of intoxication. 'If the liberties of my country are to be destroyed by a despotic and insolent majority, these liberties shall die hard,' cried the Major. The house was moved to 'great laughter'; Disraeli gave way to this 'tragic address', and the members departed in something like their normal humour after the long sitting.[21]

The debate on Biggar's amendment was resumed on 26 April. The second night was the occasion for the maiden speech of the new member for Meath, Charles Stewart Parnell, elected in the room of John Martin. It was an effort notable mainly for its forthright conclusion:

> Why should Ireland be treated as a geographical fragment of England, as he had heard an ex-chancellor of the exchequer call it some time ago? Ireland was not a geographical fragment, but a nation.

[19] *Hansard,* 3rd series, ccxxiii, 1451-8, *Nation,* 1 May, Brand Diary, 22 April.
[20] *Nation,* 1 May.
[21] *Hansard,* 3rd series, ccxxiii, 1451-90.

After several Irish members and one ministerialist had spoken, the amendment was defeated by 155 votes to 68, and the house went into committee on the bill. In committee Butt and the O'Conor Don moved the first of the fifty-nine amendments of which the Irish members had given notice. Biggar moved the adjournment, with characteristic effrontery withdrew it in order to allow Ronayne to speak, and then reintroduced it. Progress was reported.[22]

On 29 April the struggle was resumed. Amendments were introduced by Nolan, Fay, Butt, and O'Sullivan. The first three having been defeated, the chief secretary Hicks Beach promised on behalf of the government to give consideration to the fourth. Butt accordingly asked O'Sullivan to withdraw it; the latter, however, was determined to hold out for a firmer commitment until Downing intervened to remind him of ' the necessity of deferring to the expressed wish of the honorable and learned member for the city of Limerick in the interests of the house.'[23]

Amendments succeeded one another monotonously until Biggar, feeling that satiety had been reached, moved the adjournment. His speech being interrupted by 'unseemly noises', Callan rose to protest, and Sullivan also appealed to the house to hear the member for Cavan. Biggar was irked by these appeals; ' he intended to be heard. If honourable members did not like it they had their remedy, and he had his '. The motion was defeated, but the adjournment was shortly afterwards conceded.[24]

The fourth day, 30 April, passed without incident. On the fifth, 3 May, Biggar and Downing disagreed as to the pressing of one amendment, and Callan forced a division against Butt's wishes.[25] The sixth day, 4 May, was uneventful. On 6 May Disraeli complained in the house of the hindrance caused to government business by the prolonged committee stage of the bill. He made, however, no charges of obstruction, admitting that consistent with their avowed intention to offer 'unflinch-

22 *Hansard,* 3rd series, ccxxiii, 1641-83.
23 ibid., 1849. Brand Diary, 29 April.
24 *Hansard,* 3rd series, ccxxiii, 1828-63.
25 ibid., 1963-2001. It was defeated by 311 votes to 3.

J

ing opposition' to the bill the Irish members had not exceeded their parliamentary rights; he recalled that in 1843 a
coercion bill for Ireland had been held up for nine days in
committee by an even smaller minority.[26]

The committee stage of the bill ended at last on 6 May.
With the last amendment disposed of, Butt rose to make what
were probably meant to be a few concluding remarks:

> He thought at the end of the committee he ought to remark
> that the Irish members had nothing whatever to complain of
> in the manner in which the chief secretary had conducted it
> . . . They had nothing to complain of in the manner in which
> they had been received by the house, and the manner in which
> their objections had been met would have some effect in miti-
> gating the effect these coercive measures would have upon the
> minds of the Irish people. He hoped the house would not take
> objection to the manner in which the opposition had been
> conducted. The bill was unconstitutional, it vitally affected the
> liberties of the people, and its provisions were multifarious, and
> had it been applied to England it would not have passed with
> even so little discussion. He, however, believed it had been
> discussed fairly, and much as they regretted the re-enactment
> of these laws it could not be said an ample oportunity had not
> been given for the consideration of the question.

Disraeli replied: 'I think this is the best message of peace
which we have had for a long period'.

So, no doubt, Butt intended the struggle to end. But this
exchange of parliamentary compliments was incomprehensible to many of the men who had borne the brunt of the
battle.

> Mr Ronayne: I, for one, will not be a party to accepting
> from the English government chains, however gilded, or how-
> ever accompanied by courtesy, politeness, or good manners.
> Mr. Biggar: This is not, in my judgment, an occasion on
> which we ought to bandy compliments, I am not going to
> blame the house for the want of courtesy shown towards my-

26 ibid., 165-70.

self; but I must protest against a bill being forced on us un-
supported by reason, argument, or common sense.

Mr Mitchel Henry said, he did not think that was a proper
occasion for bandying compliments. He thought the question
was really too serious. He intimated that the bill would be
strongly opposed on the third reading.

On this discordant note the long debate concluded.[27] The remainder of the Irish business taken in this session can be
quickly disposed of. On the land issue all liaison between the
parliamentary committee set up by the conference, and the
home rule members, seems to have broken down. The committee insisted upon compulsory arbitration as the only legal
solution of landlord-tenant disputes, and at the same time
opposed any provision for the revaluation of rents.[28] This
attitude was quite unacceptable to Butt, whose own preference was for perpetuity of tenure at periodic revaluation, and
who did not believe that anything more radical than fixity of
tenure could be usefully put forward in an English parliament. The committee submitted their bill to Meldon on 13
April with the request that he should alter its fourth clause so
as to make arbitration the only means of settling disputes and
to repeal the relevant provisions of the 1870 act. Meldon
failed to do this, and the session was allowed to pass without
any bill being introduced.[29] In June the tenant representatives were still asking Butt to confer with them:

If you could manage to draw up your bill in a short time and
submit it to the Farmers' Clubs and even give notice to the
house that you would bring it forward at an early day next
session you would be doing good work.[30]

Butt, however, was obviously angry that a remotely-situated
tenant committee should endeavour to dictate parliamentary
tactics to him. He was also anxious not to anticipate any action
on the part of the Ulster representatives in parliament.[31]

27 *Hansard,* 3rd series, ccxxiv, 195.
28 Kettle to Butt, 13 Apr., Butt MSS.
29 ibid., and J. Byrne to Butt, 3 May, Butt MSS.
30 J. Byrne to Butt, undated fragment, 1875, Butt MSS.
31 Butt to Sullivan, undated, Butt MSS, vol. ii, MS 831.

His colleagues were no more enthusiastic. In September Henry congratulated him on regaining the 'whip hand' on the land question; revision of rents and the power of removing an undesirable tenant must certainly be conceded in any reform, added Henry; free sale, furthermore, was only a phrase, and as understood by the committee redounded only to the advantage of the tenant.[32] Falling back on a historic formula for inaction Butt finally moved, before a listless house, for the appointment of a royal commission to enquire into the working of the land act. Henry Bruen, conservative member for Carlow county, and the chief secretary Hicks Beach were the only ministerial speakers; the latter dwelt with considerable effect upon the differences between Butt's demands and those of the tenant committee. The motion was defeated by 108 votes to 41. No liberals bothered to speak, nor did any of the Ulster members.[33] The tenant committee remained wholly unsatisfied.

The other Irish measures were disposed of with equal expedition. Butt's County Boards (Ireland) Bill, which proposed the democratisation of the grand jury system, was defeated by 182 votes to 125 at the end of June in what was the most successful of the Irish debates.[34] Henry's motion for the release of the political prisoners was withdrawn after a short debate in which Parnell distinguished himself by accusing the authorities of the torture of the prisoner Daniel Reddin;[35] Downing's Poor Removal Bill was defeated by 231 votes to 65[36] and MacCarthy's Waste Lands (Ireland) Bill died by adjournment.[37] Biggar alone retired in fighting order, joining with the workmen's representatives Burt and MacDonald in opposition to the voting of a special grant to the Prince of Wales for his projected tour of India.[38]

32 Henry to Butt, 29 Sept., Butt MSS.
33 *Hansard,* 3rd series, ccxxiv, 1716-40.
34 ibid., 746-67.
35 ibid., 1198-1201.
36 ibid., 1768-96.
37 ibid., ccxxv, 1459.
38 ibid., ccxxiv, 1153-8.

So ended a session even more sterile than that which had preceded it. Butt's minor bills had been defeated or withdrawn in despair; there had been no amendment to the address, no land bill, and, above all, not even a formal proposition of the home rule demand. There had been resolution alone on the question of coercion, and it had been marked by growing dissension as to the tactics to be adopted by the party. Already public opinion was beginning to weary of parliamentary defeat, and frustration was growing in two important sections of the people; the farmers and the advanced nationalists. The land bill fiasco was ventilated in a sharp newspaper controversy between Butt and the tenant committee, which blamed the vacillation of the members of parliament for the failure to bring in a bill in the 1875 session, and accused Butt of retreating from his own resolutions of previous land conferences.[39] Butt, for his part, expressed the opinion that the Ulster tenant right should be used as the basis of all parliamentary action, and made quite clear his refusal to accept responsibility in parliament for any bill which he had not personally drafted. A British parliament, Butt obviously felt, was unlikely to concede the uncompromising demands of the committee; he made no apology, nevertheless, for persevering in the policy of argument:

I am equally persuaded that it is our duty to press upon the British parliament the legislation which we believe the pressing wants of our country need. In some instances we may—I believe we will—succeed in obtaining, it may be, partial redress for the grievances of which we complain. Every time we do so we gain some strength and vigour for the national life. But I know of no means by which we can better advance the cause of home rule than by making honest and intelligent Englishmen realise to themselves the deficiencies of their Irish government and Irish legislation. There is no subject which we ought to press more urgently than that of the necessity of giving to the Irish tenant the protection which legislation has not as yet adequately afforded him.[40]

39 *Nation*, 12 June.
40 ibid., 29 May.

Pressed home with vigour this policy was by no means in itself defeatist or futile. But the waning energy of the home rule party scarcely justified any confidence in its efficacy. Public opinion noted, with growing resentment, the steady absenteeism of the Irish members. The *Nation* drew attention to the absence of eleven home rule members from virtually all the divisions in the coercion bill committee, some of which the government had won by majorities as low as two. Less than half the party voted on Butt's land motion.[41]

Some of this lack of application was attributable to Butt's own frequent absences. Little as the party respected his authority, it seems to have been quite unable to evolve any discipline apart from his leadership. O'Shaughnessy reported from London during one of Butt's absences:

> Not a word was said at our meeting of the land act or legislation, or of any other measure except education, and all that was said about that was that nothing ought to be done in your absence . . . We have arranged to hold bi-monthly meetings, but not one word was said, and not an idea was implied, about superseding the committee in the discharge of its duties of originating or regulating action. It was agreed that individuals should explain their intended action in reference to motions appearing in their names to the meeting, in order to enlist support or have suggestions from the others, but this appears to have been aimed against guerrilla performances.[42]

O'Connor Power's proposal that a deputation of home rule members including, in O'Shaughnessy's phrase, 'the eunuchs of the party', should apply for leave to visit the political prisoners, was likewise deferred until Butt should be free to decide upon its utility.[43]

In 1875, in order to mitigate the harmful effects of Butt's frequent absences, a final effort was made to free the home rule leader from the necessity to practise his profession. In February a testimonial fund was launched with the establishment of a provisional committee in Butt's own constituency of

---

41 ibid., 15, 22 May, 19 June.
42 O'Shaughnessy to Butt, 13 Feb., Butt MSS.
43 O'Shaughnessy to Butt, 15 Feb., ibid.

Limerick; it was decided to vest the monies collected in the hands of a board of trustees with absolute discretion as to their application.[44] It was a project long planned by Butt which he at last entrusted to some of his closest supporters in the movement such as Sir Joseph McKenna, Charles Dawson, and John Ellard.[45] The gloomy prophesies of Shaw a year previously proved, however, only too accurate. Despite the efforts of its organisers to gain official clerical support at the outset, the catholic bishops for the most part held aloof.[46] To Cardinal Cullen home rule remained 'a tool in the hands of journalists and adventurers' which would 'end in smoke', and Dr MacHale still stood in solitary eminence as the nationalist zealot among the hierarchy.[47] Lacking clerical approval the chapel door collection, the only really effective means of tapping mass subscription, was denied to the testimonial; in any case, the failure of the league to raise sufficient funds to pay its own way scarcely argued the readiness of the public to subscribe to a second home rule levy. Henry wrote to Butt:

> I still do not believe that the Irish bishops wish catholic money to go into a protestant pocket and unless we can frighten them we shall get no effectual help on home rule. *They fear it.*[48]

Money came in quite quickly at first. But as soon as the contributions of the loyal supporters of home rule had been exhausted, the supply began to fall increasingly short of the demand. The chief trustees, Henry and Conyngham, had paid Butt nearly £3000 from the fund by January 1876,[49] but already the importunings of Butt were outstripping their resources, and the future receipts from the testimonial were

[44] Copy of the resolutions of the committee, 19 Feb., Butt MSS.

[45] O'Shaughnessy to Butt, Ellard to Butt, 31 Jan. McKenna to Butt, O'Shaughnessy to Butt, 8 Feb., and other letters in Butt MSS.

[46] Ellard to Butt, 16 Feb., Henry to Butt, 19 May, Butt MSS; and McAlister to Daunt, 10 May, Daunt MSS, 8047.

[47] Quoted in Bowyer to Disraeli, 9 Oct. 1875, Disraeli MSS.

[48] Henry to Butt, 5 Sept., Butt MSS.

[49] Henry to Butt, 5, 9, and 19 Sept., 9 and 17 Oct. 1875; 20 Jan. 1876, Butt MSS.

mortgaged against Henry's personal cheques.[50] By December 1875 there was hardly £100 in the four banks used by the trustees.[51] Internal divisions and jealousies in the organising committee reduced its efficiency; the paid organiser, Captain Dunne, was discharged in September, and in 1876 the conduct of the movement was placed in the hands of George Delany, an active Dublin home ruler.[52] But by that time no exertions could arouse enthusiasm in the public, and by October 1876 Butt had admitted defeat. To Delany he wrote urging him not to take the desperate expedient of publishing the names of subscribers.[53]

> The more I think of it the more averse I am to any publicity above all to any allusion to future action. Even if anything were ever to be done it could only be done by a new departure and not as a continuation of that which has been done.
> My earnest wish is that nothing more should be *publicly* done —I am led to believe that some monies will yet come in—if so so much the better but it is not the time to draw attention to the failure.

He asked Delany to lodge something as soon as possible; he had left a cheque with the bank to be drawn as soon as there was anything to meet it.[54] By 1877 Delany had succeeded to J. A. Blake's thankless task of begging on Butt's behalf from his leading colleagues in the party, his efforts seconded as Blake's had been in 1873 by the wearisome repetition of Butt's determination to retire from the leadership.[55] Butt proposed the establishment of a national committee, on the lines privately suggested by the bishop of Clonfert, Dr Duggan, to manage the testimonial fund permanently and to guarantee him an income of £2000 a year.[56] ' If men were so impressed with the necessity of my sacrificing myself—they

50 Henry to Butt, 19 Sept., 17 Oct. 1875, Butt MSS.
51 Henry to Butt, 20 Dec., Butt MSS.
52 McKenna to Butt, 3 Sept. 1875, Delany to Butt, 24 Mar. 1876, Butt MSS.
53 Butt to Delany, 30 July 1876, Hickey MSS.
54 Butt to Delany, 6 Oct., ibid.
55 Butt to Delany, 10, 13 Mar. 1877, ibid.
56 Butt to Delany, 15 Mar., ibid.

ought to guarantee me for the year £2000—£1000 to meet liabilities I might be called on to meet and £100 a month for ten months', he said to Edmund Dwyer Gray.[57] He pleaded in vain. Soon Delany, like his predecessors, was added to the list of Butt's private creditors.[58] The problem of Butt's periodic absences from parliament remained unsolved.

The apathy of the nation was unkind, but it was easily explicable. After the optimism of the 1873 conference, the movement was slow to reconcile itself to the frustrations of a minority position. The people might have accepted Butt's policy of argument and reiteration if it had been energetically pressed, if the voice of the Irish mendicant had never been mute at Westminster, if government business had been brought to a standstill by the bills of the Irish members. They knew, indeed, of no alternative policy. But it was the consistent absenteeism of the leader and the cynical apathy of so many of his followers, the diminishing energy of the party and the apparently declining volume of Irish business which caused them increasingly to lose confidence in the leadership.

If even the early supporters of the movement were losing heart, the episode of the O'Connell centenary in August 1875 showed how little it had been able to allay the distrust of the clergy and the middle class liberals. The impending anniversary of the birth of the liberator aroused much enthusiasm in Dublin, and great preparations were made to celebrate it.[59] It was unfortunate for the home rule interest that the occasion coincided with the lord mayoralty of Peter Paul McSwiney. Frustrated in all his previous efforts to gain political prominence, McSwiney determined to use his position as presiding magistrate and chairman of the centenary committee to turn the celebrations into a catholic liberal demonstration, and with the support of Lord Emly and the liberals on the one hand, and the P. J. Smyth party on the other, chose to treat the life of the liberator as if it had ceased in 1829.[60]

[57] Butt to Delany, 13 Mar., ibid.

[58] Butt to Delany, undated, ibid.

[59] Daunt Journal, 9 July 1875, MS 3041.

[60] *Nation*, 31 July; Daunt Journal, 27 July, 11 Aug., MS 3041; Daunt to the centenary committee, 27 July, Daunt MSS 8045.

J*

Cardinal Cullen, wrote Daunt in his diary, set the tone of the commemoration:

> with what he calls a ' Pastoral ', eulogising the deceased patriot as a tremendous catholic and champion of catholic liberties, but saying not one word of his merits as a nationalist or as an earnest agitator for the emancipation of the dissenters.[61]

Authorised to select the orator to deliver the memorial address at the culminating ceremony, McSwiney passed over all the nationalist leaders, and picked Lord O'Hagan, catholic lord chancellor under the Gladstone administration.

The result of this manoeuvre was what the *Nation,* with a certain disingenuousness, described as a ' wonderful uprising in Sackville Street '.[62] The amnesty men having made no secret of their determination to thwart McSwiney's intentions,[63] O'Hagan decided to stay away and the oration was committed appropriately enough to McSwiney himself. At King's bridge a hand-to-hand fight for precedence took place between the amnesty men led by Nolan and Daly and the coalporters, traditionally O'Connell's bodyguard, led by P. J. Smyth. The coalporters won the race by cutting the traces of their opponents' dray, but the amnesty men dragged their vehicle to Carlisle bridge, where they fortified themselves on the platform which had been erected upon the site of the present O'Connell statue. The poet, Denis Florence MacCarthy, had been commissioned to write an ode for the centenary, and his son has left in his diary a graphic description of the scene:

> The amnesty men with their black banners had one side of the platform all to themselves and the coalporters and carmen surrounded the others. With great difficulty I crossed Carlisle Bridge and got within hearing distance of the platform. The whole of Sackville Street, Carlisle Bridge, and all approaches to them were occupied by a dense mass of men with bands and banners. All however were in great good humour; there was no drunkenness whatever and confusion was occasioned only by

[61] Daunt Journal, 11 Aug., MS 3041.
[62] *Nation,* 14 Aug.
[63] F. MacCarthy's Diary, 30 July, MS 7251.

some of the mounted men endeavouring to force their horses through the crowd. The Lord Mayor's state coach could be seen moving slowly down through the black sea from Nelson's Pillar. At length he reached the platform, the opposite side from where I stood and therefore invisible to me. When he attempted to read Lord O'Hagan's speech, his voice was drowned in a storm of cries of all kinds, among which 'Down with Whiggery', 'No whig placemen', and 'Butt, Butt' predominated. After several ineffectual attempts to gain a hearing the Lord Mayor with difficulty regained his carriage the black flags and chains of the Amnesty Association being flaunted and rattled in his face. When his carriage was gone the cries for Butt were renewed, and A. M. Sullivan whom I observed sitting on a house top with his legs hanging over the parapet, kept shouting out Butt's name at the top of his voice. At length Butt did appear, and standing beside the white, laurel-crowned bust of O'Connell, his old opponent, made a vigorous little speech pointing down to the colonnades of the 'old house in College Green', and reminding the people of the grand centenary which was approaching in seven years time, the centenary of Dungannon and the Volunteers. O'Connor Power, M.P. for Mayo, then spoke, vehemently protesting against the selection of Lord O'Hagan as spokesman for such a national celebration. Sullivan who had descended from his perch next spoke, remarking on the attempt that had been made 'to cut O'Connell in twain', by trying to ignore his long struggle for the legislative independence of Ireland, to the honouring of him solely as the emancipator of catholics. The crowd then gradually dispersed. I got some dinner and then ran out to Kingstown and walked on the pier till 10 o'clock. There were some illuminations in Dublin, the word 'O'Connell' in large double letters on the metal-bridge coming out beautifully and being reflected back from the black waters beneath. Bands playing national airs marched through the streets almost all night, and thus the 100th anniversary of Daniel O'Connell's birth passed away into history, to be ranked among the memories of the past.[64]

64 MacCarthy Diary, 6 Aug., MS 7251.

The outdoor celebrations were followed by a banquet in the evening at the exhibition palace. At this banquet the toast of the legislate independence of Ireland was proposed by Sir Charles Gavan Duffy, who had been chosen for this honour by McSwiney, no doubt because of his avowed disapproval of the home rule movement.[65] Yells of 'Butt, Butt' drowned the speaker; Callan stopped the lord mayor from intervening by persistently calling for Butt; Butt rose, apparently intending to appeal for order; McSwiney walked out; the gas lights were extinguished, and the banquet broke up in confusion. A 'disgraceful scene', noted William Woodlock in his diary.[66] Recriminations dragged on for weeks, being given an added spice by a dispute inside the committee as to the disposal of its surplus funds. McSwiney and Smyth endeavoured to project these divisions into the future by the launching of a new repeal movement, called the National O'Connell Committee, with the motto of 'faith and fatherland', but public support was lacking, and the association dwindled into memory with its founder at the end of the mayoral year. The lord mayor himself, however, was not left emptyhanded; awarded the Knighthood of Saint Gregory in return, said hostile opinion, for his services to the whig cause, the brilliance of his red ribbon and star won for him at social gatherings the notice which had so consistently eluded him in public life.[67]

Ridiculous as this whole episode was, yet its Dickensian furies are in their way as truly evocative of the conflicts of the time as are the statistics of parliamentary defeat. They force upon later observers a realisation of the existence of a middle class which in many cases had reconciled itself increasingly to the practical comforts of the union, and, seeking to escape the insecurity of nationalist politics, was often more conscious of its religious than of its political evolution. But in contrast to this element there appears the energy of an instinctive if as yet largely negative nationalism, working warmly upon the emotions of the men with no property and no stake in the maintenance of the existing order in society. These were men

---

[65] MacCarthy Diary, 19 May, MS 7251.
[66] Woodlock Diary, 7 Aug., MSS 4498-5011; *Nation*, 14 Aug.
[67] ibid., 3 Dec. 1878; Daunt Journal, 2 Dec. 1875, MS 3041.

whose political reactions were by nature violent in feeling and not infrequently violent in execution; to disrupt an anti-national meeting they turned instinctively to the use of the fist and the club. Their dynamism found an uneasy and sporadic expression in the constitutional home rule movement.

In the centre of these two forces stood Butt. Largely rejected by the one as alien in spirit and outlook, he himself rejected the other. To one his ideas were too radical, to the other they were too conservative. Both saw in him no more than a compromise of doubtful validity; neither could see that his was an idea as organic and as homogeneous as theirs. Had he been more completely a realistic politician, he might have harnessed the energy of the nationalists to his movement by adopting their demeanour and their language. John Ferguson of Glasgow wrote to him words of sincere advice around this time:

> If I were Isaac Butt I'd gather the loyal bold and honest men of Ireland around me so firmly that no room would be found in Ireland for such opinions as O'Leary sends from Paris or any of the Luby and co party from New York. Young Ireland today wants to follow and confide in Isaac Butt. But he must be a bolder leader or he will not be followed.[68]

But already, by the end of 1875, the advanced nationalists were wearying of conciliation, and there is, finally, a special significance and a special poignancy in their participation in the centenary celebrations; this was the last occasion upon which they were to use the name of Isaac Butt as a nationalist symbol. John Daly and C. G. Doran were on Carlisle Bridge with the amnesty men in August 1875, but at the end of September Daly, who, it will be recalled, had worked for Butt ever since the 1874 election, rose before the parliamentary leader at a home rule meeting in Limerick to demand that the party should make the next session the scene of its final effort.[69] The patience of the nationalists was evaporating; they were looking for a new way. While Butt wrote

68 Ferguson to Butt, 21 Dec. 1875, Butt MSS.
69 *Nation,* 25 Sept.

openly to Biggar in April 1875 asking him to desist from 'a system of obstruction',[70] the advanced men in the movement were taking the member for Cavan and his unorthodox tactics to their hearts. Branches of the English Home Rule Confederation passed resolutions urging the home rule members to adopt a policy 'more obstructive and factious', and at a great amnesty demonstration in Hyde Park in August 1875 Biggar's reception as 'the hero of the hour' overshadowed those of all the other speakers, who included O'Connor Power, Meldon, Ward, O'Donnell, and Parnell.[71] In Mayo O'Connor Power, addressing his constituents upon the events of the late session, deplored its lack of activity and questioned the wisdom of Butt's decision not to press a home rule motion:

> In my humble opinion, nothing is more essential to the success of a good cause than that its advocates should show themselves to be in earnest . . . my individual opinion was entirely in favour of the course pursued by the honourable member for Cavan, and nothing but my desire to act in accordance with the general sense of the party prevented me from adopting to the fullest extent the tactics adopted by him during the coercion debate.[72]

Even while writing in support of the Butt testimonial John Ferguson at the same time made quite clear the desire of himself and his kind for the adoption of a bolder course in parliament.[73] In Kerry Blennerhassett, on the other hand, openly condemned Biggar's policy of 'factious opposition'.[74] The controversy was being brought into the open, and meanwhile the response of the people to the testimonial appeal gave ample proof, if not of their support for Biggar, at least of their growing apathy towards the policy of persuasion. Parnell, speaking to his constituents in Meath at the end of his first session in parliament, told them:

[70] ibid., 22 May.
[71] *Nation,* 3 July, and quoted from *Irish Times,* ibid., 7 Aug.
[72] ibid., 21 Aug.
[73] ibid., 1 May.
[74] ibid., 11 Sept.

what their representatives had to do was to attend to their own business, to watch by day and night over their national interests, and to fear nothing as long as they had the people of Ireland at their back.

'There is fire in that young man', commented the *Wexford People,* and named him as 'one of the coming men'.[75]

[75] Quoted ibid., 23 Oct.

CHAPTER X

Conciliation's Last Rally

THE SESSION of 1876 was a crucial one for the policy of
Butt. According to John Daly and C. G. Doran, it was the last
of three years granted to Butt by the fenians; in any case, it
was obvious from the growing criticisms of the advanced wing
that the present stalemate was becoming to them, at least, intolerable. The year opened hopefully enough with the issue
of a special party circular calling a conference of home rule
members in Morrison's Hotel, Dublin, on 4 January. The
conservative *Standard* prophesied that this gathering would
formally adopt the 'obstructive' policy as the tactics of the
party.[1] Perhaps it was the fear of such a development which
caused some of the less enthusiastic members to stay away; the
total attendance was only thirty-one. Twelve members were
abroad; nine absented themselves without explanation;[2] M.
W. O'Reilly sent a letter of apology. N. D. Murphy sent his
good wishes, assuring the party: 'it will afford me great pleasure if I can give my support to such parliamentary course of
procedure as you may determine upon' but declining to attend, as 'I am desirous of preserving my personal freedom of
action'.[3]

The meeting did not, in the event, adopt a policy of obstruction. It resolved, however, to bring in a home rule resolution on an early day in the session after the Easter recess. Butt
announced his intention to frame bills on the land and university questions; the party agreed also to concentrate upon
the issues of the Irish franchise, taxation, amnesty, coercion,
and grand jury reform. On Butt's suggestion a central tenant

[1] Quoted *Nation*, 25 Dec. 1875.
[2] Blennerhassett, Errington, Lewis, O'Brien, O'Conor (D.M.),
O'Leary, Sherlock, Stacpoole and Synan.
[3] *Nation*, 8 Jan. 1876.

right committee was set up to advise the party upon the defects of the land act. The discussion concluded, according to the *Nation*, after five hours of 'perfect unanimity'.[4] But a fortnight later Parnell reminded a meeting of the league that not only the people but also the members of parliament must show themselves to be in earnest on home rule.[5]

The session opened on 8 February in just such an atmosphere of resolution. On the address in reply to the queen's speech Henry, Ronayne, Ward and Parnell intervened to protest against the omission of any reference to Irish legislation.[6] Immediately afterwards the Irish members retired to their King Street offices for consultation, returning to their places in a body to give notice, one after the other, of thirteen bills, covering the topics of land, franchise, municipal, grand jury, and judicial reform, fisheries, and reclamation of waste lands, and the care of mental defectives.[7] Two days later a bill to regulate union rating was added,[8] and Butt and O'Shaughnessy finally gave notice of bills upon the subjects of university and intermediate education, and of a resolution, to be moved soon after Easter, calling for:

> a select committee to inquire into and report upon the nature and grounds of the demand made by a large proportion of the Irish people for the restoration to Ireland of an Irish parliament, with power to control the internal affairs of that country.[9]

4 ibid.

5 ibid., 22 Jan.

6 *Hansard*, 3rd series, ccxxvii, 109-14. Parnell dwelt mainly upon the question of amnesty, a topic to which he was devoting most of his attention at this time.

7 ibid., 117-24.

8 ibid., 201. There was also a Landlord and Tenant (Ireland) Act Amendment Bill, in the names of the Ulster tenant-right representatives, which aimed at amending the 1870 act.

9 The significance of the wording of this motion is discussed below, pp. 450-5. It was obviously aimed at attracting the support of sympathetic English liberals, whose number had been lately increased by the return of Jacob Bright in Manchester and Rylands in Burnley, both pledged to support Butt's motion.

On this occasion the Irish members so far forgot their customary respect for the traditions of parliamentary procedure as
to adopt a concerted organisation, and through the device of
putting up several members to ballot for the same motion,
they were able, to the disgust of Speaker Brand, to appropriate most of the Wednesdays in the session, the days traditionally reserved for the business of private members.[10] In
March the terms of Butt's land bill were published. An elaborate effort at compromise, it consisted of three sections. The
first sought to extend the provisions of the 1870 act to farms
held under the Ulster custom; the second proposed to amend
the act so as to remove the loophole which enabled a landlord, by the imposition of a new lease, either to compel the
tenant to contract out of the protection of the act or, more
simply, by breaking the continuity of his tenancy, reduce his
claim for compensation under the act in the event of his eviction. The third and most radical section broke new ground:
it proposed to allow a tenant, eligible for protection under the
1870 act, to demand instead a 'declaration of tenancy' which
would provide for the valuation of his holding by arbitration
and which would give him security of tenure at the agreed
rent. No appeal from arbitration was provided for except in
cases where fraud was established, but concessions were made
to landlord opinion in the provision for revaluation of rent
and for the ejectment of a tenant, through legal action, upon
the ground of waste.[11]

The bill aroused little enthusiasm. Daunt thought that it
gave the tenants 'far too much';[12] the tenants thought it gave
them too little.[13] Every one appears to have thought it too
complicated. Dr Magee, parish priest of Stradbally, called it
'an Apocalypse in 86 Clauses', and E. G. Dease in reply admitted that a more simple bill would have been better.[14] But

[10] *Nation,* 19 Feb., Brand Diary, 1 Mar.
[11] ibid., 4 Mar.
[12] Daunt Journal—Mar., MS 3041; Daunt to Henry, 23 Feb., Butt
MSS, vol. iii, MS 832.
[13] *Nation,* 18 Mar., '82 Club resolutions, 18 June, in J. F. X. O'Brien
MSS.
[14] M. Cahill to R. Lalor, 21 Jan. 1878, Lalor MSS, 8566.

Henry was able to reassure Daunt by reminding him that there was not 'the least possibility of its passing in any form', and the tenant representatives, for their part, endorsed the bill with some misgivings at their privately-held land conference in March.[15]

At Westminster the long process of argument recommenced. Nolan's bill for grand jury reform was introduced on 23 February, debated, and voted down by 181 votes to 153. These were not disgraceful figures, but of the minority only 24 were home rule members; the remainder were liberals. A full home rule party vote would have brought the figures almost level. The O'Conor Don spoke and voted against the bill; French, Morris, D. M. O'Conor, Sheil, and Stacpoole were in the house but did not vote.[16] On 1 March O'Gorman's bill to reform the Irish municipal franchise succumbed by 176 votes to 148. Thirty-three of the minority were home rulers.[17]

By this time the attendance figures of the home rule members were being published each week in the Nation, and their laxity aroused so much adverse comment that Butt had to issue a special circular to the party urging a greater devotion to duty[18] At the same time the first number of the Parliamentary green book, compiled by the secretary of the league, J. P. McAlister, was published, showing the attendance figures of each of the home rule members in the divisions of the previous session. On 28 March Meldon's resolution for the equalisation of the borough franchise of the two islands was defeated by 179 votes to 166, a government majority of 13; 45 home rule members voted.[19] The hostility of the administration to Meldon's proposal was scarcely surprising; it anticipated a loss of at least twelve Irish seats if the reform were effected.[20] On 29 March Butt moved his land bill, for which he had secured the support of the Ulster presbyterian Smyth.

[15] Henry to Daunt, 1 May 1876, Butt MSS, vol. iii, MS 832; Nation, 18 Mar.

[16] Hansard, 3rd series, ccxxvii, 765-88; Nation, 4 Mar.

[17] Hansard, 3rd series, ccxxvii, 1164-86; Nation, 4 Mar.

[18] Nation, 11 Mar.

[19] Hansard, 3rd series, ccxxviii, 703-66.

[20] Memo by Col. T. E. Taylor, Lord Crichton, and E. Gibson, 11 Jan. 1869, St. Aldwyn MSS.

After the first speakers on each side had been heard, the debate was adjourned, to be resumed three months later. On 22 March Ward's Coast and Deep Sea Fisheries (Ireland) Bill was disposed of by 215 votes to 131; the minority included 46 home rule members.[21]

The Easter recess caused a temporary cessation in this activity. The *Nation* was full of praise for the energy of the party: 'never before was Ireland so well served by her representatives in the British parliament'.[22] Certainly the argumentative policy of Butt was at last being energetically put into practice. But it was questionable if popular interest could survive the monotonous repetition of discussion and defeat, and the notorious absenteeism of the right-wing members of the party was throwing into sharp relief the determination of their advanced counterparts. The first part of the session had not passed without its customary incidents. On 6 March the omission of any home rule representative from the committee of referees on private bills had aroused sharp resentment in the Irish members, and Sullivan, Nolan, and other members divided the house as a reprisal upon each name in the committee. After the tenth division Sullivan gave up and asked Nolan to do the same, but the latter with Parnell, O'Gorman and a handful of supporters divided the house a further seven times.[23]

In Dublin the average popular reaction was expressed by Professor Galbraith, by instinct an amiable and conservative person, in the Home Rule League. Relating his remarks to last year's coercion struggles he said:

for his part, he was ashamed of any Irishman who would sit in the house and allow such measures to pass without giving every opposition even amounting to obstruction. To a policy of obstruction for the mere purpose of annoyance or delay he would be no party, but was he to be told that the Irish members, whose business it was to defend the rights of their country, were not to use all the constitutional forms of the house—were not

---

[21] *Hansard*, 3rd series, 428-65, 771-819.
[22] *Nation*, 15 April.
[23] *Hansard*, 3rd series, ccxxvii, 1495; *Nation*, 11 Mar.

to divide again and again to defeat or mitigate coercion for the people?

At the same time he sharply criticised the absentees and warned them that there would be a day of reckoning at the next general election.[24]

For John Daly and his incorruptibles, however, the new-found energy had come too late. A grand Easter demonstration for home rule in Limerick was attacked by forty or fifty young men armed with bludgeons. This time, however, the historic triumph of 1869 was not to be repeated; the weight of numbers prevailed, and Daly and his brother found themselves in gaol the next morning. Even yet Daly insisted that he had no objection to the holding of a demonstration in honour of Butt himself, whom he admired; what he could not tolerate was one in honour of the party. So the curious ambivalence of 1869 still persisted, and even as they drew away from his movement the advanced men for the moment retained their personal affection for its leader.[25] Immediately afterwards, however, the delicate relationship between the home rule movement and the fenians suffered a much more serious blow with the sudden death after a railway accident of Joseph Ronayne, member for Cork City since 1872. In many respects an unobtrusive member, his personal influence with the advanced men had nevertheless been of great assistance to the party; in this respect Sullivan had rated him, just before he died, as of even more importance to the cause than Butt himself.[26] His seat was lost to a conservative, and the theoretical strength of the party was brought to fifty-two.

At the same time Butt was experiencing his customary difficulty in allaying the distrust of the catholic clergy. In March Butt's bill to resolve the vexed question of catholic university education was published. It proposed amongst other things to establish the existing catholic university as a constituent college of Dublin University under the name of St Patrick's College. The catholic hierarchy, as a 'committee

24 *Nation,* 18 Mar.
25 ibid., 22 Apr.
26 Sullivan to Daunt, 10 Feb., Hickey MSS.

of founders', were to have final control over issues of faith and morals and were to have the power of appointing the rector, vice-rector, and professors of divinity; all the other professors and officials were to be appointed by a college council, subject to the approval of the bishops.[27] Whatever the merits of this scheme, the clergy were unenthusiastic; Dr Conroy, bishop of Ardagh, objected to it as having too liberal a constitution with too much lay and not enough episcopal power and in this view Cardinal Cullen appears to have concurred.[28] And it was scarcely surprising if the already known desire of Hicks Beach to associate the administration with Irish educational reform should seem a more fruitful field for negotiation than dependence upon the parliamentary strength of the home rule party.[29]

In May the parliamentary struggle was resumed. On 3 May Henry's Registration of Voters (Ireland) Bill was beaten by 235 votes to 168, of whom 35 were home rulers.[30] On 16 May Butt was given leave to introduce his university bill, but the absence of the entire Liberal party above the gangway augured badly for its chances of success.[31] The same month gave further evidence of the disunity within the ranks of the home rule party. The Irish members had got up a petition, signed by over a hundred members of parliament, including a large number of Liberals, asking the queen, in celebration of the creation for her by Disraeli of the title of Empress of India, to grant clemency to the political prisoners. Disraeli's rejection of this plea on 22 May produced another scene. O'Connor Power at once moved the adjournment, supported by Biggar and Parnell. Parnell, Butt, and Callan spoke in defence of Michael Davitt and of the men imprisoned in connection with the Manchester shooting. But Biggar caused uproar by describing Disraeli as 'alien in race and religion to the people of England'. Brooks disowned Biggar, and two English Liberals, Briggs and Waddy, withdrew their signa-

---

[27] *Nation*, 25 Mar.
[28] Butt to Henry, 16 Nov., Butt MSS, vol. iii, MS 832.
[29] This question is more fully discussed in pp. 376-9.
[30] *Hansard*, 3rd series, ccxxix, 32; *Nation*, 13 May.
[31] *Hansard*, 3rd series, ccxxix, 805-29; *Nation*, 20 May.

tures from the petition because of its inclusion of the Manchester men, and because of the language of its supporters.[32]

If the left wing had shown its impetuosity, the right wing had shewn a few days earlier its equal capacity for taking independent action when it felt so inclined. The proposal to confer the imperial title upon the queen had aroused in Butt an instinctive repugnance much out of character with that picture of him as a natural tory which was perpetuated by his contemporaries and so often accepted by later commentators. He set his face against any home rule support for the bill, even as a bargain for the concession of amnesty; such a course, he held, would alienate English democratic opinion, and in particular antagonise the radicals such as Cowen whose support had been so valuable in this session. For his part, he would have preferred openly to oppose the bill, but being unable to carry this principle unanimously in the party he was prepared to compromise on abstention.[33] His concession was in vain, for if the wishes of the home rule leader carried little weight on Irish questions, they carried none whatever upon aspects of English or imperial legislation. In the debate on the bill Butt announced his intention to abstain, and at the division walked out of the house with eighteen followers, including, to their credit, those like Biggar and Parnell who were most frequently accused of indiscipline and who had most to gain in this instance from a bargain with the government on amnesty.[34] But twenty-three members of Liberal sympathies remained and voted with the opposition, and three others voted with the government.[35]

32 *Hansard*, 3rd series, ccxxix, 1040-52.
33 Butt to Sullivan, undated, Butt MSS, vol. ii, MS 831; Bowyer to Disraeli, 10 May, Disraeli MSS.
34 Biggar, O'Sullivan, Sullivan, O'Shaughnessy, O'C. Power, Ward, Lewis, O'Clery, McKenna, Brooks, R. Power, Parnell, Fay, Collins, Kirk, Ennis, Callan, and Brady.
35 Dease, O'Callaghan, O'Byrne, O'Keeffe, Nolan, O'Loghlen, Downing, Conyngham, Meldon, Martin, Redmond, Dunbar, Stacpoole, Moore, Sherlock, Blennerhassett, Murphy, O'Reilly, Errington, Montagu, O'Conor Don, O'Conor, and O'Brien against the bill, and Morris, O'Gorman, and Bowyer for it. O'Conor Don, Morris, and Murphy, though not technically members of the home rule party, were usually listed among its camp-followers.

At the end of June Butt's campaign culminated in a last effort upon the two most vital issues of the land and home rule itself. The party whips, Nolan and Richard Power, issued a special whip calling the members to their places for the two debates.[36] On 29 June the discussion upon the second reading of Butt's land bill was resumed after an adjournment of three months duration. The bill was attacked as subversive of property by two Irish conservatives, Kavanagh and Plunket, one Irish liberal, Law, two camp-followers of the home rule party, Morris and the O'Conor Don, and one of its members, M. W. O'Reilly. It was supported by Butt, Downing, and Professor Smyth, and, in a speech of exceptional violence, by O'Connor Power. Hartington for the opposition declined to have anything to do with it, and none of Butt's radical allies were to be this time with him in the lobbies. The bill was overwhelmed by 290 votes to 56. 48 of the minority were Irish members, 45 of them home rulers. Seven home rulers were absent; one member of the party, French, and three camp-followers, Morris, O'Conor Don, and Esmonde, voted with the government.[37]

The following day the long-awaited debate on Butt's home rule motion was opened before a house which was already sated to repletion with Irish grievance. It was the first time in two years that the demand for legislative independence had been brought before the house, but in that time an important change had taken place in Butt's parliamentary tactics. Realising the hopelessness of carrying home rule in the lifetime of the existing parliament, and hoping to profit from the English radical support which had proved so useful in this session, he framed his motion to read:

That a select committee be appointed to inquire into and report upon the nature, the extent, and the grounds of the demand made by a large proportion of the Irish people for the restoration to Ireland of an Irish parliament, with power to control the internal affairs of that country.

[36] *Nation,* 17 Jun. 1876.
[37] *Hansard,* 3rd series, ccxxx, 624-714.

Butt made no secret of the fact that he had so framed his motion in order that it might obtain 'the support of honourable members who were not prepared to give any assent to the principle of home rule for Ireland'. He demanded an enquiry because a majority of the Irish representation had been returned in favour of home rule:

> It was not his intention to go into the general question of the parliamentary relations between England and Ireland . . . He had been in several parliaments, and he said consistently and sincerely that he never sat in a house in which Irish affairs were received with so much fairness and attention as they had in that. But that did not alter his opinion of the absolute necessity of changing the union arrangement . . . Give them the committee, however. That was all they asked. Let them bring the plan he proposed to the test of reason, to the test of cross-examination, that was all he asked, and then the people of England and the members of that house would probably see that their proposals were not of so formidable a character as they had supposed. But let them not shut the door in their faces, and content themselves with saying that they meant to rule Ireland by force as heretofore . . .

Butt's speech was generally accepted to have been a masterpiece at its level of quiet persuasion and in its meticulous devotion to the terms of the motion. Unfortunately, his tactics sat uneasily upon the shoulders of his more fiery colleagues. The motion's chances of even a relative success depended upon the strict adherence to its terms of all the subsequent speakers; an irate word could destroy the delicate balance of Butt's pleading. The home rule leader must have realised this, yet, according to the *Nation,* upon the conclusion of his own speech he left the chamber and the house and made no effort to control the subsequent course of the debate. In his absence, any hope that his followers might retain a self-control whose very utility they doubted was quickly dissipated by the provocative intervention of P. J. Smyth. Two years ago Smyth had given a silent vote in favour of the proposal to go into committee of the whole house to consider the home rule plan, but upon this occasion he rose immediately after Butt to propose an amendment to the effect that in the opinion of the house home rule was understood by a large proportion of the Irish people to mean the restoration of the 1782 parliament. He went on to deliver, to the delight of the ministerialists, a superbly vicious attack upon the federal plan. Why was Butt afraid to bring in a home rule bill, he asked? What, indeed, did home rule mean? It appeared to necessitate the creation of four parliaments:

> At certain fixed periods Ireland will pour 105 imperial representatives into the English local parliament, and forthwith, as if by magic, the domestic institution becomes transformed into the imperial, internal gives way to external, and all is turned inside out.

But how would this scheme provide for the local interests of Wales? Of protestant Ulster? What were internal affairs— would coercion, for example, be left in the power of the imperial parliament?

> Tried by any test that either imperial statesmanship or Irish patriotism can apply—imperial unity or national independence, constitutional principle or Irish right—precedent, authority, expediency, or feasibility—Irish home rule stands condemned. It is not restoration, it is innovation; it is not unity, it is dismemberment; it is not national independence, it is national annihilation; it surrenders the constitution of one country, and subverts that of another, in order to erect with the fragments a model lodging-house, in which the family would merge in the household, and the personal freedom of every occupant would be at the mercy of a composite majority. It can never be realised till England renounces her mission to be great, and Ireland relinquishes her title to be free.

After Smyth's intervention moderation went by the board. O'Connor Power, Nolan, and Kirk all spoke upon the merits of home rule as such. Hicks Beach made much of the differences in interpretation inside the party:

> Some time ago last autumn the hon. member for Meath made a speech in which he said that home rule and repeal meant the same thing.

Mr Parnell: What I said was that home rule would necessarily entail repeal of the union.

Sir Michael Hicks Beach: I think I quoted the hon. member pretty correctly; but the hon. and learned member for
Limerick (Mr Butt) repudiates any wish to repeal the union
and return to the old state of things. (Mr Butt: Hear, hear.)

The success of Butt's efforts, said Beach, would be the immediate signal for 'the revolt from his control of a party, who
even now give him some trouble—the nationalist party'. As
for O'Connor Power's reference to amnesty:

of all the extraordinary delusions which are connected with the
subject the most strange to me appears the idea, that home rule
can have the effect of liberating the fenian prisoners, the Manchester murderers (No! No!)—I regret to hear that there is
any hon. member in this house who will apologise for murder.

Mr Parnell: The right hon. gentleman looked at me so
directly when he said that he regretted that any member of this
house should apologise for murder, that I wish to say as publicly and as directly as I can that I do not believe, and never shall
believe, that any murder was committed at Manchester.

Beach concluded his speech to almost continual interruption
from Parnell, O'Connor Power, and O'Gorman.

The debate was wound up for the Irish by Sullivan. Speaking, apparently, against his will, he made no effort to revive
the tactics of Butt which had been buried so quickly in acri-
mony:

They declined once and for all to discuss this question from the
low level of a mere bill before the house. This was no murmur
from discontented Essex or Northumberland. This was no dissatisfaction in a county; this was the voice, the complaint, of a
nation. That was the protest of a kingdom foully robbed of all
the attributes of nationhood—of a kingdom which had never
condoned that crime, and which now in blood and in turbul-
ence, now in civil commotion, now by one means or another,
legitimate or illegitimate, had protested and would, while there
was manhood in its people, protest to the bitter end.

The house divided, and the motion was defeated by 291 votes to 61. Despite the careful wording of the motion, only eleven of its supporters were English; all of a left-wing Liberal order, they included such old allies of the Irish as Cowen, C. F. Hammond, Jacob Bright, and Burt. Of the 52 Irish members who supported the motion, four, Esmonde, Morris, Murphy, and the O'Conor Don, were not officially members of the party. As the party strength was now 52 there were thus only four absentees, Bryan, Synan, Redmond, and Montagu. The party could also boast that the hostile vote had fallen from 458 in 1874 to 291.[38]

The debate, however, was on the whole a failure. As in the past it was uncoordinated and undisciplined, and the best speakers in the party were in many cases silent. The division figures proved again that without the pressure of some extra-parliamentary cataclysm, the English member of parliament was not as yet willing to support even the most diluted expression of sympathy with the home rule proposal. The extremists in the home rule party were irked by the mildness of the motion, and by its undignified introduction as an amendment on going into supply: the point of Butt's conciliatory policy had, on the other hand, been drowned in the patriotism of his followers.

The debate over, there was little to add before the Irish contingent returned home for the inevitable inquest. As parliamentary interest became centred increasingly upon the developing war situation in the east, the attention given to Irish business dwindled. In August O'Connor Power's amnesty

[38] *Hansard*, 3rd series, ccxxx 738-822, *Nation*, 8 July. After the debate Bryan wrote to Butt:

'Since the last home rule debate, the conclusion has forced itself upon me, that the " federal scheme " is utterly unworkable, and I must say, that in my mind, the speech of P. J. Smyth is both unanswered and unanswerable—Holding these views, *you* will see, that there can be but one honourable course open to me, and that is, to lay my views before my constituents with as little delay as possible'. (Bryan to Butt, 27 July, Butt MSS). There is no record of Bryan's having publicly done so, possibly because his weak health at this time kept him largely out of politics. He may, I think, however, be regarded from this letter as in practice lost to the party.

motion was voted down by 117 votes to 51.[39] On 7 August Disraeli announced that in view of the pressure of business he proposed to move that government measures should take precedence on all the remaining Tuesdays and Wednesdays of the session. The protests of Butt against this step, which effectively disposed of the remaining Irish bills, including the university bill, were overruled by 99 votes to 45.[40] One crumb remained to the Irish members. On 7 August the Municipal Privileges (Ireland) Bill, which proposed mainly to allow Irish corporations to elect their own sheriffs, and to confer the freedom of their boroughs upon distinguished citizens, was given its third reading.[41] On 15 August, after the tribulations of three sessions, it received the royal assent and became law. The same day parliament was prorogued. For a whole session Butt and his followers had, for the first time, applied the policy of argument upon a broad front and with unprecedented energy and persistence. This was the one boon that they could carry back with them to Dublin as a justification of their labours. It was at once invoked by the Corporations of Dublin and Cork to honour the home rule leader with the freedom of their respective cities. The nation was not impressed.

39 *Hansard,* 3rd series, ccxxxi, 285-318.
40 ibid., 704-11.
41 ibid., 774.

CHAPTER XI

The Call for Action

THE RECESS of 1876-7 is in every way a watershed in the history of the parliamentary home rule movement. The futility of the policy of Butt, even when energetically pressed, seemed obvious now to a wide and representative section of the national movement. Even before the session ended the *Nation,* which had firmly defended Butt's tactics against the violence of Biggar in 1874, made clear, in a succession of editorials, its conviction of the necessity for a new approach:

> To us it appears that the rejection of the series of measures brought forward in the house by the home rule party affords full justification for a much stronger line of action than any which they have hitherto adopted.
>
> It was all very well, and quite right, up to the present time, to try the effect of conciliatory conduct and fair argument for the working out of Irish reforms, and we fully believe that the endeavours made in that way have not been altogether wasted . . . But, granting all that, we would put it as a matter for consideration to the home rule members whether the time has not come when it is advisable to do something more than merely travel slowly again over the ground that has been so lately trodden.[1]

These criticisms were developed in an editorial on 15 July, and in a series of letters which commenced in the same paper on that date.[2] The *Kerry Vindicator,* the *Kilkenny Journal,*

---

[1] *Nation,* 8 July 1876.

[2] ibid., 22 July. The change in the attitude of the *Nation* was probably caused by the increasing assumption of the control of the paper by T. D. Sullivan, by whom all these articles were apparently written (*Nation,* 21 April 1877). A. M. Sullivan qualified for the English bar

and the *Clare Advertiser* by the beginning of August had added their voices to the critics. The advanced party were outspokenly of the same view; a Glasgow demonstration presided over by Ferguson passed resolutions urging the need for bolder action and especially commending 'those Irish members who were so regular in attendance when Irish questions were discussed in the House, and who stood so boldly for the Irish people—particularly J. G. Biggar and Charles Parnell'.[3] In Castlebar in September O'Connor Power went one better in outspokenness. He expressed his personal loyalty and gratitude to the home rule leader, but as to his tactics: 'Twelve months ago he said he had faith in Mr Butt's political sagacity; but he condemned then and now the timid policy he had pursued in the presence of the enemies of Ireland'.[4] In October the publication of the second *Parliamentary Green Book* of the league redoubled the dissatisfaction of the critics of the party; party attendance in the divisions was shewn to have dropped appreciably, and fifteen alleged home rule members were recorded as having voted in less than ten of the twenty-five party divisions. Meanwhile the tenant-farmers were no more satisfied with their spokesmen; the national land conference at the Rotunda in October was only restrained by Butt's personal intervention from passing a vote of censure upon those of the home rule members who had opposed Butt's land bill in the late session.[5]

These criticisms were received with considerable vexation by the leaders of the party. Ill-feeling was unfortunately heightened by an unhappy conjunction of the editorials in the *Nation* with the appearance in Dublin of a series of articles on 'The Irish home rule movement' written by A. M. Sulli-

[3] *Nation*, 19 Aug.
[4] ibid., 23 Sept.
[5] ibid., 7, 28 Oct.

in November, and moved to London, formally handing over the editorship and proprietorship to his brother. T.D's nationalism seems to have been considerably more advanced than that of his brother; to Daunt he expressed his preference for the separatist ideal, and his belief that federalism would ultimately lead to it. (T. D. Sullivan to Daunt, 25 July (no year), Hickey MSS.)

van for the *New York Catholic World*. In the first of these articles reference was made to Butt's early fall into 'debt, difficulty, and dissipation', and later instalments were scarcely more charitable.[6] Sullivan was accused of conspiring to supplant Butt,[7] and a special meeting of the party, attended by no less than twenty-one members, passed a resolution expressing their 'unalterable confidence' in Butt's leadership.[8] The *Freeman's Journal* joined in the criticisms of Sullivan and the expressions of loyalty to Butt, and at the same time Sullivan wrote to the *Times* denying any disloyal intent.[9]

In the league Butt defended his tactics as best he could:

He would like to say just a few words about the last session. It was true they were defeated in their home session. It was true they were defeated in their home rule motion. Well, he never expected anything else, and the man who sent them into parliament expecting that they would carry, even in a modified form, a motion for home rule in the face of the influence by which they were met in the present parliament, and within two sessions, must have had a very strange notion of the influences that guide political events.

A voice: Hurrah for Rossa.

Mr Butt: If his countrymen were not possessed of that first of all qualities—the quality of not knowing when they were beaten—they would never achieve self-government in Ireland. They must have patience, they must rise against defeat. Defeat after defeat, if it were necessary, must make them only the more determined that they would persevere to the last . . .[10]

Criticisms of the party were no novelty. Now, however, the critics were for the first time united on the basis of an alternative policy. As early as 8 July the *Nation* had written: —

The time appears to us to be favourable for a more resolute course of action. The business of English legislation is now very much at the mercy of the Irish members; they can block it, stop

6 Reprinted ibid., 22 July.
7 The O'Donoghue to P. J. Smyth, 11 July 1876, Smyth MSS, 8215.
8 *Nation*, 15 July.
9 quoted ibid., 22 July.
10 ibid., 26 Aug.

it, and turn it into a mass of inextricable confusion if they choose. Again, England is at this moment involved in a maze of delicate diplomatic negotiations with foreign powers; the Irish members can, if they choose, avail of the situation to render the discontent of their country formidable to the minister. Such a course of action would, no doubt, be denounced in the English parliament and the English press as ' unpatriotic '—unpatriotic forsooth!—and some of the more tender-hearted of our members might decline to adopt it; but we feel convinced that without having recourse occasionally to strong measures, and facing some rough work, the Irish cause cannot be pushed to a successful issue in the house of commons.[11]

The following week the same paper unequivocally adopted the popular name for the tactics which it proposed:

We therefore recommend to the consideration of the Irish members of parliament and of the Irish people this ' policy of obstruction '. What is the English parliament to us but a huge machinery of obstruction? It is obstructing our national life, obstructing the prosperity of our country, obstructing our liberties; and, in short, obstructing us off the face of the earth. The substance of such objections as we have seen urged against the plan of action we have indicated is simply this—that it would make English members very angry. But we think there will have to be some anger in this business before it is settled. We would say let the policy we have supported be tried, not blindly, but skilfully and wisely; and if, indeed, laws be made to deprive Irish members of the ordinary rights and privileges of the British parliament, then let a conference of the Irish nation be called to decide what is the next step to be taken in the furtherance of the National Cause.[12]

As old a repealer as O'Neill Daunt could write to the *Ulster Examiner* in full sympathy with this suggestion; ' as the foe has deprived us of our native parliament, it is indeed a small reprisal to block up English legislation to whatever extent

11 ibid., 8 July.
12 ibid., 15 July.

K

may be necessary for our own rightful purposes '.[13] It would be intolerable, wrote the *Kerry Vindicator,* to have ' even one other session of mild and gentle appeals to that rather shadowy entity called the British conscience '.[14]

The element which was above all outspokenly identified with the proposed policy was that which might be loosely termed fenian. There were those, like John Daly and C. G. Doran, who had now, at the end of the 1876 session, totally and irrevocably dissociated themselves from constitutionalism. A league meeting in August was interrupted by Doran with a resolution calling for the abandonment of parliamentarianism, and a lecture by O'Connor Power in Manchester was broken up by extremists in a riotous scene in which Biggar as chairman paid for the sins of his colleagues with a damaged head. The subject of Power's lecture was ' Irish wit and humour '.[15]

But the active irreconcilables were few in number, and bitterness against O'Connor Power was perhaps their most coherent motive. The efforts of O'Connor Power to anticipate the new departure seem only to have aroused the most violent antipathy amongst his old colleagues of the I.R.B., who regarded him for some reason with the deepest suspicion as early as 1874. Biggar and Power were, of course, members of the Supreme Council of the I.R.B. until they left it in 1877 rather than obey an order to withdraw from parliamentary life.[16] Fenianism as a whole does not seem to have taken sides in the home rule issue. John O'Leary wrote to the *Sunday Citizen* of New York sympathising with the attitude of those who felt moved to break up home rule meetings, but deprecating their tactics,[17] and in private Kickham expressed the same view to Devoy.[18] The attitude of the advanced men inside the constitutional movement was expressed by the an-

---

13 quoted ibid., 22 July.
14 quoted, ibid.
15 ibid., 26 Aug., 16 Sept.
16 O'Brien and Ryan, Devoy's Post Bag, vol. i, F. P. O'Shea to Devoy, 17 Aug. 1874, pp. 71-4; J. O'Leary to Devoy, 13 Oct. 1875, pp. 121-2.
17 quoted in *Nation,* 11 Nov. 1876.
18 Kickham to O'Leary, 29 April 1876, *Devoy's Post Bag,* vol. i, pp. 163-5.

nual convention of the English Home Rule Confederation, which, meeting in Dublin for the first time in August 1876, unmistakeably identified itself with the policy of obstruction.

The English Home Rule Confederation was set up in 1873. It was the outcome in the first instance of a conference, called in Manchester by the home rule association of that area, with its purpose 'to take steps towards properly organising the electoral power of the Irish in England'.[19] Butt presided, and the secretary was the fenian John Denvir. It was agreed to form a union, which Butt recommended should be on the lines of the Anti-Corn Law League.[20] The conference adjourned, and meeting again in Manchester at the end of February, established the English Home Rule Confederation, to consist of five district councils for England, Manchester, Birmingham, Newcastle, Bristol, and London, together with Glasgow as the Scottish centre, subdivided into town branches, whose members were entitled to send delegates to the annual convention at which policy decisions were taken and the governing executive chosen.[21] A third conference in August, the first annual convention of the confederation, confirmed this arrangement and elected an executive committee. Two hundred delegates attended, and Butt presided over their deliberations.[22] By the time of the second annual convention in June 1874 the confederation numbered 64 branches. 37 belonged to the Manchester district, which remained continually the strongest, 13 to Birmingham, and 14 to Glasgow.[23] The other districts languished; London in particular was paralysed for several years by the disputes between the more moderate section and the working-class home rulers, who were strongly tainted by socialist principles.[24] The emer-

---

[19] —to Butt, 27 Dec. 1872, Butt MSS; *Nation*, 11 Jan. 1873.

[20] *Nation*, 18 Jan. 1873.

[21] ibid., 1 Mar. 1873.

[22] ibid., 30 Aug. 1873; Daunt Journal, 21 Aug.

[23] *Nation*, 20 June 1874.

[24] ibid., 5 Apr., 8 Nov. 1873; E. O'Cavanagh to Butt 16 Oct., T. Mooney to Butt, 8 Nov. 1873; J. Barry to Butt, 1 Jan. 1874; Dr Commins to Butt, 30 Nov., J. Goulding to Butt 3 Dec., M. Henry to Butt, 16 Dec. 1875, and other letters, in Butt MSS.

gence of these groupings within the confederation in turn
threw up key-figures in the English movement: most prominent amongst these were Dr Commins and John Barry,
chairman and secretary of the Manchester council, and John
Ferguson, president of the Glasgow council. Commins was
elected president of the confederation in 1874 and 1875, and
Ferguson and Barry vice-president and honorary secretary
respectively. The confederation quickly gained the support
of large numbers of the fenian element in England, and by
January 1876 it could number 95 functioning branches.[25]

By this time, however, the English home rulers had begun
to chafe bitterly against the frustrations of Butt's parliamentary policy. As early as July 1875 the official organ of the confederation, the *United Irishman,* was pressing the adoption of
an obstructive policy at Westminster.[26] 'The fact is, your
policy of parliamentary agitation is dying out', wrote Ferguson to Butt in January 1876,[27] and in June he expressed
the opinion that the Irish people had lost faith in the league.[28]

In 1876 the confederation resolved to make a determined
effort to force the Irish wing of the movement to take more
resolute action. Captain Kirwan, the paid secretary of the confederation, wrote to McAlister, his counterpart in the league,
expressing the desire of his executive for a joint conference of
the two bodies in Dublin to consider the state of the agitation.[29] This proposal, however, was not enthusiastically received. The leaders of the party had always feared the prole-
tarian extravagances of the English movement. 'I don't value
much the English agitation and don't expect much permanent
result from it'. wrote Shaw to Daunt in 1873,[30] and John
Martin made it clear to Daunt that it was the deliberate
policy of Butt which had kept the confederation altogether
distinct from the Irish movement.[31] Mitchell Henry in 1875

25 *Nation,* 29 Jan. 1876.
26 ibid., 3 July 1875.
27 Ferguson to Butt, 14 Jan. 1876, Butt MSS.
28 Ferguson to Butt, 20 June 1876, ibid.
29 McAlister to Butt, 27 Apr., 5 May 1876, Butt MSS.
30 Shaw to Daunt, 2 Sept. 1873, Daunt MSS, 8047.
31 Martin to Daunt, 2 Apr. 1874, ibid.

sent Kirwan a cheque for fifty pounds for the confederation funds, but he refused to agree to Butt's suggestion that he should act as league representative on the council of the English organisation—'I have some mistrust of them and their republican allies'.[32] Accused of republicanism, Ferguson and his friends made no effort to deny the charge, but retorted by organising a republican demonstration on 4 July 1876 in Dublin from which O'Connor Power and Parnell were despatched to the United States with a congratulatory address on the centenary of the American republic.[33]

This persistent adoption of an independent and extremist line by the confederation, at the same time as it constantly sought financial aid from the Irish organisation, antagonised and frightened the leaders of the party.[34] A resolution was passed by the council of the league, and conveyed to the executive of the confederation, recognising the good intentions behind the proposal for a joint conference, but expressing the opinion that 'the holding of such a conference would be contrary to the constitution of the league and a violation of the principles on which it was founded at the national conference of November 1873'. This decision did not go unchallenged by the activists in the Irish movement, eager to call in the confederation to redress the balance of the league. 'T. D. Sullivan jumped at the idea of a conference', wrote McAlister to Butt, 'and was trying to push an instant acceptance of the proposal'.[35]

Thwarted in their original intention, the English home rulers decided to proceed alone with their plans for a Dublin convention. This proposal aroused almost equal jealousy and suspicion in the Irish leaders; Butt at first refused even to attend the public meeting arranged for the evening of the first day of the convention, but gave way under pressure. Ferguson wrote to him:

32 Henry to Butt, 14 Dec. 1875, also 10 Dec., Butt MSS.
33 Ferguson to Butt, 12 July 1876, ibid.
34 Capt. Kirwan to Butt, 5 July, 12 July, Butt MSS.
35 McAlister to Butt, 2 May, ibid.

I am horrified to hear that you do not intend being at the
meeting in Dublin on 3 July! Before I agreed at all to the affair
I had your statement to tell everyone you were for it.

More than once had you not acted as Barry and I wanted you
you would have regretted it . . . take our advice this time. You
will see far more serious evils arise if you are not at the meeting
. . . than you imagine.

I have been in Ireland two weeks. My opinion is the people
have given up all faith in the league. You are still popular. We
are now about to divide at last whig home rulers one way real
home rulers the other way. The people made Isaac Butt. I hope
he will not desert them for 'respectability' and 'shopboy-
ism '.[36]

The convention of the confederation met in the Rotunda,
after several postponements, on 21 and 22 August 1876. A
large part of its work was devoted to an overhauling of the
English organisation. As a mark of respect to the home rule
leader, he was nominated to the presidency of the association
to fill the vacancy caused by the retirement of Dr Commins,
who had held the office for the preceding two years. But at
the same time the number of vice-presidents was increased to
five, and Parnell, Biggar, and F. H. O'Donnell, all members
of the extreme wing, were elected. In addition O'Donnell became honorary secretary in place of Barry, who withdrew
owing to pressure of work. The appointment of O'Donnell as
both honorary secretary and a vice-president gave him a key
position in the confederation, which he signalised a few weeks
later by the publication over his name and that of Kirwan as
paid secretary of a fierce broadside against the inactivity of
the party.[37] The delegates passed a resolution assuring Butt
of their confidence in his 'genius and determination' and of
their continued allegiance to his authority. But the crucial
resolution was number eleven:

That in the opinion of this meeting, before adopting a course
of action that *may* become necessary—namely, withdrawal—it
will be expedient for the Irish members to adopt a much more

36 Ferguson to Butt, 30 June, Butt MSS.
37 *Nation*, 7 Oct.

determined attitude in the house of commons upon all questions in which Ireland is concerned, so that the British people
may be induced to adopt the principle of division of labour in
government.[38]

The forthrightness and energy of the convention seem to
have left a marked impression upon the more realistic of the
home rule members. By the end of August Henry was writing:

> For my part I think the confederation are doing excellent work,
> perhaps the only good work now in progress relative to home
> rule—The league is in a state of suspended animation . . .[39]

The parliamentary policy which they proposed might still be
distasteful to the moderates in the party, but even Shaw could
see the fruitlessness of the last session: —

> if there is not great wisdom, coherence and decision it will be
> impossible to convince the country that we are not playing with
> the home rule question. We must remember that there is a con-
> siderable number of ourselves and a very large party in the
> country who are watching for an opportunity of dropping back
> again into whiggery . . . I feel strongly that we are at a critical
> turning-point and that we must take especial care in every step
> not only to keep the party together, but to keep it at all. No
> knowing when a general election may take place, and very
> little would so disgust the constituencies that they would let
> the majority of us go to the right about . . .[40]

Perhaps resolution in the next session could avert disaster,
and check the growing dissension in the party. But the debate
on parliamentary tactics was revealing a deep divergence in
attitude between the two wings of the movement, across
which the active moderates like Henry maintained a pre-
carious balance. The *Spectator* commented that three policies had been raised at the convention: the 'parliamentary
tactics' of Butt, the 'obstruction' of Sullivan and those who
agreed with him, and the complete withdrawal suggested by

38 ibid., 26 Aug.
39 Henry to Butt, 30 Aug., Butt MSS.
40 Shaw to Butt, 12 July, ibid.

the fenians. Of these three, it concluded, the convention, while endorsing Butt's leadership, had accepted obstruction and merely postponed withdrawal.[41] It was against the background of these now open divisions that Butt on 6 January 1877 issued his circular for the fourth annual pre-sessional conference of the Irish home rule party.

Thirty-two members obeyed Butt's summons; fifteen sent their apologies. The remainder were absent without explanation.[42] O'Shaughnessy resigned the secretaryship of the party, and Meldon and Ward were elected as honorary secretaries for the coming session. Nolan and Richard Power were elected whips. A new committee was chosen, consisting of Butt, Henry, O'Shaughnessy, Downing, Brooks, Callan, Shaw, McKenna, and Parnell. The proceedings opened with a review by Butt of the work of the party. A formal vote of confidence in Butt was moved by Sullivan and O'Loghlen and adopted with acclamation. The possibility of a crisis over the situation in the east was discussed, but no firm decision as to party policy was taken:

> As to their action in emergencies that may at any moment arise, they deemed it inexpedient to determine beforehand what course they would adopt, and resolved to maintain an attitude of reserve and observation.

This avoidance of controversy typified the decision of the conference, which virtually paralleled those of the three preceding sessions. It was decided to bring in another home rule motion, if possible early in the session. Responsibility was taken by different members for the introduction of bills upon the familiar issues of the land, university education, intermediate education, the franchise, registration, county boards, sea fisheries, and other topics, together with another amnesty motion. Upon the crucial issue of parliamentary tactics, no formal decision was taken.[43]

[41] quoted in *Nation,* 2 Sept.
[42] Blennerhassett, Browne, Digby, Lewis, O'Callaghan, O'Keeffe, Sherlock, and Sheil.
[43] This report is based on *Nation,* 3 Feb. 1877, supplemented by the leading dailies.

A few days later the league gave a banquet to Butt, at which on the eve of the new session, he reiterated his version of the policy to be followed at Westminster:

What we ought to do, and what I advised is —let us make an assault upon the whole system of English misgovernment in this country. Let us ask of the English liberals to join us in demolishing every part of the system opposed to their principles. If we carry any measure in this way, we have achieved a great triumph and can enjoy its fruits. If we fail, we have supplied another, and an unanswerable argument to Europe, to the Irish and English nations, to show that nothing but self-legislation can ever reconcile us or realise our aspirations.

This policy had been followed in the last session; it would be pursued again in the next. The franchise would be the first test—the Irish could have won on this issue last time if all the members of the party had been present. Hartington, said Butt, had refused to put out a whip for the division, but he himself upon his own initiative had circularised a large number of the Liberals, and many came down and voted with the party.[44] English opinion was moving increasingly towards the provision of local boards for Ireland, and these would represent an important step towards the principle of home rule; however, Butt added:

Never in the English parliament in pressing these measures did I utter, or will I utter, a word that would imply that we were waiving, or abandoning, or modifying the great demand of the Irish people for self-government.

Calling for the constant attendance of the party members, he made the striking admission that in the late conference they had criticised each other violently in the absence of the press; yet he believed that a real community of purpose existed. He appealed for a united national effort to sustain them; if Ireland rose with one gigantic effort at the next election, and sent them a majority—an almost unanimous national declaration—of ninety members, home rule would be attained before the centenary of 1782.

[44] Over one hundred, in fact, did so.

K*

Moving this appeal was, but reduced to essentials it seemed to the more energetic spirits to imply only the same endless round of defeat and frustration. Their critical reaction was almost as much emotional as rational; the same day Major O'Gorman said in the league:

> he begged to state, with all due deference to Mr Butt, and with very great love for their illustrious leader, that he thought him a little too soft . . . He was far too civil with these English fellows . . . he was constantly crying ' Hear, hear! ' when he should say ' No, no! ', and he encouraged them to go on with that which was not distasteful to them—the management of this country. There was only one way of getting hold of John Bull, and that was by stopping his percentages—that is, by stopping the estimates. Now in committee every member was entitled, he thought, to four votes—he would look into Sir Erskine May's book on the matter—on an item of estimates. If eight or nine of them were to combine they could wage war on them.

No one, perhaps, took much notice of O'Gorman. But now significantly the moderate Mitchell Henry rose to add his plea for action:

> He confessed he agreed with Major O'Gorman that in the next session of parliament it would be their duty to follow a very bold course. He was not in favour of shaking hands all round, of thankfulness for small mercies. What they wanted was their national rights, and they would be friends with those men who would assist them to gain those rights; they would not be friends with those who resisted them.[45]

Others, like Biggar, had come to this attitude before Henry. In previous sessions their efforts had been restrained by the opinion of the majority of their colleagues, and by the tactical authority of Butt. Indifference and absenteeism in so many of its members had, however, by now weakened the moral influence of party censure, and recurrent defeat had brought open criticisms of Butt's leadership. Faced with these issues

45 *Nation*, 10 Feb.

the party conference had resolved, in effect, to ignore as a
party the demand for fresh tactics, but that historic indiscipline of the party which permitted wilful absenteeism could
leave room, equally, for the fierce energy of a minority. For
such a display of energy a large and important section of
home rule opinion had, by the recess of 1876-7, given an unmistakeable mandate.

CHAPTER XII

The Obstruction Crisis

THE NEW policy, the policy pursued by Parnell, Biggar, and their shifting minority of supporters in the session of 1877 effectively shattered the home rule movement. It also initiated a revolutionary transformation in British parliamentary procedure which has continued into modern times. Yet there was nothing inherently original in what these Irish members actually did.

The historians of home rule have tended to think of obstruction as a uniquely novel attempt by a handful of Irishmen to delay the passage of legislation which possessed the approval of the great majority by the deliberate and cold-blooded exploitation of parliamentary liberties—liberties historically conceded in the struggle for constitutional government— liberties so prized that rather than qualify them by written restrictions English members had been prepared for centuries to unite in a gentleman's agreement not to exploit them. Parnell, Biggar, and their followers alone refused to honour this compact, and in so doing cut themselves off from the leadership of Isaac Butt and from the traditions of parliamentary government.

This traditional summary does not stand up to examination. Obstruction, defined in its broadest sense as the attempt of a minority to delay legislation which it cannot hope to defeat, was an accepted part of parliamentary tactics long before the emergence of Biggar and Parnell. All parliamentary opposition is, indeed, in a sense obstruction—it was upon precisely this point that the first attempts of the administration to discipline Parnell broke down—and the emergence in 1874 of a parliamentary third force, with neither the authority of her majesty's government nor the complementary mandate of her majesty's opposition, had an implicitly obstructive effect. The Irish party not merely criticised and opposed ministerial measures from an independent and alien point of view; it deliberately set about initiating legislation and policy motions of its own, mostly in the time and through the machinery hitherto allocated to the individual and relatively infrequent activities of the private member.

The effect of this new development can quickly be appreciated when it is recalled that by the time of its emergence the inability of parliament to cope with all its responsibilities was already being forced upon the minds of its members. Parliament was at this period in session for only six months of the year; much of its business was taken late at night, frequently after midnight, and the passage of routine legislation largely depended upon the tacit co-operation of the opposition. The intensification of this problem through the emergence of an Irish party was no mere accident. The principal aim of Butt was 'to press upon the British parliament the legislation which we believe the pressing wants of our country need'. But even if this legislation were to be rejected, he argued:

> I know of no means by which we can better advance the cause of home rule than by making honest and intelligent Englishmen realise to themselves the deficiencies of their Irish government and Irish legislation.[1]

Such a parliamentary policy produced, obviously, the secondary but important effect of overloading the parliamentary order-book with Irish business. The presence of an active Irish party at Westminster, combining to bring in its own bills, was, then, in itself an obstruction to government business. Home rule members gave notice of sixteen bills in 1876, of fifteen in 1877. In both sessions they were able to appropriate the majority of the time allowed for the bills of private members. Butt had no scruples about the legitimacy of arguing each of these bills home to its inevitable defeat. The Irish policy contributed very largely to the production of a situation of which Butt could say in 1875, 'I never remember a

---

[1] *Nation,* 29 May 1875.

session when the order book of the house of commons was so early and so hopelessly blocked', and at the end of the 1876 session Disraeli could make very much the same complaint.[2]

There were, however, limits beyond which Butt was not prepared to go. The Irish members were accused of obstruction for their deliberate persistence in amendments which had no hope of success. They could however argue that these efforts were genuinely bent towards the improvement of legislation. Butt's policy thus had this consistent theme. It involved, in theory, on the positive side, the energetic reiteration of demands for reform through bills and motions initiated and supported at length by the Irish members and, on the negative side, a determined opposition to ministerial Irish measures by voice and vote in the debates in the house and by repeated efforts at amendment in committee. Backed by a strong and energetic party, this policy might have produced both positive and obstructive effects; its main drawback was that only a minority of the Irish in fact practised it. But 'obstruction by argument' had other weaknesses. Not merely was the government unmoved by persuasion; it began also to develop a technique for mitigating the delays consequent upon the unwelcome presence of this Irish party. Ministers ceased to bother to reply to Irish arguments; successive Irish members would be listened to with a formal indifference by a house of minimum size, and their bills or motions voted down by overwhelming majorities brought in from lounges and smoking rooms by the division bell. A speaker in the North London branch of the Home Rule Confederation reported to his fellow members upon his visit to the house of commons for the debate on the fisheries bill of the Irish party in March 1876. He left the house, he said,

> more convinced than ever of the carelessness evinced by the British house of commons in the affairs of Ireland. The members seemed to have so little interest in the fishery bill, that they did not even attend while the discussion was proceeding, and it was not until the chief secretary was half-way through his

---

[2] ibid., and *Hansard,* 3rd series, ccxxxi, 704.

speech that they began to come in. But when the division bell rang, there was a rush from the lobbies . . .[3]

More important still, the so-called half past twelve rule, first introduced as a sessional order in 1871 and dropped in 1874, was reintroduced as a regular means of killing Irish bills. This rule laid down that:

> except for a money bill, no order of the day or notice of motion be taken after half-past twelve of the clock at night, with respect to which order or notice of motion a notice of opposition or amendment shall have been printed on the notice paper, or if such notice of motion shall only have been given the next previous day of sitting, and objection shall be taken when such notice is called.[4]

The time for private members' bills being extremely limited, and much of it in fact being taken in the small hours of the morning, the effect of this rule was drastically to curtail the opportunities available to Irish members to bring on their own legislation. Captain Nolan, the party whip, complained that the effect of the rule in 1875 was 'practically to put a stop to the bills of private members at that hour, without similarly affecting the government bills', and Butt complained that in the same year a bill of his was obstructed by a member who put a notice of opposition on the order paper and then went to Ireland for a month's holiday.[5] So although the Irish, as we have seen, entered an impressive list of bills on the order paper in each session, by 1876 they were experiencing the frustration of seeing the majority of them disappear without even being discussed under the pressure of government business. And the determination to fight all ministerial Irish measures was useless in dealing with a ministry which had none; as Hicks Beach admitted to Disraeli in 1876:

> our position this year with respect to Ireland might not be unfairly described as this—that we have opposed nearly every

---

3 *Nation*, 1 Apr. 1876.
4 *Hansard*, 3rd series, ccxxxii, 332.
5 ibid., 333-4.

bill or motion brought forward by private members, and passed
no bill of our own of any real importance.[6]

When the more frustrated spirits in the party turned, therefore, to seek other means of impressing the distinctiveness of
the Irish party upon the English mind, two very obvious precedents sprang to mind. The first of these was filibustering,
or the making of deliberately interminable speeches. Gladstone himself had adopted these tactics to resist the divorce
bill in 1857. Morley records that on one day in the committee
stage of this bill, Parliament sat for 10 hours in consideration
of a single clause. During this time, 'Including questions, ex-
planations, and interlocutory suggestions, Mr Gladstone made
nine-and-twenty speeches, some of them of considerable
length.'[7] This was a technique which could be used on any
stage of a bill. The second more properly belonged to the
committee stage, that is to say, the stage following upon the
passage of the second reading of a measure, at which the entire
house constituted itself a committee to consider the measure
in detail, clause by clause. In this stage each member could
speak as often as he wished—in debate he could of course
speak only once; he could moreover repeatedly move the adjournment of the committee, in the form of a motion that the
chairman should leave the chair or should report progress to
the speaker of the house. There had been many precedents
for this kind of obstruction as well; in 1870, notably in the
debates on the coercion bill, in the words of a conservative
member, 'alternative motions of the adjournment of the
house and of the debate kept them marching around the lobbies half the night on more than one occasion'.[8] In 1831 in
the reform bill debates Sir Charles Wetherall had kept the
house dividing on the adjournment until 5 a.m.; obstruction
on the bill had been methodically organised by a committee
led by Peel, and on the committee stage between 12 and 27
July, Sugden spoke 18 times, Praed 22 times, Pelham 28 times,
Peel 48 times, Croker 57 times, and Wetherall 58 times.[9] The

6 Beach to Disraeli, 30 July 1876, St. Aldwyn MSS.
7 *Life of W. E. Gladstone* (1903), vol. i, p. 571.
8 Sir Frederick Heygate in *Hansard,* 3rd series, ccxxxii, 335.
9 Quoted in *Nation,* 7 Apr. 1877.

technique was used as late as 1876 by the English radicals led by Forster, Dilke, Fawcett, and Harcourt on the committee stage of the Elementary Education Bill; in order to thwart an amendment which tended to denominationalism, introduced by Lord Robert Montagu and accepted by the government, they divided the committee on the adjournment from 10.30 p.m. until 4.30 a.m.[10]

The tactics of Biggar in the coercion debates of 1875 were not, therefore, original. And although Butt himself made no secret of his distaste for a policy of deliberate delay divorced from rational argument, there was no crisis of party discipline so long as the deviations of Biggar and his occasional allies seemed only individual acts of irresponsibility. What caused the crisis of 1877 was the employment of these tactics in a systematic campaign of retaliation against the government.

The signal for battle was the re-enactment, on 13 February, of the hated rule which provided that only unopposed business could be taken after 12.30 a.m.[11] A few days later the commons found to its fury that by an operation without precedent, wrote the liberal *Daily News,* in the history of British legislation, notice of opposition had been entered in the names of Parnell and Biggar to every important English and Scottish bill on the table of the house.[12] By this single action a large part of British legislation was effectively blocked for the remainder of the session. It was an historic step which initiated as a coherent campaign what has been called the policy of obstruction, but might better be known as the policy of retaliation. Scarcely less historically, it brought into the forefront of Irish political controversy the youthful member for Meath, after only two sessions in parliament in which, while his name had increasingly recurred in the division lists among the active fraction of the party, he had not significantly distinguished himself in speech or action. The challenge thrown down, Biggar and Parnell quickly shewed it to be no empty bluff. On 28 February Biggar talked out Chaplin's Threshing Machines Bill, a measure in which he had no in-

---

10 *Hansard,* 3rd series, ccxxxi, 476-96.
11 ibid., ccxxxii, 336-7.
12 Quoted in *Nation,* 24 Feb. 1877; Brand Diary, 7 Feb. 1877.

terest whatsoever, until 12.30 was reached and it could not be continued with; on 26 February Parnell had done the same with several government bills.[13] On 5 March Parnell moved the adjournment on the committee stage of the army estimates on the ground that his criticisms were not being listened to with proper attention; on 8 March he moved the adjournment of the valuation bill on the ground that the government was forcing too many bills upon the house; on 12 March he and Biggar moved the adjournment of the marine mutiny bill because it had not been printed.[14] These efforts were cold-bloodedly obstructive; Parnell's amendments in the committee of the prisons bill, on the other hand, if obstructive in effect, were legitimately argumentative by the standards of Butt and of parliamentary tradition.

The struggle which took place on the committee stage of the mutiny bill shewed this distinction very clearly. In the mutiny bill committee on 12 April Parnell and Nolan moved four amendments to mitigate the penal power of courts martial. All were withdrawn or defeated. The intervention of Irish members in the discussion of this kind of measure was an innovation, but real obstruction only began when Biggar, pleading the lateness of the hour, moved to report progress after the passage of clause 55, at 1.15 a.m. He was supported by Parnell, who wanted time to consider his own amendments, of which, he explained, circumstances beyond his control had prevented his giving notice. This was too much for Butt, who returned to the house to make a violent protest:

> If, at this hour of the night, any member really wished to propose a serious amendment, he (Mr Butt) would support the motion to report progress—and so, also, he thought, would the secretary for war. But when there was no amendment to a number of clauses, he must express his disapproval of the course taken by the honourable member for Meath. It was a course of obstruction—and one against which he must enter his protest. He was not responsible for the honourable member for Meath, and could not control him. He, however, had a duty to dis-

13 *Hansard,* 3rd series, ccxxxii, 1195-6, 1070-1.
14 ibid., 1439-42, 1634-7, 2018.

charge to the great nation of Ireland, and he thought he should discharge it best when he said he disapproved entirely of the conduct of the honourable member for Meath. If the honourable gentleman really had amendments to propose, he would support him; but he would not support him when he threw out vague suggestions that it was possible on some future day he might have amendments to propose.[15]

Thus publicly reproved by their leader, Parnell and Biggar for the moment gave way. On the committee stage of this and the marine mutiny bill, however, Parnell continued his course of moving amendments, but the device of the adjournment was not used again until 1 May, and this time on an Irish issue, and with evident relief the Speaker noted in his diary the 'business-like way' in which Parnell argued his amendments.[16] On 4 June Parnell opposed the second reading of the Bishoprics Bill and the Companies Acts Amendments Bill on principle because of the lateness of the hour, but gave way without a division.[17] On the prisons bill committee Parnell also moved repeated amendments, but this was a bill of strong Irish interest, and several other Irish members, including Butt himself, took part in the discussions.[18] On 19 June Biggar with Parnell and Ward talked out the Irish Judicature bill as a reprisal for the omission of the speaker to allow Biggar's amendments,[19] but there were no all-night battles, because business was not as a rule pressed on against Parnell's wishes. In May the house sat only twenty hours after midnight in a fourteen day session and in June only twenty-one hours in a twenty-one day session.[20]

Systematic obstruction by means of repeated motions to adjourn was not applied to an English measure until 2 July, in the committee stage of the army estimates. Biggar was not involved in this debate, but a new recruit for the advanced

15 ibid., ccxxxiii, 1042-50.
16 Brand Diary, 19 Apr. 1877; *Hansard,* 3rd series, ccxxxiv, 183-204.
17 ibid., 1292.
18 ibid., 1309, etc., Brand Diary, 7 June 1877.
19 *Hansard,* 3rd series, ccxxxv, 32.
20 *Return of the number of days and hours on which the house sat,* H.C. 1877, LXVIII, p. 149.

wing had been gained with the election of Frank Hugh O'Donnell for Dungarvan. Shortly after midnight O'Connor Power moved the adjournment on the ground that ' he objected to voting away public money at that hour '. Parnell, O'Connor Power, Richard Power, Nolan, O'Donnell and O'Gorman, with the support of the eccentric English member Whalley, kept the house in continuous and unproductive session until 7.15 a.m., in the course of which seventeen divisions were taken, nine on the motion to report progress, and eight that the chairman should leave the chair, before the Irish gave way.[21] Later in July the same tactics were repeated, this time on the solicitors' examinations bill.[22] In the same month Parnell gave notice of opposition to five more English bills.

Throughout all this time Parnell repeatedly denied that he had any intention deliberately to obstruct the business of the house. On 6 July 1877 he said in the house:

> He had always publicly and privately, in Ireland as well as England, repudiated any intention of obstructing the conduct of public business. Any obstruction which he might seem to the house to have committed had happened after half past twelve, when he thought business of importance should cease.[23]

His moving of amendments on the prisons and mutiny bills, if unwelcome in an Irish member, was quite legitimate, and several English members praised him warmly for the work which he had done in drawing attention to the barbaric nature of penal legislation. For these amendments, incidentally, he had taken the step, unprecedented in a private home rule member, of issuing a whip on his own account.[24] In short, the only flagrant obstruction of which he had so far been guilty lay in his notice of opposition to English bills in retaliation

---

[21] *Hansard,* 3rd series, ccxxxv, 623-662.

[22] ibid., 865.

[23] ibid., 887.

[24] *Nation,* 14 Apr. 1877. Butt himself wrote to Callan: ' The truth was obstruction has nothing on earth to do with the amendments on the prisons bill. They (the obstructives) conducted themselves most properly on this '. (Butt to Callan, 16 Sept., Butt MSS, vol. ii, MS 831).

for the use of the 12.30 rule against Irish bills and his use of the right to move the adjournment in order to hold up business after 12.30. The government were, therefore, loth as yet to limit his opportunities by a drastic revision of the rules of the house; the Speaker counselled forbearance, and the motion of J. H. Puleston (Devonport) to apply to committee business the rule followed in debate of the house, permitting each member to move the adjournment only once on any question, was not accepted by the administration.[25] But even as Parnell denied the charge of obstruction, he warned the government:

> The time would come, and had come, when the Irish people would have to consider whether their representatives should not next session enter upon a deliberate persistent course of obstruction of English measures so long as English statesmen and English measures continued to obstruct and nullify all their efforts on behalf of Ireland.[26]

The patience of the government is explicable only by the reluctance of both English parties to alter historic forms to deal with what they still hoped to be a temporary crisis. Sir Erskine May, at that time clerk to the commons, had always been readier to consider a strong line of action. On 3 July he had collaborated with Brand in the preparation of five resolutions designed to curtail the activities of the obstructives:

1. On motion for adjournment of debate or House, or for committee chairman to leave chair or report progress no member to be allowed to speak to the main question.

2. In committee of the whole house, same to apply.

3. Any member called to order more than once by Speaker or Chairman may not speak again on that question. (In Brand's handwriting).

3. Such motions as in (1) to be negatived without a division if less than twelve members stand up in support providing forty or more present. (In May's handwriting).

---

[25] *Hansard*, 3rd series, ccxxxv, 824; Brand Diary, 3 May.
[26] *Nation*, 21 July.

4. If less than one-fifth the members present have supported such a motion any member may then move that question be now put.

5. Any member who shall wilfully and persistently obstruct public business without just and reasonable cause shall be deemed guilty of a contempt of the house.

That any member so offending shall be liable to suspension from service in this house for such time during the session as the House shall determine.[27]

These resolutions would have anticipated on several points the changes ultimately to be forced on the house after the election of 1880. But for the moment Northcote as leader of the house boggled at all but the first two. These he was able to induce Hartington, as leader of the opposition, to agree to second. But Hartington added the reservation that he would prefer to postpone action until the session of 1878, and then proceed through the appointment of a committee. On reflection, Northcote and Brand came round to the same view. So, for the moment, nothing was done.[28]

At the end of July, however, the necessity to push through some important pieces of legislation provoked the inevitable climax. The introduction of the controversial South Africa Bill was preceded by the appropriation on the part of the government of most of private business time for the remainder of the session, an action which fanned Irish hostility to the measure. Parnell and his allies retaliated by delaying the passage of the bill through committee with repeated amendments and motions to adjourn. The storm broke on 25 July while Parnell was speaking on a motion of O'Donnell's to report progress:

The hon. member, who spoke amid much confusion, and who was twice called to order by the chairman, was understood to say—As it was with Ireland, so it was with the South African colonies, yet Irish members were asked to assist the government in carrying out their selfish and inconsiderate policies. There-

27 Brand Diary, 1877, 'Appendix A', 3 July.
28 ibid., 4 July.

fore, as an Irishman, coming from a country which had experienced to the fullest extent the results of English interference in its affairs and the consequences of English cruelty and tyranny, he felt a special satisfaction in preventing and thwarting the intentions of the government in respect of this bill.

To the ministerialists these last words seemed to offer the long-awaited opportunity for retribution. Northcote, the chancellor of the exchequer, leaped to his feet and moved that the words be taken down with a view to the entry of a charge of contempt. At the same time he announced that the patience of the government was finally exhausted, and that on the following Friday amendments to the standing orders of the house would be introduced to prevent a repetition of these scenes. Parnell calmly resumed, and with his allies prolonged the debate, without permitting the passage of any business, until 5.45 a.m.[29]

In the event, Northcote failed in both of his objectives. Brand, who had watched the scene from the gallery, re-read Parnell's words and realised that 'they were not strong enough to sustain the severe punishment contemplated in the resolution of the Chancellor of the Exchequer'.[30] The new rules, which were adopted on 27 July, proved equally ineffective. The intervening two days had been filled with to-ing and fro-ing. On 25 July Northcote and Hartington had been prepared to go as far as suspension, but Gladstone 'would be no party to it', and Hartington's strong tone was dropped. Without the co-operation of the Liberals, Northcote did not dare to take a firm line. 'So we raised the standard of suspension on Wednesday, and lowered it on Thursday', wrote Brand. 'This is weak . . . and is a triumph for the obstructives'.[31]

Two agreed resolutions were finally proposed : —

That when a member, after being twice declared out of order, shall be pronounced by Mr Speaker, or by the chairman of committees, to be disregarding the authority of the chair, the debate shall be at once suspended; and, on a motion being

[29] *Hansard*, 3rd series, ccxxxv, 1797-1833.
[30] Brand Diary, 25 July.
[31] ibid., 25, 26 July.

made, in the house, that the member be not heard during the remainder of the debate, or during the sitting of the committee, such motion, after the member complained of has been heard in explanation, shall be put without further debate.

That in committee of the whole house, no member shall have power to move more than once, during the debate on the same question, either that the chairman do report progress or that the chairman do leave the chair, nor to speak more than once to each separate motion, and that no member who has made one of these motions have power to make the other on the same question.[32]

Parnell did not vote on either of these motions, but took the opportunity of the debate to make a very clear explanation of his policy. He denied any intention to obstruct prior to the South Africa bill; the introduction of the 12.30 rule by the government, and their use of their English majority to overwhelm Irish measures, he said, had resulted in the situation that the only Irish measure passed by this parliament had been ' one of comparatively little importance, which had been described as being a bill to enable certain Irish corporations to present their freedom to the honourable and learned member for Limerick '. He and Biggar had used the 12.30 rule precisely as it had been used by the government: their aim was not obstruction, but simply to show up the tactics of the government. On the prisons and mutiny bills he had exercised his right as an Irish member to take ' that part in the debate on English measures which English members frequently took, with disastrous effects, in the debates on Irish measures '. At once, he said, he was accused of obstruction, but the truth was that any member who took part in any debate was an obstruction, because the house was overwhelmed with work. This explanation justified his conduct on all bills except the South Africa Bill; it involved, he said, ' constitutional principles of enormous importance to the people of those colonies ', and should have been introduced earlier, instead of at the tail end of the session, when to stifle opposition

[32] *Hansard,* 3rd series, ccxxxvi, 13-82. Brand Diary, 25, 26, 27 July.

and to get it through quickly the government adopted 'coercive proceedings' against:

> those who, like himself, wished to see that bill thoroughly debated, and that house had almost been carried into the commission of an act which it would lastingly have regretted and which would certainly have been a disgrace to a deliberative assembly.

Parnell thus was very careful to justify his policy in the terms in which it had always historically been employed, i.e., as the defence by a minority of constitutional liberties which were being flouted by a majority corrupted by its own power. O'Connor Power alone set out to justify blatant obstruction. The most shrewd observation was made by Edmund Dwyer Gray, proprietor of the *Freeman's Journal*, who was slowly coming round to the Parnellite position. The persecution of two or three members he warned, would only gain them sympathy: 'more stringent rules would have to be adopted for next session, for the party of two or three would then be increased to twenty or thirty, and after a dissolution would number, he believed, as many as eighty'.[33] In the meantime, Butt warned Northcote, Parnell and his allies would be 'quite capable of organising relays of obstructives within the terms of the resolution'.[34]

Butt and Gray proved right in their prophecies. The new rules were completely ineffective, and the government were only able to carry the South Africa Bill by a historic sitting which lasted from 5.15 p.m. on Tuesday 31 July until 2.10 p.m. on Wednesday 1 August.[35] Seven Irish members, Parnell, Biggar, O'Donnell, O'Connor Power, Kirk, Nolan, and Gray were able to obstruct the business of the house during the whole of this time. The right of the Irish members to move amendments, and their ability to make interminable speeches were unaffected by the new rules, and the restriction upon the number of adjournment motions allowed to

---

[33] *Hansard,* 3rd series, ccxxxvi, 54-7, 74-5.
[34] Butt to Northcote, July 1877, Iddesleigh MSS, BM Add. MSS 50040 f. 56.
[35] *Hansard,* 3rd series, ccxxxvi, 227-318.

each member proved useless, since each clause constituted a separate question; the seven Irish members might move the adjournment seven times on one clause, speaking at length on each motion; divide the house seven times; divide it on an amendment; divide it on the clause itself; and then start the whole process over again on the next clause. Attempts to employ the other new rule in order to suspend the obstructives were defeated by honeyed withdrawals on the part of the Irish. Abuse and interruptions only prolonged the agony. The stamina of the Irish was, in short, as before the only tangible limit upon their power to obstruct the house in committee.

From the gallery the Speaker watched the rising temper of both sides of the house. He had at first opposed the reduction of the debate to a 'physical force contest', but the realisation that the little band of obstructives was organising itself in relays to precisely this end stiffened his resolution and that of the ministry. The Irish members offered to accept all the clauses down to number forty if Northcote would concede the adjournment, but by now the government were abnormally excited and determined 'not to be beaten in the art of sitting'. 'Grilled bones, devilled kidneys, and spatchcocks' had been laid on in anticipation of the ordeal; the ministerial supporters were marshalled to come down in batches every hour after 2.30 a.m. to relieve their weary colleagues. The London correspondent of the *Irish Times* telegraphed to Dublin:

> As I write the Speaker has gone to bed. The river terrace is crowded with members, many of whom are sleeping on benches, watched over by constables waiting to call them when their relief may be required in the chamber so as to prevent the possibility of a count-out.

At 9 a.m. on Wednesday, 1 August, Brand conferred with Northcote and Forster, who was the leading Liberal present, 'Hartington being at Goodwood'. Erskine May was unable to join them, as there was no one to relieve him at the table of the house, 'the other two clerks being "relayed in bed"' The triumvirate resolved to hold out to the bitter end. In the absence of Gladstone, who had steadily counselled patience, they determined, however, to set a deadline of 2 p.m., after which the ultimate deterrent of suspension would have to be employed against the obstructives, with all the historic constitutional implications attendant upon so rare and so desperate an extremity.

But the stamina of the heroic seven was finally being worn down. At 12.30 obstruction petered out in a 'sudden surrender', induced, Brand thought, by the fear of suspension, a fear especially operating upon Captain Nolan, the only one of the little band who was a senior official of the home rule party. All sixty-three clauses were at last agreed and at 2.10 p.m. on Wednesday 1 August, after forty-five hours of continuous session, the South Africa bill was finally reported amid loud and continuous cheering. It was obvious that stronger measures would be needed if systematic obstruction were to recur in 1878, but a few days later parliament was prorogued without further incident, and the first round of the struggle was over.[36]

The historic conflicts of this session had naturally convulsed in controversy both the party and the country. Before considering this controversy it is, however, necessary to glance back briefly at the sporadic efforts of the party leaders upon the well-worn track laid down in previous sessions. Notice had been given as before of a large number of Irish bills, fifteen in all.[37] But few of these thrived even as far as the discussion stage. Grand jury reform was voted down by 62 votes to 15 on 18 March; the absence of two-thirds of the home rule members did not pass unnoticed in Ireland.[38] Butt's land bill perished by 323 votes to 84 on 21 March, the home rule leader himself being too sick to say more than a few words.[39] O'Shaughnessy brought in a strongly worded motion on education on 16 March, but in the middle of the debate his

[36] This description is compiled from *Irish Times*, 1 Aug., *Freeman's Journal*, 2 Aug.; Brand Diary, 31 July and (a) end of session note and (b) appendix 7 Aug.; also Gladstone to Brand, 9 Aug., Brand to Sir G. Grey, 15 Aug., 4 Sept., Northcote to Brand, 2 Sept., Brand MSS.

[37] *Hansard*, 3rd series, ccxxxii, 152-60.

[38] ibid., ccxxxiii, 87-89; *Nation*, 24 Mar.

[39] *Hansard*, 3rd series, ccxxxiii, 241-306.

leader decided that it was unwise, and prevailed upon him to withdraw it.[40] A further example of the disunity which prevailed even in the moderate wing of the party was given in the committee on the prisons bill on 23 March; Callan attacked Henry in language which compelled the intervention of the chair, and on the motion to adjourn sixteen home rulers voted for the government and five against.[41] Following upon the Easter recess the motion for a select committee on home rule was moved by Shaw on 24 April, seconded 'with some diffidence' by King Harman, and rejected by 417 votes to 67, the minority including 13 English liberals.[42] Butt's Voters (Ireland) Bill, which sought to regulate Irish practice in relation to registration at elections, was defeated by 125 votes to 99 on 9 May; O'Loghlen's Poor Law Guardians (Ireland) Bill was dispatched with equal expedition by 174 votes to 109 on 16 May, and Henry's resolution on Irish taxation was rejected by 152 votes to 34 on 5 June. On 11 June Butt moved a resolution calling for the appointment of a responsible minister to preside over the Irish local government boards, only to find himself criticised not only by Biggar and Parnell but by Henry, who 'objected to the patching up of this anomalous and objectionable system of government in order to weaken the claim of the Irish people to manage their own affairs'. The motion was withdrawn.[43] The best Irish division was on Meldon's motion to assimilate the borough franchise of the two islands, which fell by 239 votes to 165 on 15 June. O'Sullivan's Union Justices (Ireland) Bill, on the other hand, could muster only 36 votes on 4 July. The struggles on the South Africa Bill virtually consumed the remainder of the session; Butt's university bill was taken on 26 July and voted down by 200 votes to 55, and the home rule leader emerged from this session with nothing gained but the second reading of the Parliamentary Registration (Ireland) Bill, allowed to pass by Plunket for the government on the understanding that he reserved the right 'to oppose what he con-

40 ibid., 17.
41 ibid, 395-487.
42 ibid., 1742-1846.
43 ibid., 1585-97.

sidered a mischievous bill in its future stages'. For the exponents of persuasion it had been, perhaps, an even more
sterile session than usual.[44]

The first efforts of Parnell and Biggar in the session of 1877
gained, on the whole, an appreciative reception from the bulk
of the nationalist press. The *Freeman's Journal* denied the
charge of the *Times* that a group of Irish members were endeavouring to bring about an 'absolute stoppage' of business, and it pointed to Parnell's constructive achievements in
relation to the prisons bill. At such deliberate stoppage of
business it still boggled:

> Neither home rule nor any other good cause can be gained by
> any such madcap adventures as a stoppage of parliamentary
> business by abusing the forms of the house . . . sooner or later
> the house should protect itself from assassination, and this it
> could do only by fettering debates within certain limits. Such
> a change would have the worst effect upon the house itself, but
> it would especially weigh upon minorities, for as minorities
> trust for advancing their views to argument alone, it is to them
> that unrestricted debate is the breath of life . . . Obstruction
> is a keen, double-edged, and most dangerous weapon; it ought
> only to be used on very rare occasions and by the most skilled
> hands.

There seems to have been at first an impression in Ireland
that the tactics of Biggar and Parnell might inaugurate a new
attitude in the party as a whole, and, more important, that the
criticisms of Butt were directed not so much at the obstructive policy as at the failure of its practitioners to co-ordinate
it with official party strategy. This belief made it possible for
many Irish home rulers throughout 1877 to give a qualified
approval to the obstructive policy and at the same time to retain their loyalty to Butt himself. It was only as the home rule
leader made obvious his refusal under any circumstances to
use the weapon of obstruction that he finally destroyed his
own personal authority in Ireland.

The first blow in this controversy was struck with Butt's
condemnation of Parnell on the committee stage of the mut-

[44] ibid., ccxxxiv, 1716-34.

iny bill early in the morning of 13 April. Butt seems to have
been provoked to this action by the unexpected persistence
of Biggar and Parnell in the face of his privately-expressed
disapproval of their activities. At the beginning of April he
had mentioned to Henry his intention to write privately to
Biggar:

> I feel very confident that it will have the effect of putting an
> end (at least as far as Biggar is concerned) to all of which we
> have any right to complain . . . I hope and am persuaded that
> no appeal to the public will ever be necessary but the publica-
> tion of my letter would I think be a heavy blow and a great
> discouragement to Biggar and Parnell . . .
>
> I hope I do not exaggerate the influence I have with the
> country when I believe it strong enough to put down and con-
> trol all these evil influences. If I have it, it is a trust which
> every obligation binds me to use.[45]

Butt did, apparently, write privately to Biggar,[46] but without result, and his reluctant decision publicly to denounce
the obstructives so far from, as he bemusedly expected, in-
stantly quelling the rebellion, sparked off a controversy which
mounted in the months that followed. On the same day, 13
April, Parnell wrote to him privately:

> Dear Sir,
>   Is it true that in your concluding remarks this morning in
> the house, you expressed your belief or opinion that the amend-
> ments, which I had intimated my intention of moving on the
> mutiny Bill, had no existence.[47]

Butt replied placatingly. He had no recollection of using that
phrase, although there was little evidence for the existence of
amendments which had not been placed upon the order
paper or even stated verbally to the house:

> If however I may assume that in the question you have put to
> me you mean to ask, whether I said that your *intention* to move

45 Butt to Henry, Easter Sunday 1877, Butt MSS, vol. iii, MS 832.
46 *Freeman's Journal,* 9 April.
47 Parnell to Butt, 13 Apr., Butt MSS.

the amendments had no existence, I can at once assure you
that I neither said this nor anything that could bear such a
meaning . . . it never could have entered my mind to make such
a suggestion of a gentleman who I say unhesitatingly is of all
the men I know exactly the one that I could say is the most incapable of resorting to anything like pretence.[48]

If Butt hoped thus to close the question, he was to be disappointed. The *Freeman's Journal* of 14 April carried an
editorial on the incident. It recalled its praise of Parnell and
Biggar, quoted above, but condemned the conduct of the
former on the previous Thursday night as 'mere wantonness
and folly'; unprepared to move his amendments, 'he evid-
ently lost his temper, was called to order, and compelled to
apologise to the committee'. It concluded by expressing the
hope that he would prove his wisdom by 'resuming that line
of honourable loyalty which bound him to his leader and his
party'.[49]

These comments provoked immediate retaliation in the
shape of letters from O'Connor Power and Parnell. Power
neatly turned against Butt one of his own most cherished
principles; by what right, he asked, did the home rule leader
intervene in regard to the action of an Irish member on
English or imperial questions? His conduct, wrote Power,
struck at 'the very principle by which men differing widely
on these questions have been united on the question of home
rule'.[50] Parnell on the other hand meticulously reviewed the
events of the preceding Friday night. He asserted the gen-
uineness of his amendments and denied either that he had
lost his temper or that he had been compelled to apologise; he
had 'cheerfully' withdrawn a reference to the 'disorderly followers' of the government, on the suggestion of the chairman
that the phrase 'was not strictly parliamentary'.

Meanwhile Mr Butt, who appears to have been absent during
the evening, arrived, and sided with the government, adopting,
I regret to say, the line taken by the secretary for war as to my

48 Butt to Parnell, 13 Apr. (copy), ibid.
49 *Freeman's Journal*, 14 Apr.
50 ibid., 16 Apr.

proposed amendment—viz., that it could not be a real one because it was not on the notice paper.

In explanation for Mr Butt's strange conduct on this occasion, it is right that I should point out, that owing to his not having followed the course of the debate during the evening he does not seem to have been aware that none of my amendments were on the notice paper. When I rose to explain the position of affairs to Mr Butt I was again refused a hearing by the committee, and, many people think, was interrupted in a most unfair manner by the chairman.

The letter is concluded with a pithy summary of Parnell's attitude to the English parliament.

You say that I may have 'suffered disappointment' in the defeat of my proposed amendments. Now, to be disappointed at defeat in the present house of commons would be very foolish, and certainly I had no such feeling . . .

With regard to what appears to you to be 'the horse-laughter' of the London journals, I for one shall not allow myself to be diverted from my duty by the laughter of any Englishman, whether it proceeds from the right or wrong side of his mouth. The instinct of snobbery, which seems to compel some Irishmen to worship at the shrine of English prejudice, and to bow down before the voice and censure of the English press will never gain anything for Ireland, and will only secure for such panderers the secret contempt of Englishmen.

England respects nothing but power, and it is certain that the Irish party, comprising, as it does, so many men of talent and ability, might have that power, which attention to business, method and energy always give, if it would only exhibit these qualities.

So long as I continue to follow Mr Butt as my leader in regard to all measures upon which the Irish party are agreed to act as a party, there could be no foundation for the charge that I have desisted from that line of honourable loyalty which binds me to my leader and my party, because I, in common with every other member of the party, reserve for myself full individual liberty of action upon all matters affecting England and the empire at large.[51]

The distinction between Irish and imperial business at Westminster was to be made again repeatedly by the supporters of Parnell in the controversy which followed. It was indeed the only expedient by which they could ignore the refusal of the party as a whole to adopt the weapon of obstruction. For the moment the effect of Butt's public condemnation of Parnell and Parnell's public retort was to inaugurate a national debate upon the issue. A meeting in Glasgow under the chairmanship of Ferguson passed resolutions calling for a policy of 'deliberate and avowed obstruction', supporting Parnell and Biggar, and regretting Butt's condemnation of Parnell. At the same time Ferguson would allow no censure of Butt, and three cheers were 'heartily given' for 'our respected leader'.[52] The next issue of the *Nation* adopted a similar tone; Butt's intervention had caused 'a feeling of pain' among the mass of home rulers:

> That Mr Butt did not quite approve of the conduct in question was well known before he made the somewhat impassioned protest to which we have referred; that he was not prepared to lead the Irish party in a 'policy of obstruction'—just yet—was generally understood; but it was not expected that he would publicly, in the house of commons, reprove those gentlemen, for whose action he was not responsible, and one result of whose proceedings has been to show to the ministry and to England how powerful a weapon of parliamentary warfare the leader of the Irish party holds in his hand ready for use whenever he may deem that a fitting occasion has arisen.

It still retained the hope that the persistent rejection of his bills would bring Butt round to the retaliatory policy.[53] The *Wexford People* and the *Dundalk Democrat* added their support to that of the *Nation,* and resolutions congratulatory of Parnell and Biggar were passed by most branches of the

---

[51] ibid, 17 Apr.
[52] ibid., 20 Apr.
[53] *Nation,* 21 Apr.

English confederation. In May and June the *Kerry Vindicator*, the *Roscommon Messenger*, and the *Connaught Telegraph* joined the supporters of Parnell, and the *Galway Vindicator*, while opposing deliberate obstruction, contrasted the
'zeal and determination' of Parnell and Biggar with the inertia of the majority of the party.[54] In June the *Irishman*, bede-
villed by Richard Pigott's financial commitments to every
section of the national party, committed itself so far as to
appeal to Butt to abandon the 'whiglings' and adopt an
active policy.[55] The *Cork Examiner*, on the other hand, urged Parnell and Biggar to follow the counsels of Butt,[56] and
the 'London Correspondent' of the *Freeman's Journal* not
only ascribed to the obstructives the responsibility for the defeat of the liberal Kay in Salford, but also prophesied that the
home rule motion would now fail to get seventy votes instead
of the hundred or hundred and twenty which it would otherwise have obtained.[57] He did not elaborate upon the process
of reasoning by which he had deduced that last year's home
rule vote might have been expected to double, though his
forecast as to its eventual number was, of course, accurate.
But the *Nation* interpreted the result of this division very
differently:

> The moral we draw from the vote on Mr Butt's motion is sim-
> ply that a bolder and more vigorous line of parliamentary
> policy on the part of the Irish members is not only advisable
> but absolutely necessary for the furtherance of the cause.[58]

At the end of May, Butt sent to the *Freeman's Journal* two
letters which he had written to Biggar and Parnell on 29
March and 21 April respectively. In both letters he elabor-

54 Quoted ibid., 9 June.
55 *Irishman*, 2 June. Pigott took money at different times from,
amongst others, Butt, Henry, C. J. Fay, P. Egan, and C. S. Fortescue.
(Pigott to Butt, 2 undated letters, 1873; 31 May, 16 June, 1 July, 14
Sept., 15, 30 Oct. 1875; 18, 31 Mar., 8 Apr., 18, 20 Sept., 30 Oct., 4, 6, 9
Nov. 1876, all Butt MSS; C. Hamilton to Fortescue, 23 Nov. 1874,
Strachie MSS, Carlingford Political.)
56 Quoted *Nation*, 21 Apr.
57 *Freeman's Journal*, 21 Apr.
58 *Nation*, 28 Apr.

ated the same two arguments. Obstruction by the repeated moving of the adjournment was a device to which a minority ought not to resort 'unless they could fairly say that the majority were unfairly and tyrannically exercising their power'. In the second place, it destroyed the influence of the Irish party in the house of commons.

> I had very great hopes of a good division on the motion for a committee on home rule. I have very little now. I was perfectly confident of carrying the extension of the borough franchise . . . I am not so now. I believe that the unpopularity which attaches to us from the belief that we have adopted a policy of general obstruction will prevent many English members from giving us their votes . . .

An editorial in the same issue dismissed Biggar's denials that he was engaged in deliberate obstruction; both the enemies and the supporters of his policy were under no illusions as to its nature.

Butt's determination in ascribing his parliamentary failure to the work of the obstructives effectively dashed popular hopes that he would be converted by frustration to the policy of Parnell. It also made it inevitable that the personal affection in which he was still held even by his critics would in time be dissipated. But this hope and affection lingered on long after the justification for it had ceased. Parnell took up this position at Glasgow:

> There was no question of leadership. He would not undertake to direct such a policy. Isaac Butt was well able to do that. But the Irish people would have to induce Mr Butt to do it, if he would not do it of his own accord. Mr Butt was of a gentle and amiable nature that shrank from inflicting injury upon anything or anyone. That was one of the great reasons why he had shaped his policy in such a way as to be utterly useless for any real Irish work . . . Was there ever a thing they had gained by soft words and soft actions? No.[59]

Bitterness only crept slowly into the controversy. Parnell's letter to Butt of 14 April was now published in the *Freeman*.

[59] *Freeman's Journal*, 29 May.

Again he concentrated upon the distinction between questions of Irish and imperial policy; he reminded Butt of the
incident of the royal titles bill in the previous session:

> You will recollect that upon the only occasion when you sug-
> gested that our party should follow you on a question of im-
> perial policy it was, after long discussion, decided that each
> individual should act for himself, with the result that one por-
> tion of the party followed you out of the house, another por-
> tion followed the Marquis of Hartington, while a third portion
> did not take either of these courses.[60]

Parnell's interpretation of the party pledge was ridiculous, replied Butt:

> It would enable any professing home rule member to intrigue
> with any English party to give his vote on any imperial or
> English question to serve the interests of the faction of which
> he might be the minion, and to fulfil his pledge to his country
> by voting two or three times a year on questions on which his
> vote could not do his masters any harm.[61]

'All these things are precisely what many home rule members are constantly doing', rejoined Parnell, 'and apparently entirely without remonstrance or even attempt at restraint
by you'. As to the alleged loss of English votes in parliament:

> I recollect that last session you indulged in similar expectations
> as to the large number of English members who were going to
> vote for the home rule motion . . . Mr Biggar and I were not
> then available as scapegoats and I forget what was the precise
> reason assigned for the smallness of the home rule vote.

Now acid crept into the controversy as Parnell reviewed
Butt's leadership in the session.

> Had you exhibited any energy at the commencement of the
> session, and directed and availed yourself then of the oppor-
> tunities in the ballot which organisation can secure for our
> party, you could without fail have secured a day for the uni-

60 ibid., 26 May.
61 ibid.

versity bill, and would not now find yourself under the necessity of applying to the government for a day for the discussion
of that measure, or of throwing upon me the blame for receiving a refusal to your request.

Parnell categorically denied the adoption of any '"new
policy"', 'unless such is to be energetic, constantly at one's
post, and hostile to legislation at late hours'.

You will remember that at the convention of delegates of the
Home Rule Confederation last autumn in Dublin a resolution
was unanimously passed, to which you were a consenting party,
urging a more energetic and a bolder policy . . . The resolution alluded to above, following as it did last session, when
some real endeavours had been made to carry out this policy,
meant, if it was intended to mean anything, and if you intended anything by assenting to it, either that your policy was
insufficient, or should be supplemented.

But in fact the organisation of the party in this session had
fallen off by comparison with that of 1876:

It was quite by accident that you secured a day for the land
bill. The other measures were all of them thrown overboard or
abandoned. The grand jury question was neglected. No attempt has been made to direct the attention of the house to the
municipal franchise. The assimilation of the borough franchise, for which Mr Biggar secured a day, has not been brought
forward, because, as he tells me, you refused to supply him
with the draft of the bill. The university bill I have already
alluded to, and the fisheries bill, for which a day was also obtained, was found not to be printed when that day arrived.
Finally, the Church Lands Bill, for which I secured a day,
though drawn 50th in the ballot, and which might have been
easily carried had our party made any exertions, was lost, because I utterly failed to interest you in the question until too
late.

Nor has the rest of the session retrieved in any sense this
inauspicious beginning. The attendance of Irish members has
never been so bad, seldom at late hours exceeding five or six.
The prisons bill, of the utmost importance to Ireland, was left

to take care of itself, though for weeks in committee, during which time I urged you in vain until the last day to take any interest in the subject. At no time during the session have you shown that you had any policy at all, much less that you were carrying it out ' boldly and actively '. I should have been only too pleased to follow your lead had you led in anything but in inactivity and absence from the house. But I think it is sufficiently evident that no steps have been taken by you to carry out the resolution of the convention in which you took a leading part. I, on the other hand, am denounced because I have not joined the majority in doing nothing, in inactivity, in absenteeism—because I have shown the country that they have a power which they little knew of, to use if they desire for the enforcement of their just claims. I intended to do nothing more than show that if two members can do so much, hampered and restricted as they must be in their choice of methods by the very fact of their being only two, how vast and powerful might be the influence of a powerful party of sixty, not necessarily adopting one line of action, but at least attending to their duty and disregarding the ' feeling of the house ' when that feeling is wrong and opposed to the interests of Ireland.

Finally, Butt's lecture on parliamentary procedure was disposed of in a pithy sentence.

I cannot sympathise with your conclusions as to my duty towards the house of commons. If Englishmen insist upon the artificial maintenance of an antiquated institution which can only perform a portion of its functions by the ' connivance ' of those interested with its working in the imperfect and defective performance of much of even that portion—if the continued working of this institution is attended with much wrong and hardship to my country, as frequently it has been the source of gross cruelty and tyranny—I cannot consider that it is my duty to connive in the imperfect performance of these functions, while I should certainly not think of obstructing any useful, solid, or well-performed work.[62]

[62] *Freeman's Journal,* 28 May. The issue of 2 June contained another letter from O'Connor Power which carried still further Parnell's personal criticisms of Butt.

Of the perfect truth of a great part of this powerful indictment no active home ruler could be unaware, and its fierce tone could not fail to strike home to the emotional nationalist. But the *Freeman* deplored Parnell's 'hard if not offensive language': his clear duty was to submit the issue as Butt proposed to the decision of the party.[63] On this point Biggar had a home truth of his own to add; the home rule leader, he said, had spoken of 'the opinions of himself and the great body of the Irish home rule members':

> If Mr Butt means the members who systematically neglect their duties, I suppose he is right; but if he means the members who attend heartily to their duties, he is lamentably astray . . .[64]

A meeting of the party was in fact held on 5 June to discuss the question. On 31 May Butt issued a circular calling together the members of the party to consider the newspaper correspondence between himself and Parnell.[65] Only twenty-four responded to this summons; several of the most persistent backsliders turned up to support Butt; one of them, E. G. Dease, was compelled, however, to leave the meeting before the issue, which he had expected would be taken first, came up for discussion.[66] Parnell attended, and also wrote formally to Butt proposing that the question should be submitted to 'those who have been your most earnest assistants in the home rule movement by calling another conference'.[67] The meeting adjourned to 16 June without reaching any decision. When it reassembled tempers had cooled slightly and the only action taken was the passing of a compromise resolution calling for the holding of more frequent meetings of the party with a view to the pursuit of a course of vigorous action under Butt's leadership.[68]

But hopes of compromise were shattered by the events of July. The South Africa bill committee, besides producing the most violent scenes of obstruction, shewed a steady in-

63 ibid., 28 May.
64 ibid., 4 June.
65 In Butt MSS, vol. iii, MS 832.
66 Dease to Butt, 3 June, Butt MSS.
67 *Nation*, 9 June.
68 ibid., 23 June.

crease in the numbers of the Parnellite wing. Seven members took part in the all-night sitting of 31 July—1 August; they were Parnell, Biggar, Nolan, Power, G. H. Kirk and the newly elected Edmund Dwyer Gray and Frank Hugh O'Donnell. The most significant of these recruits was Gray. Editor and proprietor of the *Freeman's Journal* since his father's death in 1875, he had condemned open obstruction in his paper, and his return for Tipperary to fill the vacancy caused by the death of Colonel O'Callaghan was secured with the full support of Butt and only the neutrality of Parnell.[69] Gray's participation in the South Africa bill contest did not lead to the immediate endorsement of the obstructive policies by him or by the *Freeman's Journal*, but there began a gradual softening towards Parnell in its columns until by the middle of 1878 it had virtually aligned itself with the Parnellite position.

Butt's response to the South Africa bill scenes was finally to demand decisive action by the party. On 27 July he appears to have told a stormy party meeting that he would resign if the obstructive tactics were not abandoned.[70] A meeting was arranged for 6 August to consider the question. Twenty members were present;[71] three, Gray, Kirk, and O'Donnell, absented themselves as a protest against the proposed censure of the obstructives; ten of the other absentees were in London and stayed away from the meeting without explanation.[72] By the time the meeting assembled Parnell and his allies had

[69] Butt to Delany, 13 May, and undated, Hickey MSS; *Freeman's Journal*, 12 May. O'Donnell was also in the field, and as a condition for his withdrawal claimed to have exacted from Gray a promise to support a more active policy in the house. (*Nation*, 5 May).

[70] *Pall Mall Gazette*, quoted in *Nation*, 4 Aug. The *Ulster Examiner*, quoted ibid., refers to stormy scenes at a meeting on 30 July. In general, however, the stories concur; a meeting was called for 6 Aug. Through some leakage the *Irish Times* correspondent obtained a full report of this second meeting, from which the story of it below is largely taken. (See Henry's letter on this subject in *Nation*, 25 Aug.).

[71] Butt, Biggar, Callan, Delahunty, Downing, Errington, Harman, Lewis, Meldon, Moore, Nolan, O'Beirne, O'Brien, O'Byrne, O'Clery, O'Shaughnessy, Parnell, O'C. Power, Redmond, and Shaw.

[72] Blennerhassett, Bowyer, Browne, Collins, Dunbar, Montagu, O'Conor, Sheil, Sullivan, and Ward.

shown decisively in the all-night sitting of 31 July—1 August that they were not prepared to bow to Butt's wishes. Butt therefore renewed his denunciations, and McCarthy Downing and W. R. O'Byrne, two of the most consistent absentees in the party, proposed a resolution, believed to be inspired by Butt, censuring the conduct of Parnell and Biggar. An amendment deferring any decision until after the holding of a national conference, was proposed by William Shaw, in a speech which was conciliatory in tone except for a violent denunciation of his old bugbear, the English confederation. Unable to secure this compromise, he left in disgust. The meeting then abandoned itself to vituperation. Richard O'Shaughnessy said that he would vote for the resolution, but approved of the policy of Parnell and Biggar up to a certain point. Butt announced his intention of resigning unless his advice was accepted. Callan succeeded in killing another compromise motion by Nolan. Downing accused Parnell, Biggar, and O'Connor Power of obstructing the meeting; Parnell and Power on the one hand and Downing and Callan on the other almost came to blows. Power called Callan a whig placehunter; Callan accused Power of breaking his fenian oath. The meeting broke up in disorder without any vote having been taken.[73]

Unity in the party effectively ceased at that moment. The session concluded with the two factions equally determined to appeal to the people of Ireland. The obstructives resolved to pin their hopes upon the summoning of a national conference; this proposal Butt, who remained, sick, in England throughout the whole of the autumn, was determined to resist; he relied instead upon the ability of his published manifestos to produce a long-term reaction against what he considered a policy of violence. The battle for public opinion occupied the whole of the recess which now followed.

73 *Irish Times*, 7 Aug., *Nation*, 11 Aug. A round robin to the effect of Downing's resolution was subsequently signed by a number of the home rule members. (*Nation*, 25 Aug.). The almost universal distrust of Callan arose partly from his having allegedly sought place under the Gladstone administration (Fortescue to E. Lear, 20 Mar. 1874, Strachie MSS, Carlingford Political.)

L*

CHAPTER XIII

The Struggle for Power

PARNELL STRUCK the first blow with a public demonstration in the Rotunda on 22 August. From London Butt pressed Callan continuously for reports of the preparations for the meeting, but declined Callan's offer to have it broken up. 'I suspect they will break up themselves', he wrote, and prophesied the complete collapse of the 'new "revolution"'.[1] Nothing of the sort occurred. A setback was experienced when Dr O'Leary, member for Drogheda, who had agreed to preside, took fright at the last minute, but the meeting was enthusiastic and crowded, between four and five thousand persons being present. W. H. O'Sullivan took O'Leary's place, and with Parnell and Biggar, who were received with 'deafening cheers', and Kirk, four members of parliament in all attended. Letters of unqualified support were received from two more members of parliament, O'Donnell and O'Gorman, and from such well-known nationalists as Richard Lalor, Father Lavelle and, most strikingly, O'Neill Daunt. Parnell and Biggar 'have a perfect right to obstruct the obstructives', wrote Daunt, and he called for a national conference to show Butt that the people wanted him to take the lead in a new onslaught. A more qualified support was also expressed in letters from Henry and A. M. Sullivan. A man who endeavoured to hiss at the mention of Butt's name was thrown out,[2] but O. J. Carraher, vice-president of the Louth Independent Club called on Butt to face his failure or retire. Cheering crowds escorted Parnell and Biggar down Sackville Street and compelled them to speak from the balcony of their hotel.[3]

---

1 Butt to Callan, 18, 20, 22 Aug. 1877, Butt MSS, vol. ii, MS 832.
2 J. Dunne to Butt, 23 Aug., Butt MSS.
3 *Nation,* 25 Aug.

'When do you think of coming home'? appealed Butt's old friend Captain John Dunne; 'Parnell and Biggar mean to stump the country during the recess'.[4]

The following week the English Home Rule Confederation made the next and as yet the most decisive pronouncement in favour of Parnell. The annual convention of the confederation at Liverpool occupied two days, 27 and 28 August. Butt as president took the chair on the morning of the first day, but in the afternoon left for London 'on business' after a 'friendly interchange of opinion' on the subject of the active policy. The same night there was a public meeting at which Commins presided, and Parnell, Biggar, O'Donnell, Power, Ferguson, and Barry were among those on the platform. Parnell was cheered; Butt's name was greeted with hisses which were drowned in shouts of 'order'. The following day the business of the conference concluded. On the motion of John Barry, Parnell was elected to the presidency in the coming year. The outgoing president Butt had only held the office for one year, and the principle of rotation was not wholly novel. Nevertheless it was a decision capable of only one interpretation, and it was seen by the English press as a direct rebuff to Butt.[5]

With the confederation secured, the Parnellites next turned their attention to the league, which had been leading an unobtrusive and questionably useful existence in the last two years. It was unfortunate for Butt that the council of the league included a number of convinced adherents of the obstruction policy, who from their youth, energy, and residence in Dublin were able to exert a considerable influence in that body. A preliminary affray took place on 31 August on a motion by the Carmelite Father Kelly, censuring those mem-

---

4 J. Dunne to Butt, 23 Aug., Butt MSS.

5 But the moving story of Butt's tearful reaction to the election (R. B. O'Brien, *Life of C. S. Parnell*, 3rd ed., 1899, vol. i, pp. 142-6), seems to have little basis in fact. The home rule leader was quite clearly in London when Parnell was elected (*Freeman's Journal*, 28, 29 Aug., *Nation* 1, 8 Sept., *Irish Times* 28, 29 Aug. Also Healy, *Letters and Leaders of my day*, p. 54). The inaccuracy of O'Brien's information on this point makes one hesitate to rely upon the rest of his version of the incident.

bers of parliament who persistently neglected their duties. This meeting was attended by fifteen people of whom T. D. Sullivan, Patrick Egan, John Dillon, Dr Kenny and Father Kelly himself, at least, expressed opinions more or less favourable to the active policy. Callan wrote to Butt appealing to him to come back to Dublin before far worse disasters should take place in the council.

> Ignatius Kennedy and Kettle ready to back you up—if *you* were here—if any longer absent and without your presence to support them won't fight against the others. Galbraith dead with you also but *feels* your absence *sorely* . . .
>
> Now let me be plain with you—your remaining in London after the session has injured you materially—your journey to Liverpool makes the cause of your absence inexplicable. 'Tis said if you were ill—how—why—did you go to Liverpool— and then *everyone* asks why when once there did you leave before the end of the first day—why didn't you attend the public meeting—was it *sulk*?
>
> If you fancy that by your absence you are escaping injury— and that it is ' masterly inaction ' on your part you are making a grievous mistake. It reminds me of the ostrich when hunted and running from danger—hiding its head—and while leaving its body exposed—thinking itself hidden and safe. Now the sooner you face the tempest the better—from the want of a public exposition of your policy the public is veering round *rapidly* against you and in quarters you little fancy. You may be displeased—angry with me for this plain speaking. Well be it so, no true friend will conceal from you what I write . . . After today's meeting Kettle almost crying asked me to write you as I have done now—I refused and said write yourself . . .[6]

Kettle wrote as he had promised to Butt a long letter similar in tone to that of Callan:

> The leadership of the Irish people and of the Irish party are two very different things. The Irish party are a nondescript set

6 Minutes of the Irish Home Rule League, 31 Aug. (in Callan's handwriting), and Callan to Butt, same date. Butt MSS.

of men, not suited for their mission exactly. The Irish people
are in Ireland . . .[7]

But the inertia which could sometimes so strangely paralyse
Butt's will combined with his failing health to make him ignore the advice of his most loyal adherents and linger on in
England. More agreeable to him was the advice of English
friends.:

I am glad you intend to go to Buxton instead of to Ireland. To
deal with these obstructives at a public meeting is for a Gentleman to enter into a personal contest with Chimney Sweeps . . .[8]

Butt had other plans to encompass the destruction of the obstructives. Would Callan send him cuttings of all Parnell's
speeches, he asked? In particular, he asked Callan to find out
definitely if the English atheist Bradlaugh had addressed a
home rule meeting in Glasgow organised by the advanced
party.[9] He was surprised that Callan did not see how valuable it would be to establish this association:

I am not for many reasons the person to put this forward. I am
quite sure that a letter addressed to any priest in Glasgow (except perhaps one or two) asking them if it were possible Bradlaugh had been brought to lecture on home rule would bring
an answer that would finish the party in Ireland.

He thought also that the point should be made that O'Donnell was a graduate not of the Catholic but of the Queen's
University.[10]

Parnell, meanwhile, gave notice of his intention in the
council of the league:

To move that a committee be appointed to consider what further steps should be taken for the purpose of summoning a

7 A. J. Kettle to Butt, 31 Aug.
8 G. Dillon-Webb to Butt, 7 Sept., Butt MSS. Dillon-Webb had made
a brief incursion into the Dungarvan by-election only to be quickly
routed by O'Donnell. (*Nation*, 11 May 1878).
9 Butt to Callan, 7, 11, 12, 21 Sept., Butt MSS.
10 Butt to Callan, 21 Sept., ibid. Butt was not able to get the information he wanted—or perhaps his friends had too much wisdom to
find it for him.

national conference to deliberate on the present position of the home rule movement.[11]

Butt reacted with a counter-resolution referring the question of the conference to a league meeting on 11 October.[12] The two resolutions were due to come up on 14 September: Callan told McAlister to read Butt's letter first, and by this device Butt's resolution found its way on to the order paper before that of Parnell.[13] Butt's friends in Ireland renewed their frantic appeals to their leader to return to Dublin for the meeting. 'Surely Lisdoonvarna would be as good as Buxton and you would there meet people from all Ireland, priests and laymen', wrote McAlister: 'are you letting people in London in any way sway your feelings and judgment? . . . For God's sake come home' . . .[14] McAlister also warned Butt that his absence was augmenting the party on the council which had lost faith in him; he advised him to deal with the council more through Galbraith and less through Callan, who was universally distrusted.[15] Butt promised to return in time for the meeting, but at the last moment produced his doctor's orders as an excuse for staying away. He seems to have been genuinely ill,[16] and his letters for the first time shew lapses of concentration.[17] But he was able to carry the day by long-distance manipulation. He planned to 'supersede' the Council, upon which he could only obtain a sure majority through a deliberate marshalling of his forces, by the league, which could be packed with the members of parliament.[18] The success of his resolution of 14 September was essential as a preliminary to this; to secure this he drafted a lithographed circular, to be sent out by McAlister, the secretary of the league, calling his followers to the meeting when 'matters will be

11 McAlister to Butt, 5 Sept., ibid.
12 *Nation*, 22 Sept.
13 McAlister to Butt, 7 Sept., Callan to Butt, 8 Sept., Butt MSS.
14 McAlister to Butt, 5 Sept., 5 telegrams from McAlister and Callan to Butt, 12 and 13 Sept., ibid.
15 McAlister to Butt, 9 Sept., ibid.
16 Butt to Callan, 10, 12, 12 Sept., Butt MSS, vol. ii, MS 831.
17 e.g. Butt to Callan, 3 Sept., ibid.
18 Butt to Callan, 3 Sept., ibid.

brought forward upon the right decision of which the future
of the home rule cause may depend '. He planned also to call
a party conference for 9 October which he hoped would pass
resolutions which 'would put and end to the whole thing'.
Besides issuing the circular, he wrote personal letters to all
his friends asking them to come up for the meeting.[19] Some
thirty-three of Butt's supporters were thus bidden by McAlister, and more by Butt himself, including many who did not
habitually attend the meetings of the council.[20] Parnell's
supporters acknowledged defeat, and withdrew their resolution; Butt's alternative proposal was carried unanimously. In
the words of the *Nation,* the expected conflict did not develop[21]

At the same time Butt refused to listen to the appeals of
those of his friends, such as Henry, Galbraith, and Callan who
urged caution in dealing with the obstructives.[22] 'I do not
think we will ever beat them by half measures', he wrote to
Callan: 'I see that the time is coming when I must speak very
strongly and very plainly'.[23] He did so in a manifesto,
couched as a letter to Father Murphy, Curate of Ferns, and
published in the *Freeman's Journal* on 7 September. In this
letter Butt recapitulated his previous arguments: the party
had achieved much in its short life; it could not work miracles
overnight; it would have achieved still more in this session
but for the tactics of the obstructives. Obstruction was '*the
abandonment of constitutional action, and the adoption of un-
constitutional action in its stead'*; it could only alienate the
house, the English democracy, and the Irish aristocracy, and
would destroy the party.[24] The letter did not evoke an enthusiastic response even from Butt's friends. Callan, while
calling it in many respects a 'clincher', wrote:

[19] Butt to Callan, 3, 3, 9 Sept., ibid. McAlister to Butt, 9 Sept., Butt
MSS.

[20] McAlister to Butt, 11 Sept., ibid.

[21] *Nation,* 22 Sept.

[22] Galbraith to Butt, 9 Sept., Butt MSS; Butt to Callan, 11 Sept.,
Butt MSS, vol. ii, MS 831. *Freeman's Journal,* 11 Sept. Also Butt to
Delany, 21 Sept., Hickey MSS.

[23] Butt to Callan, 11 Sept., Butt MSS, vol. ii, MS 831.

[24] *Freeman's Journal,* 7 Sept.

I wish you had made it one third shorter—and not given the others any peg to hang a reply on by omitting all reference to Meldon's and Nolan's bills—Let the English parliament fight its own battles . . . for they did treat us contemptuously.[25]

'The part of it referring to the divisions is considered weak and inconclusive', wrote McAlister: 'Even the majority of your own friends do not believe the land or education divisions would have been a dozen or half a dozen better if Parnell and Biggar had conducted themselves'.[26] The *Freeman* suported Butt's motion in the council, and praised his letter as a 'masterly document'. But it added:

It displays the ingenuity of the advocate quite as much as the power of the statesman. Indeed, when the letter is criticised closely, many will think that it has more of the former than the latter quality.

It also felt the argument concerning the voting figure in the house was pressed too far; it urged Butt to come home and unite the nation behind a new and active policy.[27] The *Nation* accused Butt of using the failure of the university bill in an effort to turn the clergy against the obstructives.[28] O'Donnell rushed into print with an acid letter to the *Times* deploring Butt's refusal to hold back his manifesto until after the conference, even at the risk that he would 'give less satisfaction in anti-Irish circles'.[29]

But Mitchell Henry probably expressed the feeling of the great mass of the home rule movement in a moderate and balanced summing-up which aroused, immediately, the unreasoning fury of Butt's faction.[30] Some of Parnell's work had been praiseworthy, some wrongheaded, he wrote, but above all he had succeeded in conveying that impression of sincerity which was so lacking in the party as a whole. The party was

---

25 Callan to Butt, 8 Sept., Butt MSS.
26 McAlister to Butt, 9 Sept., ibid.
27 *Freeman's Journal*, 7 Sept.
28 *Nation*, 15 Sept.
29 ibid., 15 Sept.
30 Downing to Butt, 12 Sept., McKenna to Butt, 21 Sept., Butt MSS; Butt to Callan. 14. 16 Sept., Butt MSS, vol. ii, MS 831.

THE STRUGGLE FOR POWER

full of absentees and buffoons, who were more ready to repudiate than to cheer each other; they were taken seriously
by no one, and eighty of that type would be no more use than
their present number.

> For all this there is in my judgment but one remedy, and that
> is, as I ventured to say in a former letter, a new departure in
> Irish politics, to be planned at a conference in Dublin, and
> then really to be carried out in an orderly, methodical, and
> business-like manner. I am not an advocate for a pigheaded
> course of obstruction. . . . I am in favour of vigour and reality
> in our proceedings, and I do not hesitate to say that what makes
> Mr Parnell and some others so hateful to the English press and
> to most of the English members is that they think them for-
> midable, because not likely to be bought by office, or by what is
> quite as fatal, by personal flattery.[31]

The moderates, as this letter reveals, still clung to the hope
that Butt would agree to lead a policy of selective obstruction
at Westminster. O'Neill Daunt wrote to Henry:

> The situation is just this. Firstly, Mr Butt is indispensable as a
> leader. No other man could take his place. Secondly, the con-
> ciliatory policy is worthless, yet our indispensable leader seems
> resolved to persevere in it. At any rate he has not indicated any
> new departure, although he certainly said at a Westminster
> Meeting that obstruction *might* become necessary. Thirdly, Di-
> vision in our army would be worse than worthless; it would be
> equally damaging as the milk-and-water policy, and more dis-
> creditable to ourselves.
>
> Perhaps Mr Butt knows some distinction between the precise
> form of obstruction practised by Mr Parnell and Mr Biggar and
> the obstruction which he told his Westminster visitors might
> become necessary. If so the public should be made aware of it,
> for the present condition of matters is most unsatisfactory . . . I
> cannot see any chance of obtaining home rule by an annual
> talk on the subject in parliament unaccompanied with a sting.
> Can you? . . .[32]

31 *Freeman's Journal,* 11 Sept.
32 Daunt to Henry, 5 Sept., Butt MSS, vol. iii, MS 832.

Even Galbraith, who had little but distaste for Parnell, Biggar and O'Donnell, admitted that Parnell's tactics were an understandable reaction from the apathy of the bulk of the party, and urged the organised use of obstruction on Irish issues.[33]

But already the home rule leader had virtually destroyed the hope of such a compromise. To George Delany, secretary of the Butt testimonial, and Parnellite candidate in New Ross in 1878, he wrote: 'All their conciliation to me means is that if I put my self under their feet and manage their obstruction for them they would tolerate me as nominal leader'.[34] This Butt would never do, and so inevitably his personal authority in the country dwindled to nothing. But as yet even those who were convinced of the error of his policy retained their affection and respect for his person. 'I am outraged by attacks on Isaac Butt', wrote Daunt to Henry in October after a long, bombastic, and particularly vitriolic effusion from O'Donnell:

> Only for his genius and his patriotism the home rule movement would not even exist. I think his recent manifesto was conceived in a mistaken spirit; but his mistakes are like those of the immortal Grattan—they result from a credulous confidence in a faithless enemy. We should argue him out of them, not insult him by impertinent vituperation.[35]

The struggle for control of the Irish movement resolved itself finally in the national conference. The league meeting which was to convene it was immediately preceded at the beginning of October by a conference of the party. Only twenty-seven members attended; ten sent letters of apology. This was what was left in practice of the fifty-nine of 1874. The meeting immediately resolved itself into a discussion of the obstructive policy, but on this occasion without heat, and Butt and Parnell spoke in turn with great force. First came Butt's impassioned plea for patience:

33 Galbraith to Daunt, 18 Aug., ibid.
34 Butt to Delany, 19 Sept., Hickey MSS.
35 Daunt to Henry, 8 Oct., Butt MSS, vol. iii, MS 832.

It had been said that an obstructive policy would succeed better than one of calm debate; but had anyone expected that they would carry their measure of home rule in four years? How many measures had the great Liberal party carried in that time? They had not obtained home rule but they had been making a steady progress in the house of commons and in English public opinion in regard to all their measures. Take the franchise. They went within sixteen of carrying that, which he called a great triumph; and he called Mr Bright's support on that question another triumph. Then Mr Gladstone's speech in favour of the political prisoners was another triumph. But it was proposed that an excited popular opinion should be acted upon now—that all these things should be forgotten . . .

Having said so much, he would add that he saw pretty plainly what their policy should be in the next session. He would bring forward all their measures again. He had extracted from the government a promise that the estimates would be introduced at such a period that they might be discussed, and wherever there was an estimate involving a grievance to Ireland they ought to discuss that. Then he was disposed to think that they should move an amendment on the next address, and discuss that too . . . The government had promised them intermediate education, and they would find plenty of opportunity for discussing the whole question of education upon that, and they had also the review of the laws relating to the trial of controverted election petitions . . .

My policy is to try to bring Englishmen with us on such questions as the franchise. I believe we will carry the franchise; a year or two is little in the life of the nation. And I would ask my friend opposite to leave it to me next session to carry out my own policy. I will be as energetic as you like within the limits of that policy. . . . What we ought to do is to take up every bill that relates to Ireland, and let us consider it together. The only fault I find with Mr Parnell about the prisons bill is that he did not do it under the parliamentary committee. . . . We have abundance of work without calling each other lazy hounds; you have abundance of work to do without offering insults to me, which I scarcely think ought to have been done . . . Come to me next session; if my legal advice is of use to you,

Note

if my parliamentary experience is of use, it is at your disposal. It is not at your disposal if you resort to that parliamentary policy which will result in disgrace. I value political power, and the position in which I stand today, but rather than sanction you in letting the national cause go to ruin, I would fling them to the winds, and give up my seat.

After lunch the meeting reassembled; a series of meaningless compromise resolutions was proposed, as usual by William Shaw, and passed unanimously. The members resolved upon united and energetic action under the leadership of Butt; they agreed to retain freedom of action where there was no party decision, 'remembering the deep obligation on all individual action, both in and outside the house of commons, of endeavouring to avoid any course that would injure the influence and unity of the home rule party'. Parnell supported these resolutions in a speech which effectively summed up the crucial issues in the dispute:

> I believe that Mr Butt is capable of carrying out any policy better than any other man in our party. I am perfectly convinced of that. I should like to see him throw himself in earnest into this parliamentary warfare, because we can make it a warfare worthy of the Irish people. I think the course the Irish party have adopted in the past has not been calculated to attract the attention of the Irish people, and to make them believe in our earnestness, and if we want them to support a parliamentary policy we must show them we are in earnest, and that we are determined to carry out that policy. Whether you call that a policy of obstruction or not, I am perfectly satisfied, for I do not think there is virtue in a name; but I think it should be a policy of energy, of activity, and of opposition to the bad measures of every government in detail and generally until they consent to settle the question we have at heart.[36]

The party struggle resolved itself into compromise on the basis of the continuance of the old position exactly as before. The national conference ended in a similar stalemate. The card which the obstructives sought to play was their complete control of the English confederation. If they could secure equal representation at the conference for the English as for the Irish home rulers they would have a strong chance of forcing the acceptance of their policy upon the league and the party.[37] The meeting to arrange the details of the conference was restricted by ticket to the members of the league, and in the narrow membership of that body Butt was still able to command a majority. Admission to the conference was conceded by this league meeting in the first place to all home rule members of parliament, to be the two nominators of any home rule member in past elections to parliament and to all members of the home rule league. Butt then proposed to grant tickets to applicants from any of the following classes: clergymen of every religious persuasion, magistrates, members of corporations, town or municipal commissioners, poor law guardians and persons who had at any time been members of the old association or the league.

A bitter struggle was produced on a series of amendments to this section proposed by the Parnellite faction. Butt utterly refused to consider the admission of the branch officers of the home rule confederation and made some bitter references to that body of whose members he said in many instances 'we know nothing'. Parnell reminded Butt that he had formerly held the presidency of the confederation; in this office he should have found out something about his English supporters. The argument continued in this vein. Father Tom O'Shea said that the Irish in England had deposed Butt as their leader and now sought to come to Ireland and do the same there. At 5.30 p.m. the meeting finally accepted a compromise amendment of A. M. Sullivan's to admit fifty delegates, to be chosen by the most numerous branches of the confederation. The meeting adjourned and reassembled at 8 p.m. It was agreed to admit one representative from each trade society. Parnell proposed the admission of three delegates from each farmers' club or home rule association of six months' standing; he was forced to compromise on one delegate from each. A committee of twelve was appointed to or-

37 Telegram, McAlister to Butt, 13 Sept., Butt MSS.

ganise the conference which included T. D. Sullivan, Parnell, and Patrick Egan and it was agreed that no restriction, beyond the giving of seven days' notice, should be placed upon the resolutions to be discussed at the conference for which a date was fixed between 16 December and the assembly of parliament. Having settled all the items of contention the meeting then endeavoured to adjourn, but being unable to find an agreed candidate to take over the purely formal 'second chair', it broke up in confusion.[38]

The conference was to have been held at the end of January, but the decision to summon parliament on 17 January because of the eastern crisis compelled the committee to reconsider this date. By eight votes to four the committee decided to refer the question to the council. On the council Butt seized the opportunity to urge the abandonment of the project, but by fifteen votes to seven he was overruled, and the conference was arranged for 2 a.m. on Monday 14 January.[39] 'Those votes have virtually deposed me as far as the council of the league could do it from being the leader of the cause of the people', wrote Butt to George Delany.[40] 'As for the leader and his men—what do you say to this attempt to put off the conference altogether' . . . wrote Henry to Daunt; this scheme 'was conceived in the brain I am sure of Isaac Butt. We have far too many lawyers' . . .[41] Galbraith and John Blunden, the two long-serving honorary secretaries of the league, had both voted in the minority; immediately after the meeting they resigned together from their offices.[42] The league was collapsing even as the party had done.

Both sides submitted strong resolutions for the conference. Butt was first with a series reiterating the pledges of the 1874 party conference on united action, and concluding with a crucial proviso:

that no Irish member ought to persevere in any course of parliamentary action which shall be declared by a resolution

38 *Nation*, 20 Oct.
39 ibid., 29 Dec.
40 Butt to Delany, 29 Dec., Hickey MSS.
41 Henry to Daunt, 27 Dec, 1877, Butt MSS, vol. iii, MS 832.
42 Butt to Delany, 29 Dec., Hickey MSS.

adopted at a meeting of the home rule members to be injurious
to the national cause.[43]

T. D. Sullivan retaliated with a resolution to the effect that it
was no concern of the Irish members to facilitate the passage
of English legislation.[44] Downing wrote publicly to Butt expressing the belief that the council had called the conference
for 2 p.m. on a Monday with the deliberate intention of making it difficult for the clerical members to attend. Butt replied
that he had strongly remonstrated against the arrangement
on those grounds, and would at once move the adjournment
until the following morning.[45]

It seemed that the conference would be the occasion for an
explosion of bitterness. But moderate counsels prevailed. Sullivan wrote to Daunt that he believed his party would in fact
prevail at the conference; however, in this event, it was expected that Butt would resign, which he conceded would be
a calamity. The Parnellites did not ask Butt to lead them in
their policy, he wrote,—a notable change of attitude; they
simply wanted him to stop denouncing them.[46] A compromise was in fact arrived at on this basis by direct negotiation.

A new series of resolutions will be proposed by a neutral person, superseding Butt's resolutions and all the others. These
resolutions will go for unity, for Butt as leader, for freedom of
individual action on all questions on which the party shall not
decide to act as a party, for more earnestness, more vigour, and
better attendance of members during the next session.[47]

In other words, the status quo was restored. The only other
resolutions of importance passed were one proposed by
O'Connor Power, providing for annual holding of such conferences, and one by Parnell, calling for party consultation
with a view to united action whenever a definite issue should
arise in relation to the eastern question. The attempt of John
Dillon to bind the party to leave the house in a body on any

[43] *Nation*, 29 Dec.
[44] ibid., 5 Jan. 1878.
[45] ibid., 12 Jan.
[46] T. D. Sullivan to Daunt, 31 Dec. 1877, Hickey MSS.
[47] T. D. Sullivan to Daunt, 6 Jan. 1878, ibid.

division on this question was unsuccessful. When J. G. MacCarthy raised the issue of parliamentary policy he was ruled out of order. There were no scenes, and, in effect, no decisions. The long struggle of 1877 ended in stalemate: Parnell could not force the party or the league to adopt his policy in the teeth of Butt's opposition, and Butt, unable to force the league to discipline Parnell, did not dare to do so in the party. But Parnell made clear the precise terms upon which he had come to accept this stalemate:

> There is a different thing between believing that a change is necessary and forcing that decision upon the country. If we suppose, for instance, that I were to ask this conference today to pass a resolution calling upon Mr Butt to carry out a different line from that which he has carried out in the past; and if we suppose the conference were to carry that resolution, Mr Butt would then say that he was satisfied with his past policy, and that he could not conscientiously change it (and I assume that Mr Butt would say that, and I believe that he would do so); the conference would then find itself face to face with this position—they would either have to do an act that would deprive the country of the services of Mr Butt as our leader—to do an act which in all probability would eventuate in the disruption of the home rule party (loud applause)—or it would have to decide against the line and policy which I have recommended . . . if I refrain from asking the country today by the voice of this conference to adopt any particular line of action or any particular policy, or to put any definite issue in reference to it before this conference, I do so solely because I am young and I can wait.
>
> Mr Butt,—hear, hear.
>
> Mr Parnell,—And because I believe the country can also wait, and that a country which has waited so long can afford to be patient a little longer.[48]

So no decision was reached, and to preserve a token unity the issue was postponed until time and the general election which was bound to take place within the next two years

48 *Nation,* 19 Jan.

should resolve the questions both of policy and of leadership. In Butt's own constituency of Limerick his agent Henry O'Shea found his election committee at one in urging a more active parliamentary policy.

> I may tell you also that the eight or ten who attended on Wednesday were unanimous in their opinion in not being averse to obstruction, only they wish to have it united in order to be strong.[49]

But the home rule leader was adamant. Mitchell Henry for one had no illusions about the coming session: 'if anything is done it will be done by the obstructives and by nobody else', he wrote to Daunt at the end of December 1877.[50] But it would be done as in the last session, as a faction, not as a party. The struggle for power in 1877 achieved one thing only. By the beginning of 1878 the home rule movement had been compelled to adopt a formula which, in order to maintain its nominal existence, effectively recognised its dissolution as a real political entity.

49 O'Shea to Butt, undated, Butt MSS.
50 Henry to Daunt, 27 Dec. 1877, Butt MSS, vol. iii, MS 832.

CHAPTER XIV

Stalemate

As it transpired, Parnell and his followers did not have to wait for as long as they had feared.[1] While they waited, Parnell increasingly devoted himself to the building up of his position throughout the country by other means outside the movement; the power of the party in parliament and of the league in Ireland dwindled to nothing, and the stagnation of this last session of Butt's life was enlivened only by sporadic incidents which combined to rob him even of the personal popularity which had always been his.

The annual meeting of the party was held in Dublin on 12 January.[2] Thirty members attended, and ten sent letters of apology. The compromise of the conference was upheld with the adoption, after a long discussion, of two resolutions, one agreeing upon the introduction of an amendment to the address upon the subject of Irish grievance, the other calling for frequent and speedy consultation by the party on the eastern question, with a view to the possible adoption of united action in relation to any crisis which might develop.[3] When parliament assembled on 17 January, the Irish amendment to the address was proposed by Henry. The government put up only three speakers to reply, and on the following day voted it down by 301 votes to 48. Only 46 Irish members voted, and the Liberals, led from the house by Gladstone, took no part in the division.[4] Among the absentees was Butt himself, the

---

[1] T. M. Healy, *Letters and leaders of my day*, p. 63.

[2] Butt rejected the proposal of O'Connor Power that it should be held in London. (Butt to Power, 2 Jan. 1878, Butt MSS, vol. ii, MS 831).

[3] *Nation*, 19 Jan.

[4] *Hansard*, 3rd series, ccxxxvii, 120-53, 159-220; *Nation*, 26 Jan. 1878.

recurrence of whose ill-health made it impossible from the
outset of the session for him to attend properly to his parliamentary duties.[5]

The home rule members gave notice of twenty bills, and
O'Donnell, with typical egotism, contributed twelve notices
of motion on subjects ranging from Dunkeld Bridge to the
administration of India.[6] Before the end of January the
slaughter of these bills had begun. O'Sullivan's Union Justices
(Ireland) Bill fell by 138 votes to 38 on 21 January; the Land
Tenure (Ireland) Bill, introduced by Downing in Butt's absence on 6 February, was opposed by one home rule member,
Arthur Moore, and one camp-follower of the party, the
O'Conor Don, and beaten by 286 votes to 86, of whom 49
were home rule members. Meldon's motion on the Irish
borough franchise was beaten by only eight votes; twenty-two
home rulers were absent,[7] Twenty-five were absent from the
division on Biggar's registration bill. O'Gorman's bill to assimilate the municipal franchise of the two islands was beaten
by only five votes; more than twenty home rule members were
absent. Among these absentees was Butt himself; his ill-health
did not, however, prevent his attending regularly the meetings of the council of the Home Rule League, where every
vote was needed to exclude the Parnellites from representation in the newly-elected council. The same tale was continued for the remainder of the session; the habitual story of
defeat was remarkable only for the now callous absenteeism
of a large section of the old party. Public interest inevitably
waned to nothing. At the beginning of April Butt formally
resigned the leadership, allegedly on the ground of ill-
health;[8] he was prevailed upon to reconsider his decision,
but only on the understanding that he could not attend parli-

5 Butt to Hicks Beach, 14 Mar., Butt MSS, vol. iii, MS 832.

6 Henry, who admired Parnell up to the time of the new departure
and the Land League, thought O'Donnell was ' eaten up with vanity '.
(Henry to Daunt, 27 Dec. 1877, Butt MSS, vol. iii, MS 832).

7 The government, however, had come privately to accept the necessity to take up the issue, and even possibly that of redistribution of
seats, in the next session. (Brand Diary, 19 Feb. 1878).

8 Nation, 13 Apr.

ament consistently, and his renewed leadership brought no more discipline or organisation to the party than before. Even the more moderate of the active members began to weary of the utter futility of their parliamentary existence. The Mitchelstown evictions provided the party in March with an opportunity to exploit a popular issue, and to Gray was committed the responsibility of bringing a motion on the subject before parliament. Gray's appeals for advice and instructions met, however, with no response from his leader, until at Butt's orders the introduction of the motion was postponed until June, when it was voted down by 74 votes to 50.[9] Unable to obtain direction from their leader or support from their nominal colleagues, men like Gray grew increasingly weary of their situation. 'We were lost again yesterday', wrote Gray after the defeat of the municipal franchise bill, 'beaten by our own men—twenty-three of whom were absent'.[10] To Daunt Henry wrote desponding at the condition of the party, and to Butt he lamented: 'I believe our influence *as a party* is gone'.[11]

The obstructives, meanwhile, were unexpectedly quiet after the violence of the previous session. The threat of Parnell and O'Donnell to keep the house in session all night won them concessions in relation to the employment of child labour on the committee stage of the factories bill, and there was one all-night sitting in the committee on the mutiny bill in March.[12] There was also, ironically, an all-night obstruction of the bill for the closing of public-houses on Sunday which was led by Downing, O'Gorman, and McKenna, with the apparent connivance of the Conservative front bench.[13] From May onwards, however, there were no instances of blatant obstruction by the repeated moving of the adjournment, al-

---

[9] Gray to Butt, 4 Mar. (2 telegrams), 5, 7 Mar., Butt MSS. Also Gray to Butt, 27 Feb., in Butt Add. MSS, 10415. *Hansard,* 3rd series, ccxxxx, 1527-61.

[10] Gray to Butt, 7 Mar., Butt MSS.

[11] Daunt Journal, 26 Apr., MS 3041, Henry to Butt, 4 June, Butt MSS.

[12] *Hansard,* 3rd series, ccxxxviii, 1976-2031.

[13] ibid., ccxxxix, 1812-53, Brand Diary, 13 May.

though persistent and not wholly unsuccessful efforts were made by Parnell and his allies to amend the civil service, secret service, and education estimates in committee on supply. There were several reasons for this relative calm. Parnell had made his demonstration in the previous session and asserted his individuality; in the recess he had impressed his leadership upon Irish public opinion, but he had found it impossible to persuade the party or the league to endorse his policy. In these circumstances, and in particular in view of his expressed determination to postpone the decision of the issue of parliamentary policy until the next general election, he could gain little profit from pressing on to an open breach with the party. At the end of the 1877 session the suggestion had been made that the party as a whole should unite in obstructing the annual estimates for the Queen's Colleges as a reprisal for the persistent refusal of the government to consider the Irish demands for catholic education. This proposal had won a measure of approval not only from the Parnellite wing of the party but from the active moderates, who recoiled from Parnell's individual efforts to bring English legislation to a standstill but were prepared to consider the adoption of a disciplined course of obstruction to the ministerial Irish measures. On 18 and 19 March Biggar, O'Donnell, Martin, Meldon, Sullivan, Nolan, O'Conor, O'Clery, Richard Power, Ward, and Conyngham supported repeated motions to reduce the different items in the education estimates, and took part in six divisions in which the minority ranged from eleven to eighteen.[14] At a 'liberal' meeting in the Rotunda in May Gray and Judge Little called for determined obstruction on the estimates.[15] When the real battle came on this issue later in the session, wrote the *Nation,* and Irish members would act 'with spirit and energy'.[16] On the other hand, the proposal of Parnell that the party should obstruct all the supply estimates in retaliation for the persistent rejection of its bills was defeated by sixteen votes to eight, Gray, O'Donnell, Biggar,

14 *Hansard,* 3rd series, ccxxxvii, 1560, and ccxxxviii, 1625-33; Brand Diary, 18 Mar.
15 *Nation,* 4 May.
16 ibid., 23 Mar.

O'Connor Power, Kirk, O'Sullivan, and O'Clery voting with Parnell. O'Connor Power openly advised Parnell not to waste his time by moving the resolution:

> He was of the opinion that the only thing to do was to go on as best they could until the general election, and then let the constituencies decide the question at issue. No earthly power could induce the party at present to take any active or energetic policy, and there was no use trying to make them do it.[17]

In August the *Nation* began to call for the selection of candidates who were prepared to commit themselves to the 'active' policy in anticipation of the general election. Conyngham wrote to Butt in June:

> Would you believe it, when I tell you, that he (Parnell) and certain others talk about whom they are going to put up at the next election. This is rather too strong is it not.

According to Healy, as early as August 1878 Parnell had drawn up 'a list of men and places that he means to fight'.[18]

The refusal of the party as a whole to join in the obstruction of the education estimates would scarcely, however, have been sufficient on its own to deter Parnell from independent action. The obstructives were contenders in a drama staged before the audience of Irish opinion; in such a setting the total apathy of Disraeli's cabinet in respect of Irish legislation was striking even by the accepted standards of nineteenth century English administration, and, in turn, a display of obstructive zeal in the uniquely-respectable cause of denominational education offered unprecedented tactical advantages to the Parnellites. It was the reluctant realisation by the Conservative cabinet of the coincidence of these two factors which produced, in the Intermediate Education Act of 1878 and the University Act of 1879, the only two Irish measures of real importance passed by Disraeli's last administration. The obstructives might, and indeed did, claim therefore much of the

---

17 *Freeman's Journal*, 3 June.
18 *Nation*, 3 Aug.; Conyngham to Butt, 22 June, Butt MSS; T. D. Sullivan to R. Lalor, 24 May, Lalor MSS, 8566; T. M. Healy, *Letters and leaders of my day*, p. 64.

credit for the educational concessions of 1878 and 1879. They were not, however, given the opportunity to wring them from the government in combat.

The unique attractions of educational reform to a conservative administration averse to Irish legislation in general but above all to home rule and land reform in the particular had begun to impress themselves upon the Irish officials by the mid-70's. The total antipathy to even a back-door endowment of denominational education had always been a commandment of the Liberal rather than the Conservative *credo*. Hicks Beach, the chief secretary, was pressing the advantages of an offer in respect of education soon after his appointment, and produced a draft scheme for an intermediate education bill as early as 1876; to his voice was added by 1877 that of Marlborough as viceroy.[19] Both Beach and Marlborough were eager to see the administration legislate in respect not merely of intermediate but also of university education, either in a common 'package' bill or in rapid succession. In December 1877 Beach presented a memorandum to the cabinet proposing the introduction of a 'payment-by-results' method of endowment for catholic schools affiliated to an intermediate education board, coupled with the promise of a reform of university education either through the establishment of an examining university operating upon similar lines, or through the reconstitution of the Queen's University, the Catholic University being affiliated as a fourth college and adequate Catholic representation being conceded on the senate.[20] To Marlborough, education was the one great issue upon which legitimate Irish grievance was unsatisfied; moreover, with memories of Gladstone's abortive bill still fresh, he believed that the clergy 'would now thankfully receive smaller mercies'.[21] Denominational education was above all the cause dearest to the heart of the cardinal: 'you may remember', wrote Dr Woodlock, rector of the Catholic University, to Beach, 'how strongly his Eminence expressed his conviction that only through religious education would Fenianism

[19] Marlborough to Disraeli, 9 Nov. 1877, Disraeli MSS.
[20] 24 Dec., St. Aldwyn MSS, PCC 52.
[21] Marlborough to Disraeli, 30 Mar. 16 Dec., Disraeli MSS.

or any other kind of revolutionary organisation be checked in Ireland. '[22]

But the success of the administration in producing a measure acceptable both to the house of commons and to the catholic hierarchy was above all due to the untiring efforts of Hicks Beach. The tall, austere chief secretary might not have been the most convivial of companions; when he gave way in the spring of 1878 to the eupeptic 'Jimmy' Lowther, Lord Claud Hamilton sighed with relief at the departure of the 'six-foot icicle'.[23] But to the hierarchy Beach was the most persuasive and accommodating chief secretary of recent years, and his departure was much regretted.[24] By the time of his going, however, he had made his bill. By comparison with the product of Gladstone's self-consciously isolated cerebrations of 1872-73, Beach's measure showed the strength of the clerical contacts he had built up with little encouragement from his premier. Disraeli turned a jaundiced eye on his colleague's enthusiasm. 'The Church has educated England and denominational education was a necessity', he told Beach in December 1874:

> It's not so in Ireland: there, it is Parliament that has educated the people, and Parliament has declared against denominational education.
>
> It's very true, that, practically speaking, it, to a large extent, exists—but many are not aware of this, and many, who are aware of it, shut their eyes to the result. Any measure which advances or sanctions denominational education in Ireland, will array the whole of England against it, except a portion of the Clergy and a few country gentlemen.

Steer clear of such issues, was his advice; concentrate on something straightforward, like the remuneration of national teachers.[25]

Fortunately Beach turned a Nelsonian eye to this wisdom —not a difficult thing to do in dealing with an ageing prime

22 Woodlock to Beach, 23 Nov., 1878, St. Aldwyn MSS, PCC 64.
23 Hamilton to Disraeli, 2 Oct., Disraeli MSS.
24 Woodlock to Beach, 17 May, St. Aldwyn MSS, PCC 64.
25 Disraeli to Beach, 17 Dec. 1874. ibid.,, PCC 75.

minister to whom Irish mendicancy was continually distasteful. The Intermediate Education Bill of June 1878 was the
product not merely of long, hard negotiation by Beach with
Irish lay educationalists such as P. J. Keenan, commissioner
of national education, Lord O'Hagan, Lord Emly, and the
O'Conor Don,[26] but also of constant reference to the hierarchy itself. Bishop Conroy and Dr Woodlock were perhaps
Beach's principal clerical contacts, but both he and Marlborough was also in direct communication with Cardinal
Cullen, to whom Beach's draft bill was sent at the beginning
of 1877.[27] For a time the Cardinal boggled at the government's insistence upon the inclusion of a 'conscience clause'
allowing parents to opt their children out of religious instruction in affiliated schools, and an appeal to Rome was seriously
contemplated by the cabinet. But in March 1877 Conroy told
Beach that the Cardinal had given way, and the chief secretary at once communicated the good news to Disraeli.[28] When
the bill was finally introduced in June 1878 clerical approval
had, therefore, in principle been secured. The main provision
of the bill, which closely followed Beach's original memorandum, was the establishment of an Irish Intermediate Education Board, financed by an endowment, not to exceed one
million pounds, taken from the Church Temporalities Fund,
and empowered to make capitation grants to affiliated secondary schools in Ireland upon the basis of the results of a standard intermediate examination. The scheme did not overtly
recognise Irish demands for the endowment of denominational education, but it did devise a method of indirect state sub-
sidisation of Catholic schools. The draft scheme was 'admirable' . . . 'excellent', wrote Dr Conroy to Beach in February

[26] Keenan to Lord Emly, 5 May 1874, 8 July 1875; 2, 14 Dec. 1876;
4, 20 Mar. 1877; 13 Jan., 3 Feb., 24 Mar., 25, 30 June 1878 (all in Monsell MSS, 8317). Beach to J. T. Ball, Miscellaneous MSS, N.L.I., MS
2040.

[27] Marlborough to Disraeli, 30 Mar. 1877, Disraeli MSS. Conroy to
Beach, 15 Dec. 1876; 9, 16 Feb. 1877; Woodlock to Beach, 20 Jan., 18
Feb., 29 June 1878; Cullen to Beach, 29 Jan. 1878 (all St. Aldwyn MSS,
PCC 64).

[28] Conroy to Beach, 9 Mar. 1877, ibid.; Beach to Disraeli, 12 Mar.,
Disraeli MSS.

M

1877: 'we all owe you deep gratitude for the spirit in which you have approached this question and for the labour you have undertaken in dealing with it'; the bishops were 'most sensible of the courtesy you have shown and of the confidence you have reposed in them, as well as the fair and impartial spirit with which you have addressed yourself to so vexed a question'.[29] The hierarchy as a corporate body expressed some private reservations about the ultimate form in which the bill appeared, but while not feeling called upon to offer a formal decision upon it, they agreed that it was 'a fair and equitable measure'.[30]

In all this mutual congratulation there was little capital for the home rule party. What crumbs there were inevitably became the object of a bitter wrangle between its two factions, each claiming the measure—Butt as the fruit of his moral persuasion, Parnell and the obstructives as the outcome of their physical blackmail. Both claims had some justice, the latter slightly more, but neither much. The main importance of this sterile controversy was to shew how the tactical gulf between the two was widening as the paralysis of the party caused each in his different way increasingly to ignore its existence.

At the time of his return to parliament as home rule leader Butt's links with conservatism had been attenuated by the passing of some twenty years. Radicalism was his principal English ally in the sessions 1874-76, and as late as 1877 he could still at times treat each party on a common basis of detachment, soliciting the support of Northcote and Gladstone for his university bill with impartial unsuccess.[31] But as the party collapsed, his own health waned, and time became ever shorter, he turned more and more to the use of personal persuasion upon Beach, Northcote, and Lowther. His efforts were based upon an estimation of his own influence pathetic in its unreality, and in the long run the price he was

29 Conroy to Beach, 9, 16 Feb. 1877, St. Aldwyn MSS, PCC 64.
30 Conroy to Beach, 29 June, 7 July 1878, ibid.
31 Butt to Beach, 17, 18 May; Northcote to Butt, 18 May, ibid. Butt to Gladstone, 8, 14 Nov., Gladstone MSS, BM Add. MSS, 44455 ff 230, 244.

to pay for them was the final destruction of his position in Ireland. The greatest valuation placed by Beach upon the support of Butt was in his suggestion to Northcote in June 1877, at the height of the obstruction crisis, that the home rule leader might be bribed by concessions on university education to stand aside while Parnell and Biggar were disciplined —a proposal which was at least as great a compliment to the obstructives as to their titular leader. Beach admitted that by this device:

> the break-up of the Home Rule party would be postponed for a time: but I am by no means sure that this would be an evil. Their humbug has a good deal to do with keeping Ireland quiet—and, from a party point of view, it must be remembered that we have already received no little advantage from Butt's sympathies being Tory rather than Whig.[32]

Butt so little realised the ministerial estimate of his importance that throughout the second half of 1877 and the beginning of 1878 he increasingly pressed upon Beach his counsel and his flattery. Requested for his opinion on the drafting of an acceptable university bill, he responded in terms which represented himself as the principal spokesman of catholic educational opinion.[33] Beach can only have been amused, for he knew from his clerical contacts the real status of the home rule leader in the eyes of the hierarchy. In July he suggested to Dr Woodlock that Butt might be found a place on the new Intermediate Education Board. ' Much as I admire Mr Butt's great talents ', replied the rector, ' I am sure he would not be looked on as a representative of Catholic views, and I think his appointment as such would give dissatisfaction in many quarters '.[34] Butt, however, persisted in addressing Beach in the mysterious tones of one who could marshal massive if shadowy resources. ' I do not expect to be in the House of

---

[32] Beach to Northcote, 1 June 1877, Iddesleigh MSS, BM Add. MSS 50021 f 227. He was probably referring principally to King-Harman's election for Sligo County in January.
[33] Butt to Beach, 5 Jan. 1878, St. Aldwyn MSS, PCC 66.
[34] Woodlock to Beach, 17 July, ibid., PCC 64.

Commons much before the 1st of March', he told Beach in
January 1878:

> I wish very much I could go over at once. I [word illegible] you
> will not find the vexatious ' policy ' of last year repeated.
> I read with intense satisfaction your powerful and most con-
> ciliatory speech in the late debate.[35]

When the bill was published he wrote again to Beach:

> I have great satisfaction in thinking that at present ministers
> are regarded as the authors of a great boon to Ireland honestly
> formed with a single view to the good of the people . . . that
> such a feeling should prevail in Ireland as to any measure
> adopted by the British Parliament especially one brought in by
> a conservative ministry must produce incalculable good it may
> be in ways of which we have no idea.[36]

Butt made no effort to conceal his personal contacts with
the administration, despite their possible conflict with the
resolution of the first party conference of February 1874 that
'we should collectively and individually hold ourselves aloof
from, and independent of, all party combinations, whether of
the ministerialists or of the opposition'.[37] He rather boasted
of them as having contributed largely to the introduction of
the bill; in the debate on its second reading he declared:

> it was no secret that he had taken a very active part in pressing
> on Her Majesty's Government to endeavour to pass it this ses-
> sion. Whether his representations on the subject had any in-
> fluence on Her Majesty's Government, he did not know; but he
> made those representations as strongly as he could.[38]

Above all Butt saw the bill as cutting the ground from beneath the feet of obstruction. Its introduction was immediately followed by the publication of a letter from the home
rule leader to Dr Ward, one of the secretaries of the party,
urging the Irish members to join in expediting not merely

35 Butt to Beach, 19 Jan., ibid., PCC 66.
36 Butt to Beach, 19 July, ibid.
37 Quoted above, p. 225.
38 *Hansard,* 3rd series, ccxli, 1521.

the passage of the bill but the general business of the house. In particular, Butt wrote:

> After the introduction of such a measure, and the very distinct assurance given by Lord Cairns that it is intended only as a step to a liberal measure of university reform, I cannot but think that anything like a protracted opposition to the Queen's College estimates would be a course very mischievous to the cause of free education in Ireland.[39]

The new chief secretary, Lowther, kept Butt informed from London of the ministerial intentions in respect of the estimates, and arranged to telegraph him in the event of their being obstructed, presumably to summon his support in putting the obstruction down.[40]

The *Nation* deplored Butt's unconditional surrender of the weapon of obstruction, and Parnell for his part made it quite clear that only the introduction of the intermediate education bill and the promise of a university bill to follow had altered his unmistakeable resolve, at the beginning of the session, 'to make a very real and severe fight' on the Queen's University estimates.[41] To Butt's fury, however, the obstructives were able, with at least equal logic, to draw the triumphant conclusion that their's was the credit for having wrung the measure from the government. Nor were they alone in this interpretation. Richard O'Shaughnessy, Butt's colleague in the representation of Limerick City, a specialist upon education and a moderate but active member not previously associated with the Parnellite faction, in July openly ascribed the forward state of the bill to the demonstration of the obstructives on the Queen's College estimates. If fifty adopted the skilful use of these tactics, he said, the necessity would be removed for a few to strike out on their own.[42] The obstructionist newspapers were 'trying to represent that the intermediate education bill was brought in to prevent their opposing the Queen's College estimates', complained Butt to

[39] *Nation,* 29 June.
[40] Lowther to Butt, 24, 25 June, Butt MSS.
[41] *Nation,* 29 June, 27 July; *Hansard,* 3rd series, ccxli, 1539.
[42] *Nation,* 6 July. Also *Freeman's Journal,* 26 Aug.

Lowther, 'and to my amazement I see my colleague O'Shaughnessy lending himself to this'.[43] So widespread became the acceptance of this line of reasoning that in October the home rule leader was appealing desperately to Beach for permission to state not only that the chief secretary had drafted a bill in 1877 which the consumption of parliamentary time by the obstructives had compelled him to shelve, but further, that the ministry had on these grounds abandoned hope of ever introducing such a measure, and were only enabled to proceed by Butt's assurance that if the bill satisfied Irish public opinion he would guarantee that the Irish members would expedite public business to allow it to pass.[44] But Beach's assessment of the relative effectiveness of the two home rule factions was implicit in the memorandum in which, around the same time, he urged the cabinet to press on as rapidly as possible with the introduction of a university bill. The Irish, he argued, expected just such a sequel to the intermediate education act; denied it, they might rally to the obstruction of the Queen's University estimates in the next session. 'It is not at all impossible that the scenes of the session might be repeated over again and divisions protracted for days', with ever greater force of numbers. Furthermore, any university bill then conceded would be represented as a triumph for obstruction.[45] Lowther felt the force of this argument equally strongly; the failure to introduce a university bill in 1879 might lead, he warned the cabinet, to the blocking of the Queen's University estimates by 'a far larger number of members than those usually classified as " obstructives ".'[46]

So Beach's intermediate Education Act passed into law, and bequeathed to the Irish educational system an examinational structure whose traces have not wholly disappeared to this day. The division of the spoils between Butt and the obstructives was essentially an unconnected argument; it was scarce-

[43] Butt to Lowther, 2 July, Iddesleigh MSS, BM Add. MSS, 50040 f 118.

[44] Butt to Beach, 31 Oct., St. Aldwyn MSS, PCC 66.

[45] Undated memo, probably from the recess of 1878-79, ibid., PCC 52.

[46] Memo signed by Lowther, ' Irish legislation, 1879 ', 20 Jan. 1879, St. Aldwyn MSS, PC/PP 55.

ly one from which the home rule leader emerged victorious.
To the majority in the home rule movement Butt might hint
in vain of the dependence of the government upon his wisdom, his experience, and his capacity to restrain the rashness
of his followers; they had no doubt of the greater effectiveness
of force than flattery, and insofar as Sir Michael felt it relevant to reckon the odds in that quarter, he seems to have
agreed with them.

Two reasons have been given for the relative absence of
obstruction in the session of 1878—the failure of Parnell to
persuade the party or the league to endorse the tactics of Biggar and himself, and the introduction of the intermediate
education bill. A third influence also operated upon the obstructives in this session. A select committee on parliamentary
procedure was in constant session throughout the year to consider the framing of new rules for the conduct of business,
and Parnell seems to have thought it wiser to suspend his
more violent efforts while he was participating in its discussions. The most important issue before the committee was
the desire of Brand and Erskine May to see stronger powers
of suspension vested in the Speaker. This aim was, for the
moment, to be thwarted by the opposition of the Liberals and
the hesitancy of Northcote. In June a proposal to 'confide to
the chair a summary remedy against obstruction' was carried
only by Northcote's exercise of his casting vote as chairman
of the committee, and the government felt unable to proceed
with it before the house. In the same way the original intention to limit the number of motions which might legitimately be made on the proposal to adjourn or report progress,
and to provide for the taking of divisions on a standing count
where the minority was obviously small, was abandoned until
fresh struggles compelled its acceptance. The proposals laid
before the house in 1879 were, therefore, little stronger than
those adopted in 1877. The first to be accepted limited the
right of a private member to raise any issue of public importance as an amendment to the motion on going into committee
on supply. This was historically a much-valued privilege; it
had been used to move the home rule motion of 1876, and
its abolition was one of the first important curtailments of the

rights of the private member which arose out of the obstruction crisis. But it scarcely met the Parnellite problem. Most of
the new rules were of an equally mild nature; the most important embodied in its earliest form the rule dealing with
'order in debate'. It provided for the suspension during the
remainder of the sitting of any member named by the chair
as obstructing the rules of the house, and for the further suspension of the member for a week or more at the pleasure of
the house if he were found guilty of the same offence three
times during the same session. This rule was not in fact put
into effect until the session of 1880, and the parliament which
had seen the obstruction crisis of 1877 expired without having
framed any rules to meet a repetition of it. When obstruction
was revived in full force under the Gladstone administration
these new rules proved quite inadequate to deal with it, and
it was only with the introduction of the revolutionary machinery of the closure and the guillotine in the sessions of 1882
and 1887 that the house reluctantly accepted the necessity
effectively to modernise its procedure.[47]

The session of 1878 was, in short, characteristically unfruit-
ful of Irish legislation, apart from the intermediate education
act, and inconclusive in relation to the controversy on parliamentary tactics. One last reason remains to be given for this
state of affairs: the intense preoccupation of parliament and
of the United Kingdom with the eastern crisis. Yet it was the
issue of imperial policy which, before the session concluded,
was to produce a division in the home rule party which reacted violently upon the movement in Ireland and which,
perhaps more than any other development, completed the
destruction of that personal affection for Butt which had even
survived the rejection in Ireland of his policy. Partly through

---

47 Brand Diary, 6, 18 20 July 1878, and 'Appendix A', 21 June.
Northcote to Brand, 14 Jan., 13 Mar.; Brand to Northcote, 21 June,
Iddesleigh MSS, BM Add. MSS, 50053 f 222, 50021 ff 169, 171. *Standing
orders of the house of commons*, p. 72, H.C. 1880, (405—Sess. 2), lvi,
103 (Order in debate), and *Amended standing orders of the house*,
pp. 3-5, H.C. 1882, (429), lii, 243. *Hansard*, 3rd series, cccxv, 1594. For
a fuller treatment of this subject see D. A. Thornley, The Irish home
rule party and parliamentary obstruction, in *Irish Historical Studies*,
vol. xii, no. 45, March 1960.

the exertions of Gladstone, a violent anti-Turkish feeling had been engendered in both islands. The great mass of Irish opinion was immovably hostile to the government on this issue, and the action of Bowyer, Harman, Dunbar, Lewis, and Ward in voting with the ministry on the supplementary estimate for the armed forces at the beginning of the session had evoked severe criticism in Ireland. But Bowyer and Harman were notoriously subservient to the ministerial whip, and Lewis and Ward were also noted for their conservative leanings. Real anger was not aroused in Ireland until, when Hartington carried liberal criticisms of Disraeli's eastern policy into parliament with a formal motion of censure, Butt himself threw his weight behind the ministry. Butt had already scandalised Irish opinion earlier in the month by speaking at a public dinner in praise of the British parliament, which he called the mother of representative institutions and the seat of 'the intellect, the life, and the power of this great united nation'.[48] Now, speaking on the fourth night of the debate on Hartington's motion, he said:

I think England was losing her place in the estimation of foreign powers, and I think that was owing to our ministry being under the influence of 'peace at any price' . . . England has responsibilities already, created by her name, by what she has achieved, by the extent of the empire she has founded, and by the colonies and commerce which she has established in every part of the globe. She cannot descend from her high position and let it be believed that she has ceased to be a living and moving power, while Russia works her wicked will upon the nations of the earth.[49]

In speaking and voting as he did, Butt was simply giving expression to his unashamed loyalty to the British empire and to the conviction, which he had formed as long ago as the Crimean war, that in the expansion of Russia lay the greatest menace to European security.[50] But Irish opinion, always puzzled by Butt's idealistic imperialism, and instinctively

48 Daunt Journal, 17 July 1878, MS 3041.
49 *Hansard*, 3rd series, ccxlii, 1084-91.
50 Butt to Beach, 11 Feb. 1878, Butt MSS, vol. iii, MS 832.

M*

ISAAC BUTT AND HOME RULE

viewing these 'foreign' entanglements from the standpoint of Irish opportunity, recoiled in exaggerated horror from this panegyric of the British empire. The Irish people, said O'Clery, speaking after Butt, could have no interest in imperial affairs until the wrongs inflicted upon them by England had been undone. Sullivan was much more explicit. He felt compelled, he said, by Butt's speech to justify the vote which he intended to give against the government. Butt had been cheered, he remarked, only by the conservatives— 'Russia's lust for territory indeed.' Had he no word to say of England's?' What about Warren Hastings, he asked? Russia was inadvertently the agent of liberty in Bulgaria— had Butt no satisfaction at that? Could he not have advocated liberty and independence as the solution of the Balkan problem? Hartington's motion was defeated by 338 votes to 195; nine home rule members voted with the opposition and sixteen, including Butt, with the government. The majority abstained.[51]

In Ireland a wave of criticism greeted the news of this division in the party, and in particular of the speech and vote of the home rule leader. 'The leader of the party went over bodily to the camp of the enemy', wrote the *Nation*.[52] It was only on these major party divisions, wrote the *Freeman's Journal*, that the Irish party could hope to exert any influence; its utter disintegration on such occasions rendered it a nullity. Had the party met in an effort to secure united action, as had been recommended by the resolution of the conference last January, it asked? 'The Irish people are beginning to ask whether, as a matter of fact, the Irish party is a reality or not,

---

51 *Hansard*, 3rd series, ccxlii, 1094-6, 1114-8, 1121-5. O'Donnell also spoke and voted with the ministry; his attitude to imperial questions probably destroyed his chances of becoming one of the popular leaders in the movement. 'I wish in Imperial questions to secure the maximum of co-operation between Ireland and the English Conservatives whom I cannot but regard as the English National Party'. (O'Donnell to to Disraeli, 2 Feb. 1879, Disraeli MSS). See also Northcote to O'Donnell, 31 Dec. 1877, Iddesleigh MSS, BM Add. MSS, 50053 f 217.

52 *Nation*, 10 Aug. 1878.

and if it is, towards what its policy tends'.[53] A touch of personal venom was added to these criticisms by the London correspondent of the *Nation*: 'The spectacle of the leader of the Irish people presenting the incense of their approval at the shrine of Jingo, shows us what we have been spared by his absence on previous similar occasions'.[54] This new note of personal bitterness was not surprising in the writer, a young man called Timothy Healy now making the first of many such contributions to political controversy, at the rate of a pound a week.[55] But it was strikingly echoed by other hitherto more restrained critics of the party leadership. The executive of the Home Rule Confederation on the motion of Healy passed a resolution condemning Butt's action; several branches followed suit. In one a speaker said of Butt:

> he would not give the snuff of a farthing candlelight for all the nationality that existed in that man. It was now on the tapis that he was to be one of the paid commissioners of the new education bill, and if this was the case, he hoped they had heard the last of him—(a voice—They ought to make a judge of him and shelve him decently).

One letter to the *Nation* expressed the hope that neither Butt nor O'Donnell would ever again be allowed to sit for an Irish constituency: the popular reaction, it said, had been at first '"Were they drunk or mad"? Then, with one accord, and with bitter indignation, we exclaimed, "No! not drunk nor mad, but the veriest pair of renegades".' Meanwhile in Liverpool Lysaght Finigan called Parnell 'the *de facto* leader of the Irish people'.[56]

Parliament was prorogued on 16 August. It was to be recalled in December to consider the Afghan war, and the whole imperial issue was to be reopened amidst even more bitterness, but for the moment the last struggles of Butt's

53 *Freeman's Journal*, 5 Aug. *Saunders News-Letter*, the *Dundalk Democrat, and the Cork Examiner* also joined in the criticisms of Butt's speech. (Quoted in *Nation*, 10 Aug.).
54 *Nation*, 10 Aug.
55 T. M. Healy, *Letters and leaders of my day*, p. 56.
56 *Nation*, 17 Aug., 7 Sept.

movement were transferred again to the remnants of its Irish
organisation. The *Freeman's Journal* had doubted the continued existence of a home rule party; 'what has become of
the Home Rule League'? asked the *Nation* in September.[57]
'I am told that the Home Rule League has collapsed', wrote
P. Cahill of the Queen's County Independent Club to Richard Lalor . . . 'No association could get on after such an exposure as that of the election of the council last spring' . . .[58]
Cahill was referring to a sordid cabal which had become
damagingly public in the previous February. It will be recalled that the possession by the Parnellites of a possible
majority amongst the active members of the council had
caused considerable embarrassment to Butt in 1877. It was a
situation which his supporters had apparently resolved should
not recur. Each January the members of the league elected
fifty members to the new council. In 1878 the first ballot was
invalidated on the ground of informalities in its return;[59]
when the results of the second were announced it was found
that six members of the previous council who had been particularly active in support of the Parnellite policy in parliament,
Reverend H. Kelly, O.D.C., John Dillon, George Fottrell, Dr
J. E. Kenny, H. J. Gill, T.C., and J. W. Foley had not been
elected. Several of these men had sat on the council since
1874. Their defeat as yet aroused no controversy, as there remained, in the co-option which now followed under the rules
of the league of a further fifty members to complete the council, an opportunity which courtesy dictated should be taken
to bring on the defeated six. But when the first fifty met to
perform this operation, it became obvious, as Patrick Egan
wrote, that 'a combination had been entered into and elaborate arrangements made to keep these gentlemen off the
council'.[60] In repeated ballots the six were proposed but always rejected in favour of candidates devoted to Butt. Special
instructions were given to the secretary McAlister not to re-

57 ibid., 21 Sept.
58 Cahill to Lalor, 9 Sept., Lalor MSS, 8566. Cahill was still at this
time highly critical of Parnellite tactics in parliament.
59 *Nation*, 26 Jan.
60 ibid., 2 Mar.

lease to the press, as had been done in the past, the names of the proposers and seconders of the different candidates for the council, and the voting figures in each division. Butt himself, however, and five other members of parliament who had opposed the holding of the conference in the previous January were known to have been present, while Irish bills were being voted down by narrow majorities and Butt was pleading ill-health as an excuse for his constant absence from Westminster.

Butt secured a more docile council; the exposure of the manoeuvre by which this was achieved was, however, the last blow to the already waning fortunes of the league. In May McAlister wrote to Butt that nothing short of a revolution could set up the league again:

> Do you know that we are without money to pay our salaries this month? One party will not subscribe because of the obstructionists; the *Nation* office clique are endeavouring to prevent others from subscribing. This is done deliberately to break us down. I don't see how we are to get on . . . I am entirely despondent.[61]

'We are in debt £150', he wrote to Butt in July, 'have no money to pay our salaries and no promise of money'. Alfred Webb, the original treasurer of the league and before that of the association, had resigned several months before in view of the complete failure of the national roll scheme and the emptiness of the league's coffers.[62] His successor, T. H. Webb, could see no other course but to cut down the staff by releasing McAlister himself. 'I am in perfect despair at our prospects', concluded McAlister.[63] To Butt Webb himself wrote complaining that he was constantly being dunned by the creditors of the league.

> You will regret to hear that this time there has not been any response to the circular you drew up respecting the finances of the H. R. League. McAlister sent out some forty copies of it to a selected list of M.P's. and others on Monday and Tuesday last.

61 McAlister to Butt, 27 May, Butt MSS.
62 *Nation*, 22 Oct.
63 McAlister to Butt, 5 July, Butt MSS.

If there was still no response in a few days' time, he concluded, McAlister would have to be discharged.[64]

There was no response, and a week later McAlister wrote to Butt:

> Webb, Fay, and Galbraith have had a consultation with the result that James Collins has been called on to resign. I have been told that at no distant day I ought to do the same. In fact nearly everything is to be wound up. I do not know what to say or do or think . . .[65]

Collins, the assistant secretary, gave a month's notice, and appealed to Butt to get him a job on the staff of the new intermediate education authority.[66] A few days later the financial position of the league became so desperate that Collins was asked to alter his notice from a month to a fortnight. Refusing to do this, he was threatened with a week's notice of dismissal.[67] At the same time McAlister himself was finally asked to resign. 'Can you get me an appointment in the new Intermediate Education Office'? he wrote to Butt: 'Can you get James Collins something there too'?[68] It was ironic, this scrambling for the places created by the one Irish measure of importance passed in the lifetime of Butt's party. Another supporter of Butt's, Philip Callan, joined the list of applicants. 'Is there any chance of the post in re intermediate education?' he wrote on 7 July;[69] or in the administration of Cyprus.[70] 'The home rule movement is in my opinion broken up', wrote Galbraith to Daunt in August.[71]

As the movement finally disintegrated Butt turned more and more to the exertion of that personal influence which he deluded himself to have been so effective upon the ministry in

64 Webb to Butt, 6 July, ibid.

65 McAlister to Butt, 15 July, ibid. Collins was a protegé of Butt's, of whom he has many anecdotes in his reminiscences, *Life in Old Dublin*, (Dublin, 1913.)

66 Collins to Butt, 16 July, Butt MSS.

67 Collins to Butt, 18 July, ibid.

68 McAlister to Butt, 19 July, ibid.

69 Callan to Butt, 7 July, ibid.

70 Callan to Butt, 15 July, ibid.

71 Galbraith to Daunt, 22 Aug., Butt MSS, vol. iii, MS 832.

relation to the intermediate education bill. Now, in the twi-
light of his career, his tactical isolation, coupled with the emotions aroused in him by the eastern crisis, seem to have im-
pelled him to revive some of the conservatism of a generation
earlier. From November 1878 to February 1879 his letters
descended upon Beach and to a lesser extent Northcote, growing ever more rambling and indecipherable. From 'My dear
sir' in 1877, Beach becomes 'My dear Sir Michael' in November 1878. 'There is a great feeling among Roman Catholics that their true interest is to support a Conservative government', writes Butt in October 1878: 'I get new proofs of
it every day'.[72] 'I believe prudence on the part of the Conservative government might make it a great power for good
both to themselves and to the Empire'.

> I do not need to tell you that I am sincerely anxious to streng-
> then your hands chiefly for your resistance to Russian aggres-
> sion but also because I am disposed to think that there are men
> in the present Cabinet more likely to deal fairly with Ireland
> than any we would be likely to find in a Whig Cabinet.

To win this potential support, Butt advises Beach, the ministry must press on with the satisfaction of legitimate Irish
grievance. A university bill, a commission of enquiry into the
working of the Land Act, county boards, the assimilation of
the franchise of the two islands, a redistribution of seats—
the catalogue of reforms which has been paraded vainly for
four sessions in the lobbies of the House of Commons is now
to be solicited from a Conservative cabinet in exchange for
Irish support on the eastern question and Irish votes in the
coming general election.[73] On 2 December Beach sent on to
Disraeli a letter from Butt—probably this one. 'You will
know how much importance to attach to it', he added, 'in
the present condition of the home rule party'.[74]

In December and January Butt's appeals become more and
more concentrated upon the single goal of a university bill.
Gray in the *Freeman* is calling upon the home rule members

72 Butt to Beach, 31 Oct., St. Aldwyn MSS, PCC 66.
73 Butt to Beach, 28 Nov., ibid.
74 Beach to Disraeli, 2 Dec., ibid., PCC 13.

to work for the overthrow of the government, says Butt: he is resisting the proposal. He could do so much more effectively if Beach would allow him to proceed with 'confidently predicting' the introduction of a university bill in the coming session. Again he makes much of his influence in deciding the disposition of the Irish vote on the eastern question.[75] In January he adds the offer to drop Meldon's franchise bill as an additional inducement:
'I do not think it would be for the interests of the ministry to go to a general election in Ireland without settling the University question'.[76] An examining university will not be adequate, he insists; he knows that the hierarchy will accept nothing less than some form of endowment, if only through the payment of half-salaries for professors of secular subjects.[77]

> I feel an intense anxiety that you should settle this question on terms [which] will secure you the support of the Irish people. I wish this not for the sake of any party but of England. Any ministry upholding the honour and interests of England abroad will receive the support of the Roman Catholic people of Ireland in a struggle that cannot be long delayed. It may be needed to resist revolutionary projects at home. I believe you can have it by teaching the Irish people that your conservatism does not exclude them from the benefits which in England it guards.

If, on the other hand, the government fails to concede a university bill, he warns Northcote, it will 'throw away a grand opportunity of attaching the great mass of the Irish Roman Catholics both to Conservatism and to the ministry'.[78]
In February 1879 the stream of petitions dries up as Butt's health begins to fail. In the last analysis these letters reveal

[75] Butt to Beach, 21 Dec., ibid.
[76] Butt to Beach, 7 Jan. 1879, ibid.
[77] In his last letter to Beach, dated 2 February, Butt effects a complete *volte-face* and assures Beach that the hierarchy will, after all, accept 'a bill such as I have sketched with payment by results without the further provision for professors'.
[78] Butt to Beach, undated (Jan. 1879), ibid. Butt to Northcote, 9 Feb., Iddesleigh MSS, BM Add. MSS, 5040 ff. 136-7.

no betrayal of home rule. There was nothing intrinsically improper in Butt's wooing of Hicks Beach. No one can say how much of it stemmed from misplaced conviction and how much from tactical extremity, and Parnell's tactics of 1885-86 were not fundamentally dissimilar. It is as tactical exercises that Butt's approaches must be judged. As such, they serve only to lay bare yet again the gulf which by 1878 had come to separate this once-masterly politician from the realities of Irish public opinion. What imparts to these last letters their aura of senile desperation is that all the principals save one so clearly knew that the home rule leader had nothing left to offer.

Parnell and his followers were able meanwhile to strengthen their position in the country. In November at Ballinasloe Parnell addressed the first in a series of tenant-right meetings, under the chairmanship of the president of the local tenants' defence association. A resolution of support for the Parnellite policy at Westminster was passed, and a letter read from Dr MacHale praising Parnell, as 'the sterling hereditary advocate of Irish interests'.[79] In October the English Confederation for the second year in succession held its annual convention in Dublin. Butt refused to attend it, because he had not been consulted about its organisation, and because he and his followers looked upon the proposed 'consultative' meeting with the Irish home rulers which was to occupy the last evening of the convention as an attempt to by-pass the league and put pressure upon the Irish movement.[80] Brooks, Shaw, and Conyngham adopted the same attitude, but sympathetic letters were read from O'Shaughnessy, Kirk, and Daunt. This assembly of the reorganised convention was confined to delegates, members of the home rule 'hundred'—honorary members who paid £5 a year—and members of the executive; only seventy attended in all, and the convention bore, ironically, a more middle-class aspect than that of the previous year. But the secretary was able to report that the confedera-

[79] *Nation,* 9 Nov. 1878. This meeting preceded the Tralee meeting mentioned by R. B. O'Brien, *Life of C. S. Parnell* (3rd ed.), vol. i, p. 174.

[80] *Nation,* 26 Oct.

tion had surmounted the financial difficulties which had threatened to destroy it twelve months before. Parnell was unanimously re-elected president, but O'Donnell retired from the honorary secretaryship. The following day the consultative meeting, which was attended by nine members of parliament,[81] agreed to submit to the public meeting that evening resolutions calling upon the party to adopt an energetic policy, deploring the lethargy of the home rule council, and urging the return of supporters of the active policy at the general election. Three thousand people attended the public meeting which followed that same evening in the Rotunda. A resolution welcoming the delegates of the confederation to Dublin was proposed by Gray, who called for 'determined, persistent hostility to the government which refuses us what we are sent to demand'. The agreed resolutions were then passed on the motion of Power who openly admitted that they were directed at the return of candidates pledged to the parliamentary policy of Biggar and Parnell.[82]

The success of this meeting emboldened the followers of Parnell 'to go on and stir up the league a bit'.[83] To Daunt, T. D. Sullivan wrote:

> We mean to reform and extend that organisation, which is now almost dwindled to nothing. We mean to get new members for it, which means additional funds, and to put the machine into good working order. The first step we have to take is to call a general meeting of the league and get them to consult on the situation. In order to get up that meeting we have to send in a requisition to the honorary secretaries signed by thirty members of the league, and I have been requested to apply to you for authority to attach your signature to it.[84]

[81] Biggar, Ennis, Gray, O'Clery, O'Donnell, O'Sullivan, Parnell, O'Connor Power, and Sheil.

[82] *Nation*, 26 Oct. From this meeting arose Devoy's celebrated telegram which inaugurated the debate on the new departure which runs parallel to the story of these last months of Butt's movement. See T. W. Moody, The new departure in Irish politics, 1878-9, in *Essays in British and Irish history in honour of J. E. Todd*, 1949.

[83] T. D. Sullivan to Daunt, 25 Oct., Hickey MSS.

[84] ibid.

But the majority which Butt had so carefully secured upon the council was a permanent barrier to any such attempts at a reorganisation of the league. In September the council shelved the obligation distinctly laid upon it by O'Connor Power's resolution at the national conference in January to summon another conference of the same kind at the end of the year. According to Power this meeting was attended only by Butt himself, his son Robert, Callan, Brooks, and O'Leary.[85] But in any case, as John Dillon admitted the following February, the league could not have met the expense of a conference even if it had desired to call one.[86] In November the council was compelled by the constitution of the league to bow to the requisition, and a meeting of the league was arranged for 10 December, to be preceded on 19 November by an afternoon meeting to receive notice of resolutions for its consideration.[87]

Meanwhile in November Butt published the first of four long-promised manifestos on his parliamentary policy. They proved to be only yet another recapitulation of the arguments which had gone before. P. Cahill, who like Daunt favoured the adoption of an active policy under Butt's leadership, wrote to his friend Richard Lalor, urging him not to call a meeting of the Queen's County Independent Club to consider the issues raised at the confederation convention until it was seen what Butt's manifestos would offer in the way of 'some line of action which all may follow'.[88] He had expected a call to arms; he was disappointed.[89] In these last months of his life Butt, as he strove to counter the appeal of the Parnellite policy throughout the country, grew more and more irreconcilably hostile towards his rebellious followers. In October he was trying to arrange a private meeting with the 'moderates', who wished to maintain 'a *legal* national and constitutional movement'.

85 *Nation*, 21 Dec.
86 *Freeman's Journal*, 5 Feb. 1879.
87 *Nation*, 16 Nov. 1878; Butt to Henry, 17 Nov., Butt MSS, vol. iii, MS 832.
88 Cahill to Lalor, 2 Nov., Lalor MSS, 8566.
89 Cahill to Lalor, 4 Nov., ibid.

Sooner or later we must separate from the revolutionary party
and the time for striking the blow is only a question of prudence . . . I think it very possible the best thing may be to give
up our old party organisation and associate the moderate men
together in an entirely new formation.[90]

The publication of Devoy's telegram and the public controversy on the new departure played on his fear of revolution,[91]
and in his mind there grew increasingly the conviction of a
fenian conspiracy against him. He rejected Henry's contention that the differences in the party were mere domestic
quarrels; he believed they originated in:

a deep laid plan carried out by the paid agents of an American
junta of traitors to destroy any party of constitutional action.
Our differences are as wide and deep as the difference between constitutional action and treason.
I do not believe it possible that any way can be made for the
home rule cause or an Irish party until in some way or other
those who manage either are severed from those who identify
themselves with treason.
I think this is coming in the natural course of events.[92]

Members of the extreme right wing of the party like Bryan
and Harman were prepared to consider this step, but Henry
would have none of it.[93] The projected reorganisation fell
through.

At the end of November parliament was recalled to consider the war which had broken out in Afghanistan. Henry
wrote as usual to the press calling for a meeting of the party
to consider the issue before the opening of the special session;[94] the *Nation* reminded the party of the unique opportunity which was presented to it by the war—the Irish members could prevent a single penny being voted for supply
until some concession was made to their demands.[95] Butt,

90 Butt to Henry, 9 Oct., Butt MSS, vol. iii, MS 832.
91 Butt to Henry, 17 Nov., ibid.
92 Butt to Henry, 5 Jan. 1879, Butt MSS, vol. iii, MS 832.
93 Butt to Henry, 9 Oct. 1878, ibid.
94 *Nation,* 30 Nov.
95 ibid.

STALEMATE 373

however, thwarted in his efforts to abandon the obstructives refused pointblank to call a party meeting to confer with them, and seized the opportunity to postpone the requisitioned league meeting until the following January. At the same time Lord Robert Montagu emerged from retirement to announce his dissociation from the league on the grounds of, firstly, Butt's failure to discipline Parnell, and secondly, his persistence in introducing bills which had no hope of success.[96] The efforts of Parnell and his allies to call a party meeting by requisition were deliberately obstructed by the secretaries of the party, Ward and Meldon.[97] Instead, Butt laid down in a public letter to Ward what he considered the proper course for the party to adopt in the crisis. He did not even consider the proposal that the Irish members should threaten to obstruct supply; no hostile action whatsoever, he held, should be taken. Even to propose, as Parnell had suggested, an amendment to the address in relation to the franchise question would appear to be aimed at 'creating confusion in the counsels of a nation at a time when to do so is to help the cause of its enemies'.[98]

This letter, almost Butt's last public utterance, was decisive of his position in Ireland. To Butt any other attitude in wartime would have been treason to the empire; to any Irish nationalist convinced of the truth of the dictum that England's difficulty was Ireland's opportunity it was treason to the Irish nation. The last vestige of respect for or restraint towards the home rule leader left the public controversy on his parliamentary policy. 'Mr Butt seems to think that the policy of self-effacement on every great occasion is the way to win for Ireland her rights', wrote the *Freeman's Journal*, deploring at the same time the temporary abandonment of the league meeting.[99] The *Nation* went further: Butt had 'at last removed all doubt as to his fitness for the post of leader of the Irish national movement'. 'This old man whom we trusted',

---

[96] *Freeman's Journal*, 30 Nov. In April 1879 Montagu formally severed his connection with the party. (*Nation*, 5 Apr. 1879).

[97] *Nation*, 7 Dec. 1878.

[98] *Freeman's Journal*, 30 Nov.

[99] ibid.

was the phrase with which Healy dismissed Butt in his London letter; 'since the formation of the party', he wrote, 'no one sitting on the opposition side of the house has been of more assistance to the government than the honourable member for Limerick'. 'My personal patience is utterly worn out by Mr Butt', wrote Father Lavelle. 'Can we have misread the lines'? asked the *Cork Examiner*:

> Is it Isaac Butt, the champion of Irish nationality, who writes that there should be no obstacle placed in the way of gratifying that thirst for domination which possesses the present government? . . . After this, it is idle to conceal that the crisis in the affairs of the home rule party has come. On such a proposal it cannot consent to be led.[100]

The *Weekly News,* a subsidiary of the *Nation,* carried a cartoon depicting the reconciliation of Butt and Disraeli. But the fiercest condemnation came from O'Connor Power. When a meeting of the party was finally held on 5 December he denounced Butt as a traitor to the party and the cause, and in a letter published in the *Freeman's Journal* on 6 December he repeated this accusation. The *Freeman* deplored the violence of Power's attack as likely only to cause a reaction in Butt's favour;[101] so also did Daunt in a letter to the *Nation* of 21 December. But the executive of the Home Rule Confederation complimented Power on his 'timely warning' to Butt, and while the party as a whole repudiated it, the efforts of Ward to get up an effusive address to Butt in retaliation met with only a mixed response. Fay, Bryan, Digby, Dease, and Harman were delighted to sign it. All five had been unfailingly indifferent to the efforts of the party in the preceding two sessions; Dease had refused to attend the conference of January 1878, and Digby had been hooted at it. Brady refused to sign on the ground that the address was insufficiently condemnatory of Power. O'Clery agreed to sign it out of personal respect for Butt, but declined 'all responsibility for any political significance that might be sought to be attached to the document in question'. Sullivan, Nolan, Henry, O'Sulli-

100 *Nation,* 7, 14 Dec.
101 *Freeman's Journal,* 6 Dec.

van, and Browne apparently refused to sign it at all.[102] Butt's
loyal friends of the Limerick Corporation, on the other hand,
found time to redress the balance with a vote of confidence
in the home rule leader, before adjourning as a mark of respect to the memory of the late Princess Alice.[103] But for
Power there was a simple and unanswerable rejoinder: the
home rule leader, he said, now affected to despise the Irish
popular opinion upon which he had once rested his authority, 'because the multitudes no longer assemble in the name
of Isaac Butt, but in that of Charles Stewart Parnell'. When
the new council of the league was elected in January Henry
headed the poll over Butt.[104]

At the beginning of February Butt faced his followers for
the last time in the long-deferred meeting of the league.
There was only a small attendance, probably not much in excess of seventy.[105] The usual resolutions calling for vigorous
action in parliament and determined organisation in the
country were passed unanimously. But the decisive struggle
took place on the motion of T. D. Sullivan, reaffirming the
resolution of the 1873 conference recommending that the
home rule members of parliament should hold themselves
aloof from the English parties, and urging the members to
act up to this recommendation in the spirit of the resolutions
of the conference of January 1878 which had called for increased activity and more regular attendance. The debate
on this resolution continued all day with an adjournment for
lunch. John Dillon condemned the leadership most bitterly,
comparing Butt's current policies with the speeches he had
made 'when he was really Mr Butt'. Butt made no secret of
his conversations with the ministers—if these had not taken
place 'some of them would tell you that you would never have
had that intermediate education act in its present shape'. He
put more work into drafting bills, he said, than into walking

102 ibid., 7, 11 Dec.; Nation 14, 21, 28 Dec.
103 Nation, 21 Dec.
104 ibid., and 25 Jan. 1879. The struggle between the two factions
on the co-option of the fifty additional members was repeated, but the
Parnellites were able to improve their position.
105 The report of this meeting is taken from Freeman's Journal, 5
Feb., and Nation, 8 Feb.

matches in the lobbies, but his efforts had been undermined in 1877 just when they were gaining ground. He appealed again for the unity which had existed in the party in the coercion debates—forgetting, apparently, that the first criticisms of his parliamentary policy had been aroused by his treatment of this issue in 1874 and 1875. Henry refused to be convinced of the value of Butt's private negotiations with the government. Conciliation had failed, he said, but he was prepared, as were the people, to follow Butt loyally on one condition that he should go over to Westminster and announce 'that the time for conciliation is ended, and that we must have results'.

> Mr Butt—I won't say any such thing.
> Mr Mitchell Henry—If that is not done I look for no more good from the Home Rule League, from the meeting of Irish members, or from any attempt to keep up a united and active party.

Parnell stressed the moderation of the resolution; he did not ask the party to endorse obstruction, he said: all he sought was activity—in particular that the party should follow the advice once given him by the late Joseph Ronayne—to take part in the discussions on English business.

Despite these assurances Butt insisted upon regarding the motion as one of censure. His attitude made it impossible for men like Henry to vote against him, and an amendment substituting a simple reaffirmation of the resolution of the conference of the preceding January, calling for united and vigorous action, was carried by thirty-two votes to twenty-four. Eleven members of parliament voted with Butt and five against.[106]

The backwoodsmen of the party had thus once more helped Butt to frustrate the demands of the Parnellites for a recon-

106 For the amendment: Brooks, Browne, Butt, Callan, Delahunty, Fay, Henry, Lewis, McKenna, Martin, Meldon, and Shaw. Against: Biggar, Ennis, Kirk, Parnell, and O'Sullivan. The following week the annual conference of the Ulster Home Government Association passed a resolution endorsing the policy of Biggar and Parnell. (Nation, 15 Feb.).

sideration of the parliamentary policy of the movement, and he retired from the meeting with the year-old deadlock unresolved. The supporters of Parnell were again shewn that they could hope to achieve nothing before the general election. The meeting of the party which preceded the opening of the 1879 session could muster an attendance of only fifteen members.[107] When the ministry announced its proposals for the session they were found to make no mention of an Irish university bill. Butt had been 'sold', wrote the *Nation*, and the conciliatory policy had received its *coup de grâce*.[108] The

107 *Nation*, 22 Feb.

108 In June the government did in fact bring into the House of Lords a bill which, while leaving the three Queen's Colleges and Dublin University intact, replaced the Queen's University by a 'Royal University of Ireland', a purely examining body modelled upon the University of London. Its character essentially undenominational, the scheme aroused little Catholic enthusiasm. Of the government's principal catholic contacts, both Dr Woodlock and Bishop Conroy had pressed for the granting of some endowment to the Catholic University, Dr Conroy arguing that the establishment of an examining university would destroy educational standards in Ireland by forcing an ill-equipped Catholic University to compete with 'any little college' which could '"cram" its students for degrees'. The Earl of Granard, possibly the administration's principal intermediary with Cardinal Cullen, had sought an endowment of £10,000 per annum for the Catholic University, together with the stipulation that candidates for the degrees of the new examining body should only be permitted to come up from that college, from Trinity, or from one of the Queen's Colleges. But the successful passage of the Intermediate Education Act through all its vicissitudes persuaded both the government and the hierarchy to endorse the extension of the same principles into the field of university education. As Manning remarked to Sir George Bowyer, the Liberals 'would not if they could, and they could not if they would', do any more. And the bill did offer some indirect endowment to the Catholic University by its grant to the professors of that institution of one half of the fellowships of the new body. (The Earl of Granard to Sir Bernard Burke, 10 Feb. 1876, enclosing Conroy to Granard, 7 Feb.; Sir Bernard Burke to the Marquis of Abercorn, 10 Feb. 1876; Marlborough to Disraeli, 9 Nov. 1877; Manning to Bowyer, 7 Feb. 1879—all in Disraeli MSS. Conroy to Beach 27 Nov. 1876, Woodlock to Beach, 23 Nov, 1878, St. Aldwyn MSS, PCC 64. Also two memoranda by Beach and Lowther in St. Aldwyn MSS, PCC 52 and PC/PP 55. See also T. W. Moody, The Irish university question of the nineteenth century, in *History*, vol. XLIII, No. 148, June 1958.)

party met on 15 February to consider retaliatory action; only twenty-four members turned up, and Butt himself was amongst those absent. In the circumstances any decision was deferred. Also deferred on the same grounds was the proposal to appoint a vice-chairman empowered to summon the party together during Butt's frequent absences; the right wing of the party saw in this suggestion a device to supplant Butt's leadership, and sought time to sound the tocsin to the absentees.[109] It was their last and, as it proved, an unnecessary service to their leader. Butt's health had never recovered from his illness in the autumn of 1877. In January 1879 he complained to Henry of difficulty in breathing, and at the end of February he fell severely ill with bronchitis.[110] In March he was reported to be recovering, but at the beginning of May he suffered a stroke and on 5 May he died.[111] His death aroused genuine sorrow, but he passed on the whole quietly from the political arena in which he had become only an embarrassment. There were many obituaries, but most realistic was the youthful Healy's objective footnote to the career of the old leader:

> He gave practical direction to the national aspirations, kindled patriotic fire, and then, aided by the spirit he evoked, then?—Then he failed. Before his death so long had he accustomed Irish patriots to look elsewhere for a leader, that now these men will miss him least.[112]

---

[109] *Nation*, 22 Feb.
[110] Butt to Henry, 5 Jan. 1879, Butt MSS, vol. iii, MS 832.
[111] *Nation*, 8 Mar. R. B. Butt to Callan, 8 May, Butt MSS, vol. ii, MS 831.
[112] *Nation*, 10 May.

Conclusion

THE DEATH of Butt was not a climacteric in the history of the movement. The stalemate which paralysed the party had lasted for over a year; it could not be broken simply by the removal of the home rule leader. Butt had become little more than a symbol of the refusal of the right wing of the party to be forced into the endorsement of the Parnellite policy; the disappearance of this symbol could not alter their determination. Faced with the choice between two alternatives as Butt's successor in the chairmanship of the party, the energetic Henry and the eternal mediator Shaw, they elected the latter. It was a decision without importance; a general election was imminent and Parnell hoped for nothing from the party before it. Healy records that in the ballot Biggar voted for Henry, as the better man; Parnell voted for Shaw, 'whom he knew he could oust'.[1] The by-elections in New Ross in 1878, and in Longford and Ennis in 1879 made it obvious that Parnell would ask and in all probability obtain a popular mandate for his policy at the next election.[2] Meanwhile he continued to increase his personal authority outside what was left of the formal organisation through his contacts with the land and fenian movements. The election of Shaw was no more than another spasm in the anti-Parnellite reflexes of the home rule members; the party had been moribund since the end of 1877 and remained so.

In practice, then, the home rule party of Butt canalised the feelings of the Irish people for at most four years, from the beginning of 1874 to the end of 1877. In 1874 Butt was the unquestioned leader of the Irish people; in 1878 he was an anachronistic survival, a barrier to the development of the

---

[1] T. M. Healy, *Letters and leaders of my day*, p. 68.

[2] Parnellite candidates contested all these elections. In New Ross George Delaney with 90 votes was beaten by the conservative Colonel Tottenham with 95; in Longford Justin McCarthy and in Ennis Lysaght Finigan were elected on an obstructionist platform.

national movement, increasingly regarded as a renegade by the men who had cheered and chaired him to the representation of Ireland four years before. This was a collapse of startling swiftness. In the preceding pages some effort has been made to describe the processes by which it was brought about. It remains only to draw these threads together and to arrive at some conclusions.

In the first place, the popularity of Butt, though genuine and unquestionable, was never as firm a basis to political authority as in the case of other Irish demagogues. He gained the affection owed to a charming and humane personality; he never, perhaps, personified the racial myth as instinctively as the other olegraphed heroes of Irish history. Part of this was due to inherent weaknesses in the man himself. He lacked both the ruthlessness and the glamour, the deliberate showmanship, of the great demagogue; above all, he lacked the supreme self-confidence which enables the Parnells, the O'Connells (at least till 1843), and the de Valeras to ride tigers in the certain knowledge that they will be able to dismount at their own convenience. But partly this was his own choice, his own deliberate abdication of much of the authority which might have been his. In day to day politics he was a shrewd tactician; in his last struggle he showed he could be as unscrupulous as most political controversialists. But he was, perhaps, a man of greater intellectual breadth than most political leaders, and he possessed, consequently an ultimate vision and an ultimate sense of responsibility from which most of them are immune. Socially he was if anything less conservative than Parnell, but if, unlike Parnell, he was unable to exploit revolution, he did not choose to do so; he did not approve of revolution. Equally he could not harness the energy of separatism to his movement; but equally, unlike many of the leaders who followed him and of the supporters who attended him, he abhorred separatism. Home rule was not for him a tight-rope between English obstinacy and Irish nationalism, a compromise to be won by waving the green flag of separation in the face of John Bull; it was the best and the most honourable arrangement between the two islands. The ordinary people in the home rule movement were emotionally near to separatism; Parnell managed to persuade them that he was of their kind, their delegate, wanting what they wanted and determined to drive the best bargain on their behalf—which happened to be home rule. Butt, on the other hand, believed in the empire which Irishmen had helped to create; he believed that they could find a full national expression within its framework; emotionally he was moving towards an ideal of commonwealth which was politically in advance of his time. There was thus a fundamental dichotomy here. The people were puzzled by his imperialism in the early 70's; they forgave it as tactical; when they found he meant it they called him traitor.

But imperialism was only one basis upon which Butt built his federalism. The other was national unity. Butt learnt his nationalism in the 1840's. He learnt it from the practical lesson of the famine that the heart of empire beat too remotely from Irish misery; he learnt it, also, not from O'Connell but from the emotional, literary, and idealistic spirit of the men who followed Thomas Davis. Not for nothing did Thomas McNevin call the protestant nationalist movement which Butt typified in this period 'Orange Young Ireland'. Butt did not formally articulate his nationalism until twenty years later, but his values had been crystallised in that period, and when he founded the Home Government association he was seeking to put into practice the kindly ideal of Davis.

> What matter that at different shrines
> We pray unto one God—
> What matter that at different times
> Your fathers won this sod—
> In fortune and in name we're bound
> By stronger links than steel;
> And neither can be safe nor sound
> But in the other's weal.
>
> And oh! it were a gallant deed
> To show before mankind,
> How every race and every creed
> Might be by love combined—

ISAAC BUTT AND HOME RULE

> Might be combined, yet not forget
> The foundations whence they rose,
> As, filled by many a rivulet,
> The stately Shannon flows.

His movement, it must be remembered, was launched in the false dawn of protestant nationalism which followed on the disestablishment of the Irish protestant church. To reconcile the protestants, and to achieve his ideal of a ' united nationalist party', Butt went to the length of adopting a special formula, upon which he built his movement. The members of the home rule organisation and of the home rule party, he declared, were bound together only by their loyalty to that one principle of home rule; they were free to agree or disagree upon every other subject of political controversy.

In practice this formula was never a success. Home rule candidates, including Butt himself, found it necessary to endorse a wide variety of Irish grievances on the hustings; home rule members in parliament, led by Butt, joined in pressing for their reform. Irish conservatives were unable to see the distinction between the efforts of virtually all the members of the party acting together, and the acts of the party as such. By 1873 the battle for conservative support had been lost. Only one protestant conservative home ruler, E. R. King Harman, was ever returned for an Irish constituency, and Sir Michael Hicks Beach was able to describe him to Disraeli in 1878 as ' a "Conservative Home Ruler ", but really a staunch supporter of the government.'[3]

The home rule formula broke down before the necessity to endorse popular Irish grievances; it operated, however, sufficiently strongly to prevent the party from securing the fruits of that endorsement. In the first place, the Irish members were often accused of regarding their common membership of the party as imposing upon them only the obligation to vote for an annual home rule motion. But it was in fact inherent in Butt's formula that he could demand no more of them than this. It was not merely that he was unable to exact

---

[3] Beach to Disraeli, 2 Feb. 1878, Disraeli MSS. There is a copy of this letter in St. Aldwyn MSS, PCC 13.

pledged discipline from them; he did not choose to do so; together with men like John Martin, he regarded such discipline as intolerable to any man of principle. Inevitably, home rule members absented themselves from the divisions on his Irish bills, or even voted against them, and his policy of argument along the broad front of Irish grievance served only to illustrate the futility of, and the contradictions in, his own movement. In the second place, his fanatical devotion to an ideal of Irish national unity made it impossible for him to exploit an Irish sectarian issue, not only to the extent that Parnell was able to do so, but even so far as to mollify class interests in Ireland. Butt never secured the approval of the catholic clergy, despite his endless efforts to resolve the university question; the land conference of 1875 and the recriminations which followed in the parliamentary session of that year shewed that he had equally failed to win the loyalty of the tenant-farmers.

Yet despite these inherent contradictions, the shattering debacle which broke up the first party might not have followed if a little practical good fortune had attended Butt, and he might have died in an aura of modest success, mourned, if quickly replaced, by an affectionate people, who had never learnt the difference between their ambitions and his. But a number of practical factors destroyed the hopes of the new party even before it entered Westminster.

All these factors arose out of the general election of 1874. In the first place, this election was fought upon a franchise far more restricted than that which returned the '86 of '86'. The introduction of the ballot produced the first signs of an alteration in the class composition of the Irish representation; it was an alteration which, significantly, expressed itself most clearly in the case of the twenty-four newly elected home rule members, who included among their number men who were to prove themselves some of the most loyal and energetic of the Irish representatives. But the alteration was as yet only slight, and without a redistribution of seats and an assimilation of the franchise to that of England, it could scarcely affect the contest.

This factor was coupled with an even more fatal circumstance. The home rule movement was not established on anything like a national basis until the formation of the Home Rule League by the national conference of November 1873. The league held its first meeting in January 1874. Less than a fortnight later it was called upon to fight a general election in as little time. Inevitably it found itself totally unprepared, and above all, virtually without candidates. The effect of the sudden dissolution was, in the circumstances, disastrous. Home rule was able to destroy liberal unionism as a political force in Ireland, but the liberal members of parliament as a *quid pro quo* were able to swamp the first home rule party. When the election was over Butt could claim, technically, as many as sixty seats for home rule: but when he led his party into Westminster he found himself able to depend upon roughly one third of this number; one third were unknown quantities, and the remainder former liberals, the sincerity of whose conversion to home rule was in most cases dubious, and the majority of whom regarded their membership of the 'party' as binding them only to an annual vote upon the issue of home rule. Confronting this handful Butt found, enthroned with an overall majority, not the pliant and rational Gladstone, but the (in Irish matters) immovable Disraeli. The sterility of the party was from that moment assured.

In these circumstances there was perhaps only one course which offered a hope of ultimate success. This was to abandon the liberal deadwood of the party, and with it any hope of progress in the lifetime of the current parliament, and to concentrate upon the return of a larger, more resolute, and more disciplined force at the next election. This was the advice which sincere but realistic admirers of Butt such as John Ferguson consistently pressed upon him. He was not willing to take it. He chose instead to do the best he could with the force at his disposal, but as a part-time politician, and in his later years an ailing and prematurely aging man, he had neither the energy nor the authority to achieve anything. He was not even able to check the cynical absenteeism of a large number of his followers, and, refusing to denounce them, was tainted in Irish eyes with their insincerity. His reluctance to abandon the moderates was the logical outcome of his character and morally unexceptionable; his failure to realise that he was compelled in practice to choose between them and the advanced nationalists was a political blunder. He lost ultimately not because he failed to convince the English parliament of the justice of his cause, but because he failed to convince the Irish people of the sincerity of his party's advocacy of it. And it was on this issue, basically, that he differed from Parnell, and that Parnell won the leadership from him.

Parnell saw that the movement was losing its following in Ireland, and unlike Butt he was prepared to accept the necessity for a ruthless realignment. Obstruction was never a practical parliamentary policy; in its way it was just as futile as the patient reasoning of Butt. Butt was quite right when he said in 1873:

> If eighty men by such means could carry home rule, eighty men could carry the permissive bill, or the inspection of nunneries, or any other measure which they would conspire to force upon parliament.

Having made his demonstration in 1877, Parnell did not revive serious obstruction until the following parliament, which, once it accepted the unpleasant necessity to do so, was able relatively quickly to introduce rules to make such tactics impossible. But it is extremely unlikely that Parnell ever seriously intended to propose the adoption of obstruction as the normal policy of the home rule party: what he hoped to achieve was something quite different. By his obstructive tactics he dissociated himself from a lost cause, lifted himself above the ranks of his colleagues, and won the attention of the advanced party. Obstruction might achieve nothing practical, but the fact that the Parnellites were prepared to stay up all night infuriating the English won for them in Ireland a popular sympathy and a popular belief in their sincerity which their colleagues had, in many cases deservedly, lost. It was thus the first of the processes which led to Parnell's becoming the undisputed leader of the Irish Nation, and as such it had quite achieved its end by the time that the changes in the rules

N

of the house made it impossible. In modern political parlance it was a stunt, and as such it served its purpose.

Butt retained enough of his authority to prohibit the movement from adopting Parnell's tactics. By so doing he ensured Parnell's ultimate succession to the leadership on the terms most favourable to himself. The party did not expel Parnell, but it disowned him, and destroyed itself. From the end of 1877 there was in effect no home rule party, and virtually no home rule league. Parnell went to the country and through the land league and the new departure multiplied the authority which his parliamentary tactics had won for him. In 1880 he came back to the party and revived it by the injection of his own prestige. There is a real continuity between his movement and Butt's, but it was a continuity which expressed itself far more genuinely through the development of Irish public opinion than through the technical continuity of the chairmanship of the Party. Given authority, Parnell learnt from the lesson of Butt's failure. He did what Butt was both unable and unwilling to do—he went down into the constituencies and shewed the Irish members that they held their seats at his will, and he exacted from them in return a pledge of total obedience. Upon these twin pillars of his personal authority rested the home rule party of Parnell.

Yet if Parnell avoided the mistakes which destroyed Butt, his success nevertheless owed much to the work of the older man. The breakdown of Butt's policy has been described and analysed above; it remains to give him credit for his achievements. In 1868 Gladstone's offer of ' justice for Ireland ' had brought her people nearer, perhaps, than ever before in their history to a final acceptance of the union settlement. Above all the offer of disestablishment had won over to the support of the English Liberal party almost unanimously the catholic church in Ireland, which welcomed Gladstone as the heaven-sent deliverer of the Irish people. The clergy and the Irish liberals were able in the 1868 election to exact from the Irish representatives an unprecedented degree of uniformity with the English Liberal party, and Gladstone took office with a complete mandate from Ireland. In five years of superb political tactics Butt replaced liberal unionism by home rule as

the spokesman of Irish grievances. He canalised the emotional
nationalism of the people in the Amnesty Association, and at
the same time taught fenianism its political power; he manoeuvred the Irish liberals behind the principle of fixity of
tenure and in so doing contributed largely to the rejection of
the land bill. He was aided in this achievement by external
political developments, just as he was opposed by them in
the years that followed; but the insight and the timing of his
land, amnesty, and home rule agitations were the expression
of real political genius. In these years his was the one personality behind which all those parties were content to coalesce;
no one else could have done what he did. 'You will not accuse
me of self-conceit', he wrote to Henry in December 1873, 'if
I say that much of our present success depends on . . . combinations which I planned and carried out *alone*, and of which
in the beginning no one saw the meaning'.[4] It was no more
than the truth. It was in those years that Butt had erected his
memorial; he had summoned forth from defeat the instinctive
nationalism of the Irish people, and permanently established
the ideal of an Irish national party. Having done that, as
Healy so tersely observed, he failed. But he had moulded the
form in which Irish nationalism was to find parliamentary
expression for the next forty years, and he had ensured that
no Irish party could ever again accept anything less than
federal home rule as the ultimate solution to the Irish question. When Parnell broke away from Butt three years later
he could do so as the alternative leader of an Irish party; his
policy could be put forward as the alternative policy of an
Irish party. This was Butt's achievement, that he awoke the
constitutional nationalist spirit that was to judge him, that he
laid down aims for Irish parliamentary agitation, for the non-
fulfilment of which Parnell could accuse him before the bar
of this nationalist spirit, and finally, that he evolved the parliamentary slogan under which Parnell could regroup the
national movement in a more realistic, more disciplined, and
more effective manner. It is not then, perhaps, too much to
say that by his achievement Butt had made possible the political phenomenon of the party of Parnell.

4 Butt to Henry, 3 Dec. 1873, Butt MSS.

BIBLIOGRAPHY

A: PRIMARY SOURCES

1. Collections of private papers (manuscript)   *page* 391

2. Published collections of private papers   393

3. Newspapers and contemporary periodicals   393

4. Contemporary publications   394

5. Memoirs and histories written by contemporaries   395

6. Works of reference   396

7. Parliamentary publications   396

B: SECONDARY SOURCES

1. General histories   397

2. Biographies   397

3. Special subjects   398

A: PRIMARY SOURCES

1. Collections of private papers (manuscript)

The majority of the collections which I have used are to be found in the National Library of Ireland, in the British Museum, or in private hands. In the case of the first of these a certain confusion may arise, since the manuscript section of the library is undergoing a long-term reorganisation, in the course of which MSS numbers are sometimes changed. The most important instance in which this arises relates to the Butt papers. This collection falls into three parts:

MSS 830-2. Three bound volumes of letters from Butt to various colleagues and between the latter. Footnote references to these letters give date, volume, and MS number: e.g., Daunt to Henry 8 Oct. 1877, Butt MSS, vol iii, MS 832.

MS 10415. A small quantity of letters, purchased at the beginning of 1959. Cited as Butt Add. MSS 10415.

MSS 8686-8713. These letters, which comprise the largest and most important part of the collection, were sorted and arranged in chronological order by myself. Subsequent to my use of them they were given the MSS numbers 8686-8713, but the chronological arrangement has been preserved and letters cited in this essay can easily be traced by their date. *All references in this essay which give neither volume nor MS number are to this part of the Butt collection.*

A somewhat similar difficulty arises in relation to the Disraeli MSS which are actually in process of being recatalogued, but as all the letters which I have used are from either the Major or General Correspondence, both of which are arranged alphabetically, they can, in practice, be easily traced.

BRAND, H. B. W., Speaker of the House of Commons, letters and diaries. Property of Viscount Hampden; in the keeping of the Clerk of the House of Commons.

BRIGHT, John, letters. British Museum, Additional Manuscripts, 43385 (letters to W. E. Gladstone).

BUTT, Isaac, letters, etc. (see note above). National Library of Ireland.

DAUNT, W. J. O'Neill, journal 1868-79 (MS 3041), and letters (MSS 8045-8). National Library of Ireland.

DISRAELI, Benjamin, letters etc. Property of the National Trust, Hughenden Manor, High Wycombe, Buckinghamshire.

GLADSTONE, W. E., letters etc. British Museum, Additional Manuscripts 44086-44835.

HICKEY, collection of miscellaneous papers, MSS 10497-10533. National Library of Ireland.

IDDESLEIGH MSS. Letters, etc., of Sir Stafford Northcote. British Museum, Additional Manuscripts 50013-64, 50209-10.

LALOR, Richard, letters. National Library of Ireland, MSS 8564-7.

MCCARTHY, Justin, diary 1874-8. National Library of Ireland, MSS 3690-8.

MONSELL, William, Baron Emly, letters. National Library of Ireland, MSS 8317-9, 8629.

MOORE, G. H., letters, National Library of Ireland (of which I have used (a) vol. vii, MS 895, and (b) some loose letters, etc., MSS 899 and 8597).

O'BRIEN, J. F. X., letters. National Library of Ireland.

O'LOGHLEN, Sir Colman, letters, National Library of Ireland.

PARNELL, Charles S., a few miscellaneous letters. National Library of Ireland, MS 5934.

SMYTH, P. J., letters. National Library of Ireland, MSS 8215-6.

ST ALDWYN MSS. Letters etc. of Sir Michael Hicks Beach. Property of Earl St. Aldwyn, Williamstrip Park, Coln St. Aldwyns, Gloucestershire.

STRACHIE MSS. Include letters, etc., of C. S. Fortescue (Lord Carlingford). These are classified separately as 'Carlingford Political'. Property of Lord Strachie, Sutton Court, Somerset.

SULLIVAN, T. D., letters. National Library of Ireland, MS 8237.

DE VERE, Aubrey, letters. National Library of Ireland, MSS 13101-13139.

WOODLOCK, William, diary. National Library of Ireland, MSS 4498-5011.

2. *Published collections of private papers*

O'BRIEN, WILLIAM, and RYAN, DESMOND (ed.), *Devoy's Post Bag*, Dublin, 1948 (vol. i).

3. *Newspapers and contemporary periodicals*

Ballinrobe Chronicle.
Belfast Newsletter.
Banner of Ulster.
Clare Journal.
Daily Express.
Dublin Evening Mail.

N*

Dublin Evening Post.
Dublin University Magazine.
Derry Standard.
Freeman's Journal.
Galway Vindicator.
Irishman.
Irish Times.
Limerick Reporter.
Mayo Constitution.
Nation.
Northern Whig.
Roscommon Journal.
Saunders Newsletter.
Tipperary Advocate.

4. Contemporary publications

Butt, Isaac, *The poor law bill for Ireland examined,* London, London, 1837.
Butt, Isaac, *Rents, profits, and labour,* Dublin 1838.
„   „   *The Irish corporation bill,* London, 1840.
„   „   *Irish municipal reform,* Dublin, 1840.
„   „   *Repeal of the union,* Dublin, 1843.
„   „   *Protection to home industry,* Dublin, 1846.
„   „   *A voice for Ireland, the famine in the land,* Dublin, 1847.
Butt, Isaac, *National Education in Ireland,* Dublin, 1854.
„   „   *The transfer of land by means of judicial assurance,* Dublin, 1857.
Butt, Isaac, *The liberty of teaching vindicated,* Dublin, 1865.
„   „   *Fixity of Tenure: heads of a suggested legislative enactment,* Dublin, 1866.
Butt, Isaac, *Land tenure in Ireland: a plea for the Celtic race,* Dublin, 1866.
Butt, Isaac, *The Irish people and the Irish land: a letter to Lord Lifford,* Dublin, 1867.
Butt, Isaac, *The Irish querist: Ireland's social condition,* Dublin, 1867.

Butt, Isaac, *Ireland's appeal for amnesty*: *a letter to W. E. Gladstone*, Glasgow, 1870.
Butt, Isaac, *Speech . . . university education bill*, Dublin, 1873.
Butt, Isaac, *Irish federalism*, 4th ed., Dublin 1875.
Butt, Isaac, *The Parliamentary policy of home rule . . . address to the electors of Limerick*, Dublin, 1875.
Butt, Isaac, *The problem of Irish education*, Longman's 1875.
Dawson, C., The Irish franchise, in *Fortnightly Review*, 1880.
Grattan, R., *Isaac Butter*, Dublin 1876.
Irish Home Rule League: *Proceedings of the Home Rule Conference*, Dublin 1874.
Irish Home Rule League: *Resolutions of the national Conference*, Dublin 1873.
MacCarthy, J. G., *A plea for the home government of Ireland*, 2nd ed. Dublin 1872.

5. Memoirs and histories written by contemporaries

Collins, J., *Life in old Dublin*, Dublin, 1913.
Daly, J., Recollections, in *Irish Freedom*, 1912-13.
Daunt, W. J. O'N., *Eighty-five years of Irish history*, London, 1886.
Davitt, M., *The fall of feudalism in Ireland*, London, 1904.
Denvir, J., *The life story of an old rebel*, Dublin, 1914.
Devoy, J., *Recollections of an Irish rebel*, 1929.
Duffy, Sir C. G., *My life in two hemispheres*, London, 1898.
Gregory, Sir W., *Autobiography*, London, 1894.
Healy, T. M., *Letters and leaders of my day*, London, 1928.
H.R.N. (Capt. J. Dunne), *Here and there memories*, London, 1896.
Kettle, A. J., *Material for victory*, Dublin, 1958.
Lefanu, W. R., *Seventy years of Irish life*, 2nd ed., London, 1893.
Lucy, Sir H., *A diary of two parliaments*, vol. i, 2nd ed., London, 1885.
MacNeill, J. G. S., Isaac Butt, the father of home rule, in *Fortnightly Review*, September 1913.

MacNeill, J. G. S., *What I have seen and heard,* Bristol, 1925.
Morley, Rev. T., *Reminiscences,* 1882.
O'Brien, W., *Recollections,* London 1905. (Also Personal Reminiscences of Isaac Butt, in Butt MSS, vol. i, MS 830.)
O'Connor, T. P., *Memoirs of an old Parliamentarian,* London, 1925.
O'Donnell, F. H., *History of the Irish parliamentary party,* London, 1910.
O'Leary, J., *Recollections of fenians and fenianism,* London, 1896.
Pigott, R., *Recollections of an Irish journalist,* Dublin, 1882.
Sullivan, A. M., *New Ireland,* 14th ed., Glasgow, 1882.
Sullivan, T. D., *Recollections of troubled times in Irish politics,* Dublin, 1905.

6. Works of reference

Annual Register.
Boase, *Modern English Biography.*
Catholic Directory.
Complete Peerage (G.E.C.), 2nd ed., revised Vicary Gibbs and others, 1910-53.
Debrett's House of Commons Annual.
Dod's Parliamentary Companion.
Dictionary of National Biography.
Thom's Directory.
Vacher's Parliamentary Companion, 1876.

7. Parliamentary publications

Hansard's parliamentary debates, 3rd series, vols. cxci-ccxlvi.
Return of . . . parliamentary and municipal electors . . . and county constituencies, H.C. 1872 (17), xlvii, p. 395.
Return of the number of days and hours on which the house sat, H.C. 1877 (o. 149), lxviii, 197.
Standing orders of the house of commons, H.C. 1880 (405-Sess. 2), lvi, 103.

Standing orders of the house of commons (as amended), H.C.
1882 (429), lii, 243.

B: SECONDARY SOURCES

1. General histories

Barker E., *Ireland in the last fifty years*, Oxford, 1919.
Ensor, R. C. K., *England, 1870-1914*, Oxford, 1936.
Locker-Lampson, G., *State of Ireland in the 19th century*,
London, 1907.
Mansergh, N., *Ireland in the age of reform and revolution*,
London, 1940.
O'Connor, Sir J., *History of Ireland, 1798-1924*, London,
1934.
O'Hegarty, P. S., *Ireland under the union*, London, 1952.

2. Biographies

Ewald, A. C., *Life and letters of Sir Joseph Napier*, London,
1892.
Ferguson, Lady, *Sir Samuel Ferguson in the Ireland of his
day*, London, 1896.
Lefanu, T. P., *Memoir of the Lefanu family*, privately
printed, 1924.
MacDonagh, F., Isaac Butt's centenary, his literary and jour-
nalistic work, in *Irish Book Lover*, vol. v, Sept. 1913, and
Bibliography of Butt, same journal, Nov. 1913.
MacDonagh, J. C., *Lecture delivered at Stranorlar, 14 Dec.
1945, on Isaac Butt*, Dublin, 1946.
Moore, M., *An Irish gentleman*, London, 1913.
Morley, J., *Life of Gladstone*, 1903.
O'Brien, R. B., *Life of C. S. Parnell*, 3rd ed., London 1899.
Quin, J. F., The Moores of Moore Hall, in *Western People;*
cuttings in MS PC 320, Nat. Library, Ireland.
White, T. de V., *The road of excess*, Dublin, 1946.
Eversley, Lord, *Gladstone and Ireland, 1850-94*, London,
1912.

3. *Special Subjects*

Hammond, J. L., *Gladstone and the Irish nation*, London, 1938.

Lyons, F. S. L., *The Irish Parliamentary Party*, 1890-1910, London, 1951.

Lyons, F. S. L., *The fall of Parnell*, London, 1960.

McCaffrey, L. J., Home rule and the general election of 1874, in *Irish Historical Studies*, vol. ix, no. 34, Sept. 1954.

MacDonagh, M., *The home rule movement*, Dublin, 1920.

May, T. Erskine, *Constitutional history of England since the accession of George III*, 1912 (vol. iii by Francis Holland).

May, T. Erskine, *A treatise of the law, privileges, proceedings and usage of parliament*, 10th ed., 1893.

Moody, T. W., The Irish university question of the 19th century, in *History*, vol. xliii, no. 148, June 1958.

Moody, T. W., The new departure in Irish politics, 1878-9, in *Essays in British and Irish history in honour of J. E. Todd*, 1949.

O'Brien, C. C., *Parnell and his party, 1880-90*, Oxford, 1957.

Sadleir, M., The Dublin University Magazine, its history, contents, and bibliography, in *Publications of the Bibliographical Society of Ireland*, vol. v, no. 4.

Strauss, E., *Irish nationalism and British democracy*, London, 1931.

Thornley, D. A., The Irish conservatives and home rule, 1869-73, in *Irish Historical Studies*, vol. xi, no. 43, March 1959.

Thornley, D. A., The Irish home rule party and parliamentary obstruction, 1874-87, in *Irish Historical Studies*, vol. xii, no. 45, March 1960.

Whyte, J. H., *The independent Irish party, 1850-9*, London, 1958.

INDEX

Amnesty:
  issue, 53–6, 176, 197, 262, 273
  Committee, 53, 65–66
  Association, 53, 66–68, 73–74, 83–84,
    88, 90, 266–67
Anderson, Fr. O.S.A., 60
Anderson, Samuel Lee, 86
Armstrong, Richard, M.P., 43
Aspinall, John Bridge, 49

Bagwell, John, M.P., 179
Ball, John Thomas, M.P., 231
ballot, secret, 133
Banner of Ulster, 33, 35
Barrington, Sir John, 93, 125–26
Barry, Charles Robert, M.P., 58–61,
  72, 122
Barry, John, 141, 157, 161, 203, 292
Beach, Sir Michael Hicks, M.P.:
  and obstruction, 1875, 257
  and Butt's land bill, 1875, 260
  and educational reform, 278
  on home rule, 282–83
  on lack of Irish legislation, 1876, 304
  and Intermediate Education Act,
    1878, 351–59
  correspondence with Butt, 354–59,
    366–69
Begg, Thomas, 106
Belfast News-Letter, 35
Bellew, Lord, 116
Biggar, Joseph Gillis, M.P.:
  and Londonderry City by-election,
    1872, 133–35
  and founding of Home Rule League,
    165–66
  in 1874 election, 187, 196
  obstruction, 1874, 235–38; 1875,
    255-59, 270; 1877, 300–29 *pass*;
    1878, 349–50
  abstains on imperial title division,
    278–79

and I.R.B., 290
  elected a vice-president of Home
    Rule Confederation, 1876, 294
  and struggle in Home Rule League,
    1877–8, 330, 370; 1879, 376
  votes for Henry as party leader, 1879,
    379
  also 242, 260, 347
Blackall, Jonas, 192–93
Blake, John Aloysius, M.P., 52, 221–26
Blake, Valentine O'Conor, 42
Blennerhassett, Sir Rowland, M.P., 46,
  50, 55, 155
Blennerhassett, Rowland Ponsonby,
  M.P.:
  and Kerry by-election, 1872,
    127–30, 160, 187
  in 1874 election, 190, 196, 237
  and obstruction, 270
  also, 247, 252, 272, 279, 296, 328
Blundun, John, 128, 247, 342
Bolster, William, 31, 55, 70, 75, 249
Bourke, Father, P.P. Murher and
  Knockanure, 129
Bouverie, E. P., M.P., 153
Bowyer, Sir George, M.P., 47, 52, 178,
  187, 196, 212, 216–17, 247, 279,
  328, 361, 377
Boyle, Hon. Robert, 32, 42
Bradlaugh, Charles, 333
Brady, John, M.P., 160, 196, 198, 237,
  279
Brand, H. B. W., M.P.:
  on university bill, 1873, 152–53, 234
  on Irish tactics, 1876, 274
  on obstruction, 1877, 309–15; 1878,
    359–60
Briggs, W. E., M.P., 278
Bright, Jacob, M.P., 273, 284
Bright, John, M.P., 43, 69, 73, 273
Brooks, Maurice, M.P., 179, 200, 234,
  279, 296, 369, 371, 376

Browne, George Ekins, 94, 97, 109, 160, 183–84, 196, 213, 217, 246–47,249, 296, 328, 376

Bruen, Henry, M.P., 260

Bryan, George Leopold, M.P., 55, 75, 116, 160, 187–88, 196, 221, 247, 284, 372, 374

Burke, Viscount, M.P., 31

Burt, T., M.P., 234, 260, 284

Butler, Dr George, bishop of Limerick, 37, 122, 146, 149, 159–60, 193

Butt, Isaac, M.P.:
early career, 15–19
returns to Ireland, 20
and land question, 31, 69–82 pass., 229, 248–50, 272–75, 280, 287
and amnesty agitation, 53–54, 67–68, 73–74, 77–78
political ideas of, 20–21, 98–103, 138–39, 167–68, 269, 279
and founding of Home Government Association, 83–97 pass., 108–10
and fenians, 88–91, 122, 132, 137, 160–62, 188–89, 192–94, 203, 243–44
financial difficulties of, 20, 107–8, 219–26
and Monaghan by-election, 1871, 119–20
re-enters parliament, 1871, 121–23
defends clergy in Galway petition prosecutions, 131
threatens to resign home rule leadership, 142, 222–24, 347–48
plans for 1874 general election, 145, 173–75
and education question, 152, 182, 273, 349–59
and catholic clergy, 155, 355
and founding of Home Rule League, 158–75 pass.
on obstruction, 1873, 167
in 1874 election, 184, 188–89, 192–94, 196, 203
recruits Lord Robert Montagu, 201
calls first party conference, 1874, 212–14
moves amendment to address, 1874, 215
sits below gangway in House of Commons, 216
and election of Liberal leader, 1875, 216–18
and English radicals, 228, 234, 273, 279–80, 297, 354
moves first home rule motion, 1874, 231–34
and obstruction 1874, 234–38
hopes for general election, 239–40
and national roll, 241–42
and Mayo by-election, 1874, 247
periodic absences from House of Commons, 253, 262, 265, 346–47
in 1875 session, 253–61
and obstruction, 1875, 255–59
testimonial fund, 263–65
and O'Connell centenary, 1875, 265–69
in 1876 session, 272–85
defends tactics in recess, 1876–77, 288, 207–98
proposes local government boards scheme, 1877, 316
and Home Rule Confederation, 291–95, 369
and obstruction, 1877, 300–29 pass.
controversy with Parnell in Home Rule League, 1877–78, 330–45 pass., 371–72
replaced by Parnell as president of Home Rule Confederation, 331
declining health of, 334, 346–47, 368–69
attempts to bargain with Conservative ministry on education issue, 1878, 354–59, 361–64, 366–69, 375–76
and Eastern question, 361–63
last manifesto, 371
refuses to call party conference, November 1878, 372–73

Butt, Isaac, M.P. (*continued*)
and Afghan war, 1878, 373–75
attends Home Rule League for last
  time, 375–76
death of, 378
assessment of career, 379–87
also, 252, 296, 316, 322
Butt, Robert, 121, 192–93, 371

Cahill, Michael, 165
Cahill, P., 364, 371
Cairns, Earl of, 357
Callan, Philip, M.P.:
and land agitation, 75
and Home Government Association,
  94
and founding of Home Rule League,
  159–60
in 1874 election, 180–81, 196
elected to home rule party committee, 213, 296
and Liberal party, 217
and Butt's financial difficulties, 221
and first home rule motion, 234
obstruction, 1874, 237; 1875, 257;
  1877, 328–29
and O'Connell centenary, 1875, 268
and amnesty, 278
abstains on imperial title, 279
in struggle with Parnell in Home
  Rule League, 1877–78, 330, 332–
  35, 371; 1879, 376
seeks place, 1878, 366
Cantwell, James, 106
Carraher, O. J., 330
Catholic Union, 188, 198, 201
Cavendish Club, 216, 218
Clanricarde, Marquess of, 76
Clare Advertiser, 287
Clergy, catholic, influence of:
in early 19th century, 13
in 1868 election, 37–61
and Home Government Association,
  84–85, 96, 109, 111–23, 117–19,
  122, 127–37 pass., 139, 144–46,
  154–55

and university bill, 1873, 149–54
and Home Rule Conference, 159–60
in 1874 election, 178–204 pass.
and home rule party, 263–64, 277–
  78, 355
and Intermediate Education Act,
  1878, 351–55
also 242–44
Cogan, Rt. Hon. William Henry Ford,
  M.P., 179, 185
Collins, Eugene, M.P., 200, 237, 249,
  279, 328
Collins, James, 366
Commins, Dr A., 292, 294
Conaty, Dr Nicholas, bishop of
  Kilmore, 39, 64, 112, 159–60
Connaught Telegraph, 322
Conolly, Thomas, M.P., 34
Conroy, Dr George, bishop of Ardagh,
  159–60, 278, 353–54, 377
Conservatives:
and 1868 election, 26, 32–36
and Home Government Association,
  85–87, 92–95, 103, 109–11, 117,
  121–26, 139
and first Home Rule Conference, 170
and home rule party, 177
Conyngham, Lord Francis, 183, 196,
  212, 214, 252, 263, 279, 349, 369
Corbally, Matthew Elias, M.P., 113
Cork Constitution, 123
Cork Examiner, 59, 170, 322, 363, 374
Corrigan, Sir Dominick, 54, 110–11
Cowen, Joseph, M.P., 234, 253, 284
Crichton, Viscount, M.P., 30
Cullen, Paul, Cardinal archbishop of
  Dublin:
'charter' of, 14
and 1868 election, 28, 46, 50
and amnesty agitation, 54, 66
and Disestablishment Act, 63
and land bill, 1870, 80, 82, 84
and Home Government Association,
  128, 134, 145
and university bill, 1873, 146–47,
  150–52

Cullen, Paul (*continued*)
 and 1874 election, 180, 191
 and home rule party, 263, 278
 and O'Connell centenary, 1875, 266
 on education, 278, 351–52
 and Intermediate Education Act,
  1878, 353–54
 and University Act, 1879, 377

Daily Express, 86, 95, 108, 170
Daily News, 114, 142, 305
Daly, John, Mayor of Cork, 136, 177
Daly, John:
 and Tenant League, 71
 and Home Government Association,
  88–90, 122
 on founding of Home Rule League,
  161–62, 272
 in 1874 election, 188–89
 issues warning to Butt, 1874, 243–44
 and O'Connell centenary, 1875,
  266–69
 breaks with home rule, 277, 290
D'Arcy, Hyacinth, 117, 187
D'Arcy, Matthew Peter, M.P., 44, 75,
  160
Daunt, W. J. O'Neill:
 and 1868 election, 52, 64
 and founding of Home Government
  Association, 83, 88, 92, 103–4
 and catholic clergy, 112–13, 139,
  145, 155
 addresses Dublin Corporation, 1871,
  121
 and Mallow by-election, 1872, 132
 becomes secretary of Home Government Association, 144–45
 resigns secretaryship, 172
 on university bill, 1873, 152
 and founding of Home Rule League,
  159
 on Tipperary by-election, 1875, 254
 on O'Connell centenary, 1875, 260
 on obstruction, 289–90, 371
 and struggle in Home Rule League,
  1877–78, 337–38

 and Home Rule Confederation, 369
 and Butt's Afghan letter, 1878, 374
 also, 242
Davis, Thomas, 381–82
Davitt, Michael, 278
Dease, Edmund Gerald, M.P., 116,
  150, 152, 160, 196, 199–200, 244,
  274, 279, 327, 374
Dease, J. A., 76, 117–19, 127, 147, 200
Dease, Matthew O'Reilly, M.P., 39, 41
  179–81
Delahunty, James, M.P., 160, 328, 376
Delany, George, 187, 264, 338, 379
Delany, Dr William, St Stanislaus
  College, Tullamore, 152
Delany, Dr William, bishop of Cork,
  37, 129
Denvir, John, 94, 291
Derry Standard, 33
Devereux, Richard Joseph, M.P., 126
Devoy, John, 90, 370, 372
Digby, Kenelm, M.P., 40–41, 115–16,
  160, 196, 199, 212, 244, 247, 296,
  374
Dilke, Sir Charles, M.P., 234, 305
Dillon, John, 254, 332, 343, 364, 371,
  375
Disestablishment, in 1868 election, 21–
  24, 27–30, 37–61 *pass.* 62–65
Disraeli, Benjamin, M.P., later Earl of
  Beaconsfield:
 and 1868 election, 37, 45, 56
 friendship with G. H. Moore, 89
 and obstruction, 1874, 235–38; 1875,
  256–58
 and Tipperary by-election, 1875, 253
 and amnesty issue, 278
 complains of pressure of business in
  commons, 1876, 285
 on education issue, 352
Donnelly, Dr James, bishop of Clogher,
  154, 159–60
Doran, Fr, P.P. Rathnure, 45
Doran, Charles G., 87, 161–64, 269,
  272, 290

Dorrian, Dr Patrick, bishop of Down and Connor, 159–60
Downing, McCarthy, M.P., 31–32, 42–43, 75, 143, 160, 164, 166, 196–99, 206, 213, 233, 242, 252, 256–57, 260, 279, 280, 296, 328, 329, 343, 347–48
Dowse, Richard, M.P., 33, 36, 72, 133
Dublin Evening Mail, 86, 108, 110, 117, 119–20, 123, 128, 135, 170
Dublin Evening Post, 47, 52, 59, 96, 149–50, 155, 169–70, 191
Duffy, Sir Charles Gavan, 14, 231, 268
Duggan, Dr Patrick, bishop of Clonfert, 131, 145, 155, 159–61, 264
Dunbar, John, M.P., 200, 237, 279, 328, 361
Dundalk Democrat, 59, 321, 363
Dunne, General Francis Plunkett, 177
Dunne, Captain John, 93, 105, 112, 264, 331
Dunne, Michael, 41
Dyke, Sir W. H., M.P., 253

Eastern Crisis, 1878, 360–63
Education issue:
in 1868 election, 32–36
Home Government Association and, 84–85
university bill, 1873, 142–43, 146–54
in 1874 election, 176, 182, 185
in 1876 session, 273, 277–78
in 1877 session, 316
Intermediate Education Act, 1878, 349–59, 375
University Act, 1879, 377
Egan, Patrick, 94, 322, 332, 342, 364
Ellard, John, 55, 191–93, 263
Ellis, Hon. Leopold Agar, M.P., 179
Ennis, John James, M.P., 183
Ennis, Nicholas, M.P., 190, 196, 211, 279, 376
Errington, George, M.P., 187–88, 200–201, 237, 272, 279, 328
Esmonde, Sir John, M.P., 186, 196, 197, 212, 280, 284

Fawcett, Henry, M.P., 142, 153, 305
Fay, Charles Joseph, M.P., 187, 200, 237, 249, 256–57, 279, 322, 366, 374, 376
Fenians:
in 1860's, 14–15
and amnesty agitation, 65–66, 68
and land agitation, 70–74
and Home Government Association, 87–92, 106, 122, 132–37
and Home Rule Confederation, 141
and first Home Rule Conference, 160–62, 272
and 1874 election, 188–89, 192–94, 203
and home rule party, 1874, 243–44
and Tipperary by-election, 1875, 252
and O'Connell centenary, 1875, 268–70
and home rule party, 1876, 277
and obstruction, 287, 290–91
Ferguson, John:
and Londonderry City by-election, 1872, 134–35
criticises Home Government Association, 1872, 141
and founding of Home Rule League, 163–66
and home rule party, 269
and obstruction, 1876, 287; 1877, 321
in Home Rule Confederation, 292–93
Ferguson, Sir Samuel, 18
Finigan, Lysaght, 363, 379
Fitzgerald, Rt. Hon. Lord Otho Augustus, M.P., 179, 185
Fitzgerald, Rev. R., C.C. Ennis, 182
Fitzpatrick, John Wilson, M.P., 40–41
Fitzwilliam, Hon. H. W. W., M.P., 179
Flag of Ireland, 59
Foley, J. W., 364
Forster, W. E., M.P., 217, 305, 314
Fortescue, C. S., M.P., later Baron Carlingford, 29, 39, 41, 59, 84, 147, 179–81, 322

Fottrell, George, 364
Franchise, State of Irish, 25–27, 38–39
Freeman's Journal:
  and 1868 election, 27, 29, 48–50, 52,
    59–61, 69, 70
  and land agitation, 70, 76, 80–81
  and Tipperary by-election, 1869,
    72–73
  and Home Government Association,
    110, 114, 117, 119–21, 128–30,
    132, 135–36
  and 1874 election, 185–90 *pass.*, 199
  defends Butt, 1876, 288
  and obstruction, 1877, 317, 319, 322,
    327
  and struggle in Home Rule League,
    1877–78, 336
  and Eastern question, 1878, 362–63,
    373–74
French, Charles, M.P., 160, 200, 212,
  244, 275, 280

Galligan, Rev. P., 39
Galway Vindicator, 33, 47–50, 322
Galbraith, Rev. Joseph A., F.T.C.D.:
  and founding of Home Government
    Association, 93, 97, 106, 109, 110
  and Monaghan by-election, 1871,
    119
  addresses Dublin Corporation, 121
  campaigns for Home Government
    Association, 128, 133
  in 1874 election, 182
  on obstruction, 276–77
  in struggle in Home Rule League,
    1877–78, 332, 334–35, 338
  resigns from secretaryship of league,
    342
  also 242, 366
Gavin, George, M.P., 55
Gill, H. J., 364
Gill, Peter, 186
Gillooly, Dr Laurence, bishop of
  Elphin, 183
Gladstone, W. E., M.P.:
  and fenian rising, 14

  and disestablishment, 21–24, 62–64
  and 1868 election, 38, 43, 48–49,
    56–61
  and amnesty agitation, 66, 68, 77–78
  and land agitation, 73, 79–81
  and Londonderry City by-election,
    1872, 135
  and university question, 142–43,
    146–54
  dissolves parliament, 1874, 175
  resigns Liberal leadership, 1875, 217
  and Irish amendment to address,
    1874, 227; 1878, 346
  and first home rule motion, 1874, 231
  and obstruction, 1857, 304; 1877,
    314
Goschen, G. J., M.P., 217
Granard, Earl of, 377
Grattan, Dr Richard, 106
Gray, Edmund Dwyer, M.P., 265, 313,
  328, 348–49, 370
Gray, Sir John, M.P.:
  and 1868 election, 27–28, 50, 53, 56
  and Liberal government, 62
  and land question, 70, 75–78, 81
  and Home Government Association,
    84, 89, 109, 155
  and founding of Home Rule League,
    160, 167
  in 1874 election, 196
  elected to committee of home rule
    party, 213
  and obstruction, 1874, 237
  death of, 254
  also, 205, 248, 252
Gregory, Sir William, 15
Greville, A. W. F., M.P., 179
Greville-Nugent, Fulke Southwell,
  M.P., later Baron Greville, 73
Greville-Nugent, George, M.P., 110
Greville-Nugent, Reginald, M.P., 73,
  110
Guinness, Sir Arthur, M.P., 109

Hally, Dr, P.P. Dungarvan, 60–61
Hamilton, Lord Claude John, 131

Hamilton, Lord George, 191
Hammond, C. F., M.P., 284
Harcourt, Sir William, M.P., 205
Harman, Edward R. King, 87, 93, 103,
    106, 110–11, 113, 166, 179, 183,
    216, 221, 316, 328, 355, 361, 372,
    374, 382
Harman, Laurence King, 93, 131
Harrington, Fr., C.C. Listowel, 129
Harris, Matthew, 161
Hartington, Marquess of, 142, 147,
    157, 217, 233, 253, 280, 310–11, 361
Healy, Timothy, 350, 363, 374, 378
Heinrick, Hugh, 143, 214, 245
Henderson, W. D., 249
Henry, Mitchell, M.P.:
    enters parliament, 1871, 117
    and Cork City by-election, 1872, 137
    on university bill, 1873, 150
    and founding of Home Rule League,
        157, 160, 162
    and education question, 182
    in 1874 election, 184, 187, 196
    elected to committee of home rule
        party, 212–14, 296
    and Butt's financial difficulties, 219–
        26, 263–64
    supports home rule motion, 1874,
        233
    and obstruction, 1874, 237; 1875,
        259; 1876, 298   .
    and land issue, 260, 274–75
    and Home Rule Confederation, 292–
        93, 295
    criticises Butt's local government
        board's resolution, 1877, 316
    and struggle in Home Rule League,
        1877–78, 330, 336, 342, 345
    proposes amendment to address,
        1878, 346
    opinion of Parnell and O'Donnell,
        347
    on state of home rule party, 1878,
        348, 372
    refuses to sign address to Butt, 1878,
        376

    criticises Butt in Home Rule League,
        1879, 376
    defeated for leadership of party,
        1879, 379
    also, 252-53, 273, 278, 322
Herbert, Rt. Hon. H. A., M.P., 179
Heron, Denis Caulfield, 72
Hodnett, Jeremiah, 88
Hoey, John Cashel, 203
Home Government Association:
    founding of, 83–97
    expands slowly, 108–9, 111, 119,
        138–47
    sends delegation to Dublin Corpor-
        ation, 120–21
    and by-elections, 1871–73, 121–22,
        132–38, 156
    weakness of, 1873, 143–44
    dissolved, 172
    also 196, 199
Home Rule Confederation:
    founding of, 141, 157, 291–92
    supports Mitchel in Tipperary by-
        election, 1875, 252
    and obstruction, 1875, 270; 1876,
        292, 294–95
    Dublin convention, 1876, 292–95
    elects Parnell to presidency, 331
    and Butt's Afghan policy, 374
    also 302–3, 321–22, 369–70
Home Rule Conference, 1873, 159–69,
    197
Home Rule League:
    founding of, 169–75
    and 1874 election, 176–77, 182, 195–
        202 pass., 240–42
    struggle for power in, 331–45
    decline of, 364–66, 370–71, 373, 375
home rule party:
    discipline in, 163–69, 212–19, 221
    personnel of, 1874, 195–204, 234
    class compositions of, 205–11
    religious composition of, 210
    annual pre-sessional conference,
        1874, 212–14; 1875, 252; 1876,
        272–73; 1877, 296; 1878, 346;

home rule party (*continued*)
  1879, 377
  meeting of, 1877, 327
  refusal of Butt to call party confer-
    ence, November 1878, 372–73
  Home rule programme, 97–103, 116,
    163–64
  criticised inside party, 197, 199, 234
  attacked by P. J. Smyth, 246
Hynes, P., 177

Irishman, 59–60, 65, 78, 164, 169, 182–
  87, 197, 228, 246, 322
Irish Times, 83, 86, 95, 108, 117–30
  pass., 169, 317

Johnston, William, M.P., 36
Jones, T. Mason, 40

Kavanagh, Arthur MacMurrough,
  M.P., 280
Keane, Dr William, bishop of Cloyne,
  37, 145, 157, 159–60
Keenan, P. J., 149–51, 180, 353
Kehoe, Rev. Dr., P.P., 185
Kelly, Rev. H., O.D.C., 331–32, 364
Kelly, James, 191
Kelly, Laurence, 55
Kenmare, Earl of, 128
Kennedy, Ignatius, 332
Kennedy, Tristram, M.P., 39
Kenny, Dr, 332, 364
Keogh, Rt. Hon. William, 131, 188
Keown, William, M.P., 36
Kerry Vindicator, 286, 290, 322
Kettle, Andrew J., 94, 248–50, 332
Kickham, Charles, 90, 186, 290
Kieran, Dr Michael, archbishop of
  Armagh, 29, 42, 47
Kilkenny Journal, 286
Kirk, George Harley, M.P., 212, 237,
  279, 282, 313, 328, 330, 350, 369,
  376
Kirk, William, M.P., 44
Kirwan, Capt., 292
Knox, Major Laurence, 83, 87, 93,

  95, 124
Lalor, Richard, 40–41, 75, 116, 249,
  330, 364, 371
Land question in Irish Politics, 13–14
  in 1868 election, 30–32, 34
  land bill, 1870, 69–82
  land conference, 1870, 75–76
  and Home Government Association,
    83–84
  in Galway Co. by-election, 1872,
    123–24
  in 1874 election, 176
  land conference, 1874, 247–50
  Butt's land bill, 1875, 259–61
  Butt's land bill, 1876, 272–75, 280,
    287
Lavelle, Fr., P.P. Partry, 55, 60, 67, 94,
  106–7, 113, 184, 330, 374
Law, Rt. Hon. Hugh, M.P., 280
Leahy, Dr John P., bishop of Dromore,
  29, 44
Leahy, Dr Patrick, archbishop of
  Cashel, 112, 139
Leinster, Duke of, 248
Leslie, Charles Powell, M.P., 119–20
Lewis, Charles Edward, M.P., 133–35,
  208, 272, 328, 376
Lewis, Henry Owen, M.P., 119–20,
  200–203, 279, 296, 361
Liberals, Irish:
  and 1868 election, 25–26, 28–61 *pass*.
  and Home Government Association,
    92–96, 109–37 *pass*., 155–56
  and university bill, 1873, 153–54
  and founding of Home Rule League,
    170
  and 1874 election, 178–204 *pass*.
  and O'Connell centenary, 1875,
    268–70
  also, 279
Liberal Party, English:
  and 1868 election, 21–24, 30, 32,
    46–47
  and education question, 142, 146–53
Limerick Farmers Club, 31, 192, 243,
  247

Limerick Reporter, 46, 59, 80, 96–97
Lismore, Viscount, 186
Little, Judge, 349
Longbottom, Pearson, 186
Lowther, James, M.P., 352, 354, 357–58

McAlister, J.P., 245, 293, 334–36, 365–66
MacCarthy, Denis Florence, 266
McCarthy, Fr., Ballyheigue, 129
MacCarthy, Florence, 266–67
McCarthy, Dr John, bishop of Cloyne, 252
McCarthy, John George, M.P., 94, 132–33, 152, 155, 196, 233, 242, 249, 256, 260, 344
McCarthy, Justin, M.P., 379
McClintock, Sir Leopold, 30
McClure, Sir Thomas, M.P., 179
McDonald, A., M.P., 260
McDonnell, Canon, P.P. Listowel, 129
McElroy, E., 249
McEvilly, Dr John, bishop of Galway, 48–50, 128
McEvoy, Edward, M.P., 52, 190
McGettigan, Dr Daniel, archbishop of Armagh, 159–60, 180–81
MacHale, Dr John, archbishop of Tuam, 42, 109, 112, 115, 150, 159–60, 184, 369
McKenna, Sir Joseph, M.P.:
 and 1868 election, 47, 52
 joins Home Government Association, 154
 and founding of Home Rule League, 164
 in 1874 election, 196
 and Butt's financial difficulties, 221, 225, 263
 obstruction, 1874, 237; 1875, 256
 abstains on imperial title division, 1876, 279
 elected to committee of home rule party, 1877, 296
 votes with Butt in Home Rule League, 1879, 376

also, 242, 254, 348
MacMahon, Patrick, M.P., 75
MacMahon, P., 177
McNevin, Thomas, 17, 381
MacRedmond, Very Rev. T. J., D.D., 182
McSheehy, John, 38
McSwiney, P.P.:
 and 1868 election, 31
 and land question, 75
 and Home Government Association, 105, 121
 in 1874 election, 190
 O'Connell centenary, 1875, 265–68
Madden, John, 119–20, 177
Magee, Dr P. P. Stradbally, 40, 274
Maguire, John Francis, M.P., 55, 70, 109, 121, 132, 136
Mahon, The O'Gorman, 182
Mahony, C. R., 74
Manning, Henry Edward, Cardinal, archbishop of Westminster, 28, 80–81, 149, 180, 191, 377
Marlborough, Duke of, 351, 353
Martin, John, M.P.:
 and 1868 election, 52, 56–58
 and Liberal government, 64
 and amnesty agitation, 67
 and Longford by-election, 1870, 73
 and land agitation, 76, 249–50
 and founding of Home Government Association, 83, 92, 94, 103–8
 enters Parliament, 113–15
 campaigns for Home Government Association, 119–22, 133, 144
 and Mallow by-election, 1872, 132
 and Cork City by-election, 1872, 137
 on state of Home Government Association, 1871, 141
 on university bill, 1873, 152
 and founding of Home Rule League, 160, 164, 166
 secretary of Home Rule League, 172–73, 241–42; resigns, 245
 in 1874 election, 182, 184, 196

408   INDEX

Martin, John, M.P. (*continued*)
first home rule party conference,
1874, 212
on home rule party, 1874, 215–16,
234
and obstruction, 1874, 237
and Tipperary by-election, 1875,
252–53
death of, 254
and Home Rule Confederation, 292
also, 383
Martin, Patrick, M.P., 187–88, 200,
279, 349, 376
Marum, Mulhallen, 249–50
Mathew, J. C., 136
Mathews, Henry, M.P., 59–61, 160
Maunsell, Dr, 93
May, Sir Thomas Erskine:
on obstruction, 1877, 309–10; 1878,
359–60
Mayo Constitution, 29
Mayo, Earl of, 33
Meagher, Thomas Francis, 17–18
Meldon, Charles Henry, M.P., 185,
200, 206, 244, 248–50, 255, 259,
270, 275, 279, 296, 316, 328, 347,
349, 373, 376
Mitchel, John, 19, 65, 186–87, 252–54
Mitchelstown Evictions, 348
Molloy, Bernard C., 185
Monsell, William, M.P., Baron Emly:
and 1868 elections, 35, 37, 50–52
and disestablishment bill, 64
and land bill, 76
and Galway Co. by-election, 1871,
117
and Westmeath by-election, 1871,
118
and Limerick City by-election, 1871,
122
and university bill, 1873, 147–54
pass.
in 1874 election, 180, 191
and O'Connell centenary, 1875, 265
and Intermediate Education Act,
1878, 353

Montagu, Lord Robert, 177, 187, 200–
201, 212, 216, 227, 234, 253–54,
279, 284, 305, 328, 373
Moore, Arthur John, M.P., 200, 202,
279, 328, 347
Moore, Charles, M.P., 43, 71
Moore, George Henry, M.P.:
and 1868 election, 42, 44, 55–56
and amnesty agitation, 67
and land agitation, 76, 78
and fenians, 89–91
and founding of Home Government
Association, 89–91
also 183
Moore, Colonel Maurice, 90–91
Moore, Stephen, M.P., 254
Moran, Dr Patrick Francis, bishop of
Ossory, 188
Morell, Dr, 36
Morgan, Capt. H. F., 185
Moriarty, Dr David, bishop of Kerry,
37, 45, 62, 64, 127–29
Morley, John, M.P., 304
Morris, George, M.P., 46–50, 52, 178,
191, 200–201, 212, 275, 279, 280,
284
Mulcahy, Denis Dowling, 87, 162
Munster, William Felix, M.P., 132
Murphy, Fr., C.C. Ferns, 335
Murphy, Nicholas Daniel, M.P., 55,
136, 160, 186–87, 196–97, 212, 234,
242–43, 272, 279, 284

Nagle, D. A., 132–33
Nation:
and 1868 election, 51–52, 56–60
and Liberal government, 63–64
and land agitation, 70, 80
and Tipperary by-election, 1869, 73
and conservative nationalism, 87,
110
and Home Government Association,
115, 128, 132, 136, 143
on university bill, 1873, 152
and founding of Home Rule League,
157–58

Nation (*continued*)
and 1874 elections, 155–56, 182–87, 196, 203–4
and founding of home rule party, 214, 217
on attendance of home rule members, 216, 262, 275–76
on amendment to address, 1874, 227
on obstruction, 1874, 228, 238; 1875, 255; 1876, 286–89; 1877, 321–22; 1878, 349–50, 357
calls for action in Home Rule League, 1874, 240
on O'Connell centenary, 1875, 266
change in editorship of, 1876, 286–87
and struggle in Home Rule League, 1877–78, 336, 364
and Eastern question, 1878, 362–63, 372–73
and university education, 1879, 377
also, 245, 247
National Association, 75
National roll, 173–74, 241–42
'New Departure', 1878, 370
New Ireland, 84
New York Catholic World, 288
Nolan, Rev. Fr., 185
Nolan, John, 66, 90, 94, 106, 266
Nolan, Captain John Philip, M.P.:
and Galway Co. by-election, 1871, 117
and Galway Co. by-election, 1872, 123–24, 131–32
in 1874 election, 187, 196
appointed whip to home rule party, 214, 252, 296
supports home rule motion, 1874, 233
and obstruction, 1874, 236–37; 1875, 255–57; 1876, 276; 1877, 308, 313–15, 329; 1878, 349 and land question, 249
abstains on imperial title division, 1876, 279
and home rule debate, 1876, 280, 282

on 12.30 rule, 303
refuses to sign address to Butt, 1878, 374–75
also, 253, 275
Northcote, Sir Stafford, M.P., 235
and obstruction, 1877, 310–11, 314; 1878, 359–60
corresponds with Butt, 1878, 354–55
Northern Whig, 33
Nulty, Dr Thomas, bishop of Meath, 118, 145, 159–60

O'Beirne, James Lyster, M.P., 328
O'Brien, Dr, Dean of Limerick:
and repeal, 56–60
and land agitation, 70, 74–75, 78–79, 81–82
and Home Government Association, 94, 110, 113
O'Brien, Dr Dominic, bishop of Waterford, 60
O'Brien, Donal C., 182
O'Brien, James, 59
O'Brien, J. F. X., 72, 161
O'Brien, Sir Patrick, M.P., 44, 160, 184–85, 196, 198, 233, 249, 272, 279, 328
O'Brien, R. Barry
Life of Charles Stewart Parnell, 195, 331, 369
O'Brien, William, 88, 160–61
O'Brien, William Smith, M.P., 18
Obstruction:
repudiated by Butt at first Home Rule Conference, 167
of coercion bill, 1874, 235–38; 1875, 254–59; 1876, 276–77
call for in recess, 1876–77, 286–99 *pass.*
1877 crisis, 300–29 *pass.*
lull in 1878 session, 348–50
parliamentary measures against, 1878, 359–60
also 385–86
O'Byrne, William Richard, M.P., 200, 212, 237, 249, 279, 328, 329

O'Callaghan, Hon. Wilfred, M.P., 186, 200, 202, 212, 247, 253-54, 279, 296, 328
O'Clery, Keyes, M.P., 187, 200, 202, 233, 236-37, 249, 256, 279, 328, 349-50, 362, 370, 374
O'Connell, Daniel, M.P., 13, 15-17, 265-68, 381
O'Conor, Denis Maurice, M.P., 160, 196, 199, 212-13, 256, 272, 275, 279, 328, 349
O'Conor Don, The, M.P., 160, 163, 196, 198-99, 212, 233, 234, 244, 257, 275, 279, 280, 284, 347, 253
O'Donnell, Frank Hugh, M.P.:
  in 1874 election, 190-91
  on class composition of home rule party, 211
  becomes secretary of Home Rule Confederation, 294
  enters parliament, 1877, 308
  and obstruction, 1877, 308-29 pass.; 1878, 348-50
  and struggle in Home Rule League, 1877-78, 330, 336
  imperialism of, 362
  retires from secretaryship of Home Rule Confederation, 370
  also 270, 347, 370
O'Donoghue, Fr., P.P. Ardfert, 129
O'Donoghue, The, M.P., 59-60, 131, 178-79
O'Gorman, Purcell, M.P., 200, 229, 236-37, 256, 275, 276, 279, 283, 298, 308-15, 330, 347-48
O'Hagan, Baron, 266-67, 353
O'Hea, Dr Michael, bishop of Ross, 37, 112, 169-60
O'Keeffe, Fr., 115, 249
O'Keeffe, John, M.P., 200, 202, 279, 296
O'Kelly, J. J., 90
O'Leary, John, 19, 56, 91, 290
O'Leary, Dr W. H., M.P., 181, 196, 237, 254, 256, 272, 330, 371
O'Loghlen, Sir Colman, M.P., 54, 182-

83, 196, 217-18, 233, 247, 279, 296
O'Mahony, John, 68
O'Reilly, Myles William, M.P., 160, 163, 187-88, 196, 198, 234, 272, 279, 280
O'Reilly, Rev. R., P.P. Kingscourt, 154
Osborne, Ralph Bernal, M.P., 84
O'Shaughnessy, Richard, M.P., 189, 200, 202, 214, 217, 240, 243-44, 249, 252-53, 262, 273, 279, 296, 315, 328, 329, 357, 369
O'Shea, Henry, 345
O'Shea, Rev. Thomas, P.P. Mountrath, 60, 115, 249, 341
O'Sullivan, Daniel, 53, 55
O'Sullivan, William, 55

Palles, Christopher, 133-35
Papacy, sovereignty of, 117, 202
Parliamentary Green Book, 216, 275, 287
Parnell, Charles Stewart, M.P.:
  stands in Dublin Co. by-election, 1874, 214
  and land question, 249, 369-70
  enters parliament, 1875, 254
  maiden speech, 256
  calls for action, 1874-75 recess, 270-71, 273
  and obstruction, 1876, 276, 278; 1877, 300-29; 1879, 348-50, 359-60
  and amnesty issue, 273, 278-79
  visits U.S.A. 1876, 293
  elected a vice-president of Home Rule Confederation, 1876, 294
  elected to committee of home rule party, 296
  controversy with Butt in Home Rule League, 1877-78, 330-45 pass., 370; 1879, 376
  elected president of Home Rule Confederation, 331, 370
  and education issue, 349-59 pass.
  attempts to call party conference, November 1878, 373
  votes for Shaw as leader, 1879, 379

Party Processions Act, 36
Pigott, Richard, 55, 57, 67, 94, 246, 322
Pim, Jonathan, M.P., 30, 54, 178–79
Pim, J. E., 137
Plunket, David Robert, M.P., 109, 280
Plunkett, Alderman, 104, 105
Plunkett, Hon. George, 114, 118
Power, John O'Connor, M.P.:
  and fenians, 90, 161–62, 165
  and home rule conference, 1873,
    165, 169
  and first home rule party conference,
    214
  supports home rule motion, 1874,
    233
  enters parliament in Mayo by-
    election, 1874, 183-84, 246–47
  and Tipperary by-election, 1875, 252
  obstruction, 1875, 256; 1877, 308–29,
    pass.; 1878, 350
  and amnesty issue, 262
  abstains on imperial title division,
    1876, 279
  and 1876 land bill, 280
  and home rule motion, 1876, 282–83
  criticises Butt's tactics, 1876, 287
  and I.R.B., 290
  visits U.S.A., 1876, 293
  and struggle in Home Rule League,
    1877–78, 343, 370–71
  and Afghan war, 374–75
  also 242, 253–54, 268, 270, 278, 284
Power, John Talbot, M.P., 44, 179
Power, Richard, M.P., 200, 217, 233,
  279, 280, 296, 308–15, 328, 349
Presbyterians, Ulster:
  and 1868 election, 32–36
Preston, Hon. Jenico, 41
Protestant Repeal Association, 18
Puleston, J. H., M.P., 309
Purdon, Alderman, 93, 110

Quaid, Fr., P.P. O'Callaghan's Mills,
  54, 94, 105, 106, 171, 183
Queensberry, Marchioness of, 246
Reardon, Denis Joseph, 183

Reddin, Daniel, 260
Redmond, William Archer, M.P., 126,
  160, 196, 212–13, 252, 279, 284,
  328
Repeal of the Union:
  in 1868 election, 34, 53, 57–58
  Home Government Association and,
    87–88, 90, 103–8
  P. J. Smyth and, 246
Republicanism in Ireland, 57, 293
Rice, Canon, P.P. Queenstown, 57, 109
Ronayne, Joseph, M.P., 52, 78, 94
  enters parliament 1872, 136–37
  and founding of Home Rule League,
    160–61
  in 1874 election, 187, 196–97
  and Butt's financial difficulties, 221,
    225–26
  obstruction, 1874, 237; 1875, 258
  and land issue, 249
  death of, 277
  influence of upon Parnell, 376
  also 208, 242–43, 253, 273
Roscommon Messenger, 159, 322
Rossa, Jeremiah O'Donovan, 72–73, 90
Russell, Charles, 181
Russell, Very Rev. C. W., 150
Russell, Francis William, M.P., 55
Russell, Lord John, 41
Russell, Johnston, 170, 177, 192
Ryan, Michael, 192
Ryan, Thomas, 106
Rylands, P., M.P., 273

St. Lawrence, Viscount, M.P., 55, 191,
  196–97
Saturday Review, 155
Saunders News-Letter, 363
Shaw, George Ferdinand, F.T.C.D.,
  87, 93, 106
Shaw, William:
  and founding of Home Government
    Association, 94
  and founding of Home Rule League,
    156, 159, 160

Shaw, William (*continued*)
chairman of first Home Rule conference, 160–69 *pass.*
in 1874 election, 173, 196
and education question, 182
and Butt's financial difficulties,
219–26
and land issue, 249
and Home Rule Confederation, 292,
369
elected to committee of home rule
party, 213, 296
and struggle in Home Rule League,
1877–78, 340; 1879, 376
succeeds Butt, 379
also 242, 252, 316, 328, 329
Sheil, Edward, M.P., 183, 200, 206,
237, 247, 275, 296, 328, 370
Sheil, General Sir Justin, 183
Sheil, Richard Lalor, 183
Sherlock, David, M.P., 44, 184–85,
196, 237, 272, 279, 296
Smyth, Patrick James:
and founding of Home Government
Association, 83, 92, 94, 104, 105,
106, 110
attacks home rule programme, 116,
212, 246
enters parliament, 117–19
and founding of Home Rule League,
160–62
in 1874 election, 187, 196
and O'Connell centenary, 1875, 265–
68
speech in home rule debate, 1876,
281–84
Smyth, Richard, M.P., 36, 230–32,
275, 280
Spectator, 151, 153, 295–96
Spencer, Lord, 147–48
Stacpoole, William, M.P., 55, 182, 196,
237, 272, 275, 279
Standard, 158, 272
Stephens, James, 90
Stuart, H. W. Villiers, M.P., 156–57
Sullivan, Alexander Martin, M.P.:

and amnesty agitation, 67
and land agitation, 75, 248–49
and founding of Home Government
Association, 83, 85, 89, 91, 92–94
104, 106, 110
and Mallow by-election, 1872, 132
campaigns for Home Government
Association, 119, 128, 133, 143–44,
145
and founding of Home Rule League,
163
in 1874 election, 180, 196
supports home rule motion, 1874,
232–33
and obstruction, 1874, 235–38; 1875,
255–57; 1876, 276–77; 1877, 328;
1878, 349
criticises national roll, 242
and O'Connell centenary, 1875, 267
abstains on imperial title division,
1876, 279
in home rule debate, 1876, 283–84
resigns editorship of *Nation*, 1876,
286–87
criticises Butt, 1876, 287–88
and struggle in Home Rule League,
1877–78, 330, 341
and Eastern question, 362
refuses to sign address to Butt, 1878,
374–75
also 244, 252, 296
Sullivan, Edward, M.P., 67, 72
Sullivan, T. D., 106
and first Home Rule Conference,
140–41
becomes editor of *Nation*, 1876, 286–
87
in Home Rule League, 1876, 293;
1877, 332, 342–43; 1878, 370, 375
Sullivan, Professor W. K., 152
Synan, E. J., M.P., 160, 166, 193, 196,
198, 244, 272, 284

Tait, Sir Peter, 55, 189
Taylor, Colonel T. E., M.P., 39, 201
Tenant League, 69–79, 248

Tighe, Thomas, M.P., 184, 200, 246–
    47
Times, 151
Tipperary Advocate, 59
Torrens, McCullagh, M.P., 153
Traill, Anthony, F.T.C.D., 34
Trench, E. le Poer, M.P., 130–31

Underwood, Thomas Neilson, 90
United Irishman, 292
Universal News, 59

Vandaleur, Colonel Crofton Moore,
    M.P., 54, 183
Vaughan, Fr., Barefield, 60

Waddy, S. D., M.P., 278
Waldegrave, Lady Frances, 147
Waldron, Laurence, 97, 107, 109

Walsh, John, 161
Ward, Michael Francis, M.P., 212,
    237, 270, 273, 279, 296, 328, 349,
    356, 361, 373
Waterford Citizen, 60
Webb, Alfred, 139, 174–75, 365–66
Webb, T. H., 365
Weekly News, 374
Wexford People, 271, 321
White, Captain the Hon. Charles
    William, M.P., 43, 55, 186, 196,
    212, 232, 234, 251
Whiteside, Rt. Hon. James, 15
Whitworth, Benjamin, M.P., 55, 181
Wilde, Sir William, 93
Woodlock, Dr Bartholomew, 149–50
Woodlock, William, 268, 351, 353, 355,
    377